MIND
TRAINING

THE SCIENCE OF SELF-EMPOWERMENT

RAVINDER TAYLOR
AND *NEW YORK TIMES* BEST-SELLING AUTHOR
ELDON TAYLOR

WORDS OF PRAISE FOR *MIND TRAINING*

"*Mind Training: The Science of Self-Empowerment* is an excellent book that combines elements of brain science and theoretical research psychology with the practical applications of self-help programs designed to promote psychological health and more effective personal functioning. Deeper self-knowledge and understanding are gained by an examination of science-based principles exploring how the mind works. In a clear and concise way, co-authors Ravinder and Eldon Taylor offer the reader numerous opportunities for self-reflection and for applying self-empowering behavioral strategies using exercises contained in the book. If you want to get beyond wishy-washy feel goodism in your quest for insightful, self-determining, and authentic living, and if you seriously wish to enhance your life in a practical way informed by science-based principles, then this book is for you!"

~ **Anthony Falikowski,** Professor at Sheridan College/Adjunct Professor York University (retired) and author of *Higher Reality Therapy and Experiencing Philosophy.*

"What makes *Mind Training* different is that it is really based on research literature. It's not just anecdotes and testimonials like most self-help books. Further, the research is described, not just referred to so that the reader can see what it actually says and how it is being applied. The advice is concrete and doable. The summary and exercises at the end of each chapter are well thought out and flow from what is explained in the chapter.

"*Mind Training* also says that this is not an easy fix. Many self-help books make is seem that all you must do is read the advice and all is good. *Mind Training* makes it more realistic and therefore more valid. I especially like the discussion of placebo as a valuable tool as opposed to something that needs to be controlled for and eliminated. That view in the literature has irritated me for decades and I have written about it. Eliminating something that works because we don't quite understand how is ludicrous. I applaud this work for saying that and offering an understanding of it. I also like that *Mind Training* covers the emotional Stroop; most people and most reviews do not discuss it. I think that most are not aware of it.

"Finally, the discussion of breaking down major goals into small steps or subgoals, along with the review of subliminal research in the appendix, are both particularly good."

~ **Joel Weinberger, Ph.D.**, Professor of Psychology at Adelphi University, NY, and author of *The Unconscious: Theory, Research, and Clinical Implications.*

"I am often skeptical when considering reading a self-help book about how to train your brain. Most are trite and devoid of science. *Mind Training* does an excellent job of blending psychology and brain science, in an easily readable fashion, making real change possible."

~ **Larry D. Rosen**, Professor Emeritus at California State University, Dominguez Hills and co-author of *The Distracted Mind: Ancient Brains in a High-Tech World,* 2017 PROSE Award winner for Biomedicine and Neuroscience.

"In *Mind Training: The Science of Self-Empowerment* by Ravinder and Eldon Taylor, we are reminded through a thoughtful, readable, and evidence based scientific approach that we have much more control over our mind than most of us give ourselves credit for. The book highlights how we can maximize our mind's potential and provides a road map to a better way to live and hopefully both thrive and flourish."

~ **Thomas G. Plante, Ph.D.,** ABPP, Augustin Cardinal Bea, S.J. University Professor, and Professor of Psychology, Santa Clara University and Adjunct Clinical Professor, Department of Psychiatry & Behavioral Sciences, Stanford University School of Medicine

"We all want to be happier, and yet for many of us, the path to happiness is hard to find. *Mind Training: The Science of Self-Empowermen*t provides practical strategies, based in empirical scientific research, to guide readers in how to make positive changes in their lives. This book informs readers about the power of the mind and gives specific techniques for taking control of their thoughts in order to live happier, healthier lives."

~ **Catherine A. Sanderson,** Professor of Psychology, Amherst College, MA, and author of *Why We Act.*

"Most of our brain's activity does not take the form of conscious, verbal thoughts, so it's great to know that so much research has been done on these subconscious processes. This book gathers a broad array of that research, so we can better trace and master our own mental activity. The variety of approaches makes it easy for the reader to pull on the threads that best help them find their power over their own subconscious mind."

~ **Loretta Breuning, Ph.D.,** Professor of Management at California State University, and author of *Habits of a Happy Brain*

"Absolutely brilliant explanation for why we humans think and act as we do! Having long been in the business of joy and happiness, I often allude to the mechanics of our minds and the many ways they're simply not set up in favor of our sustainable joy. Now I finally have a comprehensive manual to recommend for thoroughly understanding and overriding this inconvenient aspect of our humanness! Thank you, Ravinder and Eldon, for your tireless contributions that shed light on these powerful truths, and for all you continue to do to move humanity in the direction of clarity, compassion, and higher consciousness!"

~ **Lisa McCourt,** author of *Free Your Joy* and other books that have sold over 9 million copies.

"Get ready to be enthralled by Eldon and Ravinder Taylor's sensational new book, *Mind Training!* This masterpiece delves into the essence of our choices and ignites our potential as genuine co-creators in life. Brimming with scientific insights and concrete data, it sheds light on various intriguing aspects, including the compliance principles. Prepare to have your mind blown as this book unveils the underlying reasons why intelligent individuals partook in seemingly irrational actions during the pandemic. Embark on this captivating read and join the community of inquisitive co-creators who seek to unlock their true potential!"

~ **Karen Kan G, M.D.,** Founder of the Academy of Light Medicine and the TOLPAKAN™ Healing Method.

MIND
TRAINING

Works by Eldon Taylor

Choices and Illusions: *How Did I Get Where I Am, and How Do I Get Where I Want to Be?*
Mind Programming: *From Persuasion and Brainwashing to Self-Help and Practical Metaphysics*
I Believe: *When What You Believe Matters*
Self-Hypnosis and Subliminal Technology
What Does That Mean? *Exploring Mind, Meaning and Mysteries*
What If? *The Challenge of Self-Realization*
Gotcha! *The Subordination of Free Will*
Subliminal Learning: *An Eclectic Approach*
Subliminal Communication: *Emperor's Clothes or Panacea?*
Thinking Without Thinking: *Who's in Control of Your Mind?*
Subliminal Technology: *Unlocking the Power of Your Own Mind*
Exclusively Fabricated Illusions
Just Be: *A Little Cowboy Philosophy*
Simple Things and Simple Thoughts
Little Black Book
Wellness: *Just a State of Mind?*
Change Without Thinking
Questioning Spirituality: *Is It Irrational to Believe in God?*

Works by Ravinder and Eldon Taylor

Motivational Nudges to Empower Your Life
Peripheral Perception via Subliminal Stimuli Desk Reference
plus, hundreds of audio and video programs in multiple languages.

Please visit: **www.mind-training.org**

MIND
TRAINING

THE SCIENCE OF SELF-EMPOWERMENT

RAVINDER TAYLOR
ELDON TAYLOR

© 2024 Ravinder Taylor and Eldon Taylor

Published by: R.K. Books and Progressive Awareness Research, Inc.
PO Box 1139
Medical Lake, WA
99022
1-800-964-3551

All rights reserved. No part of this book may be reproduced by any mechanical, photographic, or electronic process, or in the form of a phonographic recording; nor may it be stored in a retrieval system, transmitted, or otherwise be copied for public or private use—other than for "fair use" as brief quotations embodied in articles and reviews—without prior written permission of the publisher.

The authors of this book do not dispense medical advice or prescribe the use of any technique as a form of treatment for physical, emotional, or medical problems without the advice of a physician, either directly or indirectly. The intent of the author is only to offer information of a general nature to help you in your quest for emotional and spiritual well-being. In the event you use any of the information in this book for yourself, which is your constitutional right, the author and the publisher assume no responsibility for your actions.

ISBN: 978-1-62000-387-9
Library of Congress Control Number: 2024903415

Publisher's Cataloging-in-Publication Data
provided by Five Rainbows Cataloging Services

Names: Taylor, Ravinder Kaur - author. | Taylor, Eldon - author.
Title: Mind training : the science of self-empowerment / Ravinder Taylor [and] Eldon Taylor.
Description: Medical Lake, WA : R. K. Books and Progressive Awareness Research, 2024. | Includes bibliographical references.
Identifiers: LCCN 2024903415 (print) | ISBN 978-1-62000-387-9 (paperback) | ISBN 978-1-62000-388-6 (ebook : mobi) | ISBN 978-1-62000-390-9 (ebook : epub) | ISBN 978-1-62000-389-3 (audiobook)
Subjects: LCSH: Self-help techniques. | Self-destructive behavior. | Negativism. | Subliminal perception. | Self-actualization (Psychology) | BISAC: SELF-HELP / Personal Growth / General. | PSYCHOLOGY / General.
Classification: LCC BF575.E83 T39 2024 (print) | LCC BF575.E83 (ebook) | DDC 155.2--dc23.

CONTENTS

Words of Praise for *Mind Training* iii
Introduction 1

PART ONE: What to Expect 7
Chapter One: The Story of Positive Thinking 9
Chapter Two: The Power of Your Mind 15

PART TWO: Understanding Your Mind 29
Chapter Three: Models of the Mind 31
Chapter Four: The Mechanical Brain 51
Chapter Five: The Automatic Nature of Your Mind 65
Chapter Six: The Question of Will 99
Chapter Seven: Fine-Tuning the Brain 119

PART THREE: The Power of Beliefs 143
Chapter Eight: Seeing is Believing 145
Chapter Nine : The Expectation Factor 157
Chapter Ten: The Positivity Quotient 181

PART FOUR: Life on Your Terms 205
Chapter Eleven: Subconscious Controls 207

Chapter Twelve: Empower Yourself 231
Chapter Thirteen: Other Tools 255
Conclusion: The Best of Ourselves 271

ADDITIONAL MATERIALS 275
Appendix A: Subliminal Controversy 277
Appendix B: Science Review of InnerTalk 307

Endnotes 315
Acknowledgments 377
About the Authors 379
More Information 381

*To our sons, Roy and Will,
who have inspired and supported us
in ways they may never fully understand.*

INTRODUCTION

> To enjoy good health, to bring true happiness to one's family, to bring peace to all, one must first discipline and control one's own mind. If a man can control his mind, he can find the way to enlightenment, and all wisdom and virtue will naturally come to him.
>
> ~Buddha

Almost all of us are aware of the need to train our bodies. Even if we are not athletes training for some event, we know that exercising regularly will bring numerous benefits, from improved health and wellness to enhanced creativity. But have you ever considered the necessity of training your mind?

Now, when I talk about mind training, I am not referring to getting an education, learning a new skill, or training for some job. No, I am talking about training the mind much like you would tune up a car—so that it works more efficiently, and as a result, enhances your life.

There are numerous excellent books that give us insights into how our minds work, but they rarely offer us guidance for how to use this information to make positive changes in our lives. Conversely, there are many self-help books that offer us guidance, but they generally offer little scientific backing for their claims. The aim of *Mind Training* is to provide a substantial bridge between these two approaches as it presents solid science-based principles that can be put to life-enhancing use.

Evolvement

Mind Training: The Science of Self-Empowerment was conceived from a blog Eldon wrote in 2019 aptly titled, *Mind Training 101.*[1] Having been active in this arena since 1984 (I joined him in 1990), he was surprised to learn that many people do not understand what it means to train the mind. (When you are engrossed in a particular subject for decades, it can be surprising to discover how little others know about it.) In his blog, Eldon outlined the seven basic areas of examination in any mind training program:

1. Engineering your self-talk.
2. Choosing your beliefs carefully.
3. Learning the heuristics of your mind (mental shortcuts).
4. Becoming aware of patterned thinking/conditioning.
5. Utilizing physiological feedback.
6. Understanding your neurochemicals.
7. Positive thinking.

The blog was very well received, with many suggesting it be turned into a book and agreeing that it was something everyone should be taught. Eldon and I, therefore, took this outline and started working on developing this book. In time, the concepts evolved, expanding in detail and scope, and yet the core message became increasingly distilled. Soon we arrived at five steps that form the lynchpin for the philosophy behind successful mind training for self-empowerment. At their core, these steps are:

1. *Appreciate* and understand how powerful your mind is.
2. *Learn* how your mind works.

3. *Internalize* and synthesize this knowledge.
4. *Choose* to adopt strategies and choices related to that knowledge.
5. *Implement* the strategies in your everyday life.

While this may sound very basic, the process is very thorough. Information is presented in layers, with each layer providing more evidence and tools. The result is a self-empowerment program, based on a strong foundation, that works.

Reinforcing

There is knowing and there is *knowing*—we can know something on a superficial, easily forgotten level, or we can have a deeper *knowing* that creates a rippling effect through our lives. Mind training requires this second kind of knowing so that the implementation becomes second nature. There are a few approaches that assist us in reaching this goal:

- Almost every idea or recommendation has a scientific basis.
- Where possible, citations and studies are pulled from several different sources to avoid the criticism of 'fluke' results.
- In some instances, studies are dissected so we can evaluate what is truly useful for our purposes.
- Where appropriate, most chapters end by highlighting key points and offering exercises for you to do.

Mind Training combines historical background, scientific evaluations, and coursework. The best way to learn something is by doing it. As the great Star Wars character, Yoda, says, *"Do. Or do not. There is no try."* As such, you should decide if you want to take it chapter by chapter, allowing time between to gain some familiarity with the exercises, or read it all the way through and then go back to do the necessary work.

The Process

The *Mind Training* course work is broken down into four main parts.

Part One provides a foundation for what can realistically be expected from the power of the mind. Here, you will be introduced to the idea of digging deeper into stories. Overly simplified stories can be more of a disservice as they often make the student believe they are somehow deficient when they follow the teachings but fail in the goals. Inspirational stories sometimes omit some important steps. In many instances, the 'rest of the story' contains the most important keys.

Part Two looks at the mechanical nature of the mind and provides us with ways to take manual control over what are just automatic processes for most. Building on different models of the mind, we learn how experiences are embedded into our underlying programming, and how these subconscious motivations can limit our options. We also see how some automatic processes can be 'tweaked' for more efficiency.

Part Three examines the power of your thoughts and their far-reaching consequences. In many ways, it can be humbling to discover how little you know about yourself, but this process reveals fresh options and choices. Whether you are young, or not so young, you will gain some understanding of why you are where you are and how you can start making impactful changes.

Part Four offers you direct tools for taking personal responsibility for the direction of your life. All you need do here is choose the tools that best fit your preferences and lifestyle. Most importantly, it removes the mystiques that often surround self-help programs and so allows you to structure techniques that you fully understand and can personalize to suit you.

In a nutshell, *Mind Training* is a scientific exploration of the mind, specifically on how this information can be used to improve your life by maximizing your natural talents and abilities. While it is a self-empowerment book, it does not offer easy answers and quick cures. Rather, it offers a way of life that promotes a process of conscious living. Being aware of the 'whys' behind some of your behaviors will reduce the self-destructive patterns all of us are subject to, in one way or another. Understanding some of the mechanisms of brain chemistry will give you manual control

INTRODUCTION

over certain aspects so you can increase your success and overall feelings of well-being. Learning about the many automatic mechanisms of the mind will make it possible to offset the ability of others to exploit them. Understanding how the different tools work puts you firmly in the driver's seat of your life.

Mind training is a journey. Enjoy!

Ravinder and Eldon Taylor

P.S. While this book is a collaboration between the two of us, it was written in one voice to facilitate reading.

PART ONE
WHAT TO EXPECT

CHAPTER ONE

THE STORY OF POSITIVE THINKING

Our inner beliefs trigger failure before it happens. They sabotage lasting change by canceling its possibility. We employ these beliefs as articles of faith to justify our inaction and then wish away the result. I call them belief triggers.

~ Marshall Goldsmith

There is a saying that goes, "There is nothing new under the sun," and that seems the case regarding the power of positive thinking. So many popular ideas today are, in fact, regurgitations of ideas in books written decades (sometimes even centuries) ago, and in several cases, these beliefs have cycled through popular culture several times.

History of Positive Thinking

The idea of the power of positive thinking can be traced as far back as in the Bible where it states: "Therefore I tell you, whatever you ask in prayer, believe that you have received it, and it will be yours" (Mark 11:24). And, although most believe that "as you sow, so shall you reap" (Galatians 6:7) refers to your actions and karma, it could be argued that this, too, is an argument for positive thinking.

While it was Samuel Smiles' 1859 book, *Self-Help* that marked the beginning of the self-help industry as we know it today, the whole field did not accelerate in growth until the 1900s, particularly with *Think and Grow Rich* (1937) by Napoleon Hill, *The Power of Positive Thinking* (1952) by Norman Vincent Peale, and the breakout success, *The Strangest Secret* (1956) by Earl Nightingale. At the core of all these works is the idea that success begins in the mind; Earl Nightingale summed it up by saying, *"We become what we think about."* This belief was then repeated in 2006 when *The Secret* movie became a worldwide success with its message of *"Ask. Believe. Receive."*

Popular Techniques

The purpose of all these works and the vast number that have followed is to inspire the reader to think positive thoughts, and this is generally done by providing examples that illustrate the efficacy of positive thinking—who doesn't love a good, heartwarming story? The actual techniques offered, however, tend to be more limited and generally focus on:

1. Set a goal—decide what it is you want.
2. Visualize—picture yourself successful at your goal.
3. Affirm that you are already successful—write affirmations and perhaps put them in various places to remind you.
4. Eliminate thoughts of failure—cancel negative thoughts or just don't have them.
5. Always remember what can be achieved if you habituate points 1-4.

Quotes

Now, some authors may package their techniques a little differently, but they are still basically the same:

- "I claim my power and move beyond all limitations." — Louise Hay
- "We can control our lives by controlling our

perceptions." —Bruce H. Lipton
- "If you change the way you look at things, the things you look at change." —Wayne Dyer
- "Every thought is a cause, and every condition is an effect. Change your thoughts and you change your destiny." —Joseph Murphy
- "Whatever you need will just happen if you keep your energies exuberant and focused." —Sadhguru

Glittering Generalities

While popular teachings like these continue to proliferate, all saying much the same thing albeit using different words, they generally only offer glittering generalities in place of real solutions. It is certain that inspiration is a valuable tool as it can be likened to the ignition that starts the car, but you still need to know how to drive. While it may sound obvious, for change to occur in your life, you must first *choose* to change. However, we will see lots of reasons why a part of you may not want this.

Along the way, we will discover that, while positive thinking can bring many benefits, it is possible to overdo this, leading to some negative consequences. And, to confound the picture further, there are also instances where negative thinking can be beneficial.

The Rest of the Story

Paul Harvey was the ABC radio broadcaster who hosted *The Rest of the Story* radio program from 1975 to 2009. He would often present some interesting piece of information that may or may not have been widely known but would show it in a whole new light by adding some key piece of information. In so doing, he would take an already fascinating story into a whole new league. And that is the aim behind *Mind Training*—to sort the wheat from the chaff and get to the heart of the self-empowerment process.

Why?

The decades-long explosion of self-help materials into the marketplace has made a solid case for the importance of positive thinking. Unfortunately, none of them provided a real explanation for *why* people have negative thoughts in the first place. Isn't telling someone not to think a negative thought akin to asking them not to think about pink elephants, or not to touch wet paint? Telling someone to only think positive thoughts can be a sure way for their subconscious mind to fill their thoughts with negativity. Yes, it is possible to create new habits, but consciously creating new ways of thinking is a bit like creating a habit to breathe or walk differently. The old ways are so firmly entrenched that change is extremely hard (albeit not impossible). But there is a better way.

I began this chapter by saying that there is nothing new under the sun, but this is not entirely correct, at least not in the context I am thinking about. You see, while the ideas of positive thinking may have been around forever, scientific knowledge continues to open new horizons. Today, we understand much about the psychology of the human race, such as our need to be liked and how far we will go to achieve this, how easy it is for our beliefs to be nudged,[1] how drastically our moral values can be influenced by perceived societal norms,[2] and the damaging effects of negative thinking.[3] Armed with this information, we can take ephemeral concepts and turn them into concrete action.

Knowledge really is power. The only real way to limit your negative thoughts is to understand how they get into your belief system in the first place. When you understand how your mind works, how it gets programmed in negative ways, and the benefits (and I do mean *benefits*) you gain when you exhibit self-destructive behaviors, only then can you put the systems in place to restrict the entry of negativity, counteract the negativity that is already there, and give full rein to the power of positive thinking.

NOTES

Key Points

The ideas of positive thinking and self-help have been around for a very long time. It is believed that you are governed by the thoughts in your mind and that these thoughts and beliefs can enhance or sabotage your life. Very few teachings, though, show you *how* to make changes in your life—how to believe differently. The intention of *Mind Training* is to show you 'the rest of the story' as it pertains to the field of self-empowerment.

Exercise

As you will soon see, for change to occur in your life, you must first *choose* to change. Closely behind that is the need to put action behind your stated goals. Journaling is a great way to solidify both. To start then, get yourself a notebook. A physical book has the advantage that you can leave it somewhere in clear sight so you won't forget about your goals. If you prefer a digital document, then make sure you remember to look at it every day.

Start your journal by writing the date you began this new journey. Sometimes it can be beneficial to see how much progress you have made in x amount of time.

Next, think about what self-empowerment means to you. What is it that you would like to improve in your life? Please do not make this a long laundry list. Instead, think about the kind of changes that would help you feel a little happier today—a small series of mini-goals. Perhaps you would like to feel a little less stressed, a little more productive, and a little less reactive. Think about this carefully and create a list of not more than five items. Also, be very specific about these early goals. Do not write down general goals like 'be more successful.' Instead, think about what success means to you. In what area would you like success? At work? With personal relationships? With your hobbies? Imagine what the first stages of that success look like.

When you write down your list, start each of these mini-goals with the statement, 'I choose.' For example:

- I choose to be less anxious.
- I choose to be more positive.
- I choose to be happier.
- I choose to be more loving.
- I choose to be more generous.

By starting with small goals, you can see some progress early on. Seeing early progress will make it easier for you to continue on this path.

CHAPTER TWO

THE POWER OF YOUR MIND

> There are times when we are just not very kind to ourselves. The problem with our negative thoughts is that the latest science has revealed that thoughts are very powerful, even impacting us physically.
>
> ~ Elizabeth Thornton

Earlier, I said inspiration can be likened to the ignition that starts the car, and in this instance, it can provide the motivation to start the process of training your mind. But what does 'the power of the mind' really mean? What is the mind capable of insofar as influencing a person's life?

Unfortunately, while books galore have been written regarding the power of belief, many of the stories are rather clichéd with little relevance to the real-world issues experienced by the readers. In addition to this, many stories have been repeated so many times that they take on a life of their own, so much so that, even when the stories are proven untrue, they are still shared as though they were proven facts. Regrettably, this approach can lead to recommendations that don't work, while ignoring other areas that could be helpful. Here are a couple of such stories that show how a more realistic interpretation can be of greater value.

Roger Bannister

You may have heard about Roger Bannister as his achievement is frequently used to highlight the power of belief. The story, as it is commonly told, goes along these lines. Up until 1954, no one believed it was possible to break the four-minute-mile barrier. But along came Roger Bannister, who believed differently, and so on May 6, 1954, he did exactly this—running the mile in three minutes and 59.4 seconds. His achievement so inspired the world that this same feat was repeated just six and a half weeks later by John Landry who ran the mile in three minutes and 57.9 seconds. The way the story is widely told, Bannister's achievement showed the world that the four-minute mile was not an impossible achievement and that this change in belief allowed others to follow suit. Accounts on the Internet indicate that the four-minute mile has now been broken over 1,500 times, and there are even records of high school students doing the same.

Now, anyone trying to break a particular world record must *believe* they can, or they would not be trying to break it in the first place. Furthermore, this says nothing about those who are not trying to break a record but are just competing, running for fun, or running away from danger—the possibilities are endless.

Anyone who has trained for a race knows that training takes time. I experienced this when I ran my first marathon in October of 2018. My training for this race began with daylight savings earlier that year and was pretty intensive. And that is not the entire story either as, from about 1985 to 2013, I am not sure I ran at all—at least no further than perhaps across a parking lot. So, my training really began in 2013 when I first took up running, and my progress happened in increments: 5k, 10k, 12k, half marathon, and then the full marathon. Bannister started training seriously in 1946, and Landry started training in 1949. Both improved in increments until they achieved success in 1954.

Considering everything involved in training, it did not take me long to realize that John Landry's achievement had little to do with the fact that Bannister had now shown him what was possible. Both men were training for the same goal at the same time; Bannister's race just happened to come first. Yes, the belief that such a goal was possible did play a role in their achievements, but then so did the training, competition, determination, grit—all of which have a strong mind-training element—and a host of other factors that can influence the type of run you have on a particular day. The four-minute mile was not impossible, it just hadn't been done yet. In his memoir, *The Four-Minute Mile*, Bannister himself dismissed the myth that the experts all believed that the four-minute barrier was physically impossible to break—journalists simply like to paint the more exciting picture. The record currently stands at three minutes and 43.13 seconds.

Believing something is possible is the first step to putting in the effort needed to achieve it, but you must also believe you have the willpower and dedication necessary to reach your goals. You must believe that the end goal is worth all the other sacrifices you may need to make, and you must enjoy the process. While it is important to believe a goal is possible, success requires more.

Firewalking

Firewalking entails walking across a surface of hot embers or coals. It has been used by cultures around the world as a rite of passage, a test of religious faith, and a test of courage. The earliest records of firewalking date back to 1200 BC in India.[1] More recently, firewalking has been used in motivational workshops to demonstrate the power of mind over matter and for inspiring self-belief. Typically, the firewalk comes at the end of the workshop and is used as the final test of the validity of everything the individual has been taught. The idea is that the sense of achievement that comes with completing a task that sounds physically impossible will translate to a belief that you can accomplish other feats, previously thought to be impossible, in your life as well. Participants who go through this process frequently report feeling empowered and awed by their achievement. They feel unstoppable and fearless, as though they can overcome anything life may throw at them. They feel unbreakable.[2]

Now, while firewalking may sound impossible to most people, it has scientific explanations that do not involve mind over matter. When we walk across an icy path, we simply have to walk differently—we place our feet more carefully, walk more flat-footed, shuffle our feet rather than stride across, bend our bodies slightly forward, and have our arms out ready to provide us with more balance (or to protect us should we fall).[3] Firewalking requires the same kinds of principles—the coals have to be prepared correctly, the best type of wood chosen (hardwoods provide more insulation while cherry or maple also produce embers that look more impressive but do not burn as hot); the runway is raked (which spreads more cold charcoal to the surface) and patted down (to stop the walker sinking into the heat); time is allowed for the coals to dry out more; a thin layer of ash may be applied over the top; and then the participant needs to walk briskly with a light stride. Running or using a heavy step would sink the feet into the coals. Each step should last half a second or less. As long as the participant keeps on walking, each step will absorb very little heat.[4] At the end of the brief walk, the participant's feet are hosed off to stop any more heat penetration. However, you can also find real everyday examples that demonstrate some of the same principles. Transferring hot bread from one plate to another can be done very safely if light fingers and quick movements are used. In the Indian culture, rotis (flatbreads) are frequently made over an open flame using fast, delicate hand movements—something young cooks get the hang of very quickly.

Effective motivational seminars leave most people with a feeling of empowerment and the belief that their lives will be different from here on in. However, surveys conducted some weeks later will show that a large percentage of people have not even started practicing what they learned. They can report things like, *"I'll do it tomorrow," "I'm just not able to commit the time right now,"* or *"It really didn't translate well for my life (perhaps that technique just does not work for me)."*

A firewalk, though, should be empowering and have longer-lasting results. However, this is not usually the case. One researcher stated that "For days afterward, I was temporarily brainwashed, luxuriating in the achievement and not caring how it was possible that I did it. But I soon returned to my old ways . . ." Even Tony Robbins, the well-known firewalk instructor, admits that "While the firewalk can change some people's lives, for others it's merely a good pub story."[5] In reality, many participants will continue attending motivational seminars, searching for the perfect way for them.

If there is nothing magical about the firewalking technique, does this mean all the positive thinking related to it is hogwash? The answer to that is no. People attending these events (and often paying big bucks to do so) already believe within them that they can 'do better.' The first step to success at anything is always the idea that there is something to achieve. At the event, they are removed from the usual, frequently negative, environment that they normally live in and are surrounded by people who also believe they can achieve a better life if only they can find that missing key. Humans are wired with the desire to both fit in and gain the approval of those around them. Fitting into the norm is simply a way to put a cap on anything you could achieve. And when the beliefs around you are negative, it programs your subconscious to keep repeating those same negative beliefs to you. Thinking you cannot succeed will prevent you from trying your hardest to succeed, and so you accept failure as a norm. And lastly, when you achieve something that you either believed to be impossible or something that no one else in your normal circles has managed, you look at other challenges with fresh eyes—*"If I could achieve that one thing, then maybe . . . just maybe . . . I can achieve other things too."*

So, firewalking indirectly trains your mind to support your goals. It is our intention to explore more efficient and enduring ways to achieve the same thing.

Dissociative Identity Disorder

Some of the most incredible stories about the power of belief come from patients with dissociative identity disorder (DID). The stories are worth a closer look as they show us how *much* power our beliefs can have.

Dissociative identity disorder (previously known as multiple personality disorder) is thought to be a complex psychological condition likely caused by many factors, including early childhood severe trauma (usually extreme, repetitive physical, sexual, or emotional abuse).[6] What is most intriguing is there are numerous accounts of biological changes that take place in the patient's body as it switches from one personality to another.

In one instance, all the patient's subpersonalities were allergic to orange juice except for one. If the man drank orange juice while one of his allergic personalities was in control, he would break out in hives. But if he switched to his non-allergic personality, then the rash would fade, and he could drink orange juice freely.[7]

There are accounts of different personalities responding differently to different drugs. One personality can be color-blind and another not, and even eye color can change. There are cases of women who have two or three menstrual periods each month because each of their subpersonalities has its cycle. There is an account of a woman who was diabetic in one personality but not in another.[8]

While these kinds of stories are rare, these specific accounts were reported by doctors with solid reputations. Plus, the appearance of even a single white crow does suggest the possibility of even more. However, a more widely recognized area that highlights the power of the mind can be found in placebo research.

Placebo

The placebo effect is the beneficial effect of a drug or treatment, where the said benefit cannot be attributed to the drug or treatment. Drug companies must demonstrate that their new drug works better than the placebo.

One of the first people to realize that the mind played a role in healing was Dr. John Haygarth in 1799. At the time, people reported a particular treatment as effective in drawing disease from the body. The device being used was a Perkins tractor, which consisted of an expensive metal rod. Dr. Haygarth compared the effects of these rods with similar-looking rods made of wood and found that four of five patients with rheumatoid arthritis reported an improvement in pain.[9]

Since then, thousands of research studies have been carried out on the placebo effect, and many doctors admit to prescribing them.[10] They have been shown to affect a range of conditions, and their efficacy can be influenced by color, shape, and format (pill, capsule, or injection), with different demographics having their preferred format. So, in general, colored pills work better than white pills, and brighter colors are more effective than dull colors. Red, orange, and yellow are more likely to be stimulants, whereas blue and green are more likely to be tranquilizers.[11]

Drugs are also more effective when their color matches their goal, so a white burn cream works better than a red one.[12]

One aspect of research I found rather intriguing (even a little disquieting) was the interpretation of color across cultures. "In one study, Caucasians viewed white capsules as analgesics, while African Americans viewed them as stimulants. The reverse was true for black capsules: Caucasians saw them as stimulants; African Americans thought they were analgesics."[13]

"The placebo effect also varies between cultures. In treating gastric ulcers, the placebo effect is low in Brazil, higher in northern Europe, and particularly high in Germany. However, the placebo effect on hypertension is lower in Germany than elsewhere."[14]

The type of placebo is also important, with sham surgeries being more effective than sham injections, which in turn, were more effective than oral placebos.[15]

Depression

In 1998, Irving Kirsch and Guy Sapirstein published a study that showed a "substantial placebo effect in antidepressant medication and also a considerable benefit of medication over placebo."[16] The study also indicated "that the placebo component of the response to medication is considerably greater than the pharmacological effect." The authors went on to suggest that "Antidepressants might function as active placebos, in which the side effects amplify the placebo effect by convincing patients that they are receiving a potent drug."[17]

The meta-analysis showed that 75% of the improvement in the group that received the drug was also seen in the group that received the placebo and that the extra benefit gained from the medication could also be partially attributed to the placebo effect. This result proved highly controversial and sparked a follow-up study. The follow-up study showed that "82% of the drug response was duplicated by placebo." This fascinating story provides great insights into the problems behind research methods and even the FDA rules for approving new drugs and is well worth reading in its entirety.[18] Of interest to us here is the fact that the most common type of antidepressant is SSRIs—drugs that increase the amount of serotonin in the brain. However, there is another antidepressant that decreases the amount of serotonin in the brain instead of increasing it. You would expect subjects to respond differently depending on the kind of drug, but that was not the case. "It simply does not matter what is in the medication—it might increase serotonin, decrease it, or have no effect on serotonin at all. The effect on depression is the same."[19]

> (Please note, this information should not be used to influence health care choices. There are many factors involved in deciding a course of treatment and this is something your medical doctor is best equipped to assess.)

However, while all of this is most interesting, there is still the question of how far the placebo effects can go. The following story is one of the most remarkable.

Mr. Wright

A gentleman, only referred to as Mr. Wright, was seemingly dying from cancer of the lymph nodes, and orange-sized tumors had invaded his neck, groin, chest, and abdomen. Bedridden, he agreed to try a new drug, *Krebiozen*, that he was convinced would help him. Three days after his first injection, the tumors had shrunk by half, and he was out of bed and joking with the nurses. Ten days later he was released from the hospital.

Mr. Wright suffered a relapse two months later after hearing that *Krebiozen* was not as effective as had been thought. His doctor then lied to him that a more effective version of the drug was now available. He received the injection that, in fact, did not contain the drug, and once again improved and left the hospital symptom-free.

Two months later, Mr. Wright heard that *Krebiozen* was useless, and he died a few days later.[20]

Knee Surgery

The placebo effect can also be found in surgeries. In a study carried out by the Department of Veterans Affairs (VA) and Baylor College of Medicine, 180 patients with knee pain were divided into three groups. Group One received debridement, where the damaged cartilage is removed. Group Two underwent arthroscopic lavage where the bad cartilage is flushed out. The third group underwent simulated arthroscopic surgery—incisions were made but no instruments were inserted, or cartilage removed.

The results showed that:

> "During two years of follow-up, patients in all three groups reported moderate improvements in pain and ability to function. However, neither of the intervention groups reported less pain or better function than the placebo group. Indeed, the placebo patients reported better outcomes than the debridement patients at certain points during follow-up. Throughout the two years, the patients were unaware of whether they had received real or placebo surgery."[21]

Nocebo

Equally as important as the research on placebos is the research on *nocebos*. A nocebo is where the patient's negative thoughts about a treatment can cause them to experience a negative effect. About 20% of subjects who receive a sugar pill in controlled clinical trials, can report uncomfortable side effects, and this percentage can be even higher if they are asked.[22]

Several factors can be involved in the nocebo effect. It could be that the patient has become conditioned by negative effects, say from chemotherapy, and feels nauseous upon entering the treatment room. Earlier, I talked about how the placebo effect could be influenced by factors such as the color of pills and the type of procedure, such as surgery, injection, or pill. Well, it seems that these same factors also apply to the nocebo effect: "Red is associated with stimulation, blue with sedation, so red and blue pills may produce those responses as unwanted side effects."[23]

In one study, the subjects were told that a mild electrical current being passed through their heads could cause headaches. Two-thirds of the subjects experienced headaches even though no electrical current was used.[24]

Several experiments have shown the double-edged sword of the placebo/nocebo response. In one study, asthma patients were divided into two groups. A 50% improvement was seen in the group that received the bronchoconstrictor when they were told it should improve their symptoms—even though such treatment should have worsened their symptoms. The second group received the bronchodilator, which is designed to reduce discomfort in asthmatics, but were told it was a bronchoconstrictor. "The nocebo suggestion reduced the drug's effectiveness by nearly 50%."[25]

There is a two-fold conclusion to all the placebo and nocebo research; what you believe matters significantly, and most of these beliefs occur on a subconscious level. We will address this in much greater detail throughout this book.

Aging

Aging is another area heavily influenced by the power of belief. The aging process is something that concerns almost everyone at some point in their lives, so much so that, for many people, turning thirty is a sign that the best is behind them. Most people seem to accept the fact that aging comes with decline and that they need to take more care of themselves as the years slip by—*slow down, take it easy, don't push it.*

Ellen Langer (Harvard University) has done some interesting research on aging. In 1982, Langer ran a study where she took eight men in their seventies to a special retreat. These men were in good health but had definite signs of aging, such as arthritis, stooped posture, and using a cane. Once these men entered the retreat, they were taken back to 1959—the black and white TV, the shows that aired, the music playing in the background, the décor, the magazines—the experience was made as authentic as possible. In addition, the men were *treated* as though they were twenty-plus years younger, including having to take their belongings up to their rooms themselves. The men were asked not to just reminisce about being twenty years younger, but to attempt to *be* the person they were back then.

The men were tested for things such as dexterity, grip strength, flexibility, hearing, vision, memory, and cognition, both before the retreat and afterward. The results showed that the men were more supple, had greater dexterity, sat taller, and their sight improved. The same results were not found with the control group who were encouraged to reminisce, but who were not actually 'taken back' to the earlier era.[26] So just changing the mindset of the subjects was enough to reverse some of the aging issues.

While Langer never replicated this study with larger groups, in part due to costs, she ran a few other studies with interesting findings. In one study, two groups of people were put into a flight simulator. The group that put on flight suits and pretended to be Air Force pilots while guiding a simulated flight performed 40% better in vision tests than the group instructed that the simulator was broken so they should just pretend to fly a plane. So, fully embracing an acting role/experience resulted in improved eyesight—a truly interesting example of the power of the mind.[27]

In another study, healthy subjects watched videos of people coughing and sneezing and were encouraged to pretend that they, too, had colds. The subjects were not misled in any way–such as by being told they were in a germ chamber. Forty percent of those in the test group reported cold symptoms compared to 10% of those in the control group. When their saliva was tested, all the experimental subjects who reported cold symptoms showed elevated levels of IgA antibodies—a sign of an elevated immune system response. So, simply watching sick people and living vicariously through them made many of the subjects sick.[28] Does this extend to areas other than health and well-being? What do you think this says about much of the entertainment we consume?

While not very scientific, we can all find examples of the power of the mind and personal beliefs in the world around us. Some people just *know* they will catch anything that goes around, while others *know* they rarely ever fall sick. We know about these people because they are not shy about sharing their stories/beliefs. There are also those who become old at forty, whereas some others still go on adventures in their seventies. I for one love stories of senior citizens who are still very active and even winning competitions. Two of my own icons have to include Ernestine Shepherd, who holds the Guinness World Record for being the Oldest Female Bodybuilder at age eighty-one (she started body building at age fifty-six),[29] and Fauja Singh, the centenarian marathon runner.[30] These two individuals made a conscious effort to think differently—to change the *"I can't (I'm too old)"* thinking to the *"Why not? I can do it,"* attitude, and for them, success followed. The power of the mind expresses itself in some pretty important ways.

Self-Sabotage

Have you ever set yourself a goal, start out doing well, but then something happens, and you end up failing? This is the classic indicator of self-sabotage, and it manifests in a wide variety of self-improvement areas ranging from weight loss to business, education, and parenting skills. But why would we sabotage our goals?

Self-Preservation

While your subconscious mind does not intend to sabotage your dreams and goals, one of its most important tasks is to protect you. So, for the person who was embarrassed as a child when reading aloud in class, the subconscious can instill the notion of *"I must avoid public speaking at all costs."* When the person becomes an adult and has a new job or promotion opportunity that involves leading group meetings, they can suddenly reject the promotion. Or the person who associates eating with the comfort that came after having fears assuaged with a kiss and bowl of ice cream from Mom, and now always craves ice cream when stressed, even after cutting out junk food to lose weight. These examples can go on and on. However, what you should realize in all these examples is that the decision to take the action that sabotages the stated goal is coming from the subconscious.

Overcome the Negative Inner Voice

We all have self-sabotaging programming in our psyche. If you have not encountered it, that's just because you have not pushed the boundaries to find it—yet. Or maybe this very inaction is your symptom of self-sabotage. Later, we will examine how and when these restricting ideas can get embedded in your subconscious mind. Sometimes simply uncovering some of these self-destructive beliefs will make them lose their grip on you. However, we will also be providing tools to diminish or negate their power.

NOTES

Key Points

The more inspiring the stories, the more likely people will be drawn to them. But sometimes stories can be pared down so far that they become *only* inspirational—they lose the practical tools. By looking at some of these stories and then revealing the *rest of the story* behind them, we begin to see the missing elements.

Roger Bannister's 4-minute mile achievement is generally over-simplified making it seem like simply believing it was possible allowed others to follow suit. A deeper examination showed us that it also took several other mental and physical elements to achieve this goal. And this holds for most of your life goals.

Firewalking works in part by getting you out of your comfort zone and by surrounding you with other like-minded people. Having an *'I can do it'* attitude is an important element in creating success, but this can be an uphill battle when our environments contain so much negativity.

Our overview of the placebo effect is of two-fold interest. First, it demonstrates the power of our beliefs over our health and the strong role it can play in self-healing. Secondly, we get to see other ways our environments can impact us. It is very significant that one culture can view a white capsule as being an analgesic and a black capsule as being a stimulant, whereas another culture views them the other way around. We take in much information without any awareness, and this information influences how we see the world and manifests in many different areas.

The placebo effect is often dismissed as insignificant and this is a mistake. Our focus should be on ways to benefit from this effect. This idea can also extend to other areas of your life. Your thoughts can heal you or hurt you, help you succeed or cause you to fail. Appreciating the placebo effect can be the first step in realizing how much power you can have over your life.

Exercise

If you have goals that have remained elusive despite making several resolutions to change, think back to the techniques you employed. Were you just relying on will power or did you implement different strategies? Did any of these strategies include looking back to when the issue began? Did you split your goal into smaller, more achievable steps?

Now, look at the 5 goals you have outlined in your journal. For each of the goals, write down 2 steps to achieving them. Don't worry if your ideas seem superficial. At this point, we are focusing more on firming up your choice to make these improvements and adding the element of putting some action behind your goals.

Each day, focus on one of the goals and implement the two steps attached to it. At the end of the day, write down your progress and your thoughts about how it went.

PART TWO
UNDERSTANDING YOUR MIND

CHAPTER THREE

MODELS OF THE MIND

The conscious mind may be compared to a fountain playing in the sun and falling back into the great subterranean pool of subconscious from which it rises.

~ Sigmund Freud

Who am I? is one of life's big questions, one I first remember asking myself at just five years old. No one has a satisfactory answer to this question, but we keep on asking it anyway. One element of Douglas Hofstadter's exploration of consciousness in *I am a Strange Loop* is the idea that 'I-ness' arises from recognizing 'other,' and the realization that I am different from 'other.' Our differences make us all unique, but who we are can change significantly throughout our lives.

Several movies have centered on a protagonist who suffers some amnesia and their resulting experiences. One of my favorites is *Regarding Henry*. In this movie, Henry (played by Harrison Ford) is a trial lawyer who puts winning a case above every other ethical consideration. He thrives on power and is too busy for his wife and child. However, his life is upended after being accidentally shot. Suffering from retrograde amnesia and learning to regain his former independence, Henry loses all sense of who he once was; he does not even recognize his former self. With a clean slate, Henry is then able to create the kind of person he wishes to be, taking his career in a different direction and forging much healthier and happier relationships with his family.

Regarding Henry is only a story with some feel-good moments, but a fair bit of traction can be gained from the idea of rooting out characteristics in ourselves that don't serve us and creating the person we wish to be. As this information resides in our minds, the first key to successful mind training, therefore, requires some understanding of how our minds work. Minds, though, can be very tricky. While scientists can look at the brain, name the different parts, and assign different primary functions, they cannot do this with the mind. And what about the interface between the brain and the mind—how does that happen? Over the years, some of the brightest people have attempted to construct models of the mind to explain how it works. While no definitive model of the mind holds in all circumstances, the different models do give us some insights, along with some clues as to how this information can be beneficial.

Mind Divisions

While interning under French neurologist Jean-Martin Charcot, Sigmund Freud, the founding father of psychoanalysis, was introduced to the idea that subconscious processes could influence behaviors. At that time, Charcot had been interviewing patients suffering from a condition called *hysteria*. In the eighteenth and nineteenth centuries, hysteria was a commonly diagnosed affliction. While a man could be so diagnosed, it was predominantly a malady that affected women—particularly those belonging to the more affluent segments of society.

This is an important story to look at as it highlights certain issues. For one, a very long history abounds of women being defined in ways that limit their abilities, and female hysteria certainly contains within it a definition of an overly sensitive weaker sex. This very definition played a role in actualizing it for many women, restricting their potential.

Additionally, and maybe even more significantly for our purposes today, is that defining a condition can create it (or convince people that they have it), especially when the symptoms can be so varied and general. In the nineteenth century, symptoms of *hysteria* could even include a fondness for writing, post-traumatic stress syndrome, depression, or even infertility.[1] In fact, the symptoms were said to include "everything that men found mysterious or unmanageable in women" and were "evidence of both the instability of the female mind and the social function of women defined in relation to their reproductive capacity."[2]

It would be fair to believe that *female hysteria* as a condition belonged way in the past. This is not so. While the condition was not included in the first *Diagnostic and Statistical Manual of Mental Disorders* (*DSM-I*) of the American Psychiatric Association (APA), which was published in 1952, it did appear in the DSM-II in 1968. It was finally dropped in the DSM-III in 1980.[3] So, as I prepared to go away to university, *female hysteria* was still classed as a mental disorder!

A more recent example of another condition with vague symptoms that gained popularity due to increased public awareness is restless leg syndrome. In 2005, the FDA approved the first medication to treat twitching legs. A multimillion-dollar consumer advertising campaign by manufacturer GlaxoSmithKline took sales from $165 million in 2005, to nearly $330 million in 2006, and by 2007, sales were up to $491 million, with 4.4 million prescriptions written for the drug.[4] While restless leg syndrome is a real condition, according to Dr. Christopher J. Earley (Johns Hopkins University), "advertising created an overheated demand for diagnosis among consumers, while easy-to-dispense drug samples provided a convenient response for busy doctors."[5] In 2008, the FDA approved a generic version of the drug. With the end of the advertising campaign, GlaxoSmithKline anticipated a drop in sales. "It's usually a pretty sharp drop," said Mary Anne Rhyne, the Glaxo spokeswoman."[6] Since the 1980s, Eldon has spoken of the dangers in commercials with their subtle (or not so subtle) attempts to create a problem for which the advertiser has a solution.

Jean-Martin Charcot

Let's bring this discussion back to Freud's discovery that subconscious processes could influence behaviors. Charcot was dealing with female hysteria patients experiencing symptoms such as chronic pain, fainting, seizures, and paralysis. Charcot could not find biological reasons for their symptoms, but under hypnosis, he and Freud learned that many of these patients had had traumatic sexual experiences, such as sexual abuse as children. During hypnosis, remembering the incident was often followed by an emotional outpouring, after which their symptoms frequently improved. Their condition was more psychological than physical.[7]

Freud went on to develop several theories, many of which were dismissed and are even derided today, such as the Oedipus complex and penis envy. Steven Pinker (Harvard University) said that "The idea that boys want to sleep with their mothers strikes most men as the silliest thing they have ever heard."[8] However, Freud taught two concepts that are still pertinent to our present discussion. The first has to do with the divisions of the mind.

Mind Components

One of Sigmund Freud's most well-known contributions is the idea that personality is created from the interactions and conflicts between three components of the mind that he called the *Id*, the *Ego*, and the *Superego*.

- The *id* is said to be present from birth and operates on the immediate fulfillment of pleasure. If a baby is hungry, it will cry until it is fed—it will not wait for a more convenient time.[9] The *id* exists wholly in the subconscious mind.
- The *ego* develops later and is responsible for mediating between the desires of the *id* and the constraints of reality.[10] A large part of the function of the ego has to do with delaying the gratification of the *id's* desires until an appropriate time.
- The *superego* is thought to be composed of the ideals that we have internalized from our parents and society. It is the higher moral standard we believe we should live to. The superego attempts to influence the ego even if the morality is not realistic.[11]

It is common today to hear *ego* being used negatively, as though it is the selfish part of a person with illusions of greater self-importance. This is a real distortion as a healthy *ego* is one that finds a place of balance between the demands of the *id* and the pressures of the *superego*.

Important in the idea of the divided mind are the conflicts that can be created by opposing desires—conflicts that can create increasing degrees of pressure until something just gives way. With the female patients Charcot was treating, the unresolved, suppressed, painful memories led to their symptoms of *hysteria*. Freud saw this as an example of being controlled by unconscious forces.

Self-Concept

Unlike Freud, Carl Rogers, one of the founding members of the American Association for Humanistic Psychology and who is best known for his development of person-centered therapy,[12] did not believe that people were controlled by unconscious forces but rather that personality was formed based on earlier experiences. Rogers wanted to understand how personality changes occurred. He believed that the need to grow and achieve our potential is inherent in all of us and that a successful life was one where you *self-actualized*—fully became the person you were supposed to be. His personality theory focuses on the idea of self or self-concept. Rogers held that healthy individuals were better able to incorporate their experiences into their idea of self.[13] Rogers believed that our self-concept consisted of three parts:

- *Self-image* relates to inner personality, how we see ourselves right now, and the self we feel is the truest to who we really are. This is not a perfect self, but rather a real self.
- *Ideal Self* is the self we think we should be. This self is heavily influenced by the expectations of society. The ideal self may push us to become better people, may leave us feeling disappointed in ourselves, or make us angry that such things are even expected of us. We do not

choose our ideal selves, but rather it is formed from our interactions with the world.
- *Self-esteem* is how you think of yourself—how much you like, accept, and value yourself. Self-esteem depends in part on how others see you, how you think you compare to others, and your place in society.[14]

Rogers defined your self-concept as being incongruent if there was a mismatch between how you see yourself and who you think you should be, and congruent if the two images were aligned. An incongruent self-concept can negatively influence self-esteem.[15]

Four Selves

Several authors have put forward their own variations on the aspects that formulate a person's self-concept. One of my favorites, simply because I can look both out in the world and into myself and see clearly how it fits, is the one Eldon used in his book, *Choices and Illusions*.[16] Here he states the four essential views of ourselves:

- Our *Actual Self* is the self that has failed in ways we will not share with others. It is our deeply held private self. It holds the thoughts we wish we did not have, what we think of ourselves, and the acts we wish we had not performed. It holds our most secret wishes and ambitions. It is the self that most of us try to change in some way or another, at some time in our lives—or maybe perpetually. However, it is also important to note that our actual self is not our true self, but rather our self-perception, complete with every believed limitation that accompanies one's private self.
- Our *Ideal Self* is our personal construct of perfection. Our ideal self would live a perfect life, with no room for error or growth. It is a self that is so perfect it is not, and can never be, real.

- Our *Ought-To-Be Self* is full of all the "shoulds" and "oughts" that we have learned—"You should do this. You ought to do that." This *ought-to-be self* differs from the ideal self as the thoughts that construct it are not our own. They derive from the voices of society and others. Even when we know that a should or ought idea is wrong, perhaps something that has been ingrained in us by a parent, it is still hard for us to let go of it.
- Our *Desired Self* is the self we believe we can be. The desired self holds our dreams and can cause discontent if the desires have not been filled–and most of the time they aren't.[17]

All four of these selves create places of conflict and reasons to be disappointed with ourselves. In turn, these stresses can cause us to behave in ways that betray our highest potential.

Integrations

While each of them is imperfect in its own way, these three different models of the divisions of mind do show us something significant. We all have the desire to do better, to achieve more, to fly higher so to speak, but we all have insecurities imposed upon us. If there is not a healthy balance within and between these different aspects of our selves, conflicts can arise, self-destructive patterns can form, and disappointments can result. And much of this operates, without our awareness, on a subconscious level.

Levels of Consciousness

Freud believed that unconscious motivations controlled all behaviors. While we are unaware of these motivations, they reveal themselves in our dreams, through symptoms such as obsessions, in Freudian 'slips of the tongue' in which unknown truths are revealed, and while under hypnosis.[18] Freud's model of the mind has been likened to an iceberg, with the unconscious playing a more significant out-of-sight role, unlike the conscious mind.[19] In Freud's model, the mind operates on three levels of consciousness with the *conscious* mind being responsible for about 10%, the *preconscious* being used between 50-60%, and the *unconscious* being used between 30-40%.[20] I prefer to think of the mind as having four components: the *conscious*, the *preconscious*, the *subconscious*, and the *unconscious*. As you will see, by sub-dividing Freud's unconscious into the subconscious and unconscious we can focus on the area where change is possible—a significant aspect of mind training.

Conscious

The conscious mind is the part of our mind that we believe makes our decisions, performs our actions and plans, and so forth. Now I intentionally said, we believe—for you'll discover in what follows that most of our so-called volitional choices are indeed not so volitional. Indeed, the entire issue of free will is at stake when we understand just how many of our so-called choices are not coming from our conscious mind but rather from our subconscious.

Preconscious

The preconscious is the area of our mind where we store information we're not consciously attending to. It might be the lyrics from our favorite poem or song, or our childhood phone number, address, and the like. The preconscious is where we go to retrieve memories—the more we can hold in the preconscious, the better our memory is.

Subconscious

The subconscious mind is the subject of much speculation, but we know quite a bit about it. For example, in certain instances, the subconscious can be called upon to retrieve information from long-forgotten episodes in the past or simply overlooked details. Hypnosis can be a great tool for recovering forgotten memories. Eldon has had several instances where he used forensic hypnosis to discover this kind of information. In one instance, a man had been a victim of an armed robbery while at an ATM. All the man could remember was the *"big gun"* that had been shoved into his face. However, under hypnosis, he was able to also remember the make and model of the car that the perpetrator had driven up in. In this instance, the trauma of the event pushed the memory into the subconscious. It is possible that, in time, he would have remembered the details anyway, but it is also possible that he would never have remembered without the use of hypnosis.

Eldon was involved in another even more significant case that resulted in a murder sentence being overturned. In this instance, it was not fear that caused the conscious mind to forget details, but rather a self-imposed drug-induced state.

The case, as presented to Eldon, involved a troubled young man with a juvenile record. It seems he had come home from a party to discover his mother's body sprawled out on her bed. The sexual assault and murder had been incredibly brutal, and blood was everywhere. After taking a few moments to deal with the shock, the boy called law enforcement. Although he claimed innocence, the police officers did not believe him. It did not help that there had been plenty of alcohol and drugs at the party, and the kid was not only intoxicated and incoherent but also unable to provide any real details about his evening and how much time he had spent at the party. He also had a history of problems with his mother.

The police officers were pretty sure of his guilt, and after an interrogation that left the boy feeling confused about his innocence, he took a polygraph test—and failed. Later Eldon would learn that the polygraph examiner had used an illegal test—a two-needle polygraph—in addition to some other questionable techniques. As such, this testimony should never have been allowed. The boy, however, was advised to plead guilty based on the evidence and the fact that he would get a much easier sentence. This was not the case, and he was sentenced to hard time. It was after the sentencing that Eldon was brought into the case.

Using forensic hypnosis, the boy remembered that he had left the party and had cut through the park at around 2 a.m. While in the park, he saw two police officers pull in and so he hid—he did not want to get into trouble for being *high as a kite*. He watched as the officers spent about twenty minutes searching some trash cans before leaving. This information turned out to be vital as it provided him with an alibi. A search of the police records found that two officers were indeed at the park at that time searching through the trash cans. This also meant that the boy could not have been home at the time of death and could not have committed the crime. Eldon and his colleagues presented the evidence to the judge in an open hearing, and as a result, the inmate was released, and the charges dismissed.

So, the subconscious holds a great deal of information than can be very difficult to retrieve. This information, though, can influence our various *defense strategies, mental shortcuts, biases,* and the like. This is a very important subject and one we will be discussing in detail later.

Unconscious

The unconscious is the part of the mind that oversees somatic processes and the like—it handles everything from keeping our heart beating to remembering to breathe. Now before you object, the reason we named it the unconscious mind, as opposed to just dealing with specific parts of the brain per se, is that trained meditators have demonstrated an ability to control aspects of the physiology normally not thought as being accessible to the mind.

A 1982 study by Herbert Benson et al. found that practitioners of *g-tummo* (heat) yoga were able to raise "the temperature of their fingers and toes by as much as 8.3°C."[21] "Just using the power of their minds, the monks produced enough body heat to dry wet sheets placed on them as they relaxed in chilly rooms."[22] A 2011 study at the University of California - Los Angeles found that "long-time meditators have stronger connections between brain regions and show less age-related atrophy when compared to a control group."[23] So meditation can change the actual structure of the brain,[24] and for our purposes, create a pathway for improving the quality of our lives.

While it is common to think of unconsciousness as being unaware at any level, this is not true, for coma patients have recovered and reported many details about what went on around them while they were in a coma. Indeed, one individual, Martin Pistorius, reported such an experience. "Everybody thought he was a 'vegetable,' but after twelve years in a coma, not only did he wake up, but he says he remembers everything and was perfectly conscious most of the time. His body became his prison, but he was ultimately able to escape after spending years trying to communicate with the outside world."[25]

Collective Unconscious

In Freud's model though, the unconscious mind was the repository of a person's life experiences. He believed behaviors were generally controlled by unconscious beliefs and motivations, the most powerful of which were childhood sexual desires that had been repressed from the conscious mind. This is something that Carl Jung, the founder of analytical psychology disagreed with—he thought Freud was overly focused on sexual matters and, rather than seeing the unconscious mind as simply a reservoir of repressed thoughts and emotions, he thought that it could also be the source of inspiration and creativity.[26]

To Jung, there were two aspects to the unconscious mind, the *personal unconscious,* and the *collective unconscious.* The collective unconscious has been likened to Emerson's Over-Soul.[27] For Jung, the personal unconscious housed all the personal experiences, whereas the collective unconscious held inherited, deep-seated beliefs and instincts that were common to all—the past collective experiences of humanity.[28] Jung also believed that people were dominated by particular archetypes or "primordial images" as he originally dubbed them. I like the term 'primordial images' as, to me, it more clearly depicts the concept—images or constructs that existed in the early days of humanity's existence. An example of how this works would be the mother-child relationship, which is governed by the mother archetype. There is a universal view of the elements inherent to the ideal mother-child relationship. So, in Jung's model, a good mother would be imprinted by the mother-child archetype. Alternatively, a person governed by the warrior archetype would be tough, courageous, and focused on achieving goals and overcoming obstacles.[29]

With his belief in archetypes, Jung therefore also rejected the idea of the tabula rasa—an idea most attributed to the seventeenth-century philosopher John Locke—that the human is born as a blank slate. Instead, Jung believed that a person "brings with him systems that are organized and ready to function in a specifically human way, and he owes these to millions of years of human development."[30] Jung's ideas are not as popular as Freud's, perhaps because they veer into the mystical and pseudoscientific. I must admit that, after raising my children, I can see some traction in questioning the absolute tabula rasa idea; I am sure my children each brought into this life their own unique guiding principles. However, *where* these principles came from is another question. Many philosophers and psychologists also do not believe in the blank slate idea either, citing ideas and concepts that we just seem to know. One example of innate knowledge is the idea that none of us needs to be taught that there is no number to which we cannot add one. Another would be the idea that, for there to be *nothing*, there must be *something.* As a young child, I remember arguing this point with an expert at the Greenwich Planetarium, when he tried to tell me that the 'nothing went on for forever.'

Now, some metaphysical schools believe the collective unconscious is the *superconscious*,[31] and accessing it would empower super abilities. However, this, along with ideas of the seat of the soul and other such spiritual concepts, are not the purview of this book.

Subconscious/Unconscious Influences

As I said, many of Freud's ideas have been discounted or rejected, especially those on sexuality. Even as a child, I remember hearing jokes about how silly it was that Freud saw sexual aspects in everything. For example, just because something was longer than it was wide did not mean it symbolized a penis—sometimes a tie is just a tie! However, Freud's idea of the subconscious/unconscious mind exerting an influence over behavior has held true. In some cases, this influence is rooted in evolutionary adaptations. For example, the need to make a good impression on a first date could be an adaptation–like the peacock showing off its tail feathers. Generally, the more attractive you make yourself look, the more likely you will be picked to become a partner.

Other subconscious/unconscious influences can come from your past. In a longitudinal study, one-year-old infants were measured for their degrees of attachment and bonding. Using this information, researchers predicted how many friends a child would have in high school and how often they would experience close romantic breakups in their twenties.[32]

To sum it up, modern research has revealed: "that many important affective, motivational, and behavioral phenomena operate without the person's awareness or conscious intention (Freud); that they are often triggered by events, people, situational settings, and other external stimuli (behaviorism); but that these external stimuli exert their effect through their automatic activation of internal mental representations and processes (cognitive psychology)."[33]

Erikson's Eight Stages

Understanding that our subconscious mind contains all these forgotten memories, which exert unseen (unacknowledged) influences on our lives is one thing, but we need to look further at the kinds of situations that can create memories. We also need to look at the balance of power between our negative and positive experiences. It would be fair to believe that if your personal relationship was 60% good and 40% bad, you would rate it as being good overall. Unfortunately, we will see later that this is not the case. For now, though, let's look at one category of life experiences that can exert an influence on our current lives—general development.

Eldon is a little older than I am, and we find it interesting how similar my experiences are to his as I pass the same age milestones. Eldon has always said that spiritual inquiry often begins in earnest in the forties. The fifties can often be a time of assessing our lives, seeing how close we have come to achieving our goals and adjusting when necessary. The sixties bring a different viewpoint as we start to lose friends, loved ones, and peers.

In the 1950s, psychologist and psychoanalyst Erik Erikson introduced the idea that personality developed in a predetermined order through eight stages of psychosocial development. For each successful stage of development, Erikson assigned a particular virtue or ego strength.

Stages of Childhood

1. Trust vs Mistrust
Between birth and about 1.5 years of age, the primary caregiver is most important. If the child receives reliable care, they will take this security forward into other relationships. If the care is unreliable, then mistrust, suspicion, and anxiety may develop. Success in stage one leads to feelings of hope when in new situations—hope that there will be someone to help them. Failure can lead to fear and anxiety. The virtue or ego strength gained is that of *hope*.

2. Autonomy vs Shame
Between the ages of 1.5 and three, children are focused on physical skills and a sense of independence. If children are encouraged and supported, they become confident and secure in their own ability to survive in the world. If the child is overly controlled, they can develop feelings of inadequacy and suffer from poor self-esteem and shame. The virtue or ego strength gained is that of *will*.

3. Intuition vs Guilt
Between the ages of three to five, children explore their interpersonal skills and their ability to make up games. They learn how to lead and make decisions. If there is too much criticism or control, or the child feels their questions are trivial and a nuisance, the child can develop feelings of guilt. This can be a delicate balance for some guilt is necessary or a child cannot learn self-control or develop a conscience. Conversely, too much guilt will make it hard for the child to learn how to interact or be creative. They can become afraid to take the initiative. The virtue or ego strength gained is that of *purpose*.

4. Industry vs Inferiority
Between the ages of five to twelve, children go through their early school years. As they acquire new skills, they can develop a sense of pride in their achievements. Children who are encouraged and commended by their teachers, parents, and peers will believe in their ability to be successful. Failure at this stage can lead to feelings of inferiority. With the correct balance of success and modesty, a child develops feelings of competence. The virtue or ego strength gained is that of *competence*.

Stage of Adolescence

5. Identity vs Role Confusion
Between the ages of twelve and eighteen, children need to learn the role they will occupy as adults. During this stage, they explore possibilities and form their own identities and beliefs. These identities relate to both sexual

and career choices. Success at this stage brings a strong sense of self, whereas those who remain unsure of their beliefs and desires will feel confused about themselves and their future. The virtue or ego strength gained is that of *fidelity*.

Stages of Adulthood

6. Intimacy vs Isolation
Between the ages of eighteen to forty, adults focus on forming intimate and loving relationships with someone other than family members. Success leads to strong relationships whereas failure leads to loneliness and isolation.

It is important to note that each of these stages builds on the success or failure of the prior stages. In this instance, a poor sense of self (stage 5) can cause commitment problems and so lead to emotional isolation, loneliness, and depression. The virtue or ego strength gained in stage 6 is that of *love*.

7. Generativity vs Stagnation
Adults have a need to create or nurture things that will outlast them. This can be through having children or by creating something that will benefit others. Psychologically speaking, generativity refers to 'making your mark' on the world, and this becomes a priority between the ages of forty to sixty-five. Success leads to feelings of usefulness and accomplishment whereas failure leads to feelings of stagnation and disconnectedness. The virtue or ego strength gained is that of *care*.

8. Ego Integrity vs Despair.
From the age of sixty-five onwards, productivity (generally) slows down. It is a time for looking back and assessing life. If a person feels their life has been unproductive, if they feel guilty about something, or if they did not accomplish their goals, this can lead to dissatisfaction, despair, depression, and hopelessness. If they feel successful, they can look back at their life with a sense of closure and completeness. "Wise people are not characterized by a continuous state of ego integrity, but they experience both ego integrity and despair. Thus, late life is characterized by both integrity and despair

as alternating states that need to be balanced." The virtue or ego strength gained is that of *wisdom*.

One of the criticisms of Erikson's theory of psychosocial development has to do with the fact that it does not provide mechanisms for resolving conflicts and moving successfully from one stage to the next. However, it does provide a broad framework for viewing development through all stages of life.[34]

I am not fond of the term *virtue* that Erikson assigns to the successful completion of each of these stages as it sounds a bit sanctimonious and almost impossible to reach. That said, the different virtues do provide a framework to view the main benefits that can be gained on the successful completion of each stage. You should also note that there is no pass/fail type of grading system; instead, there is a continuum, and in most cases, it is always possible to do better or worse. Success should therefore be looked at more with regard to how well the learnings from each stage have served you. If there is an area in your life today that is not working for you, or if you tend to make the same errors in judgment repeatedly, perhaps you need to examine a particular stage in your earlier development again—to heal, rectify, or maybe just to accept. From a mind training perspective, definite value can be gained from looking back at the different stages of our lives.

Fight/Flight—Anxiety/Depression

Another way to look at the levels of consciousness model is with the basic instincts of *fight* or *flight*. There are no saber-toothed tigers today, so our modern adaptation for fight and flight includes *anxiety* and *depression*. That is, not many of us face real threats in our lives, and yet many of us still frequently experience the same old fight/flight responses. Adrenaline surges, blood pressure climbs, and the body has responded to a synthetic threat as though it were that tiger from the past. This fight/flight response leads to anger and aggression or withdrawal, anxiety, and depression. It is not at all uncommon for the depressed to spend extra time alone, stay in bed, and withdraw from the outside world—hide. This is a flight response, pure and simple. So, with this in mind, let's take a closer look.

Anxiety/Depression

All humans share one characteristic in particular that plays a huge role in our programming—we are herd animals. That is, we seek approval, love, engagement, and social protection. More importantly, we first seek to avoid rejection. It's not uncommon to think of acceptance as important to survival. So, what does this mean?

Our subconscious mind receives input from all our experiences—positive or negative experiences. As I said, in modern society, the fight/flight response has largely been replaced by anxiety and depression. The stimuli from the outside world can be either real or synthetic. Few of us have been presented with many real stimuli. Virtually all the stimuli that condition self-limiting responses are synthetic in the sense that they are not truly life-threatening. I opine that these stimuli are based upon an innate fear of isolation, and therefore, rejection by another human being, or the fear of this happening, conditions nearly all our responses. Our actions and responses are built upon our perception of others and our need for acceptance and understanding. Thus, behavior is purely condition/response learning. For example, we behave in one way and get an X response; we behave in another way and get a Y response. We then decide which response we preferred and exhibit the behavior thereafter, and we can quickly forget that another kind of response even exists. This is one of the processes of limiting our own choices. Only limited choice exists, and those choices result from our conditioning patterns.

Behaviorally this means we are predisposed in ways that manifest as a lack of confidence, fear of failure, internalization of stress, physical ailments, rationalization, and so forth. How can this not be so when most of our behavior comes from trying to please others and to find acceptance? And don't for one moment think that those who come across as overly confident and pushy are not also dealing with the same issue. They just use different compensation strategies.

Most, if not all, of this conditioning, takes place in primitive ways as a function of our socialization. Therefore, the old fight/ flight mechanisms of our ancestors can give rise to deeply impressed self-limiting feelings and behaviors.

Bio-Computer Analogy

Another way to look at this is to understand that every message unit one receives in a lifetime is imprinted upon the mind. This process occurs largely without discrimination, except for the lenses of interpretation, which themselves are a direct result of our primary and secondary caretakers, and from the enculturation process in general. One aspect of this can be seen in the frequently shared meme that says, "five minutes after your birth, they decide your name, nationality, religion, and sect, and you spend the rest of your life defending something you didn't even choose." This, along with the rest of the enculturation process—the gradual acquisition of the characteristics and norms of a culture or group by a person—forms the basis for our moral valuing judgments and notions of reality, together with our general aptitude regarding change or the incorporation of new ideas.

Negativity

Statistically, we have all received many more negative than positive message units during our maturation. Additionally, negative messages simply have more power over us than positive messages. Evolutionary psychologists believe this is because we once knew dangers could be lurking everywhere and we, therefore, had to pay much closer attention to negative situations (such as the rustle that told us there was a snake hiding in the grass), as our very lives could depend on it. Our society has no "rite of passage" in which a ritual or event takes place where we are supposed to leave behind the *no-don't garbage* we all heard so many times during childhood. Consequently, as adults, this type of *garbage* can become what Eldon calls a *value norm anchor* that prohibits change.

If you are in doubt, just pay attention to how you talk to yourself. How many times during the day do you tell yourself negative things? When you think about soaring financially, what thoughts come to mind? When you think about living happily and healthily into your hundreds, what thoughts come to your mind? When you think about entering a fitness or beauty event, what thoughts come to your mind? You get my point—there are many things in life that we hold from ourselves because of those old value norm anchors that insist we're not good enough, smart enough, and so forth. As such, becoming the best version of ourselves necessitates examining the contents of our subconscious mind and then finding ways to override automatic behaviors and beliefs that, while designed to protect us, actually limit our success.

NOTES

Key Points

We have now introduced the idea that subconscious processes can influence us and how widespread this can be. In our exploration of the placebo effect, we saw how a society could have a collective belief that influences how its citizens experience different colored medications. With female hysteria, we see the cultural influence of belief both on men who considered women to be the weaker sex and so expected emotional events to trigger illness and on women who accepted they were weaker and therefore more prone to experiencing illness. This is not difficult to do when the symptoms were so vague and so varied. Also, a definition that categorized women as being 'weaker' would have the effect of imposing, both by others and by oneself, limitations on potential and self-actualization, something most women are still battling in varying degrees. (Please note: while this example was regarding women, imposed definitions can affect us all.)

Another example of the power of definitions was when common, generalized symptoms were labeled *restless leg syndrome*. Public awareness of this definition resulted in many more being diagnosed with a condition—something that reversed in numbers when the marketing campaign ended.

Both stories give credence to the idea that subconscious processes can influence our health and our behavior.

When we look at the models of the mind offered by Freud, Rogers, Eldon, and in part Jung, a picture forms of how ideas and beliefs can be formed and held in the subconscious mind. The different models all point to a divided self. A healthy self needs to integrate these different aspects in a way that provides reasonable expectations. Unfortunately, our development and enculturation provide numerous places to trip us up, leaving us with feelings of insecurity and pain. If these issues are not dealt with, they can create conflicts, causing physical, emotional, and behavioral issues even though the initial stimulus may be way in the past.

Erikson's eight stages of psychosocial development, along with our anxiety/depression and bio-computer models, provide some insights into how and where these conflicts can arise. Having this basic understanding of subconscious processes will allow us to explore where issues or restrictions in our lives may have started and offers clues on how to correct them.

Exercise

Look at Erikson's eight stages of psychosocial development and rank each of the stages out of ten on how successfully you believe you navigated them. Journal your rankings along with any possible details for why you ranked it so. The more you engage in this kind of exercise, the more likely it is that subconscious connections will become conscious, leading to those breakthrough insights. However, please remember to be gentle with yourselves in this process. Life happens, and despite our best intentions everyone makes mistakes and experiences challenges. The point of mind training is not to experience feelings of guilt or regret, but rather to minimize issues to the best of our ability while accepting the fact that it is impossible to avoid every kind of problem.

Look at the five mini-goals you have outlined in your journal. Do any of them relate to how you ranked the different categories? Sometimes, the feelings that arise may be disquieting. Make a mental effort to forgive and release any negativity and focus instead on creating a better tomorrow.

CHAPTER FOUR

THE MECHANICAL BRAIN

Some automatic device clicked in her big brain, and her knees felt weak, and there was a chilly feeling in her stomach. She was in love with this man.

~ Kurt Vonnegut, Galápagos.

Brain hardwiring becomes apparent when we consider that about 90% of people are right-handed[1] and that learning to do things such as write with your non-dominant hand is difficult albeit not impossible. We also know that the left half of the brain controls much of the right half of the body and vice versa.[2] I think I was in my teens when I first learned that the eyes see everything upside down, but only recently did I learn that, rather than the brain just making a correction, and righting the image, it uses information received from the ears to calculate the rotation of the head.[3]

To highlight some of the power of this hardwiring, one of the first things we like to do when lecturing is to start with a simple exercise—one that you can do right now. From a seated position, pick up your right foot and begin to move it in a clockwise circle. While your foot circles in a clockwise fashion, raise your right hand and draw the number six in the air with your forefinger. Now check and see what your foot is doing. Most people are startled to see that as soon as they started to draw the number six, the foot would change direction and start moving in an anticlockwise direction.

This provides a doorway into the idea that, if we understand the hardwiring of the brain, even if only at a very rudimentary level, then we become open to the idea of possible places we can take manual control of these mechanisms and perhaps make them work more efficiently for our stated goals.

Specialization

Early in the nineteenth century, the German physician Franz Joseph Gall first put forward the idea that specific mental processes were correlated with specific regions of the brain. His theory of phrenology suggested that there were thirty-five 'organs' in the brain, each dedicated to specific functions. He further believed that the degree of use of these 'organs' would influence their size, and this would lead to bumps and ridges on the skull that could be used to diagnose mental abilities and personality.[4] Phrenology was quickly dismissed as being a pseudoscience and racist (it was being used to prove prevalent, but baseless hypotheses about the inferiority of non-white races[5]). However, the idea that certain functions were associated with specific regions of the brain was made apparent in the *American Crowbar Case* that involved a railroad worker, Phineas Gage. This case showed a direct link between a brain trauma (prefrontal brain damage) and personality change.[6]

Phineas Gage

On September 13, 1848, twenty-five-year-old Gage was the foreman of a crew cutting a railroad bed in Vermont.[7] He was packing explosives in a hole using a tamping iron that measured forty-three inches long, 1.25 inches in diameter, and weighed 13.25 pounds when the powder detonated.[8] The tamping iron shot through Gage's left cheek, tore into his brain, and exited his skull to land eighty feet away, smeared with blood, and stuck with bits of brain. The hole was clear enough that his doctor could insert his index fingers into both ends of the opening and have them meet. Interestingly, Gage was able to speak a few moments after the accident and, after a cart ride to town, he exited the cart unassisted and subsequently climbed up a long flight of stairs to a room for treatment. Later that evening, he even said he did not need to see his friends as he would be back to work in a day or two.[9] This would not turn out to be the case; his healing process was touch and go, and his condition became so poor that a coffin was prepared.[10] However, on November 25, about 2.5 months after the accident, Gage was considered well enough to go home.[11]

The fact that Phineas Gage survived such a horrific accident and went on to live twelve more years, traveling and even working in Chile for a while, is amazing enough. For our purposes, though, it was the complete personality change he exhibited that makes his story significant in our understanding of the human brain; a change that was so remarkable that his friends stated he was "no longer Gage," and his employers would not rehire him. Prior to the accident, though lacking a formal education, Gage was described as possessing "a well-balanced mind, and was looked upon by those who knew him as a shrewd, smart businessman, very energetic, and persistent in executing all his plans of operation." After his recovery, his physician described him as being "fitful, irreverent, indulging at times in the grossest profanity (which was not previously his custom), manifesting but little deference for his fellows, impatient of restraint or advice when it conflicts with his desires, at times pertinaciously obstinate, yet capricious and vacillating, devising many plans of future operations, which are no sooner arranged than they are abandoned in turn for others more feasible. A child in his intellectual capacity and manifestations, he has the animal passions of a strong man."[12]

Parts of the Brain

While the story of Phineas Gage provided early evidence that the frontal lobe played a role in defining personality,[13] the field of neuroscience has come a long way since. Today, we know that the brain is segmented into parts, each with its specific functions:

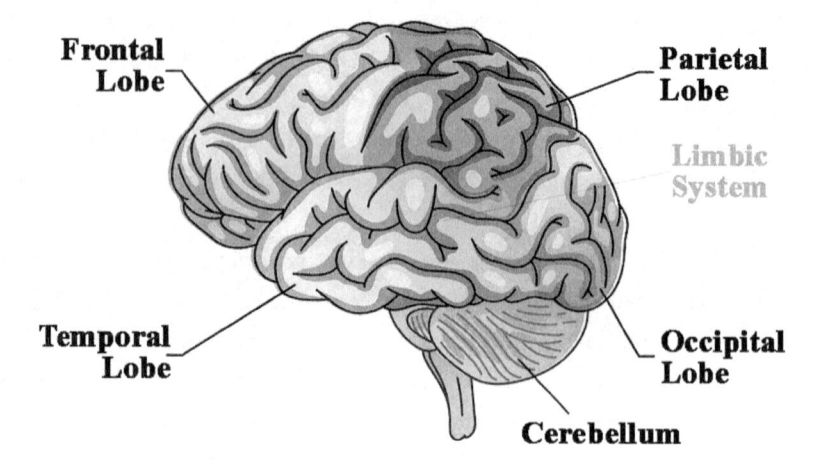

Frontal Lobe — **Parietal Lobe** — Limbic System — **Temporal Lobe** — **Occipital Lobe** — **Cerebellum**

- The frontal lobe (front of the brain) is involved with body movement, personality, problem-solving, concentration, planning, emotional reactions, sense of smell, the meaning of words, general speech, and decision making.
- The parietal lobe (upper middle of the brain) controls our sense of touch and pressure, sense of taste, and bodily awareness. It helps us identify objects and understand spatial relationships, interpret pain, and understand language.
- The temporal lobe (sides of the brain) governs our sense of hearing, ability to recognize others, emotions, and memory.
- The occipital lobe (backside of the brain) controls the sense of sight.
- The cerebellum (lower backside of the brain) governs fine motor control, posture, balance, coordination, and equilibrium.
- The limbic system (middle of the brain) controls behavioral and emotional responses, especially as they relate to survival, feeding, reproduction, caring for our young, and the fight or flight response.[14]

Of course, science knows a lot more about the functioning of the brain, but for our purposes, it is enough introduction to give us an awareness of how mechanical many processes are and how this can influence our beliefs, and therefore the composition of who we are. A serious brain injury changed Phineas Gage's personality, but this only highlights the fact that our personalities are heavily influenced by our biology. One aspect of mind training is about taking this information and making little tweaks to create changes in the kind of life we experience.

Split-Brain

While the various primary functions of the different parts of the brain may not be common knowledge, most people are aware that the two hemispheres of the brain have specific primary functions. Individuals are frequently described as being left-brained or right-brained, with the left-brained personality being more logical, detailed, and analytical, and the right-brained personality being more creative, spontaneous, and subjective. This idea stems from the split-brain research carried out by the eminent neurobiologist Roger Sperry and his colleagues.

> (Please note: Some of these studies are simply inhumane, and I apologize to anyone who is offended by this part of the discussion. Sadly, history is full of appalling animal experiments. While I support those who would call for the banning of such inhumane treatments, the verdict is still out as to whether findings from such past experiments should be ignored/forgotten.)

Sperry's earlier work investigated the hardwiring of neural circuitry. In one experiment, he transposed the flexion and extension nerves in the hind leg of a rat. Subsequently, when the bottom of the rat's foot was injured, it would straighten instead of pulling up. As the injury worsened, the rat pushed down even harder, never learning to compensate for the transposition of the nerves. According to Sperry, "No adaptive functional adjustment of the nervous system took place."[15] So, there was a hardwiring for which the brain could not compensate. Sperry's work also demonstrated that the brain is cross-wired; the right hemisphere controls the left side of the body, and the left hemisphere controls the right.

Sperry's first split-brain studies on a cat looked at interlocular transfer. The common belief was that once one eye had learned to solve a problem, the information would be transferred to the other eye. For this experiment, Sperry split the "optic chiasm so that the right eye goes to the right cerebral hemisphere and the left eye to the left hemisphere," and he also "cut the corpus callosum between the two hemispheres," so creating the "split-brain cat." With the left eye covered, the cat was then trained to distinguish between a square and a triangle and taught to select the triangle. However, when the right eye was covered, the cat had to be taught once again to distinguish between the square and the triangle. This time, though, it was taught to select the square. With two different trainings, the shape it selected depended on which eye was covered.

It should be noted that "Sperry's experiments with cats and later with monkeys paved the way for cutting the corpus callosum in humans as a treatment for severe epilepsy."[16] According to the Cleveland Clinic, this corpus callosotomy surgery "makes seizures less severe and frequent and may stop them completely."[17] So, even though thinking about the research itself makes me sick to my stomach, I am also aware of the huge impact this knowledge/surgery has had on the lives of those impacted by this serious condition.

Left Brain / Right Brain

Michael Gazzaniga, under the supervision of Roger Sperry, initiated the *human* split-brain research[18], and their subsequent work brought to light some fascinating insights into the workings of the brain.

In 1962, Gazzaniga, along with Roger Sperry and Joseph Bogen, first experimented with a split-brain human subject. The forty-eight-year-old patient, known as W.J., had recently undergone corpus callosotomy surgery to limit the spread of epileptic seizures. His behavior after the surgery suggested that the corpus callosum, rather than simply holding the two hemispheres of the brain together as had previously been thought, mediated communication between the two.[19] Several findings from the experiments carried out with W.J. included:

- W.J.'s right hand (controlled by the left hemisphere) was unable to match a set of blocks to a pattern on a flash card. W.J.'s left hand (controlled by the right hemisphere) was able to complete the task with ease, even jumping in to help the fumbling right hand.
- W.J. easily named images presented to his right field of vision (processed by the left hemisphere) but reported seeing nothing when the images were presented to his left field of vision (processed by the right hemisphere).
- Interestingly, W.J. was able to use his left hand (controlled by the right hemisphere) to point to the image he had seen on the left. This indicated that the right hemisphere was cognizant but could not speak.[20]

So, the two halves of the brain were operating independently, almost like two different minds. Gazzaniga's reaction summed up the enormity of these findings: "That was a powerful moment—to see that there were two different mental control systems competing to solve this problem," he said.[21] This is a fascinating piece of information, and we will explore some of its ramifications in more detail later. For now, it is enough to note that, just like the different lobes of the brain, the two hemispheres of the brain have their primary functions. Research has shown that the left brain is more verbal, analytical, and orderly, and is involved in:

- Logic
- Sequencing
- Linear thinking
- Mathematics
- Facts
- Thinking in words

The right brain is more visual, intuitive, and creative, being involved with:

- Imagination
- Holistic thinking
- Intuition
- Arts
- Rhythm
- Nonverbal cues
- Feelings
- Visualization
- Daydreaming[22]

By the 1960s, Roger Sperry and his colleagues had shown that "the left hemisphere is more geared toward abstract and analytical thought, calculation, and linguistic ability, while the right hemisphere is more important for comprehending spatial patterns and complex sounds like music."[23] Sperry's work had made such a significant contribution that, in 1981, he was awarded the Nobel Prize in Physiology or Medicine "for his discoveries concerning the functional specialization of the cerebral hemispheres."[24] However, that was not all the split-brain research taught.

The Interpreter

In 1976, working with a graduate student, James LeDoux, Gazzaniga showed two pictures to a patient who had undergone split-brain surgery. "The man's left hemisphere saw a chicken claw; his right saw a snow scene. Afterward, the man chose the most appropriate matches from an array of pictures visible to both hemispheres. He chose a chicken to go with the claw and a shovel to go with the snow."[25]

While the right brain is able to communicate by pointing to written words or objects with the left hand, the language centers of the brain reside in the left brain, which means that verbal communication requires left-brain input.[26] In this experiment, the left brain had seen the claw but not the snow, but the patient had selected both the chicken and the shovel. When asked why he had chosen those particular items, the patient responded, "The chicken goes with the claw . . . and you need a shovel to clean out the chicken shed."[27] The patient made up a reason.

Gazzaniga decided to call the left-brain narrating system "the interpreter," and found great significance in its ability/need to create a meaningful script, even if it was inventing reasons based on limited/flawed information. According to Gazzaniga, "We are, in fact, a confederation of relatively independent agents, each struggling to be part of our narrative that is our story. It turns out the left brain has another capacity potentially more important than language itself. The interpreter is the thing that sticks all of those parts together."[28] While not pertinent to our immediate discussion, you will see the importance of this finding in several areas as we work through the processes of mind training.

Stroop

Another related area of research involves congruent and incongruent information. In 1935, continuing from work begun in the nineteenth century, psychologist John Ridley Stroop ran an interesting study where he timed how long subjects took to:

- Read the word of a color, such as 'red,' when written in a black ink
- State the color used for a painted square
- State the color of ink used to print the name of a different color—for example, to identify the green ink used to write the word red.

Using a list of 100 words, he found that it took subjects 2.3 seconds (5.6%) longer when they were asked to *read* words that described one color while being printed in another, as compared with reading the same words when printed in black. This result was said to be unreliable. However, when subjects were asked to state the color of ink for a word that named a different color, there was a 47.0 seconds (74.3%) increase. He found that the subjects took considerably longer to identify the color of ink used when the printed word was for a different color.[29] The Stroop Test is one of the most popular examples used for demonstrating the delay in reaction time with congruent and incongruent stimuli.

While researchers do not have any definitive answers, they have a few theories for what causes the Stroop Effect. These would include:

- *Selective Attention Theory*—identifying the color of the word takes more attention than simply reading the word.
- *Automaticity Theory*—reading is a more automatic process than recognizing colors.
- *Speed of Processing Theory*—we process written words faster than we process colors.
- *Parallel Distributed Processing*—the brain creates different pathways for different tasks, and the strength of the pathway will dictate if it is easier to name the color or read the text.[30]

Lateralization

There appears to be a relationship with hemispheric lateralization in the performance of the Stroop test as a study by Lei Zhang et al. in 2014 showed an "increased information flow from the left to the right hemispheres for the incongruent versus the neutral task."[31]

Comparing verbal and spatial Stroop tasks, non-right-handers (left-handers, ambidextrous, etc.) showed a greater Stroop effect in the color-word task, but a reduced Stroop effect for incongruent spatial information (e.g., an arrow pointing in the wrong direction from its position). This would fit with the idea that non-right-handed people have "preferential access to the right hemisphere dealing with spatial material."[32]

In his work, Eldon has seen that left-handed individuals seem to be better at identifying the color of ink used to print the name of a different color and that right-handed people would be better at reading the name of the color regardless of the color of ink used. This information became one of the factors he considered when he sought to create a technology that would enhance and complement his mind training work.

The important thing to note here is that some aspects of the brain function very mechanically, but sometimes not as efficiently as we would like.

The Stroop test demonstrates the slight confusion that occurs when the incoming information is incongruent. We also see that the two halves of the brain have their preferred form of information input.

Emotional Stroop

As an aside, you may also be interested to know of a couple of variations of the Stroop test that have proved useful. The emotional Stroop test examines the subject's ability to report the name of the color of an emotionally laden word. This is not a test of congruent vs incongruent as the words now have nothing to do with the color.[33] They have also found that depressed people take longer to say the color of a negative word than a neutral word.[34] Another study found that cocaine-dependent subjects took longer to say the color of a cocaine-associated word (e.g. cocaine, crack, rocks, and puff) than a neutral word (e.g. couch, sofa, cabinet, and room).[35] This has some practical uses as the Stroop test was demonstrated to be an effective tool for identifying cocaine-dependent subjects at risk of dropping out of treatment.[36]

I found this information extremely interesting, and I wondered if the Stroop test had ever been used as a lie-detection tool. My research brought up a 2003 study by Iris Engelhard, Harald Merckelbach, and Marcel van den Hout. Of the forty subjects used, half were asked to commit a mock crime and to keep it a secret. Following the mock crime, all the subjects were administered the Guilty Knowledge Test which involves a polygraph. The subjects were then asked to perform a modified version of the Stroop Test. Here, phrases related to the crime along with phrases unrelated to the crime were printed in different color inks and the subjects were asked to identify the colors.

For the first round of the Guilty Knowledge Test, the results were 100% accurate for the innocent subjects and 78% accurate for the guilty subjects. With the Stroop test, however, no significant difference showed in interference scores between innocent and guilty subjects; knowledge of the crime did not cause any significant difference in response time when naming the colors. The researchers, therefore, concluded that the Stroop test was *not* suitable as a lie detector. It was suggested that the inefficacy could have been due to the story format of the test, but the researchers did not think it would be possible to construct such a test using just single words.[37]

Hemisphere Dominance

For the sake of clarity, know that the idea of brain function lateralization is often taken way too far when it comes to common conceptions. As I stated earlier, knowledge of the different functions of the two brain hemispheres has become so well known that it is common to hear of people being described as left-brained or right-brained, the idea being that in a particular person, one half of the brain dominates or is stronger than the other. While we have seen that certain functions primarily occur in one half of the brain—language, logic, and reason tend to be on the left, whereas artistic and creativity tend to be on the right—research carried out at Utah State University showed that people do not actually have stronger left brains or right brains.[38] In this study, data from resting MRI (magnetic resonance imaging) scans of 1011 subjects between the ages of seven and twenty-nine were analyzed for functional lateralization. The results were inconsistent with the idea that the human brain favors one brain hemisphere over the other[39]—no real differences were found between the two halves of the brain.

According to neuroscientist Jeff Anderson, "It's absolutely true that some brain functions occur in one or the other side of the brain, language tends to be on the left, attention more on the right."[40] However, "it would be highly inefficient for one half of the brain to consistently be more active than the other."[41] Another way to think about this is to realize several aspects exist for different processes. For example, while the left brain is involved in understanding language, it takes the right brain to understand the context or the tone, and although the left brain handles mathematical equations, the right brain helps with comparisons and rough estimates.[42]

The left-brain, right-brain personality narrative can become an issue if a person acts in accordance with this belief, perhaps restricting career options as a result—creating a self-fulfilling prophecy. However, understanding the left-right brain strengths can have practical applications. For example, if you have difficulty understanding or following verbal instructions (typically a right-brain characteristic), you may find it beneficial to write down the instructions. I am aware of how I can struggle when following and remembering a purely verbal narrative, particularly in lectures. Because of this, wherever possible, I make sure I take written notes. The simple act of writing down the key points enables me to remember so much more.

NOTES

Key Points

The mechanical nature of the brain is highlighted by the exercise that shows how difficult it is to rotate the foot in one direction while rotating the hand the other way. We learn that many things are just hardwired and that this can directly influence who we are. Split brain research shows us the primary functions of the two halves of the brain and reveals two different mental control systems. As we will see later, this raises some interesting philosophical questions about who we are. The Stroop test reveals another layer to this picture when we see how receiving incongruent information causes hiccups. In certain instances, the Stroop test can be used to predict subconscious choices.

While it may be humbling to realize quite how mechanically our brains operate, we should not take this information too far. Common parlance talks about the dominance of the left and right brains and how this creates a logical/creative division. As we see with the Utah research, there is no evidence for this. This belief, though, could result in a created limitation, where someone restricts their own choices based on what they *believe* their proclivities should be. It is more productive to take the left/right-brained personality idea out of the equation and instead take a more holistic approach. Put in place tactics that support your strengths and compensate for your weaknesses.

Exercise

Where do you believe you fit in the old left-brain/right-brain schema? In what ways has this thinking limited the choices you have made? What would you have tried to accomplish if you had not been subjected to limited ideas of yourself?

Think of something you would like to try that you have dismissed before because you have accepted a perceived weakness. Maybe you would like to take up art or music, or take an evening class in mathematics or software engineering. Open up your possibilities and then take some action to make it happen.

Record your discoveries and plans in your journal.

CHAPTER FIVE

THE AUTOMATIC NATURE OF YOUR MIND

> Honestly, sometimes I get really fed up of my subconscious – it's like it's got a mind of its own.
>
> ~ Alexei Sayle

What differentiates humans from animals? One of the differences between humans and the rest of the animal kingdom is the degree of ability we have to inhibit instinctive behaviors. It is common to distinguish a 'good' pet from a 'spoiled, willful' animal based on how quickly they learn what we want them to do and how often they practice these desired behaviors—how much ability they have to inhibit automatic behaviors.

I have a miniature nine-year-old Australian Shepherd. Sam (Samantha Jane) is a really smart animal and extremely loving, but she does have some *interesting* tendencies. Often, when we take the dogs outside for their bathroom breaks, she will wait until we are all ready to come back into the house, and only then will she dart off behind the house. One moment she is there and the next she is off like a speeding bullet and nothing, absolutely nothing, can stop her. Once she has gone, she can take forever to come back again, preferring to take her time doing a second bathroom duty, barking at the neighbor dogs behind us, or just sniffing around.

However, I have learned that if I pay very close attention to the tilt of her head, I can detect the instant the instinct to run makes itself known to her. From then, there is only a split second as her head begins to raise for a sharp command from me to bring her attention back and she is perfectly happy coming indoors. If I miss that split second, then I can do absolutely nothing to stop her from running off.

While most humans are smarter than my dog, it may surprise you to learn that there are many areas where we, too, exhibit automatic behaviors, with simple triggers strongly influencing our responses. Now, in this context, I am not talking about automatic behaviors such as the startle response (e.g., where we jump in response to an unexpected loud noise, or sharp movement). I am speaking of those elements in our psyche that respond automatically to certain kinds of stimuli or inputs. Robert Cialdini (Arizona State University) refers to this as "Click, Whirr,"[1] because it happens as automatically as switching on some electronic equipment and having it fire up immediately. We generally give little thought to these kinds of responses, but they most certainly influence our choices and therefore our lives.

Top Brain Bottom Brain

In the previous chapter, we discussed brain lateralization—the idea that the two halves of the brain have different primary functions—and how people can be characterized accordingly. However, Stephen Kosslyn (Harvard University) argues that the left/right brain divide is incorrect and should instead be replaced with the top brain/bottom brain model, or the theory of cognitive modes.

A side view of the brain shows the Sylvian fissure that forms a demarcation between the top and bottom of the brain. In Kosslyn's model, the top brain consists of the "entire parietal lobe and the top (and larger) portion of the frontal lobe. The bottom comprises the smaller remainder of the frontal lobe and all of the occipital and temporal lobes."[2]

Frontal Lobe

Sylvian Fissure

Temporal Lobe

Parietal Lobe

Occipital Lobe

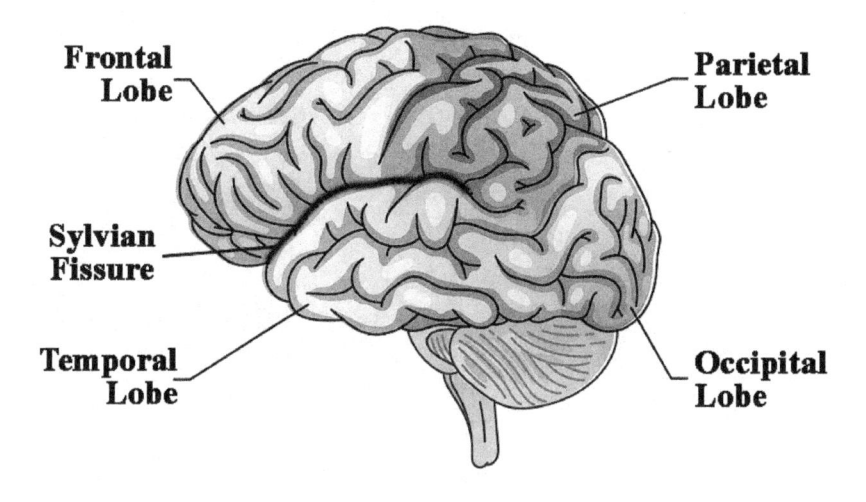

According to Kosslyn, research shows that the top brain combines information from the surroundings with other information, such as needs and emotional reactions, to figure out what goals to achieve. It creates a plan and adjusts it when needed. The bottom brain compares signals from the senses to stored memories. This allows the bottom brain to find meaning in the world. While both parts of the brain work together, they are reliable to different degrees.

Using this model, Kosslyn developed his four modes of cognition: *Mover, Perceiver, Stimulator,* and *Adaptor.*

- *Mover Mode.* Here, both top and bottom brains are highly employed together. This mode is for people who plan and then act to follow through on the plan. People who operate primarily in mover mode are well suited for leadership.
- *Perceiver Mode.* This person primarily uses the bottom brain system. They prefer to focus on making sense of what they perceive to interpret experiences and to try to understand the implications. However, they rarely initiate action or make plans.

- *Stimulator Mode.* This person is primarily top-brain oriented and is better able to think outside the box. They can create complex and detailed plans, but they don't necessarily adjust the plans when things don't go as expected. According to Kosslyn, this kind of person can be disruptive and doesn't always know "when enough is enough."
- *Adaptor Mode.* This defines the person whose access to the top or bottom brain is not highly utilized. This person is open-minded and easily involved in causes. They do not fully process or classify events so don't expect them to make plans, but they can be very responsive to local issues and get involved quickly. They tend to "go with the flow."[3]

While the cognitive modes model can be very informative, it is important to realize that, just as with the left/right brain models, the top and bottom brains do not work in isolation. So, for example, you make a plan to go somewhere (top brain), but you need to monitor conditions such as weather (bottom brain) so that you can make adjustments to the plan (top brain).

According to Kosslyn, you cannot choose the cognitive mode you operate on. However, understanding cognitive modes, in general, can put you in a better position to create effective teams or to make a team or relationship operate more effectively. More importantly, when you know your cognitive mode, you could compensate and make some adjustments in the areas where you may be prone to weakness. This is, of course, a bit of a double-edged sword. If you believe Adaptor Mode describes you the best, you may resist leadership roles (something that is better suited to Mover Mode personalities), and in so doing, create a self-fulfilling prophecy. This is the same argument we saw when we discussed left- or right-brained personalities. I believe the secret here is to be aware of the models and to compensate where necessary, but not to take them so seriously that you limit your personal growth and opportunities.

Parts Brain

Here is another example of how we process and prioritize information—and this one surprised me. A study published in the *European Journal of Social Psychology* found that *both* men and women processed men as people and women as body parts. In this study, subjects were shown images of very average-looking men and women, from head to knee and looking forwards. They were then shown two new images; one was an original image and the other was "a slightly modified version of the original image that comprised a sexual body part." The subjects were asked to identify which of the two images they had seen before. For both men and women, they found that women's sexual body parts were more easily recognized when presented in isolation than when they were presented in the context of their entire bodies. Conversely, men's sexual body parts were recognized better when presented in the context of their entire body as opposed to in isolation.[4] One idea put forward in this paper was that perhaps the men were looking for a sexual partner while the women were simply comparing attributes.

In the second part of the study, researchers found that the "sexual body part recognition bias" could be alleviated to some degree by having the subjects focus on global processing objectives first.[5] In the experiment, this priming of global vs local processing entailed looking at a large alphabet letter (e.g., 'H') built out of a series of small alphabet letters (e.g., 'F'), and being asked to focus either on the large 'H' or the smaller 'F's. In real-world situations, thinking about the complete woman (personality, background, etc.) should then reduce the tendency to focus on their body parts.

Automaticity

With the "Top Brain Bottom Brain," "Parts Brain," and brain lateralization models, there is not much room to adjust for automatic behaviors. You operate in a particular mode, or you see people in a particular way, and that is how it is. Knowing where you fit in these schemas is helpful as it provides possible ways to enhance your strengths and compensate for your weaknesses, but you cannot make any real changes. However, the situation is a little different when we start to look at 'how' we think—the processes behind our decision-making abilities.

MIND TRAINING

In his book, *Thinking, Fast and Slow,* behavioral economist and Nobel Prize winner Daniel Kahneman describes two different ways in which we think:

- *System 1* is fast, automatic, frequent, emotional, stereotypical, and subconscious.
- *System 2* is slow, effortful, infrequent, logical, calculating, and conscious.[6]

Think about that for a moment—how often do you take time to consider the ramifications, alternatives, etc. from both an introspective and a compassionate or charitable perspective before you make a decision or act? For example, being offered a choice between tea or coffee does not cause most people to weigh up all the health benefits, farming practices, cost differences, or any of the other factors that could play a role. They just make an instant decision.

Mental shortcuts, known as heuristics, allow us to solve problems quickly, and to make adequate, though often imperfect, decisions, based on past experiences and information stored in the subconscious. Careful thought is quite rare for most decisions we make. System 1 thinking is therefore responsible for running most of our lives. But should it be? System 1 thinking is sufficient and efficient in most areas of our lives, but it can also counter our best interests. System 2 thinking can provide us with better information but, according to Kahneman, it is lazy and prefers to give the reins to System 1.[7]

Malcolm Gladwell, writing in his #1 national bestseller *Blink*, shows that there is a dark side to rapid cognition as it can give rein to undesirable responses such as prejudice and discrimination.[8] One example of this can be found in politics and the joy felt by so many when Barack Obama finally achieved the highest office in the land—for too long, deep-seated biases would not have allowed for such an event. The world, however, is still waiting for the United States to elect its first female president—a bias that has yet to be overcome.

Most people make snap judgments based on limited information along with the deep-seated (subconscious) programming that limits possibilities. In *Blink*, Gladwell provides an example of where a poor or bad track record was insufficient to counteract the fact that a presidential candidate (Warren Harding) won the presidency simply because he *looked* so impressive and presidential. According to most historians, Harding was one of the worst presidents in American history.[9]

Another example offered by Gladwell shows that having more information did not lead to more accurate conclusions.[10] In 1965, Stuart Oskamp (Claremont Graduate School) ran a study to find out whether psychologists' *confidence* in their clinical decisions is justified. As the subjects were provided with more and more information regarding a possible client, confidence in their diagnoses increased. However, when asked to complete a multiple-choice test about the client, even though they made changes in their answers, their overall accuracy rate remained constant.[11] This just highlights the greater sway held by the automatic System 1 thinking—instincts too often override careful, analytical thought.

While a great deal of research has been carried out on automatic thinking, Kahneman's work shows that navigating all the pitfalls is virtually impossible, even for experts in the field.[12] However, there are research areas where gaining an understanding can offer opportunities to make some corrections. These include *defense mechanisms, shortcuts and fallacies, compliance principles,* and *definitional* and *conditioned thinking.*

Defense Mechanisms and Strategies

Anna Freud, building on the ideas put forward by her father, Sigmund Freud, defined defense mechanisms as "unconscious resources used by the ego" to decrease conflict specifically between the superego and id.[13] Defense mechanisms, then, are adopted originally to protect us from things like rejection, embarrassment, and humiliation. For these mechanisms to work, they must be unknown to our conscious minds. As such, they can also come into play in different situations where they may not be helpful and may be self-destructive. Let me give you an example.

A young boy surrounded by friends and peers finds a situation very funny and laughs out loud and hard. Those around him notice that his laughter is both raucous and it contorts his face strangely and funnily, so they laugh and ridicule him. The situation humiliates him, and an adaptation, or defense strategy, is formed. As a result, he no longer laughs. As an adult, he is thought of as a real party-pooper, the kind of guy whose presence can dampen any event. This leads to issues with friends as well as loved ones. He has become so stoic as to create a buffer zone between himself and others. After all, who wants to invite this somber, stiff-necked dude to a party?

Often, defense mechanisms can lead to over-eating, addictive characteristics, self-destructive behavior, and more. I cannot tell you how many times I have heard someone say something like, "It just seems that I have everything working great and then suddenly it all blows up in my face. I am so close to success and then bang—it's all gone!" This is almost certainly an indication that some defense strategy is sabotaging their best conscious intention.

The important thing to note here is that defense mechanisms need to be unconscious and unrecognized to work. As such, as soon as the mechanism is uncovered, it can be extinguished.

There are many different forms of defense mechanisms, and they can use different strategies. The most common defense mechanisms today include *compensation, displacement, projection, repression, denial, sublimation, fantasy formation, introjection, isolation, regression,* and *disassociation*.

Compensation

The compensation defense mechanism is where a person uses a tactic in one area to hide their inadequacy in another. While this can be beneficial, it can be maladaptive when applied inappropriately. So, for example, a shy, fearful young child may find that the best way to hide fear is to compensate by acting aggressively.

Displacement

Displacement involves taking one's emotional burden or reaction and putting it on someone or something else. For example, a person who feels inadequate and intimidated in the workplace may come home and deride or beat their spouse and children. In its extremes, this mechanism can even manifest in a serial killer who has been betrayed by one person and displaces the emotions by brutally killing others.

Projection

Defensive projection is where someone takes an undesirable trait in themselves and accuses others of having that same trait to deflect from or deny their own shortcoming—they *project* their fault onto others. Their esteem may be protected by believing others have the same fault and therefore it is normal or acceptable. An example of this would be a liar who accuses others of lying.

Eldon was once involved in arresting a young man who had just burglarized a home and was fleeing the scene. When the officers began to search the man, he repeatedly threatened them with false arrest. His defense mechanism was to accuse others of a crime rather than acknowledge his own.

Projection can take on many forms. In less violent ways, we can project our fears and weaknesses onto others. Often an adulterer will project this same behavior on their spouse, becoming suspicious and even paranoid about their mate's fidelity.

Repression

Repression is an unconscious process that blocks painful memories, impulses, and emotions from the conscious mind. While initially, this can be seen as helpful and calming for the individual, it can cause other issues later. For example, a person who has repressed memories of abuse may find it difficult to build new relationships later in life. Repressed emotions have also been implicated in several health conditions, including high blood pressure, skin conditions, fatigue, obesity, headaches, dizziness, and back, neck, chest, and abdominal pains, along with stress, anxiety, and depression.[14]

Denial

Denial is perhaps the most widely-known defense mechanism. Plain and simple, denial is exactly what it implies, the act of denying reality, and though it is among the best known, it is also dangerous. Denial most commonly occurs where great risk accompanies certain behaviors. For example, a form of denial sometimes referred to as the law of psychological self-exemption often takes hold of the smoker who denies the health risks involved with smoking.

Sublimation

Sublimation is an interesting defense strategy for many reasons and a very useful one from a societal standpoint. Take this example as one of the ways this mechanism serves communities. Our desire to breed can be very strong, but breeding with whomever, whenever, and indiscriminately leads to trouble. We, therefore, sublimate our desire to breed with as many as we are attracted to through marriage. Now we can enjoy all the sex we want, partners consenting, without guilt, shame, or fear. Also, the social fabric condemns infidelity and punishes abusers when they are discovered in a variety of ways. This may be less true today than fifty years ago, but it is still true.

Another common form of sublimation may manifest where our unhappiness or frustration is taken out in some fashion such as strenuous physical training or art. Many famous artists have led unhappy lives but used their art to escape the unhappiness.

Fantasy Formation

Imagining a successful outcome can be a great motivational tool for getting through the work necessary to achieve a specific goal. Fantasy formation, though, occurs when fantasizing is used to simply escape real-world problems. Many people live in their fantasies, imagining themselves as happy, prosperous, and powerful, sometimes using computer games. But whether it is in gaming or excessive day-dreaming and senseless wishing, fantasy formation is a problem when used in lieu of taking direct action to deal with the uncomfortable or unsatisfying parts of life.

Introjection

Introjection is most often encountered when as parents we do the very things we swore never to do with our children. Introjection is all about internalizing the characteristics and traits of others—making them our own. Remember, these mechanisms must be unconscious to be successful. Therefore, all the oath-taking to never act as our parents did can be quite fruitless.

Isolation

Isolation can result from severe depression and in this sense can be seen as the modern adaptation of the fight/flight paradigm, where complete withdrawal and isolation is the flight purpose. That said, isolation is usually viewed as how we avoid feelings by isolating them from our consciousness. Complete emotional detachment is a form of isolation and can underpin disorders such as affective attachment disorder. For example, a child who experienced much pain in their family environment because of emotional and physical abuse may go on to develop a compensation mechanism that incorporates isolation. Hence, they are unable to attach emotionally to anyone. They go through life able to walk away from any relationship, not look back, and feel no real pain about it, all to ensure that the pain they felt as a child never controls them again.

Regression

Regression is defined by Freud as a mechanism that leads to reverting to an earlier age to avoid dealing with the problems of an adult. This mechanism can involve play, sexual pleasure or libidinal urges, and other primitive activities. Regression is commonly seen in someone who has suffered psychological trauma as they will typically curl up in a fetal position, sometimes rocking and crying. This mechanism can also be used to gain control over another, so the spouse who is afraid to drive, regressing to childhood fears, gains control over their mate who must now take them everywhere.

Dissociation

Many people have experienced this mechanism without ever being aware of it. Driving down the freeway seemingly unaware of what you are doing until that exit sign appears is an example of dissociation. Another example is that conversation you had with a friend where you were nodding in agreement with what they said and yet you were not engaged.

Dissociation can be found underlying many different disorders. In a healthy individual, this mechanism may have you saying something like, "I find my body doing things different than my mind would have it do." This mechanism also helps us forget. We go off at someone and can't remember what we said or why. This mechanism usually kicks in when the nervous system reaches its capacity to handle stimulation. For example, shutting down emotions to avoid feeling pain or rage when an authority figure starts yelling at you about a mistake. While this can be helpful at the moment, it does not let you deal with the situation itself.

Self-Destructive Patterns

A quick search of the literature will bring up several other defense mechanisms. However, the point here is not to get bogged down in the different kinds of defense mechanisms, but rather to understand that the subconscious mind uses various techniques to protect the individual from pain. While many of these strategies may be effective in the immediate situation, over time they can become the source of self-destructive or self-sabotaging behaviors. So, perhaps someone always finds reasons for not applying for that better job because they were mocked when they were younger, or another person walks away from relationships too soon because they are subconsciously afraid of becoming too involved and getting dumped. The triggering event(s) are forgotten, and the self-protection mechanisms are automatized. The defense mechanisms will still be in play later in life, even though their use may no longer be beneficial and may even hold the person back.

Where Erickson's Eight Stages of Development focused on learning specific skills at specific ages, defense mechanisms provide us with some of the processes that may have been used to deal with the different perceived failures. In some instances, therapy is the best way to deal with past, buried traumas. However, for the myriad of small improvements most of us wish to make in life, simply being aware of a defense mechanism and asking yourself honest questions will open the door for the answers to come to you. Questions such as "Why do I do X? What do I get out of it? What am I hiding from? When did this issue begin?" can be a great way to start the process. Some of the answers you get may seem silly at first. However, over time, it will become easier for the real reasons to make themselves known.

Shortcuts and Fallacies

Another set of thinking processes that can distort information is heuristics and fallacies. These strategies can be extremely useful as they generally allow us to make decisions quickly and so enable us to move on with our lives. Unfortunately, they can often lead to incorrect conclusions and choices.

One of my favorites is the sharpshooter fallacy, and no one fleshes this out better than David McCraney in his book, *You Are Not So Smart*. This has been shared widely on social media so you may have encountered it.

What do you think when you learn the following corresponding facts about the deaths of Presidents Abraham Lincoln and John F. Kennedy?

> Both were shot by men with fifteen letters in their names—Lee Harvey Oswald and John Wilkes Booth. Both presidents were killed on a Friday while sitting next to their wives. John F. Kennedy was shot in a Lincoln car made by Ford, and Abraham Lincoln was shot in the Ford Theatre. Their successors were both named Johnson—Lyndon Baines Johnson for Kennedy and Andrew Johnson for Lincoln. Both Johnsons were born in an '08 year—President Lyndon Baines Johnson in 1908 and President Andrew Johnson in 1808.[15]

To many people, this information must be more than a coincidence. Unfortunately, a lot of reasoning going on in our world is built from this kind of association. We jump to a conclusion without considering the many differences between the men. We seek to find a pattern, and when it emerges, we say, *"Look—there must be something to this!"* No one knows this better than those who would sell you a product or a political platform, cherry-picking the bits of evidence that best fit their views and acting like it provides a complete picture. This is called the *Texas Sharpshooter Fallacy* for it's a little bit like someone shooting up the side of a barn. Then, instead of looking at all the bullet holes, we single out some small area with many closely related holes, draw a circle around them, and then argue that there must have been a real sharpshooter to keep a pattern that tight. When you *do* consider differences, everything changes.

Many of these shortcuts lead us astray. Some are as simple as hindsight bias, an attitude that expresses itself in these words altogether too often, *"I knew that would happen."* These shortcuts can be misleading to us all and include such processes as the *Dunning-Kruger Effect* or the *Bystander Effect* (also known as the *Genovese Effect*).

The *Dunning-Kruger Effect* is where a person with low ability at a task overestimates their ability at that task. I have seen individuals who read one book on a subject such as quantum physics or psychology and suddenly came to believe they are experts on the subject—even arguing with an expert holding a Ph.D. in the subject.

This next one, *Genovese Effect,* is painful to even think about—named after Kitty Genovese, who, according to the report, was raped, beaten, and murdered while onlookers did nothing.[16] It turned out the reporting was incorrect for there was "no evidence for the presence of thirty-eight witnesses, or that witnesses observed the murder, or that witnesses remained inactive."[17] Nevertheless, the *Genovese Effect,* also known as the *Bystander Effect,* is real. Results in the 1969 seminal paper by Bibb Latane and John M. Darley showed that if a person was a sole bystander, they would render aid. However, only 62% of participants intervened if they were part of a group of five bystanders.[18]

This reduction in aid given when in the presence of others has been reported in a number of studies, including in serious accidents, noncritical situations, on the Internet, and even in children.[19] Several news reports have also shown the *Genovese Effect* in play—ranging from the cars that carefully drove around an injured man in the street,[20] to patients in a hospital waiting room not calling for help when another patient was in extreme distress and eventually died. Sometimes it is tempting to put these stories in special categories, such as *'It happened a long time ago and therefore wouldn't happen today,'* or *'It happened in some faraway place with different values, etc. so it could not happen here.'* Unfortunately, that is far from true as you can see from the most recent example I found—again, this involves a rape with witnesses. This event occurred on Wednesday, October 13, 2021, on a Pennsylvania train heading toward Upper Darby. A woman was sexually assaulted by a stranger. According to the authorities, the assault could have been stopped sooner if one of several bystanders had just called 911.[21]

Current research has revealed that this *Bystander Effect* most often occurs when there are many witnesses.[22] It appears that, when there are others around, everyone assumes someone else will do something and no one does. While most people would deny they would do such, these events are a lot more common than we would think.

Many such shortcuts and fallacies can lead us astray. Let's take a quick look at the most common and best-known.

Hindsight Bias

Hindsight bias can be easily seen when we catch ourselves saying something like, *"I knew you were going to say that"* or *"I knew that was going to happen."* This sort of bias is usually nothing more than fanciful thinking expressed in 20-20 hindsight—we gain a feeling of power in having foretold a situation, even when it is not valid.

Confirmation Bias

Confirmation bias is where we look for information that favors our views and opinions and dismiss or minimize information that goes against them. This can even result in two people with opposite ideas hearing the same presentation, yet both coming away feeling validated as they cherry-picked the parts that confirmed their pre-held opinions. Confirmation bias also plays a significant role in most people's preferred news source—their first-choice pundit or commentator will be someone most likely to provide information that confirms their pre-held beliefs.

Normalcy Bias

Normalcy bias often manifests in emergencies. Here, a person underestimates the present danger. One example would be the individual who refuses to leave their property when imminent danger is present. The idea is simple: since nothing has happened before, it's not likely to happen now. It's worth noting that the opposite of this bias is the *worst-case bias*, expecting the worst possible outcome to occur.

Introspection Illusion

Introspection illusion is a cognitive bias based upon the false belief that a person has direct access to his or her inner thinking, motives, and so forth. The person laboring under the introspection bias also believes that others do not have this same access to their inner self. Even professionals can find themselves guilty of this bias. Take this example: Eldon once interviewed a Harvard professor who is a psychiatrist. She experienced a supernatural phenomenon at a very young age. She was on the radio show to discuss her scientific evidence for psychic phenomena. When Eldon asked her about bias perhaps influencing her science, she denied the possibility of having any bias.[23] How can that be when this professor also insisted that they had experienced phenomena? Science recognizes the unintended influence of bias as the reason for the gold standard of research, the double-blind study. As a Harvard professor, she of all people should have acknowledged the very real possibility of bias.

Straw Man Fallacy

A *straw man fallacy* occurs when a person exaggerates or completely makes up some distorted argument to make their argument more credible. This sort of thing happens in politics all the time.

Candidate A may say that the national debt is obscene and must be contained by cutting spending and increasing taxes. The opponent quickly twists or spins this and says something like, "Candidate A wants to drastically cut social programs like welfare, Medicare, and Social Security, putting your grandmother on the street. And this is what they think America is all about?"

Alternatively, Candidate B may say something like, "We must recognize that the people who crossed the border without papers are simply seeking to improve their lives and care for their loved ones." The opponent then lashes out with, "Criminals, you are defending criminals! They come into this country and commit crimes, and you want to give them sanctuary. Honest people wait in line, and you just don't care about justice!"

Both straw man examples are obviously exaggerations. Nevertheless, many people fall into the trap of accepting the straw argument as valid.

Ad Hominem Fallacy

The *ad hominem fallacy* is the practice or mental shortcut of deciding based on a personal attack—confusing the message with the messenger. This, too, is especially common in politics. Attack the person as dishonest, provide some credible-appearing examples of their dishonesty, and it's easy to dismiss their other statements as misleading and false. So, Hillary Clinton claimed she landed *"under sniper fire"* during a visit to Bosnia and then we learn that this did not happen.[24] Now her opponents have sufficient ammunition to poison people's minds regarding her character. Crossing the aisle, when George Bush stated on national television that, "Iraq has aided, trained, and harbored terrorists, including operatives of Al Qaeda," no one, including members of the U.S. government, seriously believed there was any real connection between the Islamic fundamentalist and Saddam Hussein.[25] This, however, enabled Bush's opponents to quickly condemn *everything* about the Iraq war as a war built on lies.

Just World Fallacy

The *just world fallacy* is based on the hypothesis that the world is just and therefore whatever action one may take will have just consequences, at least at some point, even if they are delivered in the afterlife. This fallacy also insists that rewards await those who act honorably and justly. This is both a psychological and theological cognitive bias. Some may argue that this is not really a fallacy and that may well be true when we add the afterlife into the equation; however, while it may comfort us when bad things happen, such as the sudden loss of a child due to some freak accident, it leaves us empty when it comes to justifying our loss. Sadly, many who find themselves in this place can feel abandoned by the God they have worshipped, and as a result, they lose both their faith and their child. In this sense, the fallacy can be very harmful.

Self-Serving Fallacy

The *self-serving fallacy* is a cognitive distortion of our self-worth. This mechanism can distort our past, justifying actions in the name of restoring or maintaining a healthy sense of self-esteem. This fallacy raises its head often when we blame external factors for our failures and praise our efforts despite the failure. Most parents have observed this in their children for they will often attribute a good grade to their hard work and a bad grade to their miserably incompetent teacher.

Critical Thought

Where these are the most common fallacies that daily influence us, again, it is not a complete list. The relevant point here is this: fallacies haunt all of us in one way or another and undermine critical thinking. What's more, both fallacies and mechanisms emerge from subconscious programming and are both part of System 1 thinking. Later we will be exploring ways to change this inner program, but for now, here is a quick, simple way to engage more conscious reflective thought—frown while assessing information.

According to Kahneman, smiling induces cognitive ease and therefore makes System 1 thinking more likely. Conversely, frowning causes cognitive strain, which engages more System 2 thinking. Evolutionarily, this would make sense. It is okay to relax when all is well with the world and vigilance can be eased as mistakes will not be critical. When there is a possibility of danger, though, you need to ensure your finest thinking faculties are engaged so you can respond as necessary. The influence of smiling or frowning even holds when the expressions are fake, such as the false smile created by holding a pencil sideways between your teeth or the forced frown from holding a ball between your furrowed brows. As Kahneman says, "Maintaining one's vigilance against biases is a chore—but the chance to avoid a costly mistake is sometimes worth the effort."[26]

Compliance Principles

The next area of automatic thinking I wish to share with you has a darker, more manipulative side to it. Billions of dollars have been spent learning how to get us to behave as desired (comply) while we labor under the notion that we are doing what *we* choose to do. To that end, certain compliance principles, as they are known, have been identified. A compliance principle taps into some of our subconscious societal needs to exercise its power. The compliance principles I would like to look at are *consistency, authority, reciprocity, scarcity, social proof, association, liking, drives,* and *justification*.

Consistency

People have an inherent need to be consistent, and sometimes they will go to great lengths to achieve this. In one study, they found that 76% of the people who signed a petition to keep California beautiful later agreed to place a billboard advertising safe driving on their front lawn. This was as opposed to the 17% who agreed to the billboard but who hadn't been asked to sign the earlier petition. The first petition had sparked a desire to be civically minded and involved in the community, and this fed the desire to be consistent and therefore agree to the billboard.[27]

A good salesperson knows how to take advantage of the customer's need to be consistent. When a customer enquires if the store has a particular product, an effective salesman knows exactly how to nudge them into purchasing that (or a better, higher priced) item. They play on the customer's need to be consistent—if they did not want the item then why did they waste the salesperson's time asking after it?

Authority

How often have you made a decision based on the word of an authority, perhaps your doctor? Not long ago, doctors not only recommended smoking, but also shared their recommended brands. How often are our so-called authorities wrong?

In 1949, the Nobel Prize for Medicine was awarded to the Portuguese neurologist Egas Moniz for prefrontal lobotomy. Today this procedure is considered barbaric, but at the time, it was even employed with President John F. Kennedy's sister Rosemary. Physicians around the world recommended it to treat schizophrenia, manic depression, and bipolar disorder, among other mental illnesses. This went on until a better understanding of the brain was gained, and then they all turned on Moniz.

Unless conscious efforts are made, the presence of an authority figure can strongly influence vigilance and skepticism when judging the truth and importance of what people say. In a 2011 study, Uffe Schjoedt and team used fMRI (functional magnetic resonance imaging) to investigate brain activity in response to an authority figure. They looked particularly at the frontal regions known to play a role in attentional processing and executive function.[28]

Eighteen secular and eighteen Christian subjects were asked to listen to three speakers; a non-Christian, a Christian, and a Christian known for their healing powers. In subjects who identified as Christian, where there was a significant increase in activity in response to the non-Christian speaker, there was a massive deactivation in response to the Christian speaker known for their healing powers.[29]

The authors of this paper believe that this mechanism is likely to be present in other interpersonal interactions as well. Previous studies have shown that "during hypnosis subjects inhibit their executive system as they 'hand over' the executive control to the hypnotist," and that "instructions received during hypnotically induced inhibition influence how subjects subsequently perceive and relate to stimuli."[30]

The power of the authority figure can be compelling and here we see a mechanism to account for it. Experts, though, can occasionally be wrong, may be taking inappropriate shortcuts, and may also be making decisions based on incomplete information. Turning our power over to the authority figure is therefore not always in our best interest. A couple of ways to temper the power of the authority figure would include checking their credentials and making sure their input only relates to their area of expertise. More importantly, having an awareness of the power of the authority figure and making a conscious effort to assess for yourself the information you receive.

Reciprocity

Have you ever wondered why charities send you gifts when they ask for money? The simple reason is that it generates a sense of indebtedness, and most recognize this. So here comes a dime or even a dollar in the mail with a request to assist the poor and needy, the disabled or disadvantaged, and so forth. We can't get ourselves to throw the money away, so we keep it, and that tends to either induce a form of guilt or create the need to give. How do you respond to this one? From the so-called "warm handshake" to "inside information" and the "free" things offered today, a gift given implies a gift in return.

Most people succumb to compliance principles all the time, and if it is pointed out to them, then they will generally be vociferous in their denials—even when they should know better. One day, Eldon and I were out driving in a touristy area when we saw a small store that specialized in Native American products. We stopped to explore this store, and quite honestly, it was one of those off-the-beaten-path kinds of stores with some old clutter for products and not much else. However, the owner of the store exchanged a few pleasantries before asking me if I wanted to see a couple of wolves he had in the back. I don't remember why he had them—if they were pets or what—but I was intrigued. I don't think I had ever seen a real-life wolf. I then turned back to the products on display and found a small map of America that showed the locations of the Tribes of the Indian Nation. I purchased the map and soon after the gentleman took me out back to see a dog run with two wolves in it.

Later, Eldon pointed out to me that I had only purchased the map because the guy had offered me something—a viewing of his wolves. I adamantly denied this. I love history and believe it is important to learn about and honor the Native Americans, and that was the only reason I made the purchase. The more Eldon pushed me on this, the firmer I became that the two events were unrelated. To prove this to Eldon, I hung the map in my office, where it has stayed for about a decade. The thing is, in my heart of hearts I knew that purchasing the little map was more about 'paying' for something I had been offered. I often look at this map and think about reciprocity. You may also be amused to learn that, to this day, I have never admitted this to Eldon; he will learn about it when he reads my addition to this book.

Scarcity

Scarcity is the common compliance principle used in most sales events today. The local retailer has an item on sale, and quantities are always limited. Sometimes it's a loss leader and there are only a few. We rush to get in line on Black Friday to take advantage of the great deal. We're nearly the first in the store, but they are already sold out. This motivator gets us into buying action. Get it while you can before it's gone! We have unconsciously entered a mental state that is no longer rational. We are not carefully deciding because if we do, the item may be gone when we come back. No—the subconscious urges, "Get it now! Get it before it's gone!" And for some, this is what they call thinking when indeed it is simply rationalizing away our behavior after the fact.

Social Proof

Of all the compliance principles, *social proof* seems to carry the most weight in modern society. According to Robert Cialdini, author of *Influence: The Psychology of Persuasion*, "we view a behavior as more correct in a given situation to the degree that we see others performing it."[31] So particularly in situations where we are unsure what to do, we assume that those around us (celebrities, experts, friends, etc.) have a better opinion than we do.

In marketing, you are made to feel deprived if you do not have XYZ gadget that is the rage and used by everyone. Just think about the number of commercials that show someone hearing about the latest, greatest 'thing' they should have, and as they run to get it, others follow until there is a raging sea of people trying to obtain this wonderful object.

Celebrity endorsements are also incredibly powerful. If a super successful celebrity believes in XYZ, then that proves it must be good. Maybe there is also a little voice inside us saying that our path to success could start with following the celebrity's example. Even though it can sound nonsensical to put it that way—just because a celebrity uses a particular retirement program does not mean it is the right program for you—this remains an effective tool to get people to comply.

Association

Association seeks to link favorable feelings with a product or aim. We see politicians with apple pie, babies, and the American flag. We see stunning men and women in the most unlikely of places, with the most unlikely of apparel, just to connect this image with a product. As with all these principles, you can look beyond the obvious. Take, for instance, a study that sought to measure the influence of major credit card logos on buying. In this study carried out by Richard Feinberg, subjects would spend 29% more on mail order items when they could see a major credit card logo. Another study by the same researcher showed that college students gave money to charity more often when they could see a credit card logo in the room. 33% of the students gave to charity where there was no credit card logo in the room, while 87% gave with the logo present. This occurs even though credit cards were not accepted. The association alone increased spending.[32]

Advertisers also use sound. Sound, particularly music, has long enjoyed renown for its affective power. Perhaps you are old enough to remember an old Marlboro television commercial that used the theme music from the classic movie, *The Magnificent Seven*. This associated feelings from the movie and the music with smoking Marlboro cigarettes.

Television producers use canned humor to punctuate comedy. Many people don't notice it. In our culture, people often consciously overlook sound, but sound moves upon our primordial nature. Our first knowledge of the outside world comes from sounds we hear in the womb.

The Liking Principle

The more each of us identifies with another, and feels comfortable with that other, the more we like them, and the more often we comply with their requests. The liking principle has nuances unfamiliar to most of us though, including its mechanical features.

The science of neuro-linguistic programming (NLP) often starts with the mechanics of rapport. It breaks rapport into matching, pacing, and leading. Match by adopting the speaking style, physical mannerisms, and so forth of an individual. Pace by continuing with them. Lead by making a new gesture, or by shifting your tone of voice. So long as they follow your lead, you can continue to lead them. You have rapport. Liking often develops under conditions of cooperation. This undergirds the "politics make for strange bedfellows" truism and the "common enemy" strategy.

Drives

Behavioral specialists have identified four basic human drives. They are *fight, flight, feeding,* and *fornication*. Advertisers and motivators are aware of our drives, and they work them against us all the time. Fear is frequently used in political campaigns with both parties focusing on issues at the forefront of the voters' minds. They want the fear tactic to be powerful enough to override the fact that other planks exist in their platform. Fear feeds the fight/flight aspect of our drive mechanisms.

All those ads that present food and sex are obvious appeals to our drives, and they typically work. Inherent in all this advertising is the implied proposition that you are somehow deficient. Why? Because if you were not deficient, didn't need that hair sheen, or makeup, or workout equipment and so on, you wouldn't buy it. Ergo—you must not be as beautiful as others in some way and so forth. Again, this appeals to our subconscious and not so much our conscious mind, for when we become fully aware of these techniques and strategies, they lose their power.

Justification

Justification is the principle that acts on the rule that extenuating circumstances can justify radical actions. Indeed, a tenant of our jurisprudence system allows for exactly this. That is why there are such acts as justifiable homicide, self-defense, etc. This principle is probably the most often overlooked compliance tool. However, an excellent example of its power exists in an older television commercial. The viewer sees a woman performing the many tasks of a frantic day—shopping, cleaning, caring for the children, banking, and so forth. At the end of the day, she (a very beautiful and seductive woman) relaxes in her bath covered by bubbles. The commercial advertises a bubble bath and ends with the statement, "Let XYZ product take you away." It's an excellent commercial and employs more than one compliance principle. Still, it is the notion of a justified indulgence that makes this commercial so powerful. How else do you sell bath bubbles?

Human beings need reasons to act. In his book, *Man's Search for Meaning*, Holocaust survivor Victor Frankl sums it up with a quote by the

German philosopher Fredrich Nietzsche: *"He who has a why to live can bear almost any how."*

Vigilance

As I said, billions of dollars have been spent researching ways to make the consumer compliant. The principles are commonly used in sales, whether it is to persuade you to purchase a product or to vote for a candidate. These tactics are designed to pull at your psyche and cause you to act in a particular way. Without a certain degree of vigilance, these tactics can turn you into a puppet under the control of marketers. Understanding this, though, will cause you to pause and rethink what is being offered. Discerning the compliance principles being used on you can even be fun. This process can assist you in turning on System 2 thinking as you ask yourself questions such as, "Do I really need this product? How much hype is being used here? What aren't they telling me? What are the downsides to this issue or this product?"

Definitional and Conditioned Thinking

Now, before we finish up, there are two more processes I wish to touch upon briefly. These processes deal with *context* and *framing*. We can be run on automatic pilot simply by how information is presented to us and how we expect it to be presented.

Context

Context is all-important to how we process every bit of information. For example, a spouse may use vulgar profanity laughingly and it's taken in a light-hearted vein, but when the same word or phrase is used with an angry face, the meaning completely changes.

Here is an exercise for you to try right now. First, think about the saliva in your mouth. Give it a rating—are you glad you have it, or would you prefer your mouth to be dry? Having enough saliva in the mouth is important. When Eldon and I are involved in public speaking, saliva in the mouth becomes particularly important, otherwise speaking would be difficult. We rate saliva 10 out of 10. So, take a moment and think about the saliva in your mouth. Rate it before you continue.

Now imagine you have a shot glass, the kind found in a bar. Imagine that you deposit some of that saliva into the glass. Look at the spit in the glass for a moment, observe the bubbles floating in it, and then knock it on back (drink it). Now, if you're like most people, the idea of drinking spit in a glass is gross. Some can even gag at the very thought, but why? Spit in the glass is not saliva in the mouth, even though it's your own and was in your mouth just seconds before. The context has changed, and in only a few seconds something that was perfectly comfortable and necessary has become disgusting. Context is everything.

Even something as simple as hand sanitizer can change your views. Take this little context experiment. Researchers randomly selected students to fill out a questionnaire surveying their political attitudes. "They found that the students endorsed more conservative attitudes when they stood next to a bottle of hand sanitizer or near a sign reminding them to wash their hands."[33] So, if you smell cleaning chemicals when you go into the voting booth, you may want to think carefully if you have the urge to change your choice.

Another simple example of our subtler context evaluations comes from a study done with parents. According to research by Richard Eibach (University of Waterloo, Canada), just thinking about children can make people lean conservative. In a 2009 study published in the *Journal of Experimental Social Psychology*, Eibach found that simply reminding parents of their children triggered harsher evaluations of people who engaged in distasteful but essentially harmless [sic] behavior, such as a dwarf-tossing event.[34] A 2006 General Social Survey showed that parents judged premarital sex as more morally wrong than nonparents. According to Eibach, "When you are a nonparent, you can afford to have a fairly lax attitude toward morality so long as someone isn't harming someone else . . . When you're a parent—or reminded of being a parent—you can't afford to ignore rude or uncivil or unpleasant behavior because it can potentially corrupt your children's character development."[35]

Context can be all-important. Changing the context can change opinions.

Framing

Most people give little thought to labels and definitions, which can be a significant mistake.

Framing is a perception-management tool that is used from time to time. This is because *how* something is said and the *context* in which it is framed becomes all-important in how the information is perceived. Think back to the saliva example; the context changed but so did the frame. The first frame was saliva in the mouth, but what made it potentially so vile was placing it in a glass and changing its name to spit. Now while we're comparing spit with saliva, think about how much grosser it might have been if we called it drool or gob. Labels have power.

In *Thinking, Fast and Slow* Kahneman provides a fascinating example of the power of framing. To experience the full power of this process, please take a moment to think about what your choices would be in these two scenarios before moving on.

In a study, subjects were told to imagine that the U.S. is preparing for the outbreak of an unusual disease that is expected to kill 600 people. Two programs have been proposed to combat the disease:

- If Program A is adopted, 200 people will be saved.
- If Program B is adopted, there is a $1/3^{rd}$ probability that 600 people will be saved and a $2/3^{rd}$ probability that no one will be saved.

Which of the two programs would you favor?

A clear majority of respondents choose option A, preferring risk aversion.

A second variation of the study was run, still looking at the same kind of scenario. However, this time:

- If Program C is adopted, 400 people will die.
- If Program D is adopted, there is a $1/3^{rd}$ probability that nobody will die. and a $2/3^{rd}$ probability that 600 people will die.

Now, which of these two programs would you favor?

In this study, most of the respondents chose option D, preferring risk-seeking. However, seeing the two studies together, we can see that both variations provided the same options, they were just framed differently. This difference in framing led to different choices. These techniques, as Kahneman says:

> ". . . can also be exploited deliberately to manipulate the relative attractiveness of options. For example, Thaler (1980) noted that lobbyists for the credit card industry insisted that any price difference between cash and credit purchases be labeled a cash discount rather than a credit card surcharge. The two labels frame the price difference as a gain or as a loss by implicitly designating either the lower or the higher price as normal. Because losses loom larger than gains, consumers are less likely to accept a surcharge than to forgo a discount. As is to be expected, attempts to influence framing are common in the marketplace and in the political arena.[36]"

Eldon has argued for years that if you can control the definition, you will control the argument. Elite marketers know this, and so they contrive names and labels, often relabeling, to advance their cause. For example, the recent relabeling of "illegal immigrants" to "undocumented workers." These two labels are intentionally different as one leads to judgment and punishment, and the other compassion and understanding. Think about some well-known labels such as *Pro-Life* or *Pro-Choice* or *Operation Iraqi Freedom*. The labels often are the argument.

Real World Applications

In 2021, Elon Musk tweeted a graphic outlining something he believes should be "taught to all at a young age." The tweet was titled, *50 Cognitive Biases to Be Aware of So You Can Be the Very Best Version of You.*[37] When

Eldon wrote his blog outlining the focus of *Mind Training*, he stated that these were tools everyone should be taught in schools. This has been the direction of the work Eldon and I have been doing for over thirty years now.

Musk's tweet outlined fifty biases. We covered thirty-one in this chapter. Some of them overlap, and some are different. If you do some additional research, you will find more. This is a great deal of information, and it would not be surprising if you feel a little overwhelmed; how can you possibly remember all of these and monitor them in your daily lives? You can't, and you don't need to.

When I was in my mid-teens, my brother brought home a video of *The Exorcist*. He had watched it in the theatre, something I was too young to do at the time, and told us how scary it was. Now, he looked forward to watching me while I watched this movie, convinced that I would be petrified and so make a complete spectacle of myself. For some reason, I decided the best way to handle this was to put on my analytical cap, so to speak. I did not know anything about videography, but I knew that lots of special effects would be used. As I watched the movie, especially the scarier parts, I just wondered how they had put together those shocking scenes—did they use clever make-up, special wires, and video editing? I did not have any answers, but just being in this frame of mind took away any fear factor the movie could have had. In the same way, just having a general understanding of the automatic nature of the mind and how it can be manipulated should change your perspective enough to allow you to become more of a dispassionate observer.

Additionally, once you have a familiarity with these biases, defense mechanisms, shortcuts, compliance principles, etc., then you can start looking for patterns. If you watch a political event, you now know they will use many of these principles to swing your vote in their direction. If a salesclerk approaches you in the store, it won't matter if they went to school to learn these techniques, or if they just learned them through the school of life; they will still use them to persuade you to make a purchase. Friends, family, colleagues, and more will all use these techniques, without even being aware of them. And you will fall for many of them. However, having an awareness of these concepts is enough to make you ask questions. And just like with the story I shared with you at the beginning of this chapter about my dog Sam, that little pause to question can be enough to stop your head from rising all the way and perhaps to inhibit a charge to action fueled totally by automatic responses.

NOTES

Key Points

In his 1994 documentary, *An Inconvenient Truth*, Vice President Gore attributed to Mark Twain the quote, "It ain't what you don't know that gets you into trouble. It's what you know for sure that just ain't so." However, according to the *Center for Mark Twain Studies*, this attribution is wrong[38] and despite extensive research by others,[39] we are still unsure who said it first. Nevertheless, there is great value to this quote, especially when you consider our most basic assumptions, that we know what we know and that we make our own choices.

We have now looked at numerous ways in which we run on automatic pilot, and we do this almost all the time. Heuristics are mental shortcuts, and this *fast* thinking has developed to help us (individually and as a society) run more efficiently and productively—to save time and to stay safe. However, this mode of operating can be detrimental, causing us to race ahead based on incomplete or inaccurate information. This creates a two-fold problem. Firstly, we are operating on old programming that may (or may not) have benefited us in the past but will no longer do so. Secondly, we can lose ourselves in the process while we betray our best interests. Numerous research studies have been carried out to learn the automatic processes of the brain, and the findings are frequently being used against you, to persuade you to do something or to believe something that suits another's agenda.

Even if you do not wish to remember all the different processes that can distort your thinking, you should have gained a certain degree of humility in knowing about this by now. How can you be passionately for or against some issue if you cannot be certain that you have chosen for yourself? How can you be honest with yourself when you have these undercurrents and unknown needs and desires? But it is in this state of humility that you gain the ability to engage more in System 2 thinking—thinking through problems again rather than relying on a certainty that you already have all the answers you need.

The idea is not to master all of this, but rather move you along the continuum so that *more* of your decisions are made with System 2 thinking. Being aware of this information is the first step to making this change. The more you do this, the more you will uncover your real self and the easier it will become to move along the path toward self-realization. It is a process that will build upon itself.

Exercise

Take at least one day for each of the exercises below. Be sure not to rush the process. Give each of them careful consideration and enter your thoughts and discoveries into your journal.

1. Consider the four modes of cognition as developed by Kosslyn: *Mover, Perceiver, Stimulator,* and *Adaptor.* Where do you think you fit? How can you compensate for your weaknesses and maximize your strengths? How about the people you interact with? Are you experiencing any conflicts because someone operates in a cognitive mode not ideally suited to your expectations of them? For example, do you expect your partner to plan an excursion when they are more suited to being a follower and a supporter? What adjustments can you make to your interactions to maximize their strengths and minimize their weaknesses?
2. Look again through the various defense mechanisms. Try and find examples where you may have used each of these techniques. Have your trusted friends and family ever provided you with hints regarding some of the mechanisms you rely on? As you give these mechanisms careful

thought, you will find that some almost inconsequential events will surface in memory. The more you acknowledge these closer-to-the-surface events, the more likely your subconscious is to allow you access to more-deeply-buried events. Next, think about an area in your life that you may struggle with. Is it possible some defense mechanism is at play here? This is not an easy process but the more open you are to the idea, the easier the process will become. In time you will be surprised by some of the ways you have avoided an issue.

3. We all fall prey to fallacies and biases but determine to remember this the next time you get into a disagreement with another person. Stop and think, are your values and reasonings as solid as you believe them to be? Are you being blind to other alternatives? Are your choices being massaged by a confirmation bias? Try frowning as you think through a debate—this will assist you in really thinking through the issue again. Perhaps you could try this exercise with a friend who holds a different viewpoint to yours.

4. Compliance principles are being used on you all the time, whether it is by the natural salesman or family member who always manages to get their way, or by the media, marketers, and news organizations. Try to spot the techniques that are being used. A little skepticism will assist you in evaluating the information being presented to you. In the political and media arena, words certainly have been carefully honed to encourage your compliance. Watch some ads on TV and see how understanding compliance principles changes your perception of the ads. You can apply this same exercise to watching your favorite political show or politician.

5. Think about some of the causes you support. How have they been defined? What labels have been put on them?

Consider the other side. What definitions and labels do they use? Look at the issue again and work to accommodate both sides of the argument while eschewing the extreme ends. Now, redefine what it is you are supporting or denouncing. Have your views changed at all? If you put serious effort into this exercise, you will find value in some of the arguments for 'the other side.' I am not saying you will have changed your mind, but you will now have more information and more choices available to you.

CHAPTER SIX

THE QUESTION OF WILL

"Life is like a game of cards. The hand you are dealt is determinism; the way you play it is free will."

- Jawaharlal Nehru

Not long ago, Eldon attended a continuing education course (CEU) presented by Dr. Brian King and sponsored by the *Institute for Brain Potential*. One of Dr. King's specialties is the study of habit formation, and Eldon attended the course titled, *How the Brain Forms New Habits: Why Willpower Is Not Enough*. His work, together with that of dozens of other scientists, teaches us that the area of the brain known as the nucleus accumbens is associated with unconscious behaviors, particularly as they relate to habits and addictions. Essentially, our prefrontal cortex is our conscious decision-maker and is connected to the nucleus accumbens. However, the evidence shows that this connection alone is not nearly enough to override habituated patterns. As an anecdotal piece of self-disclosure, King illustrated this point with his *Krispy Kreme* story.

Habits

King decided he was going to lose weight. He knew how to do this since he had just moved to a city without a *Krispy Kreme*. Although he loved *Krispy Kreme* donuts, he surmised that if he went without his usual box of donuts every day, this would help him lose weight. This strategy worked for a few weeks until he had to drive out of town one day. Along the route was a *Krispy Kreme* store. He told himself there was no harm in getting a donut because, after all, he intended to get coffee anyway. This seemingly innocent thought led to an internal argument. He began talking to himself something like this:

You know if you stop, you'll get more than one donut.

No, I can go with only one, but if I got two or three that would be no big deal.

It would be a big deal—you know how habits work.

Yeah, maybe, but I have been good, so I sort of deserve it.

No, you set a weight goal and relenting once opens the door and you know that.

Well, I'll just get the coffee then.

No—once there you won't be able to resist, and you know it.

Now the dialog continued like this until he realized he had already exited the freeway and was pulling into the *Krispy Kreme* parking lot.

Most of us have decided at one time or another to give something up. Perhaps it was chocolate or wine or tobacco. Most of us can relate to King's internal conversation. I have on occasion given in to an urge I justified on the basis that it was only this once, or I deserved it, or—and the "or" goes on and on.

Neurons That Fire Together

A popular saying among neuroscience circles today goes, *"Neurons that fire together wire together."* Think back to Kahneman's *System 1* and *System 2* forms of thinking. System 1 is automatic, and the activity of the nucleus accumbens is one of the aspects that regularly contribute to this thinking, especially regarding habits and addictions. For example, you visit a restaurant for a nice evening meal but do not plan on ordering wine as you have resolved to give it up. However, at another table, you see some people enjoying wine with their meal. Your mirror neurons almost literally have you tasting the wine as well—it just feels so good. The next thing you know, the waiter arrives, and you order wine too, for what is the harm in one glass.

I have my own examples of this. As I head home from work, most days my thoughts are either on the work I have left behind or my plans for the evening. I am rarely thinking about food. However, the moment I walk into the house and step into the kitchen, my mind immediately asks what I can eat right away. After dinner, we generally sit on the sofa and watch television. Even though I may have resolved not to have dessert, I cannot prevent those thoughts from knocking, and my thoughts then follow Dr. King's self-talk closely.

I don't want dessert.

But does it really matter?

What if I only had a small piece?

But you know that's a slippery slope.

But I will be strong this time. Plus, I've had a rough day, so I deserve a little indulgence.

Okay, I'll be strong and only have just half a cupcake.

Oh, there is so little left I might as well finish it. That way it won't tempt me tomorrow.

I associate home with time for myself and sitting on the sofa is a time when I focus on taking care of myself, resting and unwinding. Food is associated with both events, so the super-highway of my brain says that food and treats are the goal. The nucleus accumbens then kicks in with its constant urging to give in to the habit/addiction.

Now, this is a bit of an oversimplification; we know other elements are involved in addictions such as drugs. However, it is accurate for self-empowerment and mind training. The idea here is that, even when we engage our frontal cortex to make that healthy, conscious decision and turn away from those delicious *Krispy Kreme* doughnuts, or that smooth glass of wine, our nucleus accumbens often wins the battle. According to Dr. King, the estimate gives the decision to the nucleus accumbens 90% of the time.

If you take a moment to think about it, you can surely find some real examples of this kind of story in your own life. Neurons that fire together wire together. Once a habit is established, it can be hard to break but not impossible. Understanding how this works can be liberating because we can then choose to wire a new pattern or habit together instead of fighting indefinitely with older wired patterns. So the smoker can find something else to busy their hand with or something different to put into their mouth. For myself, if I don't want to get up and do something else to distract myself from urgings to indulge in some dessert after dinner, I will frequently busy my hands with some project—perhaps drawing or sewing. Later, we will cover other techniques to take conscious control over these pre-programmed unconscious behaviors.

King said he recognized what he had done and pulled out of the parking lot instead of going in. What would you have done before reading this?

One Mind

We like to think of ourselves as having one mind. Research, though, suggests that this one-mind model is a gross over-simplification. We have already discussed the components of the mind (conscious, preconscious, subconscious, and unconscious), and hemispheric specialization, but it is worth revisiting in a different context.

Earlier, we discussed some of the split-brain research carried out by Roger Sperry and his colleagues. One study we looked at was run by Gazzaniga and

LeDoux where a split-brain patient was shown a chicken claw to his left hemisphere and a snow scene to the right. Afterwards, "the subject chose the most appropriate matches from an array of pictures visible to both hemispheres. He chose a chicken to go with the claw and a shovel to go with the snow."[1]

In another study, the right hemisphere saw the word "egg." When the subject was asked what they had seen, they said "nothing." When the subject was asked to reach behind a partition with their left hand and select from a variety of objects the item they said they had not seen, they chose the egg. It seemed that, if the left hemisphere was prevented from seeing it, the subject could not name the item they held. If the subject was then shown the egg and asked why they selected it, they invented a reason such as, they had eggs for breakfast that day.[2]

Note that while the egg was properly selected according to what the right eye saw, the left hemisphere made up the reason. In other words, the so-called conscious response, and I say so-called because of the typical emphasis on communicative abilities as defining consciousness, is telling a story to justify the behavior. Michael Gazzaniga called the left-brain narrating system "the interpreter."[3] According to Roger Sperry, each hemisphere is "a conscious system in its own right, perceiving, thinking, remembering, reasoning, willing, and emoting, all at a characteristically human level, and ... both the left and the right hemisphere may be conscious simultaneously in different, even in mutually conflicting, mental experiences that run along in parallel."[4] This leads us to some interesting questions.

Split-Consciousness?

As neuroscientist and philosopher Sam Harris points out in his excellent book *Waking Up*, sometimes substantial differences, one might even say, *arguments* occur between the two brains. Harris provides an example I'll paraphrase here. A young boy who has had his hemispheres separated and who has some language skill in his right hemisphere is asked what he wants to be when he grows up. His spoken (left brain) answer is something like a chemist. He provides his right-brain answer using cards, and it disagrees—it wants to be a racecar driver. Harris asks an interesting philosophical question: these two brains disagree with each other so what is the ethical solution when the patient, tired of the right brain interference, asks for it to be removed? Would that constitute murder at some level?[5]

Evidence suggests that both the right and left brain have their own subconscious or unconscious operations, but then what sense does it make to address the unconscious operations of some part of our being that we're not conscious of, as in the case of the boy above? In that sense, the problem of one mind is further exacerbated.

The reason for this discussion is to make it clear that the subject of mind remains a frontier. Many processes influence our conscious minds every day in so many ways. We may never come to a place of understanding ourselves, but we'll get much closer when we are informed of the processes and the actors, so to speak, behind the scenes.

Research

Mind programming and brainwashing—to the vast majority, these can sound fictional, or fodder for conspiracy theories. But how much truth is there in these ideas? A plethora of research is being carried out to discover why we do what we do, and the power elite are devouring (and often funding) this information. From the government to marketers, there is no shortage of people and organizations who wish to tweak your psyche to suit their aims—to get you to vote in their direction, buy their products, and even organize protests and demonstrations that suit their agenda. Eldon covers a great deal of this kind of research in his book *Gotcha! The Subordination of Free Will*, but here are a few examples for you.

Sample Studies

Earlier, I pointed out that in the presence of a bottle of hand sanitizer, students endorse more conservative attitudes. The same holds if a sign nearby reminds them to wash their hands.[6] A waitress who is dressed in red will receive larger tips, and not just from male patrons.[7]

Are you aware that people consistently prefer firsts? We are all more likely to choose our first option. This means that the order of contestants in a talent show is significant, as is the order of college acceptance letters received by an applicant, and the position of your resume in a pile of resumes.[8]

Studies have found that smokers want to smoke more after seeing the surgeon general's warning. With temporal distance, participants who had seen an ad that included the surgeon general's warning purchased more than those who had only seen an ad touting the benefits. Temporal time was defined as either being told that the products would be delivered in the future, or the orders being taken 2 weeks after exposure to the ad with the surgeon general's warning. Trustworthiness seemed to be the key. By being open about the risks, the advertiser (and therefore their product) was considered safer.[9] Is this why cigarette companies have no problem with making these warnings larger and more lurid? The same results were found for erectile dysfunction and hair loss drugs.

Covid-19

This kind of research goes on all the time and sometimes can appear to be very valid/beneficial. During the Covid-19 pandemic, governments and private institutions alike were racing to find both treatments for the sickness and vaccines against the virus itself. Many parts of the world spent time in total lockdown, and even when these restrictions eased up, the social distancing recommendations and rules still imposed huge burdens on both our personal and community lives. While everyone wanted to see an end to the Covid restrictions, many still didn't believe the end justified the means—how far does the need for civil liberties go?

For the pandemic to truly be over, immunity levels needed to be high enough in our communities. One way to achieve this was by making sure that as many people as possible got the vaccine as soon as possible after it became available. For this to happen, the Covid-19 vaccine needed to be marketed as efficiently as possible.

In this study sponsored by Yale University, ten different messages and their effects were tested. These messages focused on:

- Personal freedom
- Economic freedom
- Self-interest
- Community interest

- Economic benefit
- Guilt
- Embarrassment
- Anger
- Trust in science
- Not bravery

Immediately after hearing their specific message regarding the Covid-19 vaccine, the subjects were asked about their likelihood of getting the vaccine within three months and six months of its availability. They were then also asked to score their feelings on:

1. Vaccine confidence scale—the impact of the messages on vaccine confidence.
2. Persuade others item—their willingness to persuade others to take the Covid-19 vaccine.
3. Fear of those who have not been vaccinated—how comfortable they would be with an unvaccinated individual visiting an elderly friend after a vaccine becomes available.
4. Social judgment of those who do not vaccinate—how trustworthy, selfish, likable, and competent are those who choose not to get vaccinated after a vaccine becomes available?[10]

This study is interesting as there can be no confusion about the intent and how the results were to be used. How would you feel about this kind of study being run to boost political agendas? Could this kind of research be used to cause even greater divisions in our country—strengthening one side while demonizing the other?

This is just a minuscule view into some of the studies being carried on around the world to learn how your mind works. Globally, marketing companies use this kind of research to influence your buying decisions. Major elections also utilize this research. The use of focus groups in politics and general marketing has become the norm, but this kind of research has become even more intense in recent elections—President Obama used a 'dream team' of social scientists to help him win his election, and President Trump used Cambridge Analytica for the same purpose.[11]

With this going on, the Delphic maxim, "Know Thyself," becomes more important.

Unconscious Choices

Imagine a science fiction flick where minds are connected remotely to some auditing computer that images the brain's activity in real time like today's fMRI technology. In our imaginary scenario, a human auditor monitors the computer recording your every choice before you make it. With unerring accuracy, your decision is known in advance, and should that choice be objectionable to the social structure of the day, the monitor orders intercession, and some remote feedback loop corrects your decision by stimulating another area of your brain. Can you imagine this little entry into the world of science fiction as a real possible future? Well, this possibility is much closer than you might think.

Benjamin Libet

While Hans Helmet Kornhuber and Luder Deecke in 1964 discovered the readiness potential[12]—electrical activity in the brain that precedes voluntary activity—Benjamin Libet in the 1980s investigated how this related to the *decision* to perform the voluntary action. Libet used an electroencephalogram (EEG) to detect brain activity when subjects made a *choice* to move their finger. He found that brain activity occurred several hundred milliseconds before the subject expressed the conscious desire to move. Libet himself said this does not prove the lack of free will, for there was still time for 'free-won't' to change the action—150 milliseconds remain during which Libet thought the agent could "veto" the urge to move.[13] However, other researchers have continued the debate, providing further evidence for the actual choice being made in the subconscious mind.

John-Dylan Haynes

In 2007, John-Dylan Haynes, a neuroscientist at the Bernstein Center for Computational Neuroscience in Berlin, used functional magnetic resonance imaging (fMRI) to reveal brain activity in real time as the volunteers observed a screen showing a succession of random letters. The participants were asked to press a button, using either their right or left index fingers, whenever they felt like it and to remember the letter showing on the screen at the time. They found that although the conscious decision about which hand to use was made about one second before the actual act, their brain activity predicted this decision by up to seven seconds. So apparently "that consciousness of a decision may be a mere biochemical afterthought, with no influence whatsoever on a person's actions." As Haynes says, "How can I call a will 'mine' if I don't even know when it occurred and what it has decided to do?"

Haynes' experiment was more precise than Libet's. Libet used EEG to look at a limited area of the brain, whereas Haynes used fMRI to look at the whole brain. Libet's subjects decided when to move, whereas Haynes' subjects had to choose between one of two options. Nevertheless, critics still pointed out that Haynes and his team could only predict the right or left button press choice with a 60% accuracy.[14]

Itzhak Fried

This line of research did not stop there. In 2011, Itzhak Fried (University of California, Los Angeles and the Tel Aviv Medical Center, Israel) implanted electrodes in the brain, which allowed much more accurate readings than Libet's EEG and Haynes' fMRI techniques.

> "Fried's experiments showed that there was activity in individual neurons of particular brain areas about a second and a half before the subject made a conscious decision to press a button. With about 700 milliseconds to go, the researchers could predict the timing of that decision with more than 80% accuracy. 'At some point, things that are predetermined are admitted into consciousness,' says Fried.

The conscious will might be added on to a decision at a later stage, he suggests."[15]

The research here is complex, but it repeatedly shows that activity in the subconscious mind precedes a conscious choice. Using sophisticated equipment, a technician can watch your brain activity while you make a decision and know what you will consciously choose up to seven seconds before you are aware that you have even made a choice, and do so with an 80% accuracy rate.[16] This tells us that the subconscious mind is doing the choosing, while the conscious mind is inventing likely reasons to justify the decision. The technology necessary to augment the first part of our imaginary sci-fi scenario exists today. We can only ask how this information may be used in the future.

Free Will

Not long ago, Eldon and I were discussing practical reasoning versus theoretical reasoning, and I confess that I had some problems with this, especially as the topic we considered was 'is it *irrational* to believe in God?' My educational background is very much grounded in science, and so I understand theoretical reasoning, but our discussion turned to the many benefits, physical and mental, that came from a belief in a higher power, religion, and spirituality. I had a hard time understanding that it could be perfectly *rational* to believe in God just because of the *benefits* such a belief would confer. (As this is not the place to have that complete discussion, I would simply ask you to check out the book Eldon wrote on this subject, *Questioning Spirituality: Is it Irrational to Believe in God?*) However, I do see an interesting correlation in the arguments regarding free will. While the science behind the argument that there is no such thing as free will is solid and has the support of many prominent researchers and experts, problems arise in *believing* that we do not have free will.

Dis-Belief

In 2008, Kathleen Vohs (University of Utah) and Jonathan Schooler (University of Pittsburgh) ran a study to see whether differences in abstract philosophical beliefs would influence people's decisions. They took two groups of subjects; one was asked to read a paragraph arguing that free will was an illusion, while the other read a more neutral paragraph on the same subject. They found that, on a math test where it was easy to cheat, the group primed not to believe in free will was more likely to cheat. When able to steal, this same group pilfered more. In fact, on a range of measures, Vohs and Schooler found that "People who are induced to believe less in free will are more likely to behave immorally."[17]

This same effect was also observed outside of the laboratory. In another study, Tyler Stillman (Florida State University) and colleagues took a group of day workers and first measured the degree to which they believed in free will. They then examined the supervisor's reports on the job performance of these workers. Those who believed in free will were more likely to show up for work on time and were rated as being more capable. "In fact, belief in free will turned out to be a better predictor of job performance than established measures such as self-professed work ethic."[18]

Roy Baumeister (University of Florida) took this research further and found that a weaker belief in free will led to students being less willing to help their classmates or give money to a homeless person. They also experienced increased stress, less happiness, and a lower commitment to relationships. A weaker belief in free will also led to poorer academic performance.[19] The research further showed that a weaker belief in free will reduces creativity and gratitude, boosts conformity, and reduces the likelihood of learning from mistakes.[20]

A study carried out by a team of psychologists at UC Santa Barbara showed that disbelief in free will corrupts intuitive cooperation, leading to impulsive selfishness,[21] while another study carried out at Texas A&M University showed that disbelief in free will led to increased aggression and cheating while decreasing feelings of gratitude.[22] Additionally, the lack of belief in free will positively correlates with a diminished sense of self-awareness and an increased feeling of self-alienation.

Belief

Although the benefits of believing in free will are apparent in the studies cited above, it has also been shown to influence at an even deeper level.

In 2011, Davide Rigoni et al, "showed that shaking people's belief in self-mastery impairs their brain's readiness to act, even before they're aware of the intention to move."[23] In this study, the experimental group was told to carefully read a text that said scientists had discovered free will to be an illusion, whereas the control group read an article on consciousness with no mention of free will. The subjects then took part in a Libet-style experiment—pushing a button and indicating when they decided to act. The EEG results showed far lower activity in the group who did not believe in free will during the unconscious phase of the readiness potential. It seems that "deep in the brain, the gumption to act flagged along with the belief in self-determination." As Davide Rigoni said, "If we are not free, it makes no sense to put effort into actions and to be motivated."[24]

So, when we believe that something will make a difference, that we can achieve something through our efforts, we put in much more effort. Conversely, if you think you will fail, you will never try your best to succeed. Your beliefs matter.

Hiding the Facts

Even though so many reputable scientists say on record that free will is an illusion, a strong belief prevails that this information should not be made available to the public, for to do so could be harmful to society.

Saul Smilansky (University of Haifa, Israel) said "We cannot afford for people to internalize the truth" about free will. "If the public are naïve enough to believe in free will, let us not disabuse them of their mistake when such a mistake helps maintain the existing social order."[25]

According to Michael Egnor (State University of New York, Stony Brook), "Denial of free will, in a culture of pervasive surveillance, is the straightest road to totalitarianism."[26]

Paul Davies (Macquarie University, Sydney) thinks "These ideas are dangerous . . . there is an acute risk that they will be oversimplified and used to justify an anything-goes attitude to criminal activity, ethnic conflict, even genocide."[27] Davies has even called for an absolute suppression of the idea that there is no free will.[28]

Steven Pinker, cognitive psychologist and popular science author, says that "'Free will is a deception society must be built on,' although he prefers to call free will 'an idealization' rather than pejoratively calling it a deception."[29]

So, according to these experts, there are very practical reasons for promoting a society that believes in free will.

Silver Linings

Not everyone thinks free will, or the lack of it, is all doom and gloom. One idea suggests that not believing in free will can make one realize that successes and failures come down to luck rather than talents they have developed within themselves or choices that they consciously made. Crediting luck for your success could also lead you to experience emotions such as gratitude and love for the circumstances (genetics or social experiences) that brought you this good fortune. It also makes it easier for you to learn from your mistakes when you experience failures.[30]

When it comes to our views on criminality, Sam Harris, neuroscientist and author of *Free Will*, makes a great argument—one that to me highlights the spiritual side of the self-proclaimed atheist. The science behind the lack of free will is so robust that it is being used in legal proceedings, stating that the criminal acts committed by the defendant were not their fault, but rather the fault of their genes or their circumstances.[31] While Harris still believes that criminals should be punished, he says that doing so with an eye to the lack of free will the defendant has, will lead to more compassionate punishments that could result in more effective rehabilitation: "Blaming people makes us angry and vengeful, and that clouds our judgment."[32]

Forgiveness

In many ways, this reminds me of the work behind the *Forgiving and Letting Go* InnerTalk program. While working with the Utah State Prison, Eldon interviewed many inmates before deciding on the best affirmations to include in a program that they would test to try and reduce aggression and recidivism. A common story from these interviews came down to blame; the inmate invariably blamed someone or something else for their criminality—something along the lines of, *"My mother was a hooker, my father beat me, and the neighborhood boy hung heroin on me when I was twelve, so what else could I do?"* After a great deal of thought, Eldon settled on three affirmations that we now refer to as the *Forgiveness Set*: "I forgive myself. I forgive all others. I am forgiven." These affirmations were included, along with other affirmations designed to lower hostility and aggression and to increase the chances of rehabilitation. The results from the study were so robust that the Utah State Prison put in a library of InnerTalk programs and other prisons followed suit.[33]

We often speak of this study during public presentations, and invariably someone will express the concern that forgiving themselves for having committed the crime would perhaps encourage the inmate to recommit—as though they needed to blame themselves to feel any remorse. This was not the case. Freedom from blame appeared to give the inmate room to choose differently instead.

Recognizing that blame affects us all, and not just criminals, we decided to take things a step further. Blame assigns responsibility to someone else, or, in the case of self-blame, to an aspect of ourselves we have little control over. If it is not *our* fault, then there is nothing we can do about it. "The world sucks and then you die" attitude, the "it's not my fault" approach, and so forth, strips individuals of the power to affect their world.[33] Not only have we been giving the *Forgiving and Letting Go* program away for free since 1990, but we also include the *Forgiveness Set* on every single InnerTalk program.

What Does it Mean?

But back to the question of free will; what are we to do with all this information? According to the discussion Eldon and I had on practical versus theoretical reasoning, it certainly seems perfectly *rational* to believe in free will, even though science says it does not exist. Believing in free will improves the quality of your life while simultaneously building a better, more coherent society. However, in our opinion, we can take the free will story a step further.

We know that both nature and nurture play a role in the free will argument—whether we have it or not. The body can be likened to the hardware of a computer while the mind can be likened to the software. Both operate on automatic pilot most of the time. The mind and body can react automatically to various stimuli, with the body using biochemical processes and the mind using psychological predispositions. Both, though, can be influenced; just as we know that alcohol and drugs can cause shifts in judgment, and brain traumas can cause huge personality changes, we also know that our peers and enculturation influence many of our tastes. Genetics also contributes, providing perhaps a tendency towards an addictive personality, a genius capable of some out-of-the-box kind of thinking, a person driven by compassion, or a person likely to become a criminal.

Epigenetics

Even though epigenetics has seen a fair amount of work, many people, particularly in the new age arena, have extended this information to extremes that hold no validity. The scientifically accepted definition of epigenetics is "the study of heritable phenotype changes that do not involve alterations in the DNA sequence."[35] It means nothing in the arena of self-improvement and personal empowerment—the very theme of this book. This is not to say that positive thinking is not good for you and that living a healthy lifestyle will not cause positive expressions of your DNA and genes, but rather that the term epigenetics is being misused when applied to the field of self-help. Focusing on changing your DNA for sure is not the panacea for all your day-to-day challenges in navigating life.

Luck

So, let's look at the nurture side of the equation. Yes, there is so much that we have no control over, including the country in which we were born, our families, and our life experiences. However, the fact that you are reading this book at all would indicate that something in your life has influenced you to believe that such a thing is even possible—that you can make conscious changes, eliminating or minimizing problems in your life while maximizing opportunities. Maybe you know someone who has done this—so a life experience has taught you that it is possible—or you have some natural proclivity/interest in exploring the mind and the meaning of life. Whatever the reasons (or pure luck) behind your interest in this kind of reading material, you have it and are therefore capable of taking the next step and actualizing it in your life.

Choose Your Personality
Friedrich Wilhelm Nietzsche, the German philosopher, made some interesting and powerful suggestions, one of which can be found in his essay titled, *Twilight of the Idols*. Nietzsche implores us to ask ourselves whether we are living authentic lives or lives derived from the template of others. He encourages us to examine our values and our personality and to consciously choose who we want to be.

Changing your personality may seem like a tall order, especially if you have been taught to believe that your personality is fixed. However, according to research carried out by psychologists at the University of Manchester and London School of Economics and Political Science, not only can personality change but "Compared with external factors, such as a pay rise, getting married or finding employment, personality change is just as likely and contributes much more to improvements in our personal wellbeing."[36] Also, according to Kateri McRay (University of Denver) in a CEU course titled, *Developing Positive Emotional Habits*, "Change is possible, but first you must believe that you *can* change."[37]

Reinforcing Cycle
The work of Benjamin Libet and those that followed clearly show that the contents of your subconscious mind play a significant role in your choices. Luck may have brought you to this point in your life, but as you gain some understanding of how all these work, you will become empowered to take conscious control over at least some of the contents of your subconscious mind. You can change these contents to create new experiences and beliefs that reinforce the positivity in your life. Free will is not something given to you, but rather something you must take and make a reality in your life. Just remember, it cannot be turned on or off with a switch, but rather it happens in increments. Reinforce the positive and more positive experiences will come to you, creating a reinforcing cycle. All you need to do is take the first step, and that is the

realization that you *can* program your subconscious mind. And the benefits may extend further. As you learn to program your subconscious in a way that suits you, your life will improve. As your life improves, others will see what is possible, and maybe they too will use these kinds of tools to improve their lives. And so, these ideas can spread far and wide.

NOTES

Key Points

Many of the brightest minds have looked at the idea of free will and decided it does not exist. Biology, enculturation, social pressure, past experiences, and other such factors all exert an influence that negates free will. However, believing we have free will brings a host of benefits, including increasing morality, gratitude, academic performance, relationships, and more. Can we just act like we have free will and ignore the research that shows us otherwise? Of course—society is based on that. But mind training requires that we take this further, to find ways of exerting free will wherever we can.

We see how 'neurons that fire together wire together,' and how this explains some of our addictions or seeming lack of willpower. Here, we gain some ability to make changes. For example, if you are trying to lose weight and have decided to cut back on having dessert after your evening meal, then try changing what you do immediately after having your main course. Use different activities to replace the routines that normally trigger the weakening of your resolve to make changes.

In a prior chapter, we spoke about defense mechanisms, shortcuts and fallacies, compliance principles, and definitional and conditioned thinking. All of these contribute to the automatic System 1 thinking that Kahneman refers to. The more you learn about how these things work and develop strategies to negate them, the greater your chances of exhibiting a degree of free will.

Research has repeatedly demonstrated that we make our choices on a subconscious level. According to this research, we have only milliseconds to alter the choices made by our subconscious. But what if we start taking responsibility for the information programmed into our subconscious mind? In part, we have already started this process as we put into place exercises to engage more System 2 thinking. Later, we will be looking at more direct ways to program our subconscious mind in a manner of our choosing.

There is a value to looking at free will that goes beyond just self-empowerment. As we make small changes within ourselves, we open the door to making bigger changes in ourselves, and soon these changes can cause a ripple effect in the world. Maybe there is more truth to the admonition, "Be the change you wish to see."

Exercise

Look back at the exercises outlined at the end of chapter 5. Work through them again. The more you can habituate the new ways of looking at the world and reacting to it, the more you will be able to claim free will for yourself.

Think about the idea of 'neurons that fire together wire together.' In your journal, write down one of the habits you wish to change. Decide how to change your routine to prevent your habit from being triggered. Each day, note down the kinds of changes you are seeing. If your new pairing is not working for you, look for a different tactic. Once you have succeeded with this, you can move on to the next habit you wish to change.

This idea can also be extended into other areas. For example, when I need to remember something, especially when it was the kind of thing I would forget in the past, I first *choose* to remember (just as we saw in the exercises for chapter 1). Sometimes, all you need do is to tell yourself "I choose to remember that . . . ." Next, I will create some kind of pairing. I may tell myself, "When I see *x-object*, I will remember to do *y*." Sometimes I will change my jewelry over and wear the bracelet I usually wear on my right wrist on my left wrist, telling myself I will remember *y* whenever I become aware of the bracelet now on my left wrist. I consciously create a pairing for myself. Think of how you can use this kind of tactic in your own life.

In the morning, identify five areas in your life where luck and good fortune occurred. Write them in your journal and take a few minutes to experience gratitude for them. As your day progresses, pay attention to how this gratitude attitude influences the kind of day you have. Did you find yourself behaving differently? Did the day turn out better than expected? Make this gratitude exercise part of your everyday morning routine.

CHAPTER SEVEN

FINE-TUNING THE BRAIN

You can't change who you are, but you can change what you have in your head, you can refresh what you're thinking about, you can put some fresh air in your brain.

~ Ernesto Bertarelli

Most of us own cars and drive regularly. However, there is driving and there is *driving!* For some people, a car is simply a way to get from A to B; apart from making sure it is full of gas, checking the oil once in a blue moon, and making sure it gets serviced semi-regularly, they take little interest in knowing anything about the mechanics. That is how most people treat the workings of the brain, not understanding anything about the mechanics and how it can influence operations.

Some drivers, though, truly love to drive. They understand the mechanics of the car, including the gear ratio and optimal differential torque in relation to the rpm of the engine. They understand the fuel system and how the injectors or the old-style carburation system works. They know the horsepower of the engine and other details right down to the cylinder bore, piston size, length of stroke, the lift of the camshaft, valve lifter action, etc.

And they know how to get the maximum out of the car, including mounting tires compatible with how they will drive. You may see someone who knows how to operate a vehicle like this doing stunts in a movie; one minute the car is at high speed going north, the driver checks his speed, pulls the emergency brake (because this locks up only the rear wheels), releases the brake, and floors the accelerator, all without the slightest loss of control. (The maneuver is called a J-Turn.) These drivers know how to stay safe while getting the maximum out of the car, and so it is with understanding the workings of your brain and maximizing its output.

Now I am not suggesting that you embark on an intensive training regimen with heavy-duty neurology classes just so that you can take control of your brain. Nor am I assuming that you even want this degree of power over your mind. Most people just want to live happier lives, reducing conflict while increasing success. And for this, harnessing the power of the brain to support your goals is relatively simple.

We've already covered the fundamental areas—providing various models of the mind and highlighting its automatic nature regarding psychology. We can infer how difficult it can be to develop ideas that are truly ours. The only way around this is to gain an understanding of the mechanics so you can exert some conscious control. This also holds for some of your neuro molecules.

Brain Chemicals

Four brain chemicals are commonly referred to as *the happy chemicals*. Feeling happy is not only a good thing in and of itself, but it also improves many other areas of our lives, from our health to our productivity. Life is just smoother and easier when we feel happy.

However, from an evolutionary standpoint, these happy chemicals all have a survival purpose—we are rewarded when we do things that increase our chances of survival, and the lack of a reward can feel like a punishment. In today's world, survival is not about protecting ourselves from a saber-toothed tiger, but rather about our standing in society. Do others approve of us? Can we get ahead? How well can we provide for ourselves and our families? Unfortunately, these same automatic chemical processes can addict us to failure.

Just as understanding some of the basics of your psychological makeup allows you to take manual control over your actions and reactions, so it is with these happy chemicals. On their own, they will switch on and off in reaction to stimuli that you may not understand. But when you know what the triggers are, you can use them to your advantage. These four happy chemicals are *endorphins, dopamine, serotonin,* and *oxytocin*.

The story of these happy chemicals is usually over-simplified in popular literature, especially when it comes to self-improvement and motivation. When you dig further into the scientific literature, you will find that the story is not always as rosy as is generally portrayed, but then, what in life is 100% good in every circumstance? We aim to show you that this is still very pragmatic information that, if used correctly, can fast-track your life empowerment journey.

Cortisol

Before we delve into the happy chemicals, we must first look at the unhappy, or stress chemicals, particularly cortisol, which is secreted by the adrenal gland in response to stress.

Your body is designed to protect you from threats, like a built-in alarm system. However, it does not distinguish between physical threats, such as being faced by an aggressive dog, or just the stress of overcomplicated lives, bills, work, families, etc. In both instances, it releases adrenaline and cortisol as part of its fight response. Adrenaline increases heart rate and blood pressure and boosts energy supplies. Cortisol increases glucose in the bloodstream and the availability of substances to repair the body.[1] It inhibits insulin production so that glucose won't be stored but will remain available for use, narrows your arteries, and works with epinephrine to force your blood to pump harder so you can deal with the crisis. Cortisol can also shut down non-essential functions and anything else that can interfere with the fight/flight needs, such as immune systems, digestion, reproductive processes, and growth. Under ideal conditions, cortisol levels drop once the danger has passed. However, under chronic stress it can persist with detrimental effects, causing anxiety, depression, heart disease, sleep problems, weight gain, and memory impairment. Low levels of cortisol, though, can play a role in alcoholism, chronic fatigue, etc., and can also cause memory loss as you age.[2]

Relieve the Threat

By nature of evolution, we have inherited a threat-focused brain that promotes survival. This translates to accepting that our natural way is to expect threats. Loretta Breuning (California State University, East Bay), author of *The Science of Positivity*, explains it this way, "Our natural threat chemical alerts us to evidence of threat so we can act to relieve it. Cortisol feels awful because it prompts action to escape the threatened feeling. Relieving a threat feels good, and wires the brain to repeat any behavior that has previously relieved a sense of threat."[3]

However, today's world contains very few real threats compared to our ancient ancestors and their original need for constant threat assessment/expectation. How then do we reverse this high-level alert mode that can cause more harm than good? Let's begin by looking at what we can do to wire new pathways that make us feel good.

Endorphins – Natural Opiates

Endorphins are generally considered the body's natural opiates and are used to mask physical pain and boost happiness. Evolutionarily, endurance was a good thing as our ancestors often had to work through pain to be successful in the hunt—the group's survival was at stake. So, feeling good enabled us not only to continue until we were successful but also gave us the incentive to do it again.

Endurance

Today, endorphins explain the *runner's high*—the almost euphoric feeling that can keep the long-distance runner going until they cross the finish line. Virtually everyone who looks at photos of me at the end of my first marathon comments on how relaxed and happy I looked, and I had no problem whatsoever walking to where our car was parked, even though it was some distance away. But endurance athletes are not the only ones who benefit from this as intense exercise will also cause a burst of endorphins.[4]

Various studies have implicated endorphins in alleviating depression, reducing stress and anxiety, boosting esteem, reducing the amount of pain, helping in weight loss,[5] and inhibiting cancer cell growth.[6] And all of this is in addition to simply feeling marvelous when endorphins are released.

Humor

Many options abound to increase your endorphin levels. Laughing and crying stimulate small bursts of endorphins. Even the anticipation and expectation of laughter can induce endorphin release.[7] So when a colleague sends a link to you, telling you that you will find it funny, don't hesitate to click on it for it could well increase your work productivity as well as boost your health. Social laughter has been shown to increase endorphins,[8] as has dancing and sex.[9] Music is also a good way to increase endorphins, and this holds whether you are performing or composing, and whether you are singing, dancing, or drumming.[10] Sunlight,[11] meditation,[12] dark chocolate,[13] and spicy food[14] have all been shown to increase endorphins, as has aromatherapy, particularly the smell of lavender.[15]

Dopamine – Effort Rewarded

Dopamine is both a hormone and a neurotransmitter and plays several important roles in the brain and body. It is responsible for the feeling you get when you achieve a goal or are making real progress toward achieving a goal. From a survival perspective, it is responsible for the joy of a successful hunt or food find, and it pushes you when it sees an opportunity to repeat the success. Procrastination, self-doubt, and lack of enthusiasm, however, are linked to low levels of dopamine and can result in a person taking the easiest option.[16]

What is interesting about dopamine is that the more uncertain the reward is, the higher dopamine production goes, urging you to persist at the task. "Dopamine is not about the happiness of reward. It's about the happiness of pursuit of reward that has a decent chance of occurring."[17] Once the reward of effort is achieved, a second burst of dopamine can reinforce the goal and keep you looking for another opportunity to achieve it.

Social Networking

Dopamine is responsible for addictions as it turns on when it sees a way to get more of the addictive substance, whether it is alcohol, points in a computer game, or a chance to get 'lucky.' I must confess to being amused as I dug further into the mechanisms of addiction. We tend to think of addictions primarily as they relate to issues such as substance abuse, but we all have things we are addicted to. Today, a common addiction is social networking, or simply scrolling through 'feeds' and 'walls.' Many people check their social network sites several times a day, even while they complain that they repeatedly see the same stories. I, too, have commented on the fact that so much time could pass while I scanned social sites looking for interesting posts or connections I rarely found. Generally, these social networking work-breaks were not refreshing at all and sometimes could be downright depressing. However, as I reminded myself about the role of dopamine and addictions, I realized what was going on and so found different ways to take work breaks. While this kind of solution may not be as simple for more serious addictions, understanding some of the chemistry behind them could provide the incentive to search for different options/distractions.

Failure

Interestingly, addiction to failure exists. According to Breuning, "A bit of dopamine is released when the brain finds evidence that confirms its predictions. Negativity helps you make predictions you confirm, so it's a reliable way to enjoy a little dopamine."[18] In other words, you can become addicted to expecting to fail, as the act of failure will confirm that you were *correct* in expecting to fail—you get rewarded for failing. A key part of succeeding at any of your goals is to believe you *can* achieve your goal. This certainly explains something that Eldon and I have taught for decades: If you believe you will fail, you will never try your best to succeed, therefore increasing the likelihood that you will indeed fail. This one aspect is a key foundation stone behind the efficacy of our InnerTalk technology, something we will discuss later.

Smaller Steps

As dopamine rewards effort and urges you forwards, it is key to achieving your goals. The secret, however, lies in breaking your bigger goals down into smaller ones and then ticking them off the list as you accomplish them. This will keep you on track and give you small rewards along the way. Many of us seem to intuitively understand this as people often realize they have completed a task that was not on their list, only to then go and write it on the list just so that they can tick it off. I have certainly done this and can attest that I got a little jolt of pleasure from it, along with the energy and enthusiasm I need to tackle the next task on the list.

Creating a to-do list is the best way to keep me on track and keep my productivity up. I also find it helpful to create tomorrow's to-do list before winding off each day. This way, I can see all my accomplishments from today and build up enthusiasm for tomorrow's workload. For employers and leaders, making sure to thank your people for their work and commending them whenever possible is a great way to keep them motivated and on task.[19]

Low dopamine levels have been implicated in weight gain,[20] sleeping troubles, mood swings, an inability to focus, low sex drive, feelings of hopelessness, low energy, and much more. Unhealthy diets and a lack of sufficient protein are among the causes of reduced dopamine.[21] Foods high in tyrosine, such as dairy, soy, legumes, and turkey, can increase dopamine levels, as can reducing saturated fat intake. A healthy lifestyle that includes exercise, yoga, sunlight, meditation, music, and good sleep habits has also been proven to increase dopamine levels.[22]

Serotonin – Self-Confidence

Serotonin is both a hormone and a neurotransmitter. While it serves many purposes, ranging from controlling bowel movements to assisting in blood clotting, we are interested in its effects on the brain. Serotonin is thought to regulate anxiety, happiness, and mood. Low serotonin levels are associated with depression.[23]

Serotonin flows when we are feeling important.[24] If you are wondering how this promotes survival, remember we are born helpless. Our survival is dependent upon attention. Even though we become self-sufficient as we age, the old patterns remain. Your brain continues seeking serotonin as it makes you feel good, which means you are always looking for ways to feel important. A classic example of serotonin in action can be seen during awards and commendations. The recipient makes sure to thank all those who made their success possible, and they will have as many of these people in attendance for the presentation.

Parental Pride

I remember when our eldest son Roy graduated from the University of Washington in 2016; the ceremony took place at Husky Stadium, and the place was packed with graduating students and their loved ones. Even though there were far too many graduates to say their names individually, and even though I could only see our son when I peered through the high-level lens on my DSLR camera (and even then I only found him when looking at the photographs afterward), there was no way I was going to miss the event—and dress for the event rather than the weather, which for Seattle predictably turned to rain. In addition to celebrating the culmination of Roy's academic life, Eldon and I were blessed further in this event because Roy had been a part of the Associated Students of the University of Washington (ASUW), having been elected director of University Affairs. When the ASUW president gave his address and thanked all the parents of the members of his board, a family picture appeared on the giant screen behind the stage—a photograph of Eldon, me, Roy, and our younger son Will. I almost cried with pride, and even as I share this story with you, my heart still overflows. Serotonin in action indeed. And while I enjoy this happy chemical boost, I also experience the other benefits of serotonin, from stress reduction to clearer thinking.

However, the achievements aspect of serotonin extends even further. Not only does it urge us to do our best for our own sake, creating better students, leaders, parents, teachers, etc., but it also creates better followers. When you are an effective group member, credit to the leader brings its own serotonin boost. For example, even though you may not be the leader, you will still get a serotonin boost when your group leader receives a commendation because you participated in the project.

Deficiencies

Low serotonin levels are associated with anxiety, depression, insomnia, low self-esteem, poor memory, and more. It may also be associated with disorders relating to eating, social anxiety, panic, etc.[25] Research has shown that low serotonin levels could predispose individuals to impulsive aggression.[26] This could also be why some people fall into gangs as they seek recognition and importance.

Serotonin is also crucial for memory. Scientists are currently working on ways to use this information to aid in age-related cognitive decline.[27]

Increasing

A study carried out by Perreau-Linck and colleagues found that "self-induced changes in mood can influence serotonin synthesis."[28] While more work is needed in this area, it certainly highlights the importance of understanding the happy brain chemicals as they relate to mind training. You are not at the mercy of your biology, experiencing mood states that are beyond your control. While serotonin influences mood, your mood may also influence your serotonin levels. Taking conscious control over this could reap significant benefits.

Remember earlier, when we were talking about the unconscious mind and we learned that "long-time meditators had stronger connections between brain regions and show less age-related atrophy when compared to a control group."[29] Well, another study found that engaging in spiritual practices also raises serotonin and endorphin levels.[30]

Boosting our serotonin level has many benefits, from mood to health to cognitive abilities. While we cannot control the world, we can train our minds to recognize our importance. An effective way to boost serotonin is simply to remember happy events. Just taking a few minutes every morning to not only recall happy moments but live them again in your mind will significantly change the mood of many people.

Other ways to boost serotonin in the brain include spending time outdoors and exercising.[31] Dietary ways include consuming food high in tryptophan, such as peanuts, pumpkin and sesame seeds, milk, chicken, and cheese.[32] And if you enjoy aromatherapy, then lavender is another great way to increase serotonin and endorphins.[33]

Oxytocin – Bonding

Oxytocin is a hormone and a neurotransmitter secreted by the pituitary gland. In women, oxytocin plays a crucial role in childbirth, signaling contractions during labor, and releasing milk during nursing so the baby can feed. In men, oxytocin plays a role in moving sperm and the production of testosterone.[34]

However, for our purposes, let's focus on its role in social recognition and bonding.[35]

Contact

Humans are herd animals—the vast majority of us need to have contact with other humans, and we gain security from being part of a group. Oxytocin plays a huge role in this as it is responsible for love, trust, friendship, and the warm fuzzy feeling we get from helping others.

Oxytocin is so important that it forms its own production loop—the more affectionate you are, the more oxytocin you produce and therefore the more affectionate you *want* to be. This show of affection does not have to be with a partner as research shows the same effects from hugging your pet. I always feel that special warm glow whenever my dog Jessie looks up, sees me looking at her, and immediately comes bounding over for a cuddle. Even if you don't own a dog, simply seeing one you know and like can also cause an oxytocin boost. And for dog lovers, this same boost may be seen whenever an opportunity presents itself to pet a dog.[36]

While hugging, kissing, holding hands, etc. all boost oxytocin production, we should note that unwanted physical contact does not have the same effect—for this increases stress and cortisol release.[37]

An interesting benefit to oxytocin is that it increases fidelity. According to a study reported in *The Journal of Neuroscience*, oxytocin caused men in monogamous relationships to keep a much greater distance between themselves and other attractive women. This did not hold for single men and it was unclear if it aided the maintenance of monogamous bonds after they had formed. Also interesting to note was that oxytocin is known to promote trust, but it did not make the men who were in committed relationships more trusting of the women used in the experiment, even though they reported them as being just as attractive as reported by the males in the control group.[38] So, the more you hug your partner, the greater the chance they will remain faithful.

Here is another interesting finding. In the classic Trust Game experiment, two strangers communicate via computer. Person A receives $10 and is invited to electronically send some of it to Person B. There is an incentive as any money sent will be automatically tripled. Person B can then send some of it back as a thank you. Both participants are aware of all the rules. They found that 90% of the A participants sent money, and 95% of the B participants sent some back. Blood analysis showed an increased oxytocin level when A sent the money—they exhibited trust. Being on the receiving end of trust also causes an increase in oxytocin in B, motivating them to be generous in return. The same oxytocin boost was not seen when someone just came into a windfall.[39] So generosity is infectious too.

Benefits

There are other benefits to promoting oxytocin production. In addition to simply feeling good, hugging, kissing, snuggling, and cuddling have been shown to help you lose weight, lower blood pressure, fight off sickness, and more.[40] A study carried out by Kathleen Light and colleagues showed that women who hugged their partners more often had a lower resting blood pressure than women who rarely engaged in physical touch.[41] Oxytocin has also been shown to play a role in faster wound healing.[42] According to Paula S. Barry, MD, a physician at Penn Family and Internal Medicine Longwood, "It is important to remember that oxytocin is part of a complex system of neurohormones, but when it's released by physical touch, it can have many benefits including laying the foundation for cognitive, social, and emotional well-being, and strengthening emotional bonds and trust."[43]

The Darker Side

Now, you should also know that there is a darker side to oxytocin. A review written by Andrew Kemp and Adam Guastella found that oxytocin also increased envy and gloating. They believe that oxytocin is involved in 'wanting something' as opposed to 'shrinking away'. As such, they say that more research is needed before oxytocin could be used as a psychiatric treatment.[44]

Unfortunately, cynicism can also give you an oxytocin boost. According to Loretta Breuning, "Cynicism can stimulate oxytocin by creating the feeling that 'we're all in this together.'"[45] So while the oxytocin may make you feel more empowered, in this instance, it does little to positively influence your life's progress.

A study by Carsten de Dreu (University of Amsterdam, Netherlands) showed that oxytocin can increase the feeling of bias towards people who are in the 'out group'. This experiment utilized the classic trolley problem, where a runaway trolley is coming down the tracks and you must decide whether to allow it to proceed on its current track where it will kill five people or divert it to another track where only one person will be killed. While this may seem to be an obvious choice, it becomes more complicated when the single person is someone you love. However, this experiment was designed to look at the effect of oxytocin. They found that the subjects, who were all Dutch, were just as likely to sacrifice the lone person if they had a Dutch, German, or Arabic name. That was until oxytocin was administered. Under the influence of oxytocin, the subjects were *less likely* to sacrifice the lone person with the Dutch name, but this did not change their willingness to sacrifice the lone person if they were German or Arabic. So, under the influence of extra oxytocin, more subjects would be willing to sacrifice five people if it meant saving one of their own.[46]

Boosting

Fortunately, most of us do not have to make such difficult decisions. We can focus on all the positive benefits of oxytocin while bearing in mind some of the negative effects and canceling them where appropriate. So, what are some of the ways to boost oxytocin?

Dr. Paul Zak, author of *The Moral Molecule*, "recommends a minimum of eight hugs a day (pets count, too); massage and even soppy movies seem to work: he has done the blood tests. Interactions on Twitter and Facebook seem to lead to oxytocin spikes, offering a powerful retort to the argument that social media is killing real human interaction: in hormonal terms, it appears, the body processes it as an entirely real kind of interaction."[47]

So loving, hugging, cuddling, kissing, connecting, appreciating others, and the like are all ways to give you an extra oxytocin boost. As is remembering and reliving some of those special moments in your life in your mind. Just as a little aside, for me, the most memorable oxytocin boost came at the birth of our second child. Towards the end of my pregnancy, I became increasingly concerned; how could I love a second child without subtracting some love from my first? Nature has a way of handling this, though, and like so many mothers before, the moment my youngest was born, my ability to love doubled instantly, and I put behind me all the challenges of labor. While I do not, of course, suggest that everyone go out and have a/another baby, I use this as an example of the immense power that lies in the happy brain chemicals. There are many ways to influence the release of these chemicals to increase the quality of your life and to make success, in whatever area is important to you, more possible. When you understand how it all works, when you stop believing that you are at the mercy of your biology, and when you start to use this information to benefit your life, your life will only improve.

The Warm Fuzzy Feeling
For decades, Eldon has taught that the real value in life comes from going to the aid of another person, finding the kind option, or doing something nice for someone else, especially if it is not expected. He has often talked about the *warm fuzzy feeling* you can get as you lie in bed at the end of the day recalling these kinds of events. I can't think of a nicer way to fall asleep than with an oxytocin boost.

When you think about creating and collecting your own warm, fuzzy moments, remember the time factor. Sending someone a 'thank you' text is good, but writing a letter is better, and calling them on the phone is even better yet. But best of all is making the effort and taking time out to actually go see them, and perhaps give them a thank you hug at the same time. Remember, in these kinds of interactions, both the giver and the receiver experience an increase in oxytocin. I am sure you can find plenty of other examples where time and effort can magnify the resulting oxytocin boost.

Combinations and Benefits

The four happy brain chemicals of importance in your self-empowerment journey are endorphins, dopamine, serotonin, and oxytocin. As we went through each of these, you should have realized that several activities can increase the production of more than one of these happy brain chemicals. High-intensity exercise can increase endorphin, while regular exercise can also increase dopamine and serotonin.[48] Exposure to sunlight can increase both serotonin and endorphins.[49]

We already know much of this information. It has become common to say that if you are feeling bad or down, then straightening your back, lifting your shoulders, holding your head up high, and smiling will make you feel better . . . at least to a degree. Unfortunately, this almost sounds like your parents insisting that you eat all your vegetables. Knowing the right thing to do and putting it into action on a reliable basis can be challenging. The biggest issue I have with this kind of advice is that sometimes I want faster, clearer results. So, let's discuss two very basic techniques for boosting your happy brain chemicals, and some of the surprising science behind them. To test this out, I ran my own experiment and had some pretty incredible results that I will share with you shortly. The two techniques are smiling and deep breathing.

Smiling

The simple act of smiling causes your brain to release neurotransmitters, such as dopamine, serotonin, and endorphin. Not only does this make you feel better, but it also boosts your immune system. In one study, children in an infectology hospital ward had their blood tested half an hour before and one hour after being visited by tale-tellers, puppeteers, and handicraft artists. The experimental group showed an increase in white blood cells.[50]

We all understand that there is a wide range of smiles: the polite smile, the nervous smile, the reassuring smile, the half-smile, the full smile, the ecstatic smile, and on and on. One kind of smile that has garnered the interest of several scientists is the Duchenne Smile. "Discovered by French anatomist Duchenne de Boulogne in 1862, the key difference between this 'real' happy smile and a 'fake' happy smile lies in the orbicularis oculi – muscles that wrap around the eyes."[51] A genuine smile reaches the eyes, causing them to crumple into crow's feet. Now, this distinction between real and fake is not necessarily that clear-cut as some people can fake it, but this does not change the produced effects.

A 2014 study by Gunnery and Hall showed that those who could put on a Duchenne smile were more persuasive than those who could not.[52] Another study found that people producing Duchenne smiles were rated more positively (i.e., authentic, genuine, real, attractive, trustworthy).[53]

In several studies, smiles were created by simply having the participant hold a pencil or a chopstick in their teeth. In one such study, "All smiling participants, regardless of whether they were aware of smiling, had lower heart rates during stress recovery than the neutral group did, with a slight advantage for those with Duchenne smiles."[54] Another study used fMRI (functional magnetic resonance imaging) to compare brain images of those holding a pen using only their teeth (to facilitate a smile) with those holding a pen using only their lips (to inhibit a smile). Findings show that "Engaging the muscles you use to smile stimulates parts of your brain that control emotional responses."[55] Yet another study found that holding a pencil in the mouth to facilitate the Duchenne smile led to a "more positive experience when pleasant scenes and humorous cartoons were presented."[56]

In an interesting twist to the research designs, a small study carried out by Michael B. Lewis (Cardiff University, Wales) showed that treating frown lines with Botox reduced depression. Conversely, using Botox to treat crow's feet or laughter lines increased depression and reduced sexual function. Botox treatments also interfered with the subjects' emotion-recognition pathways—a reduction occurred in the accuracy with which emotional facial expressions were recognized.[57]

In case I have not yet managed to persuade you to smile more often, here are two studies that seem to say that smiling will also help you live longer. In a 2009 study, Ernest Abel and Michael Kruger (Wayne State University) found that using photographs taken from the Baseball Register for 1952, longevity could be predicted by simply analyzing the subject's smile intensity. "On average, the players with no smiles lived for 72.9 years, a full two years less than those who exhibited partial smiles. Those with full smiles lived to 79.9 years."[58] In another similar study, scientists analyzed the smiles in yearbook photographs taken between 1958 and 1960. They found that "the genuine smile group were more likely to get and stay married and had higher score evaluations of physical and emotional well-being more than thirty years after the college photos were taken."[59]

I wonder if I have always instinctively known this information; one of my favorite childhood songs was Nat King Cole's *Smile*, and it was more than just his beautiful, rich voice. Some part of me always knew that smiling would help me cope with heartaches and sadness. Now we know it can boost our happy brain chemicals, improve our immune system, clear our thinking, make us look more attractive and trust-worthy, live longer, have a happier marriage, and so much more.

Breathing

In moments of fear or panic, the first advice given is usually, "Take a deep breath." Constant advice of this nature and life experiences show us that taking manual control of our breathing, just forcing ourselves to breathe calmly and evenly is the first line of defense in moments of stress. Now we know that deep breathing is a great way to engage the parasympathetic nervous system; to turn off the stress chemicals such as cortisol, adrenalin, and norepinephrine; and turn on the happy brain chemicals endorphin and serotonin. A study by Valentina Perciavalle et al. showed that deep breathing exercises could lead to nearly a 50% reduction in stress levels as measured both by self-evaluations and objective parameters such as heart rate and cortisol levels.[60] There are other effective ways for reducing stress levels, such as meditation, yoga, music, and massage,[61] but for now, I will focus on breathing exercises as this can be done anytime and anywhere.

In times of stress, and as just a natural part of growing older, our breathing tends to become shallow, utilizing only our chest. Diaphragmatic or belly breathing allows for more complete oxygen exchange.[62] As the name suggests, diaphragmatic breathing involves the diaphragm, the large muscle that sits under the lungs. Here is the technique as recommended by Harvard Medical School:

1. Lie on your back on a flat surface (or in bed) with your knees bent. You can place a pillow under your head and your knees for support if that's more comfortable.
2. Place one hand on your upper chest and the other on your belly, just below your rib cage.
3. Breathe in slowly through your nose, letting the air in deeply, towards your lower belly. The hand on your chest should remain still, while the one on your belly should rise.
4. Tighten your abdominal muscles and let them fall inward as you exhale through pursed lips. The hand on your belly should move down to its original position.[63]

Once you have learned what diaphragmatic breathing feels like, you can do it anywhere and at any time—there is no reason to lie on the floor. Here is the process I like to use:

1. Breathe in slowly while focusing on my diaphragm.
2. Feel my diaphragm expand and lift while my lungs fill with air.
3. Breathe all the way in until my diaphragm is at full stretch.
4. Pause briefly.
5. Then relax and slowly exhale.
6. Again, focusing on my diaphragm at is relaxes and lowers.
7. At the bottom of the exhalation, pause briefly before starting again.

I also like to bring in my imagination as I do this process—

1. Picturing the energy of the inhalation running up my back.

2. Feeling the energy circling over my shoulders during the pause at the top of the inhalation.
3. Then allowing the energy to flow down the front of my chest and stomach along with the exhalation and lowering of my diaphragm.

The whole process is slow and easy so there is no chance of hyperventilating. Plus, I generally only do this for about three cycles—three slow controlled breaths. I find this process such an effective way of calming down tension and creating an instant relaxation response that I do it a few times during the day. I also do this once I am in bed and ready to sleep. Most nights I fall asleep a few minutes after completing the three cycles.

Putting it Together
Simply placing a pencil between your teeth will cause the release of dopamine, serotonin, and endorphin. Putting on a full Duchenne smile will increase these benefits, even if the smile itself is not genuine. Diaphragmatic breathing releases endorphin and serotonin and can result in a 50% drop in cortisol levels. Both techniques have been shown to reduce stress levels, but what does this mean in practical terms?

To explore this a little further, I decided to do another little experiment. This is not a scientific method, only a little personal test, but I wanted to see if I could quantify the difference these two little techniques alone could make. I must also confess to having had a certain amount of skepticism when I first heard of the pencil-between-the-teeth and the artificial Duchenne smile techniques for boosting happy brain chemicals.

All my life I have had excellent blood pressure; regardless of the stress I found myself under, my blood pressure was always around 106/68. In 2020, my brother passed away and I could not be there for him due to Covid restrictions. Several other things occurred, and my stress level increased; it is hard being unable to go to the aid of loved ones who need you. Often, a bit of time may pass before we even realize that a significant problem has developed. It was my husband who saw a problem and recommended that I check my blood pressure. For the first time in my life, it shot up to

180/100. I immediately started practicing every technique I knew of—most of them are included in this book—and very quickly I got frequent readings of around 125/85. But that was not good enough for me; I would not stop working on this until I get it back to my norm. So I decided to use this to test out the diaphragmatic breathing and the Duchenne smile.

- Sitting down, telling myself to relax while breathing evenly, my readings were 128/95.
- I then did the diaphragmatic breathing and pasted on as big a Duchenne smile as I could (fortunately I was home alone so no one could see my funny face), and within two minutes my blood pressure reading was 100/68.
- I went back to breathing normally and removed the Duchenne smile, and two minutes later my blood pressure reading was 105/70 – starting to creep up again.
- I went back to the diaphragmatic breathing and Duchenne smile, and a minute later my blood pressure reading was 99/68.

As I said, not a very scientific experiment, but it did show me what was possible. We have spoken about the mechanical nature of the brain and how we can take manual control over some aspects; my little experiment highlighted to me quite how significant an effect these techniques can have.

You should note that I repeated this same experiment several times around that time. Sometimes the results were just as striking and at other times they were not. But they worked well enough and often enough to demonstrate that we have more control over our stress levels, blood pressure, health, and happiness than we may have thought. Also, as with many of those things that health care professionals recommend, such as meditation, exercise, eating healthily, etc., done regularly, the positive benefits will accumulate. Today, I am back to frequently getting excellent blood pressure readings.

So, create habits that incorporate these techniques into your daily life; go for a walk (alone or with friends), take a quick break at work and share some humor with your colleagues, share your accomplishments and celebrate those achieved by friends and family, enjoy the outdoors whenever possible, take some time to focus on your breathing, and always remember to smile.

NOTES

Key Points

The journey of self-empowerment is all about finding ways to be happier, healthier, more productive, and more successful. One of the easiest routes to this is to engage in activities that will turn on our happy brain chemicals and turn off the stress chemicals.

Endorphins

Ways to increase endorphins include:

- Exercise—endurance exercise or short intense exercise,
- Laughing and crying,
- Dancing,
- Sex,
- Singing,
- Drumming,
- Sunlight,
- Meditation,
- Dark chocolate,
- Spicy food,
- Lavender, and
- Spiritual practices.

Dopamine

Ways to increase dopamine include:

- Create a 'to do' list and tick items off as they are accomplished,

- Foods high in tyrosine, such as dairy, soy, legumes, and turkey,
- Reducing saturated fat intake,
- Exercise,
- Yoga,
- Sunlight,
- Meditation,
- Music, and
- Good sleep habits.

Serotonin

Ways to increase serotonin include:

- Do your best—for yourself, your team leaders, your partner, and your family,
- Engaging in spiritual practices,
- Spending time outdoors,
- Exercise,
- Eating food high in tryptophan, such as peanuts, pumpkin and sesame seeds, milk, chicken, and cheese, and
- Lavender.

Oxytocin

Ways to increase oxytocin include:

- Hugging,
- Kissing,
- Holding hands,
- Snuggling,
- Cuddling,
- Hugging a pet,
- Trusting,
- Being generous,
- Receiving trust,

- Massage,
- Soppy movies, and
- Connecting with and appreciating others. (Please be sure that the recipient of physical contact from you is open and willing.)

Exercise

Look through the ways you can increase your happy brain chemicals and write down in your journal the techniques that appeal to you the most, or that you believe will be easier to implement in your lifestyle. Be sure to find at least one item from each of the lists. Write your preferred techniques in your journal, adding how and when you will include them in your day-to-day life.

As you can see, there is some overlap in ways to boost each of the chemicals and there are also ways you can combine exercises.

Here are some ideas to get you started:

- If you can, get up right now and go and hug a loved one.
- Put on a Duchenne smile and take three consecutive diaphragmatic breaths.
- Step outdoors and take a moment to appreciate something—the fresh air, the quiet, the world outside, etc.

If possible, figure out how you can get eight hugs daily. (Remember, hugging pets counts as well.) However, try not to get too clinical about this. Hugging is a fun way to express affection, and that should be your primary focus. This is what will strengthen your connection with your partner and family.

Ask your friends and family how much of a smiler they think you are. Look at photos of yourself and see how often you are smiling and how natural it looks. Since paying attention to this aspect, I have been surprised at the number of people who do not smile much. Think about how you greet people. Do you smile at them? How warm and genuine is the smile? It may help to focus on how seeing someone smile at you makes you feel—appreciated, valued, etc. *Choose* to make others feel this way too and reap the benefits of smiling for yourself too.

Plan to watch movies, particularly comedies and sad stories, with friends and family, and share jokes and memes. This will give you opportunities to laugh and cry more.

Cultivate the warm fuzzy feeling that comes with doing something nice for someone else. Go out of your way to open the door for others, smile when you greet them, and generally show people you care. Sending someone a 'thank you' text is good, writing a letter is better, and calling them on the phone is even better yet. Best of all, make the effort and take the time to go see them, and perhaps give them a thank you hug.

The more affectionate you are, the more oxytocin you produce and therefore the more affectionate you will *want* to be. If you are not a naturally physical, touchy person, just start with the occasional contact and build it up.

Dopamine's role in addictions will include alcohol, computer games, and even social networking. If you find too much time in your workday disappearing due to social networking breaks, try stepping outdoors, walking around the office, or watching a couple of funny video clips. Don't forget you can also be addicted to failure. Pay attention and correct yourself if you say anything regarding expecting to fail, or that you knew something would not work out for you.

Creating 'to-do' lists can assist in triggering dopamine. As you create them though, remember to break your bigger goals down into smaller steps so there is more to tick off as you accomplish them. It can also be helpful to create tomorrow's 'to-do' list before winding off each day. This way you can see (and appreciate) all your accomplishments from today and build up enthusiasm for tomorrow's workload.

For some, it may be worth it to guard against the role oxytocin plays in how outgroups are treated. Think about your biases against certain groups of people. Ask yourself, are the biases real or just a habituated way for you to get more oxytocin? Remember, mind training is also about living consciously.

While we can often reject the commonsense advice all of us have received in our lives, that is a big mistake. Getting outdoors, exercising, eating healthfully, smiling, deep breathing (diaphragmatically), etc. will all assist you in your goals.

PART THREE
THE POWER OF BELIEFS

CHAPTER EIGHT

SEEING IS BELIEVING

There is an optical illusion about every person we meet.

~ Ralph Waldo Emerson

How good are your observational skills? While some people are better than others—Eldon certainly spots the police cars running radar detection way more often than I do—as a rule, we all tend to think the world around us is as we observe it to be. But should we?

Category Thinking

Some have argued that we cannot see that which we have no language for. Research psychologist Kevin Dutton states in his book *Black-and-White Thinking*, "Hard though it is to believe, language is an hallucinogenic. Not only does it make us see things that *aren't* there . . . it also makes us see things that *are*."[1]

An example Dutton provides for his statement is the 1974 Car Crash Study carried out by Elizabeth Loftus (UC Irvine) and John Palmer (University of Washington). In this study, after watching a video of a traffic accident, the subjects were asked about the speed at which the vehicles were going. The question, "About how fast were the cars going when they *smashed* into each other?" elicited higher estimates for the speeds than when the verbs *collided, bumped, contacted,* or *hit* were used in place of *smashed*. In a retest one week later, the subjects who had been asked the 'smashed' version of the question were more likely to answer yes to the question, "Did you see any broken glass?" This, even though there was no broken glass in the film.

Dutton's use of the word 'hallucinogenic' is a bit of a stretch, although for these subjects, thinking back to the video they had seen the week prior caused them to 'see' something that was not there. It may be more accurate to say that using the word 'smashed' resulted in the mind filling in some additional blanks to create its own version of the story. Researchers Loftus and Palmer concluded that "These results are consistent with the view that the questions asked subsequent to an event can cause a reconstruction in one's memory of that event."[2]

Nol

Dutton uses another example that brings us closer to the idea of seeing or not seeing something based on language. Native Berinmo speakers (an indigenous language of Papua New Guinea) find it easy to distinguish slight variations in the color green as they have different names for them, whereas native English speakers struggle with this task. Native English speakers can easily distinguish blue from green, whereas the Berinmo speaker finds this difficult, if not impossible. This is because they have a single term, *nol,* for the colors we describe as blue and green.[3] According to Sandra Waxman (Northwestern University), "The particular categories we impose on our experience of the world are shaped by the language we speak. And this has consequences for thinking and memory."[4]

In an interesting study, nine-month-old infants were shown colorful cartoon-like creatures on a screen. Each appeared on the center of the screen and then moved in one direction or another according to their type. Some of the infants were given the same novel word for all the characters, regardless of their type. Other infants were given two different names. The experiment was designed so that one kind of creature would move across the screen in one direction, and the other kind of creature would move across the screen in the other direction. In the next stage of the experiment, a creature would appear on the screen, and the researchers watched to see if the infants would anticipate the direction the creature would move. It was found that the group of infants who had been taught two different names, and had therefore created two categories of creatures, were able to predict the direction of movement, whereas the infants who only learned one name were not.[5]

I am reminded somewhat of something I experienced when I first started working in a microbiology path lab after graduating from university. One of the first tasks I had to master was distinguishing red and white blood cells in urine samples. At first, looking down the microscope, I was only able to see blood cells that all looked roundish. However, after about a couple of weeks, it was as though a light went on. Now, the red cells appeared to me more defined and almost looked like they had a halo around them whereas the white blood cells looked kind of fuzzy on the inside. My eyes had become trained to see the difference. But this had nothing to do with categories; I knew about red and white blood cells (two different categories), I just had to learn to discern the differences when looking down the microscope. I wonder how long it would take a native Berinmo speaker to be able to discern the difference between blue and green once they associated different names with them.

We see then that language can influence how we see things, and that small differences can be hard to detect without some practice, but what about those everyday things we see clearly?

Eyewitness Accounts

Little evidence is more compelling during a trial than when the witness points to the defendant and states clearly, "He (she) did it!" We tend to trust our senses, so unless we have evidence to suggest that a witness is lying, we trust the evidence they provide for they saw it with their own eyes. DNA evidence, however, has upended this confidence. According to the *Innocence Project*, whose mission is to free innocent people who are incarcerated and to reform the system responsible for the unjust imprisonment,[6] of the 358 people who had been convicted and sentenced to death only to be later cleared by DNA evidence, 71% had been convicted by witness misidentification and had served an average of fourteen years before their exoneration.[7] Much as this statistic horrified me, the information did not surprise me.

Dinner in London

In my early twenties, I went out one evening for dinner in London with a group of friends. In my experience, London restaurants are only a little less crowded and hectic than restaurants in New York City; the tables placed extremely close together, the cacophony of conversations, orders being shouted, and the clanging of serving dishes and banging doors, made conversation at our table challenging. Back then, though, it was all just part of the fun . . . a lively atmosphere indeed.

At one point during our meal, a party of four or five men walked past our table heading for the exit. As they passed, one of the men stumbled, his hand hitting our table as he stopped himself from falling to the ground. In a flash, he righted himself and left with his group. My friends and I immediately checked for our bags and purses, but everything was in order. Except that not one minute later, a diner at the table behind us called out in alarm: "My bag, my bag . . . they took my bag!"

It turns out that the technique they had used was to kick a bag sitting beside a diner at the next table, pushing it so that it was on the floor alongside our table, and then the fake stumble at our table had allowed the thief to pick the bag up without anyone realizing anything was amiss. But here is the interesting part. The man had stumbled at our table; we had all had a good look at him; he had looked us in the eye in fact, yet we all provided the police with *totally* different descriptions, each of us certain about what we had seen. No time had passed for memories to fade or become distorted, and no cognitive issues that would have impaired our observation skills. We had even been alerted to be more careful, yet glaring differences emerged in our descriptions as provided to law enforcement. Are our senses less reliable than we believe?

Illusions

Cognitive dissonance is where a person can simultaneously hold two opposing views without even realizing it, and an example of this can be found in how we think of eye-witness testimony. We trust eyewitnesses, but most of us have watched enough television shows about crime and law enforcement to know that eyewitness accounts are fallible. However, even though most people are aware of the fallibility of eyewitness testimony, they categorize it specially. As such, the gold standard for discerning truth can still be summed up in the statement 'seeing is believing.' The common belief is that there is no denying what is directly in front of your eyes. But should we?

At this point in our mind training presentations and workshops, Eldon loves to pull out a collection of illusions, some of which can elicit exclamations of awe and wonder from the audience—especially when one technique leads to an image of Christ appearing on a blank wall.

It is interesting how illusions can be so well-known—almost everyone has seen the maiden and the hag, or the faces and vases illusions—yet very few stop to think about the brain mechanisms responsible for them and what this tells us about our perceptions. Let me describe just a few I found that will make you question the truthfulness of your senses.

The Break of the Curveball

On a green background are two balls. The blue ball is static, while the black and white spinning ball is falling. When you focus your attention only on the black and white ball, you will see it is falling straight down. When you focus your attention on the static blue ball, the falling ball is still clearly visible but now, rather than falling straight down, you will see it veering off to the left as though falling down a slope. (This illusion, by Arthur Shapiro et al. won first prize in the 2009 *Illusion of the Year* contest.[8] If the illusion is no longer available at the internet address provided in the endnotes, a simple search for "break of the curveball illusion" will show you several versions.)

This illusion seems to explain some of what we call the curveball phenomenon in baseball, where the pitcher throws a ball that seems to curve as it crosses the plate, causing the hitter to miss. It seems that not all curve balls really curve; they only *appear* to do so when the arc moves from one part of the batter's vision to another—central vision to peripheral vision.[9] (Note: Some curve balls actually curve. There are several explanations for this including the way the threads of the ball move the air around them[10] and the Magnus Effect.[11])

3D Schröder Staircase

In this illusion, the creator, Kokichi Sugihara (Meiji University, Japan) created a 3D model from the classic 2D Schröder Staircase where the stairs appear to be leading down regardless of whether the picture is upright or upside down. In the video demonstrating this illusion, an object is placed on the top step of a staircase. However, when the model staircase is rotated 180 degrees, the same object now appears to be sitting on the bottom step. What makes this illusion even more uncanny is that when the entire model is viewed in a mirror, the object can be seen simultaneously on the top step (on the actual model) and the bottom step (viewed in the mirror). This illusion won first prize in the 2020 *Illusion of the Year* contest and is worth checking out. (An internet search for 3D Schröder Staircase will bring up several videos).

The explanation for this illusion seems to be that the dark tones *imply* shadows and depth, and converging lines are *usually* a measure of distance. The brain then takes a *shortcut*, creating a storyline that seems to make sense of the shapes that usually mean a staircase, even though in this instance they do not.[12]

Motion-Induced Blindness

I do enjoy illusions where the viewer can interact and change parameters; it is interesting to see how far some aspects need to be changed before the illusion is no longer there.

Michael Bach (Freiburg University, Germany) shares the *Motion Induced Blindness* illusion on his blog. This illusion is set against a black and grey-striped background. Three yellow circles form a triangle and over this is a rotating grid of blue crosses, with the central pivot point marked with a small circle that slowly flashes red and green. If you focus your attention on the central green/red circle, even though the three yellow circles are still clearly visible and remain constant, they still seem to blink at seemingly random intervals; sometimes one, sometimes two, and sometimes all three of them will simply disappear. A quick refocusing of your eyes will show you that the yellow circles are still there. In this illusion, you can change the color of the dots, the color of the blue crosses, the rpm of the blue crosses, and the size of the dots. I was amazed at the extreme nature of the changes I could make, and still the illusion held.

The simple explanation for this illusion has to do with something known as the *Troxler* effect, a local adaptation by the retina that some have referred to as fatigue. This occurs when you fixate on your vision; the rotation simply adds even more background noise, and so enhances the effect.[13]

It is well worth taking the time to check out the above illusions, Internet addresses for which can be found in the Endnotes, not only so you can experience them for yourselves but because they will lead to other incredible illusions that will give you even more pause for thought. Not only are illusions fascinating but when you look at the science behind them, you get to see the various mental shortcuts your brain makes. Note that it is not necessary to understand the science behind the illusions, especially as some of the explanations can be very complex. However, it *is* important to know that the brain uses many such mechanisms to find quick solutions, and while these can be extremely helpful in the right situations, sometimes they can provide us with a wildly distorted view. This phenomenon becomes even more fascinating when we look at examples that relate to everyday situations.

The Gorilla in the Room

Several years ago, I saw a video on YouTube entitled *Selective Attention Test*. The video shows a group of people bouncing and passing a basketball. There appear to be two teams of three, one team dressed in white and the other in black. The instructions at the beginning of the video ask the viewer to count the number of times the players wearing white pass the basketball. The task took a little concentration but was still relatively easy; I got the correct answer of fifteen passes. However, the video does not stop there, and the next question simply astonished me. The narrator asks if the viewer saw the gorilla. *What gorilla?* The video is then rewound and played again. This time, I saw a person dressed in a gorilla suit saunter into the frame from the right, stand in the center, pound its chest, and then exit left.[14] How could I have missed something so glaringly obvious?

According to researchers Daniel Simons (University of Illinois) and Christopher Chabris (Geisinger Health System), my experience is common. They state that 50% of the people who watch this video miss the gorilla.[15]

The Illusion of Attention

Chabris and Simons provide several examples where people simply do not see what is right in front of them, ranging from drivers who miss seeing a motorcyclist to Commander Waddle of the nuclear submarine USS *Greenville* missing the Japanese fishing vessel *Ehime Maru* during emergency training maneuvers. This last example resulted in the death of three crewmembers and six passengers.[16] How could an experienced captain in a state-of-the-art submarine have missed it?

In their fascinating book *The Invisible Gorilla*, Chabris and Simons explain how often we only see what we *expect* to see. While we believe we will consciously see whatever confronts our visual system, the truth is that we can often miss glaring details when our attention is directed elsewhere.[17] Simons explains this in his Tedx Talk titled *Seeing the World as it Isn't*. According to Simons, rather than seeing the complete world in front of us, we only clearly see the small sliver in the center of our view—all the rest is out of focus. Our view of real focus appears much wider because our eyes are constantly moving around.[18]

In the case of the gorilla experiment, we were instructed to count the number of *basketball passes* the people in white made. Everyone is moving about on the screen, and concentration is required to follow the ball in question. This effort narrows our field of focus—our eyes are no longer wandering around capturing images from the entire scene—and as we focus only on the basketball in question, we easily miss major events such as the gorilla.

Inattentional Deafness

This phenomenon is not restricted to visual situations. A study carried out by Nillie Lavie (Institute of Cognitive Neuroscience, UK) and James MacDonald (University of Oxford, UK) found that focusing one's attention on a demanding visual task can lead to a failure to *hear* an otherwise obvious sound.[19] In two variations of this experiment, the subjects were tasked with discerning details as they appeared on the computer screen. The subjects also wore headphones as they were told this would help them concentrate more. During the study, an audible tone was played through the headphones, sometimes against a background white noise, and sometimes all by itself. The more difficult the visual task, the less likely the subjects were to hear the audible tone, even when it was played all by itself.[20]

Inattentional Blindness

Brian Scholl et al. (Yale University) ran a variation of the gorilla experiment where subjects were tasked with tracking multiple objects on a dynamic screen. On the fourth trial, an unexpected event was introduced; a fully visible object enters and passes across the screen. After the experiment, the subjects were all questioned to see if they had noticed the unexpected event; 30% of the subjects missed it—they were *inattentionally blind*. The experiment was then repeated, but this time the subjects did the test while also talking on a cell phone. Talking on the phone did not affect the subjects' *multiple object tracking* ability, but the rate at which they missed the *unexpected event* shot up to 90%. The study concluded that "visual *awareness* is particularly impaired by cell phone conversations, above and beyond any smaller effects on visual performance."[21]

Research by David Strayer and William A. Johnston (both at the University of Utah) provides more details. Using a simulated driving task, they found that driving ability was not impaired while listening to the radio or an audiobook, even when the subject was holding a cell phone. However, an unrestrained phone conversation, using either a handheld phone or hands-free, resulted in a "twofold increase in the failure to detect simulated traffic signals and slower reactions to detected signals." The authors suggested that "Cellular phone use disrupts performance by diverting attention to an engaging cognitive context other than the one immediately associated with driving."[22]

Real-World Ramifications

As you can see, these studies are not only intriguing on a theoretical level, but they also have very real everyday ramifications. For example, the person texting while crossing a road may not hear a car approaching, and talking on the phone (even hands-free) while driving may cause one to miss unexpected actions by another driver. In the latter example, keeping both hands on the steering wheel will not preempt the consequences of attention being directed toward the phone conversation conducted while driving. Sometimes those split seconds of warning we get while fully attending to our driving can make a huge difference.

However, this is not a lecture to dissuade cell phone use while driving, but rather to highlight the fact that our ability to pay attention is nowhere near as infallible as we generally believe. Chabris and Simons call this the *Illusion of Attention* because we believe we are paying close attention when, in fact, we are not, and this *inattention* can cause us to become blind or deaf to events outside our primary focus. Simon's explanation of how we only really focus on a small section of our view could well explain, at least in part, the different descriptions my friends and I provided after the bag theft in the London restaurant. Very possibly in the stress of the moment, we focused on different slivers that may not have been related at all—perhaps the person behind the perpetrator was wearing the blue scarf, or the person who jostled past at that very moment was wearing the denim jacket.

Undergirding all of this is our belief that we know and understand our senses. But what if you learned that your beliefs about someone else can affect the quality of their life, just as their beliefs about you can affect yours? Our beliefs impact our experiences in so many ways.

NOTES

Key Points

Just because we see something with our eyes, or hear it with our ears, does not mean we have the complete picture. We have now learned that language itself can influence what we see, and how things are defined can influence how we remember an event.

By looking at and examining a few illusions, we gain some idea of how mental shortcuts and beliefs can create a picture and a false understanding of our world. For example, the mental shortcut that says dark tones *imply* shadows and depth, and converging lines are *usually* a measure of distance, can cause us to wrongly interpret what we see.

We also learn that paying attention has greater importance than we might have thought. Sometimes we can be so focused on one thing that we miss some glaring pieces of information. Alternatively, the belief that we can function effectively when multi-tasking and dealing with today's constant digital stimulation is false.

Once again, there is room for some humility when we learn we cannot even take our senses for granted. All of this speaks to a greater need for more careful thought, even in more mundane situations. Discarding the assumption that we can talk on our phones while driving through heavy traffic could certainly lead to fewer accidents. But it also raises the question regarding paying attention in other situations, such as when your partner is speaking to you—your lack of focused attention may cause you to miss some important detail. An awareness of this—a respect for your own limitations—points again to the need for more conscious living. If we can miss such obvious things, what other information in our daily lives are we missing?

Exercise

Go online and check out the illusions referred to in this chapter. You can find the internet addresses for them in the endnotes, or you can search using the name of the illusion.

Do a general search for illusions and explore some more. See if you can find out why these illusions work.

Take a moment to realize fully what this says about your observational skills. While you may not understand the science behind the illusions, you do want a firm handle on the idea that some of your brain mechanisms seem to distort your reality.

CHAPTER NINE

THE EXPECTATION FACTOR

"It is our attitude at the beginning of a difficult task which more than anything will affect a successful outcome."

~ William James

"What you expect is what you get." Is there any truth to this saying, or is it just another one of those tired clichés with little real-world relevance? Most of us have had at least some experiences that would confirm this statement, even if these confirmations come primarily from viewing the actions of others rather than our own. However, we have all certainly experienced times when circumstances did *not* go as expected, when they went significantly better than we expected... or significantly worse. So how *much* truth is there to the statement, and what are the factors that influence it?

Microscopic Cues

In 1904, the *New York Times* reported on a horse that would become known as Clever Hans. It seems that Hans' owner, Wilhelm Von Osten, had trained the horse to count, distinguish between coins, perform mathematical computations, spell out the name of someone he had been introduced to earlier, and much more.[1] Hans would provide the answers by tapping his hoof or by indicating letters on a blackboard. At first, this was all believed to be an incredible hoax, and that the horse responded to cues provided by its owner. However, it was soon found that the horse could perform just as well regardless of who asked him the questions. A special commission was formed to study Clever Hans, and after 1.5 years, the German board of education concluded no hoax was involved.[2]

In 1907, Biologist and psychologist Oskar Pfungst finally found the explanation. Pfungst discovered that Clever Hans could only answer questions if the person asking the questions knew the answer, and the horse was able to see the questioner's face. It turned out that Clever Hans was reading microscopic signals on the face of the person asking the questions. Pfungst also learned that, however hard he tried, he was unable to control these cues as the horse always answered correctly if he could see Pfungst's face.[3] It is fascinating to realize how much information we can reveal without being aware or regardless of how hard we try not to.

Hound Dogs

A 2011 study by Lisa Lit et al. (UC Davis) also demonstrated this effect in dogs trained to sniff out drugs and explosives. In the experiment, the handlers were told that the search area may contain three target scents and that in two of these cases, the scents would be marked with pieces of red paper. None of the search areas contained the scents of either drugs or explosives, although two of the targets contained decoy scents (hidden sausages). Of the 144 searches, only 21 came up clean—the dogs did not signal they had picked up a scent. In total, the dogs alerted their handlers to 225 false positive results. When broken down, the numbers showed the human handlers were not only influenced by the red pieces of paper, but they transmitted this information to the dogs, who then responded accordingly.[4]

In both accounts, the animals registered microscopic cues that their human handlers were unaware of transmitting and responded accordingly. So, are there microscopic or subconscious cues that we respond to?

The Thomas Theorem

In 1928, William Isaac Thomas and Dorothy Thomas stated that *"If men define situations as real, they are real in their consequences."* They used the example of a prison guard who went against orders and refused to let a particular prisoner go outside the prison walls. The prisoner had killed several people who had the habit of talking to themselves. To this prisoner, when he saw their lips moving, he believed they were saying vile things about him, and he acted on his beliefs.[5] While this is an extreme example, the idea that actions are taken based on a person's *subjective* interpretation of a situation rather than the *objective* interpretation became known in sociology as the *Thomas Theorem*.

Another popular example of the Thomas Theorem can be found in the oil crisis of 1973. A rumor started that a toilet paper shortage was coming, which resulted in panic buying and stockpiling of toilet paper. This action ended up causing the shortage the public had feared.[6] Most of us can find wry humor in this example as this is exactly what happened at the beginning of the Covid-19 pandemic. For months many stores were unable to keep such paper products (toilet paper, paper towels, and facial tissues) on the shelves for more than an hour after delivery. Not until about a year after the pandemic began did our local Costco finally remove the signs over their paper products limiting purchases to one per customer.

Self-Fulfilling Prophecies

A self-fulfilling prophecy is generally used to describe the idea that a person's expectations could lead them to behave in ways that would bring about the desired or expected outcome. Expanding on the story of Clever Hans and the Thomas Theorem, the term *self-fulfilling prophecy* was first coined in 1948 by American sociologist Robert K. Merton to mean more specifically a '*false* definition of the situation evoking a new behavior, which makes the originally false conception come *true*.'[7]

Oedipus

A classic example of a self-fulfilling prophecy can be found in the Greek mythology story of Oedipus. A few versions of this story exist, but basically

King Laius and Queen Jocasta of Thebes have a child. Laius then consults an oracle and learns that not only will his son kill him, but the son would then also sleep with his wife, the boy's mother. Laius wants the child killed and gives him to a slave to abandon on Mt. Cithaeron, which is haunted by wild beasts. The slave is unable to do this and instead hands the baby to a shepherd, who then gives it to King Polybus of Corinth. King Polybus and Queen Merope decide to adopt the child and raise him as their own.

As a young man, Oedipus learns that he was adopted and decides to consult the oracle at Delphi to find his real parents. The oracle instead informs him that he will mate with his mother and kill his father. Oedipus vows not to return to Corinth and instead travels to Thebes. On the road, Oedipus gets into an altercation with another traveler and ends up killing him, not knowing that this is King Laius.

When Oedipus gets to Thebes, he manages to free the city from the legendary Sphinx that has been devouring travelers unable to answer its riddle. When Oedipus provides the correct answer, the Sphinx throws itself from the cliff, and as a reward, Oedipus is granted the kingship of Thebes and the hand of the dowager Queen, Jocasta. In so doing, Oedipus fulfills the last part of the prophecy.

One might think that the lesson in this story is not to trust oracles, but it is more than that. In believing that something specific will probably happen, we can end up taking actions that cause that very thing to happen. King Laius believed he had to give his child away to prevent the prophecy from coming true, and in so doing, he created a situation where Oedipus did not know that Queen Jocasta was his mother. Oedipus in turn tried to thwart the prophecy by leaving Corinth. In doing so, he created the circumstances where he unknowingly killed his father and married his mother.

In the examples used for the Thomas Theorem, you can see the same kind of patterns. The belief that banks would run out of money caused people to withdraw their money and so created the money shortage. At the beginning of the Covid-19 pandemic, people believed the rumor of an upcoming shortage of toilet paper, and the panic-buying and hoarding caused this very shortage to occur. But self-fulfilling prophecy can go a lot further, as one person's false belief has been shown to directly influence another person's experience.

Pygmalion

In the 1913 George Bernard Shaw play *Pygmalion*, which was later made into the movie *My Fair Lady*, Professor Higgins states his belief that in just six months he can take Eliza (a poor flower girl in London with a curbstone cockney English accent) and pass her off as a duchess at an ambassador's garden party. Overhearing this, Eliza pushes to become Higgins' student when she realizes that speaking better will gain her employment as a lady in a flower shop.

After some extremely intense training, Higgins is afforded the opportunity to test his work at an embassy reception, where he meets a former student of his, Count Aristid Karpathy. The count has now gained a reputation for being able to identify high society lineage by a person's elocution. Higgins is ecstatic when the count identifies Eliza as a princess and takes full credit for the transformation with little regard for the girl's huge commitment and the emotional bond created between them.

While in the movie the moral of the story had more to do with appreciating the internal value of a person, this story is of significance to us here due to the effect the *expectations* of the teacher (Professor Higgins) had on the student (Eliza). Without his belief that she could be taught to speak and act like a lady, she would never have even tried. But this is much more than just a cute movie idea.

The Pygmalion Effect

The *Pygmalion Effect* (also known as the *Rosenthal Effect*) is a psychological phenomenon where a person's performance is influenced by the expectation of their leader or superior; it is a form of self-fulfilling prophecy.

Study with Rats

In 1963, Robert Rosenthal and Kermit Fode (both at Harvard University) ran an experiment using rats labeled as very smart or very unintelligent. When students tested how quickly the rats could learn how to navigate a maze, the *smart* rodents performed twice as well as the *dumb* ones—even though all the rats were the same. Researchers concluded that the students' expectations influenced how they interacted with their rats, which in turn, influenced the outcome. Rosenthal suggested, "So when the experimenters thought that the rats were really smart, they felt more warmly towards the rats. And so, they touched them more gently."[8]

Classroom study

Rosenthal and elementary school principal Lenore Jacobson then experimented in a public elementary school to see if the same kind of effects could be observed in the classroom setting; would the teachers' expectations of their students influence how the children performed?[9] The research was carried out at a school in South San Francisco and involved grades one through six. There were three classes in each grade, making a total of eighteen teachers.

At the beginning of the study, all the children were given an IQ test called the *Test of General Ability (TOGA)*, a non-verbal test that did not rely on school-learned skills of reading, writing, and arithmetic. The teachers, however, were told that the test administered was the *Harvard Test of Inflected Acquisition* and that it was a predictor of academic blooming or spurting. The teachers were then provided a list of the students in the top 20%. The lists were not real; the students included were simply picked at random.[10]

The same test was administered to the students a total of four times, and at the end of the study, the changes in IQ between the first and last test were calculated. When the results were viewed for the entire school, the IQ of students in the control group (those not included in the list of students expected to do well) increased by an average of 8.2 points, whereas the experimental group's IQ increased by 12.2 points, giving the experimental group a four-point advantage. The results became even more significant when they were broken down by grade level. The point gain advantage for the experimental groups was as follows:

- First Grade   15.4%
- Second Grade   9.5%
- Third Grade   0.0%
- Fourth Grade   3.4%

- Fifth Grade   0.1%
- Sixth Grade   -0.7%[11]

As you can see, the effects of the teachers' beliefs were most noticeable in the lower grades. A few theories were put forward to explain these results, including:

- Younger children are thought to be more malleable—or perhaps the teachers believed that younger children are more malleable.
- The younger children do not already have an established history in the school—the teachers have not already seen or interacted with them, and no reputation has formed about how bright these children may or may not be. The teachers could only work with the information provided to them, i.e., the list of students who purportedly tested as having greater academic potential.
- Younger children may just be more sensitive to the different ways in which teachers interact with them.
- The lower-grade teachers could differ in some way from the higher-grade teachers.[12]

When the study was first published, mainstream media sensationalized the results with headlines such as, *Study Indicates Pupils Do Well When Teacher Is Told They Will* (Leo, *The New York Times*, 1967),[13] and glowing reviews such as, "Jose, a Mexican American boy . . . moved in a year from being classed as mentally retarded [sic] to above average. Another Mexican American child, Maria, moved . . . from *slow learner* to gifted child . . . The implications of these results will upset many school people, yet these are hard facts. (Kohl, *The New York Review of Books*, September 12, 1968)."[14] The Pygmalion study was even used by plaintiffs in several court cases. In one Washington, D.C. case (Hobson v. Hansen. 1967), the plaintiffs won the case to restrict the use of group tests for placing students in ability tracks. As a result, the school district abolished its ability-track program.[15]

In 2014, the liberal advocacy group Center for American Progress used the Pygmalion effect to argue in favor of the new, more rigorous Common Core State Standards adopted by more than forty states since 2010. Using national education data, the advocacy group said that "all else being equal, 'tenth-grade students who had teachers with higher expectations were more than three times more likely to graduate from college than students whose teachers had lower expectations.'"[16]

Controversy

However, a few dissenters argued vociferously against the Rosenthal-Jacobson study. The controversy went on for over thirty years with numerous public statements being made—some of them incredibly harsh. Robert L. Thorndike, psychometrician and educational psychologist, said about the Pygmalion study, "Alas, it is so defective technically that one can only regret that it ever got beyond the eyes of the original investigators!"[17] Richard E. Snow (Stanford University)[18] said, "Pygmalion, inadequately and prematurely reported in book and magazine form, has performed a disservice to teachers and schools, to users and developers of mental tests, and perhaps worst of all, to parents and children whose newly gained expectations may not prove so self-fulfilling."[19] Although Snow and Thorndike appear to be the loudest of the dissenters, there were many others.

So, what was it about a study run by a highly reputable professor of psychology, who taught at Harvard University from 1962 to 1999, became the chair of the department in 1992, and the Edgar Pierce Professor of psychology in 1995,[20] and who, according to the American Psychological Association, is one of the top 100 eminent psychologists of the twentieth century,[21] that could incur such strong sentiment, and what kinds of criticisms were put forward? As stated earlier, the debate continued for over thirty years, with Janet D. Elashoff (University of California), along with Richard E. Snow writing an entire book, *Pygmalion Reconsidered*, critiquing the Pygmalion study.[22] A few examples of the criticisms made included:

- The adequacy of the *Test of General Ability*, particularly when used on children from lower socioeconomic

backgrounds.
- Arguments were made regarding the improbable pretest results, which in many cases were too low, and the extrapolations of some of the high post-test results as these were higher than the TOGA allows for.
- The study was more about test-taking than increasing intelligence.
- The teachers did not remember the names of the children on the list of those expected to be 'academic bloomers.' (Two possible explanations put forward by Rosenthal and Jacobson were that the names were registered unconsciously, or that "whatever mediated the effects of teachers' expectations operated early in the academic year."[23])
- The TOGA was an unreliable test for youngest children at pre-test so the only test results that should be compared would be test 3 and test 4 – in which case no change was found.

On the other side, Rosenthal and Rubin ran a meta-analysis of 345 studies on interpersonal expectancy effects and showed that self-fulfilling prophecies reached statistical significance in 37% of the studies, something that would be virtually impossible if the effect did not exist.[24]

Lee Jussim and Kent Harber (both from Rutgers University) summarized all the available evidence on teacher expectation effects. They concluded that self-fulfilling prophecies exist and estimated that "expectations generate self-fulfilling prophecies in about 5-10% of pupils."[25]

The real division in opinions seems to be between social psychologists who found the results of the Pygmalion study to be consistent with their knowledge of errors in social perception, and educational psychologists who believe that intelligence is a fixed factor dictated by genetics and early brain development.[26] So the entire debate seems to hinge on Rosenthal's assertion that "teacher expectancy could affect pupils' *intelligence*," something that also put untenable pressure on the teachers' role.[27] If you disregard this particular assertion regarding IQ levels, then you are left with the idea that, if the teacher believes a child will be successful, then that child does better in the classroom as indicated by test results, an idea that the most vocal dissenters had no problem with:

- "I would expect the phenomenon {self-fulfilling prophecy} to appear most clearly . . . in those areas that are most directly teacher-based and school-dependent, such as learning to read, to write, and to cipher." (Thorndike, 1969.[28])
- "I agree that general evidence shows that interpersonal expectancies exist as psychological phenomena, and that teacher expectancies, as an example, can influence classroom teaching and learning, at least sometimes." (Snow, 1995.[29])

Quite frankly, how significant is your child's IQ number to you (assuming you have a child)? Wouldn't you just be thrilled if they went from struggling at school to finding it easy to achieve higher grades? Think what this would mean to their confidence and development to say nothing about their further education and career prospects.

Further Studies
However, the Pygmalion effect is not just important in child development, for it has now been demonstrated in a wide range of other arenas such as in the gym, leadership/management, sales, manufacturing, industry, and the military.[30]

Teachers
First, though, you should note that Pygmalion in the Classroom is not a one-way street, for findings show that the teacher's presentation was affected by the students' expectations. When the students expected the teacher to be cold, they rated them as being tenser and less competent. When the students expected the teacher to be warm, their ratings for the lecture performance reflected this.[31] I wonder if the adage, "When the student is ready the teacher

will appear," should be changed to "When the student is ready the *right* teacher will appear." I certainly had experiences in my younger school days where a teacher, more often a substitute teacher, would be unable to control a class. The students believed the teacher to be a pushover, so the teacher became that pushover. And in my college days, perhaps that super boring lecturer who put everyone to sleep was just responding badly to our blank faces. While we can question how *much* we may have affected a teacher's performance, there is no doubt we did, at least to some degree.

Workplace

In 1961, Alfred Oberlander, manager at a life insurance company in Rockaway, saw that new insurance agents performed better when placed in the outstanding agencies. He then grouped his superior agents into one unit and challenged them to produce two-thirds of the premium volume achieved by the entire agency in the previous year. Due to the efforts of this one super-group, the agency saw an overall improvement of 40%.[32] It seems that being a member of the well-known super-group inspired everyone in that group to push themselves to much greater heights.

Military

In 1982, Dov Eden (Tel Aviv University, Israel) and Abraham Shani (California Polytechnic State University) designed an experiment to replicate the classroom Pygmalion study but this time using trainees for a combat command course with the Israeli Defense Forces. There were 105 trainees and four experienced training officers. The officers were told that data had been compiled for each of the trainees including psychological test scores, sociometric evaluations, grades in previous courses, and ratings by previous commanders. Using this information, the command potential (CP) for each of the soldiers had been assessed, and they had been rated as having high, regular, and unknown potential. The officers were told that this classification was correct 95% of the time. The instructors received the list of their trainees and were told to learn the names and their CP scores before the soldiers arrived. At the end of the course, the soldiers were given four tests, three of which were multiple choice, and the fourth was evaluated by an impartial examiner from corps headquarters. The examiner knew nothing about the experiment. The results showed that those soldiers who had been rated as having high command potential scored about 15% higher than those rated regular. The unknown group scored about midway between the high and regular command potential groups.[33]

Manufacturing

In 1971, Albert S. King (Northern Illinois University) replicated the Pygmalion study in the manufacturing industry by designating four welders, five pressers, and five mechanics as high-aptitude personnel. The instructors expected superior performance from them. At the end of the study, these individuals obtained higher test scores, higher supervisor and peer ratings, shorter learning times, and had lower dropout rates. This study once again demonstrated the Pygmalion effect.[34]

The Space Race

One of the most inspiring examples of the Pygmalion effect is from President John F. Kennedy. At that time, many were concerned about America falling behind in the Space Race. When, in 1961, President Kennedy stated his firm belief that America could, in that decade, both land a man on the moon and return him safely to Earth, he galvanized the best scientists, engineers, managers, and other workers to make this a reality, while at the same time elevating the nation's support for this most exciting endeavor.[35]

Cautions

It seems that repeatedly, these kinds of studies clearly demonstrate the need for good leadership, regardless of the area of work or study. In yet another study, salespeople with average sales-aptitude test scores were nearly five times as likely to succeed under managers with good performance records than under managers with poor performance records. Those with high sales-aptitude scores were twice as likely to succeed under high-performing managers.[36] However, as exciting as these kinds of results can sound, a few issues here should concern us and induce caution.

Realistic

First, for the Pygmalion effect to work, the desired results of the leaders must be achievable. In the case of elementary school students, believing the children capable of writing college-level papers by the end of the year would be considered ludicrous. The key here is to find the right balance—the point at which the students or workers can stretch themselves and still achieve their goals. If goals set are simply too high and unachievable, this can cause people to quit trying, and subsequently perform at a lower level. Unrealistically high expectations can lead to high rates of attrition, either voluntary or involuntary.[37]

Before President Kennedy gave his famous 1961 speech, he had already ascertained the availability of the resources, technology, and talent necessary for accomplishing the high goal of landing a man on the moon and bringing him back safely—all he had to do was let the American people know he believed in them (and provide the funding, which reinforced his belief). With his words, President Kennedy inspired the entire nation to believe in their ability, and in 1969, Neil Armstrong became the first person to walk on the moon as he uttered the famous statement: "That's one small step for (a) man, one giant leap for mankind."

Burnout

Constantly setting high goals for subordinates can also create the problem of burnout.[38] It is possible to so inspire people to reach higher that the stress level causes productivity and achievements to fall apart. For the Pygmalion effect to be truly effective at increasing standards and performance, the expectations need to be realistic and balanced. It is also important that the rewards from reaching higher should match effort as much as they match performance.[39]

Golem

We must remember that there are two sides to a coin. So, today there is little doubt that when the authority figure believes their subordinate will be successful, then that subordinate is likely to perform to a higher level. Unfortunately, the opposite also holds; where the authority figure does not believe that their trainee or student is capable of high achievement, then that is exactly what happens. This is known as the *Golem Effect*. (In 1982, Babad, Inbar, & Rosenthal borrowed this term from Jewish folklore,[40] where Golem was a clay figure brought to life. Originally created to defend the Jewish community from anti-Semitic attacks, it became so violent and fearsome that it had to be destroyed.[41])

In the Rockaway study mentioned earlier, while the superior group was responsible for the 40% increase for the entire agency, the productivity of the weak group declined, and attrition among them increased. By dividing the agents into three groups and defining one group as being weak, their weaknesses became exaggerated, and they produced below their capacity.[42]

The authority figure's beliefs are so significant that, in some studies, their deeply entrenched personal opinions caused the Pygmalion effect study to fail. In another test, one manager divided his subordinates into superior, average, and low groups. However, he did not believe this categorization, stating that all his people were either average or incompetent. As a result, his test failed.[43] If positive expectations are not communicated, whether this is due to the manager's style or their belief, then improved performance does not happen.

Something else you may well know is that negative expectations are communicated more frequently, or they are simply more powerful than positive expectations. We will discuss this more later, but for now, know that negative feedback almost always trumps positive feedback.

Necessary Lies Or . . . ?

So what does all this mean? Would we all perform at a higher level if authority figures at least feigned faith in our abilities? Can we get our subordinates, students, children, employees, etc. to perform to a higher level by simply pretending to believe in their abilities?

In the original Pygmalion classroom study, great efforts were made to convince the teachers that the test the children took could predict their likelihood of academic blooming. Rather than telling the teachers that the tests given to the children were the *Tests of General Ability*, they were told that it was the *Harvard Test of Inflected Acquisition*. This was a much more impressive-sounding name and eliminated any familiarity the teachers may have had with the test. The teachers were also told that the National Science Foundation supported this test, which while true, still gave more prestige to the results.[44] Why was all of this lying so important? Couldn't the teachers have been asked to simply pretend with certain students? Apparently not.

The key here is that the authority figure must *really* believe it—they cannot *pretend* to do so. Just as the dogs trained to sniff out explosives responded to cues their handlers did not intend to give, and Clever Hans picked up on cues even when Oskar Pfungst tried to disguise them, so we all communicate a great deal of information in cues we are generally unaware of. I see this with our dogs. No matter how much I work to disguise the fact, our dogs always know when I am about to let them out, give them a treat, or whatever else it is they like. I can tell them to sit and wait at the other end of the room, I can have my hand on the doorknob, I can look aimlessly around humming to myself, but a split second before I start to turn the doorknob, there they are, at my feet, competing to be the first one out.

According to Paul Ekman, an expert on emotions and facial expressions and six times one of *Time* magazine's *100 Most Influential People*, we communicate high hopes by the degree to which we show attentiveness; a fixed gaze and raised eyebrows shows attention whereas a wandering gaze and bored expression show the opposite.[45] Rosenthal suggested that the teachers communicated their higher expectations by:

- Warm, friendly behavior
- Giving the students more attention
- More frequently calling on the students for answers
- Providing more helpful feedback

Educational researcher Christine Rubie-Davies used video recordings to show instructors some of the ways they communicated to their students via their mannerisms—a frown here or a headshake there could speak volumes. Robert Pianta (University of Virginia) has done the same thing to highlight the winces, shrugs, and frowns the instructors were unaware of.[46] Results show that no matter how hard we all try, our true beliefs will find a way to be expressed.

Why Does This Matter?

You may be wondering why I am spending so much time discussing a matter that seems to be out of our control. Science clearly shows that we do better when the authority figure believes in us. But doesn't this just make sense anyway? Most of us have stumbled on a task when under the watchful eye of someone we deem to be critical of us. (Yes, some people double down in their determination to prove their critic incorrect, but this takes a great deal more effort and may still be ineffective.) We have also worked harder to please someone who believed in us . . . or to prove them right for having faith in us and our ability. In one way or another, we have all experienced the Pygmalion effect ourselves. Having a better understanding of the extent of this effect should cause us to think more carefully about how we interact with others—smiling at someone is so much more valuable than frowning at them, and encouraging them will enable them to do better—but how does any of this relate to how we can improve our *own* lives? We are not in charge of what others think of us or how they treat us. Does this mean our successes and failures depend on the whims and fancies of other people? Are we nothing more than Ping-Pong balls bouncing between two paddles with no control over anything? The answer can be found in those areas where studies of the Pygmalion effect failed.

Where Pygmalion Fails

In the original Pygmalion in the Classroom study, definite effects were seen in grades one and two, with the effects falling off until a negative result was shown for the sixth grade. Among the possible suggestions for why this was the case was the idea that perhaps younger children may be more sensitive to the different ways in which teachers interact with them.[47] For young people starting school for the first time, the entire experience can be very scary. It makes sense that those children who are encouraged and supported more would also thrive more. Also, they would not already have preconceptions about where their abilities lie in relation to the other students in the class. They would have little need to doubt the validity of their teacher's expectations for their progress, and every desire to prove the teacher right—their very sense of security could come from pleasing the authority figure in charge. This is not the case for older children, for they have their own ideas of what they are capable of based on their earlier experiences.

This same effect is observed in the workplace, where managerial expectations had the greatest effect on the younger agents. As the workers gained their own track records, they were less likely to be influenced by their manager's expectations.[48] Resistance to Pygmalion effects can therefore be found when the subjects already have firmly crystallized expectations.[49]

Gender

To examine self-fulfilling prophecies as it relates to gender, Dvir, Eden, and Banjo ran a study with trainees in the Israel Defense Forces. Once again, they looked to see if the trainees' performance could be influenced by the expectations of their training officer. In the first study, they used female cadets led by a woman. Even though the researchers successfully raised the expectations of the trainers, this did not increase the performance of the trainees. A second experiment was then run, this time using gender-segregated groups. The Pygmalion effect was seen in the all-male group run by a man, and in the all-women's group run by a man, but not in the all-women's group run by a female. The authors concluded that the Pygmalion effect can be produced among women but perhaps not by women, but is this fair?

In the Pygmalion in the Classroom study, the effects were seen with female teachers. Is it possible that adults are just biased against women leaders and therefore their opinions are taken with a grain of salt? It would be a sad situation if women themselves were unable to accord their female leader the same respect they would give to a male leader. Does it have to do with the generally supportive roles women play in their parenting style? Could it be that, generally at least, Mom is always going to support us, so her opinion isn't valid? Certainly, more studies need to be run before concluding. A study needs to be run with an all-male group led by a female—interestingly, this aspect was not included in the study.

Note that the paper for these studies was published in 1995. In the last ten years, the Western world at least has made huge strides when it comes to gender equality. If the same study were run today, would they find the same results? These interesting questions still need to be answered. However, for our purposes here, the important thing to note is that resistance to the Pygmalion effect is real.[50]

Galatea

To find the most interesting result from the Pygmalion studies, though, we must return to the series of studies carried out in the Rockaway Life Insurance Company. Grouping the top salespeople under the top manager increased the entire office's productivity by 40%, demonstrating a strong Pygmalion effect. Grouping the weakest salespeople under the weakest manager resulted in reduced productivity and a high rate of attrition, demonstrating the Golem effect. But the third group's result was unexpected.

This group consisted of the average salespeople and the average manager, who were expected to show an average performance, but this did not happen. It turns out the assistant manager refused to believe she was less capable than the manager of the top group, or that her people had lesser ability than the agents in the top group. Her belief was so strong that she succeeded in stimulating her group to attempt to outperform the top group. As a result, this group increased its productivity by a greater percentage than the super-sales group, although they did not attain the high dollar volume.[51]

This is known as the *Galatea Effect*, the idea that the person's positive performance is caused by their own belief in themselves, unlike the Pygmalion effect that relies on the belief of a superior (boss, teacher, parent, etc.). With the Galatea effect, one's belief in themselves and their ability outweighs the effects of beliefs held by others. (In Greek mythology, Galatea was the name of a statue so beautiful its sculptor fell in love with it. He believed in and loved it so much that, with the help of the goddess Aphrodite, he brought it to life.)

Dov Eden (Tel Aviv University, Israel) and Gadi Ravid (Netanya Academic College, Israel) ran another study to see if they could create the Galatea effect. The study design was similar to the one used with the combat trainees, but this time:

- 25% of the trainees were reported to the instructors as having high potential.

- 25% of the trainees were designated as having regular potential – and so serving as the control for the high-potential group, and
- 50% were designated as having unknown potential due to incomplete information.

This last group was then divided into two trainee expectation conditions—Galatea and Galatea Control. All the members in this group underwent a five-minute personal interview by a military psychologist at the beginning of the course. After asking some basic questions, the psychologist ended the interview with the Galatea subjects with the following statement: *"To conclude, I wanted to tell you that, in light of data we've gathered about trainees with the aid of the military psychology unit, you have high potential for success."* The Galatea-control trainees received the same interview except that it ended with: *"You have regular potential for success."*

As expected, the subjects in the Pygmalion condition group showed an increasing level of self-expectation based on how they were treated by the instructors. However, subjects in the Galatea group also showed substantially rising self-expectations that could only have come from their expectations as the instructors had been told that they were unclassifiable and as such, had no expectations about them. Analysis of the scores at the end of the study showed that the Pygmalion group had an increase of twelve points and the Galatea group had an increase of eighteen points—both significant when compared to the control groups but not significantly different from each other.[52] This would indicate that the Galatea effect and the Pygmalion effect led to very similar degrees of results.

Potential and Challenges

The Galatea effect turns out to be the linchpin for any self-empowerment program. Since 1985, this has been the focus of the work we do at Progressive Awareness—how to strengthen self-belief and so eliminate the self-sabotaging strategies that can restrict us. So many things in life are out of your control but activating the Galatea effect is where you can take firm control over your own life and start creating successes. You can never become the best version of yourself until you truly believe in yourself. Regardless of your goals and dreams, or the amount of determination and willpower you put into achieving them, if you do not believe you *can* be successful, you will never try your absolute hardest to get there. And when you fail to achieve your highest best, you will find some way to justify it.

Lesson from Biking

Several years ago, Eldon and I decided to join our sons in one of their favorite outdoor activities—biking. When our youngest was still very small, biking was no problem for me, as I would hang back to keep him company and encourage him to keep on going. Boys quickly turn into young men, though, and seemingly overnight our youngest went from asking me to carry his backpack after school to doing chin-ups and push-ups with ease. Before long, my three men would leave me in their biking dust—I simply could not keep up. For the sake of my self-esteem, I would frequently remind myself that *'Eldon uses the exercise bike all winter, so he finds biking easy,'* and *'Men are naturally stronger than women,'* but this did not make me feel better. In time I upgraded my bike, but no matter hard I tried, my men could still leave me in the dust whenever they chose. And boy, sometimes they would choose to do exactly that—laughing all the way!

We liked to ride a route close to our home. The boys reveled in seeing how fast they could go on the steep downhill slope, but then we had to face the uphill slope. For the longest time, I knew I was highly unlikely to ever make it, and I invariably got off my bike when I was about one-third up the hill—pretty much when the uphill grade increased a fraction more and I felt that tiny bit of increased resistance. I knew I was not trying as I was never out of breath when I quit, but no matter how much I told myself I could do better, I always stopped at about the same point because some part of me *knew* I would not succeed.

Real Perseverance

One year, rather than having Dad tune the bikes up as usual, our oldest son asked if we could take them into the bike store to have them professionally serviced. When we picked the bikes up, the technician in the store informed me that I had been riding with my brakes partially on and that I should find it a lot easier now. I most certainly did! It was still hard work to keep up, but now I could do it. You have no idea how good this felt. I don't know if all my previous bikes were defective in some way, or if I had simply gained strength and stamina with the biking we had done, but now I was no longer the weakling I had thought I was. (I do also have to recognize that the suggestion alone could well have played a defining role in my newfound success.)

Then I came to this hill—the same hill that had been defeating me for years. What do you think I did? Well, I now *knew* I was strong and capable and that my bike was in tip-top condition—and I so very much wanted to succeed. I went down the steep hill and then up the steeper hill. I reached the one-third mark where I had always quit before, but I had lots of lung power left and my legs felt fine. At the two-third mark, where the incline increased again, pedaling became extremely difficult—but still, I pushed on. I proceeded incredibly slowly but I was still on my bike and making progress. One push followed by the next until, lo and behold, I had reached the top where I could cruise a little, catch my breath, and rest my achy legs.

What Could You Achieve?

The power of self-belief indeed. When I believed I would fail, I simply quit early. I did not give it my all. I knew I would fail so I didn't even try. But when I *knew* I could succeed, I tried my utmost best. I worked so hard; every fiber of my being ached with the effort—and I succeeded. But what could I have achieved before my bike was tuned if only I had *believed* I had a chance of succeeding? I most certainly would have worked harder, and I would have gone further. In this instance, I could always manage the first third of the hill, the second third of the hill could have become possible due to fixing my brakes, but the last third of the hill was pure effort. I biked with pure determination because I *knew* it was possible—I knew I could do it. This meant that believing in myself gave me the ability to achieve 33% more.

What could you achieve if you were 33% more successful at whatever you tried to achieve? Would you stick to that diet more easily? Would you find the courage to ask for that promotion at work? Would you study a little harder for that exam . . . and pass? Would you find your perfect partner or enhance your personal relationship? And, as with the Galatea effect, would you become immune to those people in authority who do not believe in you?

Negativity Bias

Unfortunately, we all hold negative beliefs of some kind. According to the work by Roy F. Baumeister (now at Queensland University, Australia), bad events are more powerful than good events, whether this is in everyday situations or major events.[53] Bad information is processed more thoroughly than good information, meaning bad feedback and negative comments have more sticking power. Even though we may receive many positive comments, the negative comments and feedback hold more sway. The power of negative over positive is so significant that psychologists call this the *Negativity Bias*, which means we can stew about the one negative comment in our work review and almost disregard the other positive comments. Negative beliefs have staying power, and they can come from any number of sources. Maybe a comment from a friend who said you were 'crap' at football and so you shouldn't even try out. Perhaps a loved one told you not to worry about your weight as losing weight after forty is impossible anyway. The sources of these negative, self-sabotaging beliefs are everywhere, and we cannot pretend they don't exist. Many of these negative beliefs come from our childhood—comments from parents, teachers, friends, etc.—and they can have a firm hold on us.

Just as with the Pygmalion effect, where the authority figure (teacher, boss, etc.) had to *truly believe* they were dealing with someone of high potential, the Galatea effect requires that we *truly believe in ourselves*. How can we do this when the negativity bias is so strong? Simply telling ourselves that we are good, capable, successful, etc. will not stop that inner voice, that inner belief, from expressing itself and saying, "No I'm not!" The answers lay in changing the negative programming that lies deep within our subconscious mind, and we will soon be looking at how to do that. But first, let's look at some of the other impacts of negative beliefs.

NOTES

Key Points

Non-verbal information is revealed, even if we try to hide it. We can all pick up on microscopic cues, as can our pets, and this information influences our choices and our behavior. Acting on our beliefs, whether consciously or subconsciously, directly influences our life experiences.

The Pygmalion effect brings these two elements together, whereby students pick up on microscopic cues from their teachers, and work, albeit subconsciously, to fulfill this belief. This can be beneficial when these microscopic cues impart confidence and faith in the student's abilities but can create a problem (the Golem effect) when the belief communicated is one of expected failure. This also holds in many other subordinate/superior relationships such as employee/employer, follower/leader, etc.

There are limitations to the Pygmalion effects as the desired goals need to be reachable and realistic. If the goals set are too high, a person could give up. Constantly reaching too high can also cause burnout, and once again cause a person to quit.

Microscopic cues though, cannot be faked. For the Pygmalion effect to work, the superior must *truly believe* in the abilities of the subordinate, just as the subordinate needs to believe in the judgment of the superior.

So, we are influenced by what others think of us. Sometimes, others' beliefs can form our stepping-stone for higher achievements, but sometimes these beliefs can place a ceiling on what we can achieve, based on ideas that may not even be true. The most powerful way to deal with all of this is to create the Galatea effect in yourself—to find ways to create an inner self-belief so strong it neutralizes external input. This can be challenging when we consider the power of negativity and how it can lodge in our subconscious mind—but it is possible. In the coming chapters, we will be looking at ways to change our subconscious programming, both directly and indirectly, to minimize the negative and maximize the positive.

Exercise

Think back over your life and the authority figures (teachers, bosses, leaders, etc.) you have encountered. Think about where you performed the best and try to ascertain the characteristics of your authority figure that aided your success. Remember to note this in your journal. Also, make a note of some of the positive comments you have received that were particularly impactful.

Whatever influential position you occupy (boss, manager, parent, etc.), look for places where your followers show their greatest strengths. The more you focus on the positive aspects of those you lead, the more easily you will bring out the best in them. Write some of these in your journal and plan how you will try to bring out the best in those around you.

CHAPTER TEN

THE POSITIVITY QUOTIENT

The only person who can pull me down is myself, and I'm not going to let myself pull me down anymore.

~ C. Joybell C.

"Look on the bright side," is a piece of advice all of us have received sometime in our lives. Most of us have certainly been brought up to think that positive thinking is some kind of magic key to success and happiness. But this belief is not as deeply ingrained as we may think. I have seen movies where we are introduced to some self-help teacher/expert who preaches 'just believe' to a rapt audience. However, most of these movies end up showing us the shallowness of the teachings and the hypocrisy of the teacher. In real life, the super positive attitude is often derided for being unreal, inauthentic, or just plain annoying. How much truth is there to the power of positive thinking?

Hopelessness and Helplessness

One aspect of the negativity/positivity spectrum deals with helplessness and hopelessness as opposed to hopefulness and self-empowerment. Hopelessness is the lack of hope, optimism, and passion. People who feel hopeless generally do not expect future improvements or success—they see no point in trying as there is no chance of success. Hopelessness is a core component of depression.[1]

Here are two experiments that highlight the significance of the negative effects of extreme hopelessness and helplessness. Unfortunately, both sets of studies involved the mistreatment of animals, and the accounts can be rather distressing. Please remember that both Eldon and I are strong advocates for animal rights. That said, while putting an end to future abuses is our strong desire, ignoring the teachings from earlier studies does nothing to further the cause. As such, please do not equate our discussing the results of these studies with even a modicum of approval for the fact that they were carried out.

Drowning Rats

In a 1950s paper, psychobiologist Curt Richter (Johns Hopkins University) begins by discussing an article by Walter Cannon in which he describes various occurrences of sudden/unexpected death in humans from causes that include voodoo or an extreme reaction to breaking some kind of taboo—the kinds of situations where the *absolute belief* in the power of an external source to cause death caused the death. Cannon believed the deaths were caused by the continuous outpouring of adrenaline. Richter offered a different explanation based on his studies with rats, where deaths occurred due to the total elimination of hope.

In his experiment, Richter placed rats (one at a time) into a jar of water and timed how long they would swim before they gave up and drowned. Although you may be familiar with this rat study, something particularly gruesome happens when we see the extent to which Richter made sure the rats had no possible chance of escaping. Richter used "specially designed tanks—glass cylinders thirty-six inches deep, standing inside glass jars eight inches in diameter and thirty inches in depth. A jet of water of any desired temperature playing into the center of each cylinder precluded the animals' floating, while the collar of the cylinder itself prevented escape."[2]

In the first round of experiments, Richter took twelve domesticated rats, clipped their whiskers, and placed them, one by one, in the jars of water. The first three rats died in just a few minutes, but the remaining nine rats swam for forty to sixty hours. (No real explanation was given for why the first three rats died so quickly). Richter then took thirty-four wild rats, clipped their whiskers, and subjected them to the same experiment. It was theorized that these rats would fight even harder for survival as they were "characteristically fierce, aggressive, and suspicious . . . constantly on the alert for any avenue of escape and reacting very strongly to any form of restraint in captivity." However, all thirty-four died between one and fifteen minutes after immersion. Richter examined several factors that could have explained this, including the fact that trimming the rats' whiskers destroyed "possibly their most important means of contact with the outside world."[3] This could have been so disturbing to the wild rats as to cause their deaths.

Richter then tweaked the experiment by again immersing the rats in the water but then *saving* them right before they were expected to die, holding them for a short while, and then putting them back into the water. These conditioned rats then managed to swim just as long as the domesticated rats or longer. Richter attributed this to the "elimination of hopelessness"—the rats learned that maybe they were not so doomed, and that help could come, and they kept on swimming.[4] With the power of hope, they were capable of amazing feats.

> (As recently as 2019, evidence emerged that a variation of Richter's experiment was still being carried out on mice, rats, gerbils, guinea pigs, and hamsters. The *behavioral despair test*, also known as the *forced swim test*, is used to test the efficacy of anti-depressant medications. However, even with the most prescribed Prozac, consistent results with the *forced swim test* have not been found.[5] The horror of these experiments is only magnified when you think back to our earlier discussion on placebos and depression, in which it was found that "82% of the drug response was duplicated by placebo."[6])

During Richter's studies, EKG results showed that the rats that died quickly experienced a *slowing* of the heart rate, not the increased heart rate that would have occurred if Cannon had been correct in his attributing the deaths to a surge in adrenaline. Richter also found that the body temperatures dropped, and respiration slowed. When hopelessness was eliminated, the rats recovered with remarkable speed and did not experience the same effects again. Richter went on to suggest that when freed from the voodoo, the human individual would recover just as quickly, even though just moments prior they would have been very close to death. Furthermore, having survived once, the voodoo curse would not have an effect a second time. The power of hope indeed.

Now, some may choose to disregard our discussion on Richter's work, thinking that they don't believe in voodoo or any such things and so the information cannot apply to them, but other instances of sudden, unexplained death have occurred:

- Researchers in Denmark and the U.S. found that "the death of a child is associated with an overall increased mortality from both natural and unnatural causes in mothers, and an early increased mortality from unnatural causes in fathers."[7]
- The risk of dying from a heart attack or stroke soars immediately after a cancer diagnosis.[8]
- The likelihood of a heart attack or stroke would increase with the severity of the cancer diagnosis—the worse the cancer was, the greater the chance of dying from a heart attack or stroke.[9]

Additionally, it is not uncommon to hear stories where one spouse died shortly after the death of the other spouse. Psychogenic death, also known as 'give-up-itis,' "describes people who respond to traumatic stress by developing extreme apathy, give up hope, relinquish the will to live, and die, despite no obvious organic cause."[10]

Hope is not only necessary in perilous circumstances. There is no question that hope is important in all areas of our lives. Hope gives you the power to keep on going, to try once again, to work that bit harder. With hope, you still have a chance to succeed, regardless of what your specific goal may be. As hope diminishes, so does the quality of life, and as we have seen, fatal consequences may result.

Helpless Dogs

The second of the series of animal experiments I wish to share with you occurred in the late 1960s when Martin Seligman (University of Pennsylvania) ran a series of experiments that demonstrated *learned helplessness*. For the first phase of the experiment, they restrained three groups of dogs in a hammock, where they were administered electric shock. The first group learned that if they pressed a panel with their nose, the electric shock would be turned off. In the second group, two animals were yoked together. One of the animals had already learned how to turn the electric shock off and would do precisely this. The animal it was yoked to did not see this connection and had no idea how to turn the shock off or what stopped the shock. To the second animal, the turning off of the shock was random. The third group of animals received no shock at all.

The next day, the animals were tested in a shuttle box, where half of the floor was wired to deliver shock. There was a small divider separating the two halves of the box and the dogs could escape the shock by simply jumping over this low barrier. What they found was that, of the animals who had learned to turn off the shock, and those who were never shocked in the first place, 90% easily learned how to jump over the wall and escape the shock. However, of the group of dogs who had learned that the shock was random and they could do nothing about it, 66% made no attempt whatsoever to escape the shock.[11] They simply lay down and whined. From this study, the researchers decided that helplessness was a *learned* characteristic. While at first glance, this study can seem cruel and pointless, according to Maier and Seligman, this line of experimentation may have substantial implications in the treatment of depression.

Interestingly, in a 2016 follow-up study, Maier and Seligman discovered that the process works the other way around; the default unlearned response of the brain is that of helplessness, and animals learn control. Prolonged aversive events can then lead the animal to *unlearn* the belief in its ability to control.[12] However, this does not alter the importance of the lessons learned in the context of understanding how your mind works so you can guard against it.

It is also worth noting that, in this latest 2016 paper, the researchers also stated that they found this entire experiment to be a harrowing experience as they were both dog lovers. For this reason, they stopped running the experiment on dogs as soon as they could and instead used mice, rats, and people with the same pattern of results.[13]

Choices

In another study, Hiroto and Seligman tested the effect of the lack of control over aversive noise – an uncomfortable noise was played while the subjects tried to perform mental tasks. Those who were able to turn off the noise rarely did so, but still performed their work better than those who had no control over the situation.[14] So just feeling that they had an option enabled the subjects to work better under difficult circumstances.

This information brings an added sense of importance to Eldon's *New York Times* bestseller *Choices and Illusions*. In that book, he demonstrated how circumstances (such as enculturation) can cause us to believe we have far fewer choices than are available. The main takeaway here is the importance of hope, choice, and agency—feeling that we can do something about our circumstances.

We should also remember the addictive nature of failure. In our earlier discussion on brain chemicals, we learned that dopamine is released to urge you to an achievable goal, and a second surge is experienced on the successful completion of that goal. So the person who believes there is no hope, that their attempts to make a change will fail, will have a release of dopamine at the time of failure.[15] While that may seem counter-intuitive, it changes when you realize that the person's *prediction* came true—they expected to fail and they failed. So they were right, and they receive a brain reward for it. Again, this highlights the importance of believing in yourself, for without self-belief, you will always hold yourself back.

Optimism vs Pessimism

Another, more generally applicable way to compare the effects of positivity versus negativity is to look at optimism and pessimism, which is how people view future possibilities. Positive thinking covers more than just future events, but quite a bit of research has been carried out on optimism vs pessimism and this makes the advantages and disadvantages easier to see.

Pessimists tend to see the worst aspect of things or believe that the worst will happen—they have a lack of hope or confidence in the future. Optimists exhibit hopefulness and confidence about the future. Optimism versus pessimism, however, is not an either/or situation, but rather a spectrum of attitudes, and positive thinking covers a lot more than just expectations for future events.

Pessimists may cling to their pessimistic viewpoints as they believe that expecting the worst can prompt them to take action to prevent the worst from happening. This is not full pessimism as there is still hope (optimism) that if they take the right actions, then disaster may not strike. At the extreme though, the pessimist can be miserable. Optimists may dream big and, as a result, push themselves further even in the face of some setbacks. But they can also be less likely to plan for challenges and so able to avoid them. At the extreme, the optimist may be detached from reality.

Numerous studies show a link between optimism and good health and longevity. One of the possible explanations for the correlation between optimism and longer lives is that optimists tend to engage in healthier behaviors like exercising frequently, eating fruits and vegetables, and avoiding smoking. However, whether optimism precedes healthier behaviors or if there is some other shared common cause is unclear. Another argument is that the pessimistic approach could also lead a person to engage in healthier behaviors as they do not dare take their good health for granted.

Negativity

We know that negative thinking can trigger the fight/flight, or stress response, leading to an increase in heart rate, quickened breathing, a tightening of muscles, and a rise in blood pressure. In small doses, this response can assist us in getting out of danger, such as slamming on the car brakes to avoid hitting another car. But sometimes raised stress levels are ongoing, a reaction to fears that may be out of proportion to the stimuli. Long-term stress may lead to mental health problems, cardiovascular disease, obesity, and more.[16] But even when the negative thinking does not rise to the level of causing physical harm, it can still take a toll on our lives, leading to a lowered ability to see opportunities or even talking yourself out of trying to succeed.

We have also seen the reality of the negativity bias—how negative experiences can hold more power over us than positive experiences—but the degree of power held over different people can vary significantly. Some people prefer to focus on the part of the glass that is half full so they can enjoy what they have rather than lament what they lack. Others choose to focus on the half-empty glass so they can be prepared for the bad things when they inevitably will happen. Both choices bring their own opportunities or ramifications, so which way is best? Does being happy lead a person to be more successful or does being successful make a person happier? Or is this a chicken and egg kind of question?

The Power of Positive Thinking

Many people believe that if only they had a certain thing—perhaps the perfect job, the right partner, or in the case of our children when they were young, that most sought-after toy—then they would be happy. To them, happiness comes from the achievement (or acquisition) of something specific. The shallowness of this approach was most apparent in our children when we saw how quickly their enthusiasm for that shiny new item waned in just a matter of days. Where they had declared "If only I had x, then I would be happy forever," we learned how quickly 'forever' passes. Are adults really that different? Maybe we don't declare that we would be 'happy forever' if we only achieved some goal or acquired some gadget or other, but in a remarkably short time we stop scrubbing every speck of dust off our new car, or the enthusiasm for a new promotion soon devolves into complaints about the increased pressure. Several decades ago, Eldon put forward the idea that, rather than success bringing happiness, it was, in fact, happiness that brought success.

A study published in *Psychological Bulletin* looked at this very question, "Does Happiness Lead to Success?" In this study, the researchers argued that not only does success make people happier, but that being positive engenders success. Looking at 275,000 people, the researchers examined the idea that positive moods and emotions "lead people to think, feel, and act in ways that promote both resource building and involvement with approach goals." What they found was that "happy individuals are more likely than their less happy peers to have fulfilling marriages and relationships, high incomes, superior work performance, community involvement, robust health, and a long life."[17]

Longer Life Better Health

Remember earlier when we looked at studies that showed the simple act of smiling was a predictor for living longer? Well, the same correlation has been found for positive thinking. Researchers from the University of Kentucky examined the handwritten autobiographies of 180 nuns with a mean age of twenty-two. The biographies were scored based on the emotional content and then compared with the rate of survival from ages seventy-five to ninety-five. They found that as the rankings for positive emotion in early life increased, the risk of mortality decreased. Comparing the groups in the top 25% of emotional rankings with those in the bottom 25%, they found a '2.5-fold difference' in the risk of dying, indicating that positive emotions in early life was strongly associated with longevity six decades later.[18]

Heart Disease

Living longer is one thing, but what about living healthier? What about if you already have a health condition, or if there is some genetic factor that makes it more likely you will develop a health condition? Can positive thinking have an impact there or are you just fighting too many headwinds?

Johns Hopkins' report on the link between positivity and the likelihood of heart disease gives us some insight here. What they found is that "people with a family history of heart disease who also had a positive outlook were one-third less likely to have a heart attack or other cardiovascular event within five to twenty-five years than those with a more negative outlook. . . The finding held even in people with family history who had the most risk factors for coronary artery disease, and positive people from the general population were 13% less likely than their negative counterparts to have a heart attack or other coronary event."[19] So, across the board, a more positive attitude will significantly reduce your chances of developing heart disease.

Another study delved even deeper into the correlation between optimism and health. Using data obtained between 2004 and 2012 from the Nurses'

Health Study, a long-running study that tracks women's health via questionnaires every two years, they found that "The most optimistic women had a 16% lower risk of dying from cancer; 38% lower risk of dying from heart disease; 39% lower risk of dying from stroke; 38% lower risk of dying from respiratory disease; and 52% lower risk of dying from infection."[20]

Pessimism and Health

Across the board, positive thinking and optimism are actively good for health and longevity, but what about pessimism and negative thinking? How much impact do they have? A thirty-five-year longitudinal study of Harvard students looked at this specific issue. They found that pessimism in early adulthood was a risk factor for poor health in middle and later adulthood. Researchers Peterson, Seligman, and Vaillant examined open-ended questionnaires completed by ninety-nine graduates all aged twenty-five. They found that a "pessimistic explanatory style (the belief that bad events are caused by stable, global, and internal factors) predicted poor health at ages forty-five through sixty, even when physical and mental health at age twenty-five were controlled."[21]

Personality Types

In his 1992 book *Wellness: Just a State of Mind*, Eldon investigated the whole issue of the mind's role in wellness. Originally written as a paper to be presented at a symposium, Eldon took the information and simplified it into a bit of a detective story. It is a very easy read and well worth looking at. I bring it up here as the current discussion reminds me of his discovery that personality types were linked to different kinds of health conditions.

- Madeleine Visintaines (University of Pennsylvania) has linked helplessness to cancer.[22]
- Researchers at Duke University have shown that hostility and mistrust are key predictors of heart disease and early death.[23]
- H. J. Eysenck found that personality variables were more predictive than smoking in the occurrence of lung cancer.

So smoking was virtually a prerequisite for getting lung cancer, but only the emotionally repressive types seemed to contract the disease.[24]

- Karl Goodkin (Stanford University) found, amongst other characteristics, that being overly optimistic to the extent of being in denial of reality was part of the cancer profile for women.[25]

I found this last one to be particularly interesting in our current context; being overly optimistic to the extent of being in denial could be another way of saying they buried their pessimism in a false layer of optimism.

Cognitive Advantages

When looking at some of these studies, we may be tempted to slip into the (pessimistic) trap of thinking 'it's too late for me.' If smiling and being more positive in my teens and twenties means I will live longer, doesn't that mean I may have started too late? I don't believe so. Do you remember earlier when I spoke about the power of smiling and diaphragmatic breathing? Using these techniques, I dropped my blood pressure numbers significantly in a matter of minutes. Positive thinking would only add to this kind of process. However, health and longevity are not the only benefits of positivity; there are also cognitive advantages. Positive emotions make people feel better, but it goes further than that as positivity can extend into the future.

Upward Spirals Effect

Barbara Fredrickson (University of Michigan) and Thomas Joiner (Florida State University) researched deeper into the effects of positive thinking, both in the present and in the future. The study design involved 138 students. At the beginning of the study, the students were asked to complete measures of affect and coping. Five weeks later they completed identical measures. They found that experiencing positive emotions will increase the odds of people feeling good in the future. Fredrickson and Joiner called this the "upward spirals effect" and linked it to the broadened thinking that accompanies positive thinking.

Although an isolated experience of positivity is unlikely to have much impact on wellbeing and longevity by itself, these positive emotions will accumulate and compound, and this 'upward spirals effect' results in increased well-being and longevity. "Individuals who achieve such upward spirals not only enjoy improved emotional wellbeing but also build their coping arsenal for handling future adversities."[26] Over time, the upward spirals effect can "build psychological resources and optimize people's lives." Positive thinking therefore builds your skill set as well as your self-confidence.

Mind training is all about building an expansive arsenal for dealing with life's many challenges. Some situations require what I refer to as the 'kitchen-sink' approach, where many tactics are used to control negative situations. When positive thinking becomes a persistent manner for managing our thoughts, our expectations change, which in turn, influences our perceptions and, in the end, reveals new opportunities to express our lives. I like the term *upward spirals effect*—that the more positive you are, the more positive you will be. So, making the effort to be positive today will have a ripple effect on your tomorrow's life quality.

Frequency

A paper published in 2022 by Lewina O. Lee and team (Boston University) looked at a specific aspect of the effects of optimism on wellbeing, which could well explain at least part of why this ripple effect may occur. They wanted to know if optimism would preserve well-being by limiting exposure to daily stressors and/or if higher optimism reduced emotional reactivity to daily stressors and made the recovery from them easier. So, do optimistic people not experience as many stressful events, or do they just not react as strongly when they occur?

The researchers followed 233 older men who first completed an optimism questionnaire in 1986/1991. Fourteen years later, they asked the participants to report daily stressors along with positive and negative moods on eight consecutive evenings up to three times over eight years. What they found was that the more optimistic participants "reported not only lower negative mood but also more positive mood (beyond simply not feeling negative). They also reported having fewer stressors, which was unrelated to their higher positive mood but explained their lower levels of negative mood."[27] So, being more optimistic did not affect how older people emotionally reacted or recovered from day-to-day stressors, but it did limit *how often* they experienced stressful situations or changed the way they interpreted them. So they were more easily able to pass off as a minor event, something another person would count as significantly stressful—their perspective changed and these minor events were no longer able to detract from their overall quality of life.

Too Much

Some believe that if a little of something is good, then more of it would be better. However, this is not the case when it comes to optimism and positive thinking. As we discussed, Karl Goodkin's research (Stanford University) showed that being 'overly optimistic to the extent of being in denial' was part of women's cancer profile.[28] The importance of realism was highlighted in another study announced by the University of Bath in the UK, where researchers looked at people's financial expectations and then compared them with the outcomes eighteen years later. What they found was that "Overestimating outcomes was associated with lower wellbeing than setting realistic expectations." In this study, pessimists also fared badly when compared with realists. Some of this information may be welcomed by those who object to the constant push to climb on the positivity bandwagon—where anything not mega-positive is frowned upon. One researcher, Chris Davis, went on to say, "I think for many people, research that shows you don't have to spend your days striving to think positively might come as a relief. We see that being realistic about your future and making sound decisions based on evidence can bring a sense of well-being, without having to immerse yourself in relentless positivity."[29]

Perhaps this study explains why positivity can get a bad rap—some circles can push Pollyanna thinking so far that it can belie real-world experiences. Worse than that is toxic positivity, where empathy is replaced by dismissal of negative emotions, and so causes more angst for the distressed individual. Thus, being positive can bring great benefits to all aspects of your life, but just be sure to season it sufficiently with some realism.

The Power of Words

When looking at positivity, it is important to consider the actual words you use or are used on you. When I was a child, it was very common to hear children in the playground responding to an argument with, "Sticks and stones may break my bones, but words will never hurt me." We quickly realized this was not true. Several decades ago, Eldon wrote the more accurate version, "Sticks and stones may break my bones, but words will slice and dice me."

Racism

Words can have great power. Growing up in the United Kingdom during the '60s and '70s, encountering racial taunts was very common. Just walking down the street could result in strangers, generally groups of kids/young adults, throwing racial epithets at us (me and my Indian family and friends), and laughing about it. Sometimes, if we knew there was no *real* danger, we might respond with a patronizing, "I'm not from Pakistan, I'm from India," as though highlighting the blatant ignorance of the racists could make any difference. But words have power. Simply hearing that one word would result in an increased heart rate, a tensing of the muscles, and a lowering of esteem. To this day I still despise that one word, even when it is said in jest with no malice intended. Anyone who has experienced this kind of racism will know exactly what I mean. One derogatory word, heard enough times and in enough places, can invoke the same stress response many decades later.

Aging

But words don't have to be hateful for them to gain power over you, and responses aren't always stress-based. Some words can cause a behavior change. In a 1996 study, John Bargh (New York University) and his team, discovered that priming people with words that are typically related to old age in the U.S., such as 'bingo,' 'wrinkle,' and 'Florida' caused the subjects to walk more slowly than the control group. Bargh and his colleagues also found that subjects primed with rudeness "interrupted the experimenter more quickly and frequently than did participants primed with polite-related stimuli."[30]

If you are familiar with the field of social priming, you may know it became quite controversial, largely due to a *Nature* article that discussed a failed replication.[31] Eldon asked Professor Bargh about this directly during an interview on *Provocative Enlightenment Radio*, and was told that too many variations were present in the method for it to be considered a real replication; the replication study tested primes that were used at a much lower frequency, was carried out in French, and the participants were directed to leave the room.[32] The selected primes would be very significant. While there is no indication of what the actual primes were that were used in the replication, in Bargh's study, 'Florida' was one of the primes and so it could only work in this kind of study on participants who already relate Florida to the idea of old age, snowbirds, etc.

In a 2015 paper, Michael Ramscar et al. (Eberhard Karls University, Germany) provide a detailed analysis of the problems inherent in replicating studies on priming effects in other languages. One of the factors Ramscar points out is that that the distribution of adjectives and nouns differ "between the two languages, with 28% of English nouns being preceded by at least one adjective, as opposed to just 10% of French nouns."[33] As a result, the subjects in the study run by Bargh would have had around 6 times the experience of encountering the priming words with the nouns as compared with the subjects in the French replication.[34] In his summary, Ramscar states that "the dynamics of learning (and related cultural and linguistic change) present serious challenges to the scientific study of priming, yet these factors are overwhelmingly ignored by researchers."[35]

However, the entire controversy regarding the veracity of social priming became moot following two reviews supervised by Dolores Albarracín (University of Pennsylvania) . The 2015 meta-analysis examined 133 studies that used only words for priming and found "a small behavioral priming effect which was robust across methodological procedures."[36] The 2022 meta-analysis examined 357 studies, mostly using words as primes, and demonstrated there was "strong support for the existence of a priming effect by showing its robustness across different contents and contexts."[37]

There are real world implications for the priming effect when you consider their use to nudge human behaviors in areas such as student motivation, behavior, altruism, along with other economic and social issues. While the effect size of behavioral priming from the 2022 "meta-analysis may appear small, its effect on the scale of thousands or hundreds of thousands of individuals could yield a sizable difference."[38] As such, Eldon could be correct when he suggested to Professor Bargh the possibility of a money motive behind the resistance to the idea of social priming and behavior manipulation. If such a technique was widely believed to be ineffective, then those in the 'know' could continue using it.

Negative Words

Other studies also show the power of words. In a 2010 study, Maria Richter and colleagues (Friedrich Schiller University Jena, Germany) used functional MRI to study the brain's responses to auditory and imagined negative words. What they learned was that pain-related words caused the release of stress and anxiety-inducing hormones.[39] So, just hearing or imagining a negative word could cause a physical reaction.

In another study, researchers looked at preadolescent children's self-talk under conditions of mild anxiety. They found that "Increased levels of anxiety were associated with higher rates of negative self-talk, but not clearly associated with other types of self-talk. These results suggest negative self-talk plays a role in the generation or maintenance of anxiety in normal children."[40] Negative words not only cause situational stress but can also contribute to long-term anxiety.

To bring the discussion back to the use of words and aging, a study published in *Aging and Mental Health* showed that priming with negative aging stereotypes led to increased feelings of loneliness as well as an increase in dependency in the subjects.[41] In another study, adults aged fifty-five and older were asked to read mock news articles that portrayed the elderly as being either an asset (positive prime) or a burden (negative prime). The subjects were then asked to recall a list of thirty words. Those primed with negative messages exhibited worse memories than those primed with positive messages.[42]

Brain-Changing Words

Andrew Newberg (Jefferson University Hospital, Philadelphia) along with

Mark Robert Waldman (University of Pennsylvania) have reported some interesting results when the brain was exposed to specific words. Using an fMRI scanner, they found that simply flashing the word 'No' for less than one second resulted in the immediate release of stress-producing hormones and neurotransmitters. "These chemicals immediately interrupt the normal functioning of your brain, impairing logic, reason, language processing, and communication."[43] Anger adds even more impact to the use of negative words, causing an interference of the decision-making centers of the brain, thereby increasing the likelihood of the individual acting irrationally.[44]

Conversely, words like peace and love can strengthen areas in the frontal lobe, giving rise to increased cognitive function and even arguably influencing the expression of our genes. In their book, *Words Can Change Your Brain*, Newberg and Waldman report their findings this way:

> "The longer you concentrate on positive words, the more you begin to affect other areas of the brain. Functions in the parietal lobe start to change, which changes your perception of yourself and the people you interact with. A positive view of yourself will bias you toward seeing the good in others, whereas a negative self-image will tend you toward suspicion and doubt. Over time the structure of your thalamus will also change in response to your conscious words, thoughts, and feelings, and we believe that the thalamic changes affect the way in which you perceive reality."[45]

So optimists will generally use positive words when they think of themselves and their circumstances, and pessimists will generally use negative words, and as a result, their actual perceptions can be influenced. This sounds like a confirmation, at least to some degree, of the old saying, *what you expect is what you get*. But changing how you talk to yourself is not that simple. Negative situations imply danger, so the brain grabs hold of that information and remembers it. Positive information is nice but not potentially life-threatening. It takes many more repetitions of these statements to cancel out the negative. Marcial Losada (Meta Learning) and Emily Heaphy

(University of Michagan) looked at the effect of the positive/negative ratio regarding business teams, and they found that it took "at least *five* positive messages for each negative utterance you make. ("I'm disappointed" or "That's not what I had hoped for" count as expressions of negativity, as does a facial frown or nod of the head.)"[46]

Increasing Positivity Techniques

Positivity matters, but what can you do if your personality leans to the negative/pessimistic side? Are you stuck with the hand that you have been dealt? It seems not. While it may take a little effort, at least at first, there are several ways to enable a change in your life's positive/negative ratio. Here are a few ideas to get you started

Imagine a Positive Outcome

In an interesting 2015 study carried out at Kings College in London, researchers tested the effects of positive thinking on 102 subjects who had been diagnosed with a generalized anxiety disorder (GAD). Dividing the subjects into three groups, they asked the first group to visualize the positive outcome of something they were worried about, and the second to verbalize the positive outcome. The third group, which was to function as the control, was asked to picture positive images unrelated to their cause of worry. What made the results particularly interesting was the fact that *all three* groups showed benefits, with reductions in anxiety and worry. The results showed that any form of positive ideation could effectively counteract worry.[47] So when you have a negative thought or concern, try imagining a positive outcome, or simply turn your mind's focus to something you like or enjoy. Maybe you have a favorite memory of a special vacation or time with friends. When you are feeling anxious, try thinking about the fun you had. This simple activity will reduce your anxiety level and make it easier for you to move forward.

Journaling

We have seen where researchers examined the writings of nuns, scored the writing for degrees of optimism, and then correlated it to longevity. Journaling has long been seen as a good way to get your thoughts and feelings on paper—to give you a different perspective. So why not take this a step further? Try keeping a journal, but then go back and look at what you have written down and find ways to look at the same situations more positively. Kaitlin Hagan, co-lead author of the 2016 Harvard study that found optimism may help people live longer, gave similar advice. Hagen suggested having "people write down and think about the best possible outcomes for various areas of their lives, such as careers or friendships."[48]

Canceling Negativity
Many positive thinkers do not automatically think positive thoughts—they actively work to cancel negative thoughts. When I was young, I was overly passionate and cared too much. As a result, I was often upset when things did not go as I expected (or people did not behave as I thought they should). It was a religious time in my life and, seeing me upset one day, a friend told me I should turn my worries over to God. I did this well—I could picture in my mind the 'lap of God' and could see myself handing him my bundle of worries. At first, I did this exercise frequently. In the process, my life became incredibly calm. However, I also learned that most of the things I would have worried about never happened at all, and those that did were not as bad as I expected.

Now, you should know that this process does not need to involve religion or spirituality, for you can just decide to create a mental box for your concerns. The important part here is to *choose* to hand your worries off. The more you do this, the easier it will become. Today, I have rejected formalized religion, but that early training still holds strong—I make a conscious choice to focus on a positive outcome, and if the outcome still turns out to be negative, then I will deal with it at that time. Why waste the time fretting over it now when there isn't anything I can do about it, and it may not happen anyway?

Contagious
Motivational speaker, Jim Rohn, is most often credited with saying "You're the average of the five people you spend the most time with." American businessman Dan Peña said, "Show me your friends and I will show you

your future." This idea also extends to your positivity quotient. Some people like to dwell on the negative, sharing stories and competing to see whose life is worse. In *Choices and Illusions*, Eldon describes these people as "*bad-luck fortune cookie collectors,* riding the elevator of life seeing how many of these cookies they can collect." However, negativity is contagious. If you are around people who complain all the time, soon you will be complaining too. If you find it difficult getting your friends and associates to talk about the good parts of their lives, maybe you need to expand your circle of contacts to include people who prefer to look on the brighter side.

Form a New Habit

Recognize that negative thinking can be a habit. Negativity can take many forms. Maybe you find yourself constantly criticizing yourself or others, choosing first to be distrustful or cynical about others' motives, filtering out the good part of an experience and focusing only on the bad, always expecting the worst, and other such things that reinforce the negative. Not only does this impact your health and well-being, your chances of success, and your relationships, but it also creates and strengthens the negative neural pathways in your brain, making it easier for you to make the negative choice.

There is a popular idea that states it takes twenty-one days to create a new habit. This came from a misinterpretation of Maxwell Matz's work on self-image, but the idea became so popular that many believe it to be true.[49] In his bestselling book *Psycho-Cybernetics*, Maltz said that it would take a 'minimum of twenty-one days,' but many self-help instructors have chosen to make this number more definitive. However, according to a study by Phillipa Lally and team (University College London, UK), creating a new habit can take as little as eighteen and as much as 254 days. The median time to reach 95% of the new habit automation was sixty-six days. Missing one opportunity to perform the behavior did not materially affect the habit-formation process.[50] So remember this when you start your positivity practices. At first, it may seem like it does not work, or the results are too faint or fleeting to be worth anything, but the *upwards spirals effect* will help the positivity accumulate. Keep on working at it and a little patience will reap significant rewards.

NOTES

Key Points

In Richter's drowning rats' study, the power of hope made it so that, rather than dying in minutes, the wild rats kept on swimming for 60 hours. In Seligman's study, the dogs who felt helpless just endured the pain whereas the hopeful dogs would find a way to move to a more comfortable place. When there is hope, we gain opportunities to find solutions.

There is a spectrum of attitudes ranging from extreme pessimism to extreme optimism. Both ends of the spectrum can be detrimental to health, well-being, and quality of life. The point of nurturing optimism is not to deny the possibility of bad things happening, but rather to realize that the likelihood of the worst possible scenario occurring is not high and that it is more beneficial in the meantime to keep an eye on the more positive outcomes.

Regardless of the aspect of life being considered, including health, relationships, success, and prosperity, an optimistic approach was found to be the most beneficial. However, it is important to maintain some realism. Optimism to an extreme is not optimism but rather denial—pessimism in disguise. All the denial does is prevent you from looking for other solutions. Extreme or toxic positivity is where empathy is replaced by the dismissal of negative emotions, so causing angst in others.

A related issue can be seen in the value of words. Negative, harmful words can increase anxiety and loneliness, cause memory issues, and have other undesirable effects. Speaking positively to yourself is important, as is speaking to others in the same way.

The idea of the *Upwards Spirals Effect*, coined by Fredrickson and Joiner is of key interest to us. This kind of idea is something we have now seen several times. In our discussion regarding free will, it was suggested that taking proactive steps to claim free will as well as taking steps to address the contents of your subconscious mind, was the path to gaining more free will, and even to allowing these ideas to spread to others. Free will may be limited but the more you claim, the more you get. A good exercise routine is known to have accumulative benefits for your health and well-being, and this also holds for finding ways to increase your positive brain chemicals. In my instance, regular use of diaphragmatic breathing and Duchenne smiling got my blood pressure numbers back under control. Very little is to be gained by practicing positive habits only once or twice. The key is to create habits to make these practices part of your everyday routine for the benefits just accumulate, just as with the *Upwards Spirals Effect*.

Exercise
In the evening, journal the positive things that happened that day. It may take a little bit of thought, especially if your mind has been focused on everything that went wrong but keep working on it. With practice, this process will become easier.

Next, take something you are worried about and write down the ways your worries may not come to pass and how something positive could come as a result. In this latter situation, remember to write down that the feared outcome may not happen at all, or if it does happen, it may be mild. Then focus on the best possible outcomes.

Below are several strategies you can implement in your daily life. For the next week, read these through both in the morning and in the evening. In the morning, plan to use these strategies as much as possible. In the evening, think back to your day and note where you used them and the kind of difference they made. If you forgot to use them, then think back to negative interactions and visualize applying them in retrospect. If you actively chose not to use them, then think carefully through why you made that choice. Was it based on some old programming? Looking again at Erikson's eight stages of psychosocial development may assist you here. Sometimes, simply remembering the initial triggering event that led to your utilizing a particular pattern of behavior can be enough to neutralize its power. This can allow you to make fresh choices that work better for you at your current stage of life. Additionally, looking at where you actively chose not to implement these strategies can enable you to plan how to make the more beneficial choice next time, such as taking a few diaphragmatic breaths and smiling (even if just forcing it by holding a pencil between your teeth).

- *Choose* to hand off your worries. You can do this through religion, such as with prayer, or in a secular way by just creating a mental box. Make a conscious choice to instead focus on a positive outcome, and if the outcome still turns out to be negative, then deal with it at that time. Why waste the time fretting over it now when there isn't anything you can do about it and it may not happen anyway?
- Pay attention to your thoughts. When you hear your inner voice saying something negative, turn it around and say something positive. Try to find someone in your life to assist you with this, maybe a friend or a partner. Determine to speak positively about yourself and others. Ask them to remind you when you start on a negative downward slope.
- Make empathy a priority in your life and remember that this includes you. When you care about others, you will find that they care about you more. In doing this, you will be able to avoid the toxic positivity slope for yourself and be able to identify those who may bring you down.
- If you experience difficulty getting your friends and associates to talk about the good parts of their lives, explore ways to expand your circle of contacts to include people who prefer to look on the brighter side.
- *Nostalgizing*, or thinking back on positive events, has been shown to boost spirits, counteract loneliness, and reduce anxiety. A few minutes of nostalgizing in the morning can improve relationships, inspire creativity, enhance coping abilities regarding stressors at work, and bring a greater sense of meaning to life.[51] Each morning, take some time to think about things you like or enjoy.

When anxious, thinking about some fun you had will reduce the anxiety level and make it easier for you to move forwards. And when something good happens in your life, add it to your collection of events to nostalgize about later. Collect your happy moments.

- Make 'this too will pass' your mantra. When life does not go the way you would prefer, take a big diaphragmatic breath, put on a smile, and repeat to yourself, 'this too will pass.' Then focus on the good in your life.

PART FOUR
LIFE ON YOUR TERMS

CHAPTER ELEVEN

SUBCONSCIOUS CONTROLS

Human beings, by changing the inner attitudes of their minds, can change the outer aspects of their lives.

~ William James

Your subconscious mind has a better memory than you do. While not strictly true as your subconscious mind is of course a part of you, it *is* nevertheless a repository of all your experiences and learning, most of which you will have (consciously) forgotten. This information, though, influences your entire life, including your various defense strategies, mental shortcuts, biases, etc.

Positive/Negative Ratio

We are herd animals—we have a strong need to be accepted, loved, and feel like we belong, and if we cannot feel special, we want at least to be considered *normal*. When we have a negative experience, our subconscious mind will try to create strategies to protect us from repeating this *mistake*—the avoidance of pain. Because of our negativity bias, these negative experiences have more power than our positive experiences, even when the positive experiences are more plentiful. Corroborating the work discussed earlier by Losada and Heaphy working with business teams,[1] according to John Gottman (University of Washington) and Robert Levenson (UC Berkeley), when it comes to relationships, for every negative interaction, a stable, happy relationship needs to have five (or more) positive interactions. Using this ratio, they were able to predict which couple's marriages would not last.[2] So if you have done something to upset your partner, then a simple apology is not enough—it needs to be followed up with four more demonstrations of love.

There are exceptions to this five-to-one rule. Most of us have heard some inspirational story about a super-positive encounter that had long-lasting results, but these events are incredibly rare. The *frequency* of small, positive acts can be critical—and most of us do not have enough, and/or there are certain areas in our lives affected by this kind of imbalance.

Stream of Consciousness

It was the philosopher/psychologist William James who first introduced the idea of a *stream of consciousness*. For most people today, their stream of consciousness is full of what Dr. Aaron Beck (father of cognitive therapy) coined *Automatic Negative Thoughts* (ANTS)—in the privacy of our minds we often become our harshest critic. This almost non-stop stream of internal chatter can be viewed as a mirror of our true inner beliefs, and what we believe to be true can easily become a self-fulfilling prophecy. In many ways, it can seem like a sentry is standing guard—a sentry all too quick to jump in and block our success. The intention is not to sabotage our conscious goals but rather to protect us from pain—the problem is, the sentry frequently uses information that is no longer appropriate.

A Million Dollars?

Eldon likes to demonstrate this when he is doing a presentation by asking the audience to raise their hands if they would like to make a million dollars. Invariably, most people raise their hands. Eldon then explains that to make a million dollars, they will have to do something different than what they have been doing in the past (unless they are already making millions). They may need to quit their job, take out a mortgage on their home for seed money, borrow from friends or family, get an education in specific areas, etc. They will need to put action behind their goal. But first, they must believe—truly believe that they will make one million dollars this year before they stand any chance of being successful. Why don't you try this exercise for yourself? Right now, say aloud to yourself slowly, meaningfully, and with as much sincerity as you can put behind it, *"This year I am going to make one million dollars!"* Remember, you're *making* one million dollars, not winning some jackpot or lottery.

What happens when you do this? When doing this in front of a live audience, Eldon and I frequently see the atmosphere change—people start to shift around, smile nervously, laugh a little, and chatter with those close by. Many people report hearing their inner voice answer back with comments like, *"Yeah, sure—what are you going to do, rob a bank?"* What does your own inner belief tell you when you declare something like this? Do you hear your self-talk returning negative thoughts that stream disbelief and doubt?

You might be surprised at what your self-talk will reveal to you when you begin a serious declaration process. Often, a declaration such as, *"I am good,"* can return a stream of self-talk reminding us of ill-begotten deeds we may have done or participated in. The self-talk will often return thoughts like, *"Really? Good at what? Good for what? Do you remember when . . . ?"* etc. A declaration such as *"I'm going to stop eating, or smoking, or getting angry, and so forth,"* may trigger a response such as, *"Sure—I've heard that before. Who are you kidding? What makes you think this time is different?"* Or perhaps instead, it equivocates with you as opposed to directly challenging, and you hear that inner voice say things like, *"Sure—maybe, but not today. One more piece of chocolate, one more cigarette, one more whatever,"* and so forth.

Positive Affirmations

The use of positive affirmations (declarations) has become a mainstay in most self-help training. You can purchase special affirmation posters, décor items, journals, cards, audio programs, etc. Positive affirmations are often printed on items of clothing and other personal items. Even if you don't purchase special items, a common recommendation is to create your own positive affirmations cards, or *Post-It Notes,* and stick them up everywhere in your home. However, when you consider the many ways subconscious strategies can trip you up, does this mean that the use of positive affirmations is a total waste of time?

We have seen that to create the Pygmalion effect in another person, the authority figure must *truly believe* that the student/trainee/subordinate is capable of great things. For the Galatea effect to play a role in negating negative influences, the individual must *truly and deeply believe* in themselves. The more hurtful a negative comment or feedback, the greater the influence it can have on your subconscious defense mechanisms. Repeating positive affirmations to yourself is highly likely to trigger responses that will nullify the statements—especially in those times of stress when you need to believe in them the most.

Perhaps the five-to-one positive-to-negative ratio would lend some credence to the use of positive affirmations—inundate yourself with positive statements to cancel out the negative—but the positive statements you repeat to yourself cannot compete with the pain you may have experienced when a loved one said you were worthless, ugly, stupid, or whatever. These could be canceled by your loved one telling you five times that you are worthy, beautiful, smart, etc., but many times, the utterer may be oblivious to the pain their thoughtless comment inflicted. And some people can just be plain mean!

It is always beneficial to try to keep a positive mindset, so having affirmations around to remind you can be a good thing. However, they can be of limited value when it comes to making real-life changes, especially in areas where some significant negative event or belief has already carved its home in your subconscious mind.

Free Will

In our discussion earlier regarding free will, we learned there is activity in the subconscious mind before we make an active choice—the subconscious mind makes our choices and the conscious mind comes up with the reason for the choice, making it up if necessary. So, in this instance, free will is illusory—but not totally. Benjamin Libet himself said there was still time for "free-won't" to change the action—the subconscious mind makes the decision, and the conscious mind has 150 milliseconds to *veto* the action. I don't know about you, but 150 milliseconds do not give me the feeling of real hope.

Conscious Control

Employing more thoughtful (System 2) thinking can be helpful, and you already have several ways to do this. We have examined various defense mechanisms (compensation, repression, denial, regression, etc.) that can cause us to hide from ourselves. We have seen the shortcuts and fallacies (normalcy bias, introspection illusion, just world fallacy, self-serving fallacy, etc.) that can limit our ability to think through problems and see the real world for what it is. We have some understanding of our psychology and the techniques (compliance principles) we can succumb to so we can at least feel that each of us is a *normal* and acceptable member of the human herd, such as consistency, reciprocity, justification, etc. We are also aware of the vast amount of research being done not only to understand these automatic ways we function, but also to find ways they can be tweaked to suit the goals of entertainers, marketers, and politicians. The more you become aware of this kind of information, the easier it will be to question your own choices and to come closer to finding your authentic self.

Being aware of these mechanisms and paying attention to those times we may employ them, allows us to decide if this is what we want to do. But it is not practical to rely only on these techniques—automatic thinking is just so much faster and more efficient in most instances. So, what can we do about the source of our automatic responses, all the information that is already in our subconscious mind, all the experiences that have shaped our choices, and all the negativity that seeps in from our environment despite our best intentions? How do we undo the negative, limiting program already there and replace it with positive, empowering programming that will allow us to become the best version of ourselves—to consciously create the Galatea effect in ourselves? Based on 30+ years of research and experience, Eldon and I know that subliminal messages can play an important, albeit not exclusive, role in this process.

Subliminal Communication

Most people have heard of subliminal messages, but some have very confusing and contradictory beliefs about it. These same people often state that subliminal messages in the media are illegal, that they don't work, but they are still being used. This does not make sense. If subliminal messages don't work, how could they be illegal? If they are illegal, how are they still being used? Why would major companies invest so heavily in a technology that has *supposedly* been proven not to work?

The creation of the controversy around subliminal messages is a fascinating story with lots of layers to it, including several (overt) tactics that were used to convince the public that this technique does not work. However, while it is worth looking at in some detail, discussing it here would take us away from the purpose of mind training. As such, for those readers who may be suspicious of subliminal communication, I have provided a full accounting of this story in Appendix A.

Also, whether we are looking at the contrived controversy or the benefits that can be gained from the correct use of subliminal technology, you should know upfront that Eldon and I have significant skin in this game. Over 30 years ago, after carrying out extensive research, Eldon created the InnerTalk subliminal self-help technology, had it patented by the U.S. government, and invited independent researchers and private and public institutions to study it. Numerous double-blind studies—the gold standard for research as it eliminates the bias of the researchers—have demonstrated the efficacy of InnerTalk programs for priming self-talk and thereby changing the user's life experience. Eldon also participated in one of the attempts to create laws that would require informed consent for the use of subliminal messages and has testified as an expert court witness on the subject. For the past few decades, Eldon and I have been creating and using InnerTalk programs to assist people around the world in taking charge of their inner beliefs (subconscious programming), so they support their stated goals as opposed to sabotaging them.

So, with the full disclosure out of the way, let's look at *how* subliminal messages could be useful to us.

Asclepius

How far back does the idea of programming the subconscious go? We cannot know for certain, but in ancient Greece, there were many healing temples dedicated to Asclepius, the Greek god of healing. Priests and physicians at these *Asclepeions*, as they were called, believed ill health resulted from a combination of social, environmental, psychological, spiritual, emotional, and physical interactions, and their treatments attempted to bring back balance in these areas—a holistic kind of approach.[3] Cleansing, diets, purgation (both physical and emotional), and exercise were common, although surgeries were also sometimes performed. Transcendental or mystical rituals were also used to reinforce the patient's belief in the healing god or to stimulate the innate human ability for self-healing.[4] Were they using the authority figure to stimulate the placebo effect?

Many years ago, I was told that the priests and/or physicians in these Asclepeions would whisper to the patients as they slipped into sleep and this guided their dreams, either to reveal the answers from their subconscious (as in hypnosis) or to lead them to Asclepius, who would then provide them with solutions. While I was unable to verify this specifically, I did learn that the final part of the healing treatment entailed the patient going to the Abaton, where they were put into a hypnotic state and encouraged to dream. Several accounts say that the hypnosis was probably induced by hallucinogens, but based on what I had heard previously, it could just as easily have been done by the priests or physicians whispering to them. Patients then would report either being healed automatically (divine intervention) or they would awaken with information that offered the cure.[5] It is possible that, rather than a drug-induced hypnotic state, the patient could have heard a whispered hypnotic script or maybe even self-healing affirmations.

Early Research

Most accounts say that the first real research into subliminal information processing was carried out in 1863 by M. Suslowa. Using an esthesiometer to measure the threshold (distance) at which the subject could distinguish a two-point contact, Suslowa found that electrical stimulation would inhibit the subject's ability to discriminate, even when the electrical stimulation was below the level of conscious perception.[6] So, using an esthesiometer, the subjects became less able to distinguish a two-point touch from a one-point touch when a subliminal electrical stimulus was applied.

In 1884, Peirce and Jastrow found that their subjects could "detect consciously imperceptible weight differences at confidence levels significantly beyond chance, although they had 'zero confidence' about their judgments."[7] So the weight differences were so slight they were subliminal, but the subjects were still able to 'guess' which was the heaviest even though they had no idea why.

In 1917, the Austrian neurologist Otto Poetzl reported the reappearance in dreams of images or information previously subliminally presented. In this study, Poetzl asked his subjects to make a drawing of a picture he presented. Using a tachistoscope, a device that projects an image too fast to be consciously recognized, this picture also included 'hidden' or subliminal images. The subject's drawing did not contain any of the hidden images. However, when Poetzl asked the subjects to make drawings of their dreams after exposing them to these subliminal images, their drawings contained the hidden images.[8] The Poetzl Phenomenon is the ability of subliminal terms or images to show up in imagery or dreams shortly after.[9]

In 1958, Howard Shevrin (University of Michigan) and Lester Luborsky (University of Pennsylvania) ran a study to measure preconscious perception in dreams and images. Their results significantly supported the Poetzl theory that the subjects dream about the originally unreported parts of a picture. Again, these 'unreported' parts had been presented using a tachistoscope.[10] Another replication by Charles Fisher in 1988 found that subliminal representations were utilized in hallucinations, again confirming the Poetzl Phenomenon.[11]

So, subliminally presented information is perceived and this, in turn, influences the individual, but to what degree, and are there any practical applications?

1984 Congressional Hearing

Subliminal messages were the focus of the August 1984 congressional hearing before the *Subcommittee on Transportation, Aviation, and Materials of the Committee on Science and Technology.* The subcommittee was exploring areas that could concern the public in a kind of Orwellian sense simply because this was the year 1984. The committee acknowledged there had been 'a number of scientific advances in the area and an increase in its application in recent years,' and mentioned that this technology was being used by 'a large number of stores throughout the county to discourage shoplifting,' as well as in areas of self-help, such as weight loss, smoking cessation, enhancing memory, etc.[12]

Included amongst the expert witnesses called to testify were Dr. Hal Becker, president of Behavioral Engineering Corporation; David Tyler, president of Proactive Systems; Howard Shevrin, Ph.D. (University of Michigan); and Lloyd H. Silverman, Ph.D. (New York University).

Hal Becker shared information regarding the use of his "Black Box," to deliver anti-theft subliminal messages in "department stores, supermarkets, drugstores, real estate agencies, professional placement agencies, automobile dealerships, computerized apartment rental agencies, and medical and dental clinics." Becker reported great success using his technology with anti-theft messages, and in a few therapeutic settings. In his testimony, Becker made it clear that he was *not* using subliminal messages for advertising purposes.[13] (In Appendix A, you will learn how the controversy regarding subliminal communication began with reports of its use in marketing. This would have played a role in Becker's need to distance his use of this technology from the advertising arena.)

David Tyler stated that his company had been in the retail theft prevention market for three years. He also shared information about some therapeutic areas they were in the early stages of researching, such as for reducing depression in cardiac patients or for relieving stress in a stockbroker's firm. However, his primary area of success occurred in the anti-theft market, where he had achieved success rates of a 30-50% reduction in theft.[14]

Howard Shevrin indicated he had been researching the nature of subliminal perception for thirty years and stated that "pictures or words flashed so quickly that the person could not report seeing them, nevertheless registered in the mind unconsciously and influenced consciousness without the person being aware of it."[15] However, he also believed that "There is no substantial evidence that a subliminal stimulus can effect motivation resulting in a change in behavior important to the individual."[16] In other words, subliminal messages need to meet a congruent drive or desire to cause an effect.

Shevrin went on to share some research that showed how presenting subliminal information and tracking brainwave activity could even be used as a sophisticated lie-detection technique.[17]

Lloyd Silverman introduced his testimony by saying "I think it is fair to say that any reasonable review of the literature over the past thirty or so years would convince an unbiased observer that this [subliminal] is a real phenomenon." Silverman's early interest in subliminal messages was for examining the "Freudian unconscious." One study found that people with guilt-related depression would respond to guilt-related subliminal messages, such as "I have been bad," but not to loss-related subliminal messages such as "I have lost Mommy," and that the opposite reactions were found in people with loss-related depression.[18]

A fascinating area of research carried out by Silverman is his work with unconscious fantasies or ideas. Positive results were found in several studies using the subliminal phrase "Mommy and I are one." This idea first arose from his work with subjects suffering from schizophrenia and the belief that the cause could lie in the subject's issues with their mother. Silverman then extended this into work with subjects suffering from depression, and then into the self-help arena. During his testimony, Silverman shared the results using his "Mommy and I are one" message with a self-help program for smoking cessation. He found that:

> "A month after the program ended, 13% of the people who had received the message 'People are walking' [the control] were still abstaining from cigarette smoking which the program itself brought about, but only 13% were able to sustain this gain after a month's time while 67% of those who got the message, 'Mommy and I are one" were still abstainers. These were pretty striking results."[19]

So, the stop smoking subliminal program was effective. One month later, though, of the subjects who received the additional subliminal statement

"People are walking," 13% were still abstaining. This contrasts with the subjects who received the additional subliminal statement "Mommy and I are one," where 67% were still abstaining. This indicates that subliminal self-help programs can work, but differences in the techniques used to create them will affect efficacy.

Both Silverman and Shevrin made it clear in their testimonies that subliminal messages are perceived and can cause behavioral changes in the right situations.[20]

Just as an aside, Eldon spoke with Joel Weinberger (Adelphi University), who had trained under Lloyd Silverman, about the "Mommy and I are one" message on our *Provocative Enlightenment Radio* show. When asked, Weinberger was unsure exactly *why* the message increased efficacy across so many different domains and was most interested in Eldon's belief that, rather than being related to the subject's relationship with their own mother, it related to the archetypal mother—the time in the womb when the subject only knew comfort and security.[21] As we have seen, feeling safe and secure plays a significant role in creating success, whatever aspect of life we are looking at. This idea became an important factor when Eldon designed his own InnerTalk technology.

Further Evidence

I met Eldon at the end of 1989. At the time, he had gathered an account of all the research he could find done around subliminal communication and preconscious processing. Together we compiled this information into the *Peripheral Perception Via Subliminal Stimuli Desk Reference*. This tome consists of some background information plus 234 pages of citations and brief descriptions of the studies.[22] (While this book is now out-of-print, you can still read it yourself by going to https://progressiveawareness.org.)

Today, the research has only continued to proliferate with more and more studies demonstrating both that subliminal perception is real, and that it can have an affective influence on the subject. I share a few more of these in Appendix A. However, here is another study by Paul Whalen et al. (Dartmouth College) that Kahneman wrote about in his book, *Thinking, Fast and Slow*. This study is about the negativity bias and the speed at which the amygdala responds to negative images. The study is of extra interest to us here as the stimuli, images of the whites of the eyes in a black background, "were presented to people lying in a brain scanner. Each picture was shown for less than 2/100 of a second and immediately masked by "visual noise," a random display of dark and bright squares. None of the observers ever consciously knew that he had seen pictures of eyes, but one part of their brain evidently knew: the amygdala, which has a primary role as the "threat center" of the brain . . ." There were two sets of eyes shown, one wide in terror and the other expressing happiness, and they were presented subliminally. "Images of the brain showed an intense response of the amygdala to a threatening picture that the viewer did not recognize."[23] So, the negativity bias, an evolutionary mechanism to protect us from threats, even responds to subliminally presented information.

Better research studies use larger numbers of subjects to allow for abnormal results. A meta-analysis is a research process that merges the results from multiple studies and uses statistical methods to calculate overall results or effects. These have also been used to examine the validity of subliminal information processing.

In a 1990 meta-analytic review, Robert Bornstein (Adelphi University) looked at studies that had been published between 1966 to 1989. This review aimed to examine the magnitude of behavior change produced by subliminal vs. supraliminal drive-related stimuli—how different was the degree of response when the stimuli were presented below the level of conscious detection (subliminal) as compared to above it (supraliminal)? The analysis revealed that the subliminal presentation of drive-related stimuli produced significantly stronger effects on behavior than the supraliminal presentation of the same stimuli.[24]

In 2009, Eva Van den Bussche (KU Leuven University, Belgium) presented her doctoral thesis titled *The Mechanisms of Subliminal Stimuli: A Meta-Analysis and New Experiments*. For this thesis, she ran several of her studies along with a large-scale meta-analysis where published and unpublished masked priming studies conducted between 1983 and 2006 were statistically combined. She states that "while less than two decades ago it was still highly debated whether unconscious information could influence our behavior at all, it now becomes increasingly clear that unconscious processing does not only exist, but it also extends to a sophisticated cognitive level."[25]

Different Technologies

When it comes to subliminal self-help programs, some other issues can arise, ranging from outrageous claims to ineffective technologies. Because of his research, Eldon has been privy to a fair amount of inside information from various subliminal self-help companies. He learned that subliminal self-help programs from different companies vary in several ways, such as:

- There may be no affirmations on the program at all. In one instance, the owner of a company thought the results were all due to the placebo anyway.
- Affirmations may be recorded as much as 50 db beneath the primary carrier. This is too low a level for regular players to even pick up.
- Affirmations may be recorded in the second person (*You are good*) as opposed to the first person (*I am good*). This is an important distinction. When you hear fully audible coaching, someone else is encouraging you. When the affirmations are presented subliminally, they become part of your stream of consciousness. When this self-talk is saying 'you are good,' that only tells the individual that other people are good, and this can have a deleterious effect on their esteem if they think everyone else is better than them.
- Affirmation formatting is important. Short and to-the-point affirmations are more effective than long, convoluted ones. Affirmations also need to be well thought out; an affirmation such as "Ten cigarettes a day is more than enough for me," could be turned around and interpreted as "More than ten cigarettes a day is enough for me."
- Some companies believe that 'more is better' and they

advertise that their programs contain millions of affirmations. There are several ways to do this:
- Have a hundred people say each affirmation simultaneously. However, it is much more difficult to understand what is being said when many people are speaking at the same time.
- Speed up the affirmations. Nothing indicates that the subconscious mind understands speech that has been sped up. Depending on how much the speech is sped up, it can be difficult to impossible to understand even when fully audible.
- Layer the affirmations – perhaps at 5 db, 10 db, 15 db, and so on beneath the primary track. However, there is an optimal range beneath the primary carrier where the affirmations can be detected. Any more than that is like asking a violinist to go to the other side of Los Angeles and still expecting to hear their music.

Independent Research

With such a wide variety of subliminal technologies being used to create subliminal self-help programs, it becomes important to ask about the research that has been carried out on the different brands. But even here, caution is needed. Some companies cite research backing their programs. However, in many instances, they cite generic research as opposed to studies carried out on their programs. (In some instances, they have cited research carried out on InnerTalk, while the programs they market utilize a different technology). Where studies have been carried out on their programs, the research was generally carried out in-house, which can lead to cherry-picking of the results to suit the company's agenda.

With InnerTalk, not only have we carried out our own research, but, as stated earlier, we have also made our programs available to independent researchers to study. For example:

- Thomas Plante (Stanford University) together with Michael DiGregorio, Gerdenio Manuel and Bao-Tran T. Doan (Santa Clara University) evaluated the effect of InnerTalk on test anxiety. The statistical data significantly supported the hypothesis that the InnerTalk subliminal technology could be an effective tool for lowering test anxiety.[26]
- A study carried out by Rainer Pelka (Armed Forces University, Munich, Germany) on an InnerTalk program for weight loss, showed average weight losses of thirteen pounds in subjects who used the program without following any other kind of diet or exercise regimen.[27]
- At the University of Southern California, Diana Ashley studied the effect of InnerTalk on academic achievement. She found a significant increase in learning among students in the experimental group.[28]
- Patricia Galbraith and Brad Barton carried out a study at Weber State University on the effects of the InnerTalk program, *Freedom from Stress*. The psychological test results showed a significant decrease in stress.[29]
- James Reid carried out a double-blind study at Colorado State University using the InnerTalk program *Freedom from Depression*. It was found that using the program for more than seventeen hours led to a significant decrease on the Beck Depression scale. This study not only shows the effectiveness of the InnerTalk program but also indicated that the program's effectiveness was related to dosage.[30]

(For a more complete list of studies that have been carried out on InnerTalk, please see Appendix B).

Further, thousands of testimonials from individuals and organizations have produced a tapestry indicating that 1) it's never too late to change, and 2) you can change almost any area of your life. We have repeatedly seen that self-sabotaging beliefs hold people back and that changing these beliefs can lead to success.

Personal Experiences

For me, though, mind training is more than just an academic exploration. While I enjoy learning about how the mind works and what makes us tick, I am also interested in the practical applications for my own use. As such, I have worked with all the tools outlined in this book at one time or another. Now, I would like to share some of my own experiences—some of the challenges I have faced and the choices I have made.

Esteem

When I first met Eldon in 1989, I considered myself practical and down to earth. I accepted who I was, knew my faults and shortcomings but, overall, I was happy just being me. Eldon, however, saw through this right away. Shortly after we first met, he gifted me the InnerTalk program, *Soaring Self Esteem*, and told me to stop putting myself down. I must admit, I laughed when I opened this package—I thought Eldon was joking. However, trusting the new relationship developing between us, I played the esteem program continuously all evening.

By the time Eldon called me that evening to say goodnight, I had worked myself up into a real state. Of course, at the time I did not realize the positive esteem affirmations were in confrontation with the defense mechanisms I had erected over the years—information that was buried in my subconscious programming. Instead, I believed the music on this program was the worst I had ever heard, so bad in fact that it was an offense against humanity itself! You would not believe how vocal I was at expressing my contempt for this monstrosity masquerading as music that Eldon had chosen to put on a program designed to help you appreciate yourself.

Not long after this, I happened to listen to another InnerTalk program, and this time I found the music to be purely divine. The music was so smooth and melodic that it seemed to call to my very soul, inspiring me to reach for ever-greater heights. Imagine my shock when I learned that this was the same music on the esteem program I had complained about so vociferously. The music was by Emmy award-winning musician Jim Oliver and since then no single piece of Jim's music has failed to lift my spirits.

By this time, I was ready to listen to Eldon's explanation of how it was not the music that had upset me when I first listened to the esteem program, but rather it was resistance to the specific set of affirmations that were directly challenging my inner beliefs—beliefs constructed by my subconscious to protect me from pain and disappointment. Unfortunately, by not believing in myself, I had been avoiding situations where I could potentially fail, and in that process, I had also missed chances of success and real achievements.

I continued to play *Soaring Self Esteem* and it was not long before my resistance to the new way of thinking dissipated.

Layers

An analogy that can be used for self-empowerment is peeling back the layers of an onion—there is often another layer. Over the years, I have found this with my esteem issues, with life experiences revealing more layers. As such, I have found myself reaching for my *Soaring Self Esteem* program several times, and each time I have reached a little higher and achieved a little more. Since this journey started, my life has changed immensely. From assisting in our business with all the bottom-rung tasks (packaging products, cleaning, etc.), I have worked my way up to running the marketing department, from simply laying out the page designs for each new book, I now do a great deal of the heavy-duty editing, research and fact-checking. To date, my biggest achievement of all is researching, studying, and writing this book.

Speaking

There was a time public speaking terrified me, so much so that I refused to do any. One time, we were in a recording studio prepping for a radio interview that Eldon was to give. This was not long after Eldon's *Choices and Illusions* hit the New York Times bestseller list and he was doing lots of radio interviews, both on the dial in major markets, and online with specialty networks. In this instance, the hosts were our friends and they suggested that I join in the conversation—*"It's just the four of us chatting around the table,"* Elaine said. I was so afraid they would stick a microphone in my face that I made sure I was sitting at the far end of the room, away from any kind of equipment.

Over the past decade or so, I have supported Eldon on our *Provocative Enlightenment* radio show. Those of you who have been listening in since the start may be aware that I progressed from merely uttering a couple of words, to saying a few complete sentences, to having full discussions. However, you should note that our part of the radio show is held in our office/studio—a room we sit and chat in almost every single day—and where we can connect remotely with the radio station in Seattle. Talking to my husband from across the table makes it very easy to forget we have an audience.

Joint Interviews

In time, I also participated in a few joint interviews with Eldon with the same hosts I mentioned earlier. For these interviews, rather than being in their studio, our end was carried out in our office/studio—so we were, in essence, talking with a couple of friends, using headphones that were jacked into a telephone line. Also, because it was just audio and not video, I could signal to let Eldon know whenever I was stuck and had no idea how to answer a question. Being the perfect gentleman and experienced radio guest, he would simply pick up the slack for me. His hardest part here was not laughing out loud at my antics as I silently pleaded for his help!

Hosting the Show

Then, one day Eldon had planned to host the radio show while on the road. All the arrangements had been made for a private room at Ruby's Inn in Bryce Canyon where he would originate the broadcast. Unfortunately, car troubles meant he was unable to do this, so I was left with a choice—arrange to re-air an earlier show or host the show myself. Eldon had the show all prepared, right down to the questions he wanted to ask, so if I had to, I could simply read from a script. While that little internal voice first screamed out *"No way,"* it was quickly replaced with a quiet, *"Can I really do this?"* And soon the entire internal dialog was changing from, *"No way!"* to *"Why not?" "I hate public speaking"* to *"Why not just look at Eldon's notes?"* Well, the long and the short of it was that I hosted the show and had a fascinating conversation with Larry Rosen (California State University) regarding his book, *iDisorder: Understanding Our Obsession with Technology and Overcoming Its Hold on Us*. So, I was not speaking to to a lightweight. Yes, I did have a pre-written script that I could fall back on, but I was also aware that not long ago that would have been of very little consolation to me. As it turned out, I used the script very little as the conversation just flowed naturally.

Flying Solo
Not long after that, best-selling author and radio host Caroline Sutherland asked for an interview with me alone. Once again, there was an internal conversation/argument that went on: *"No way . . . why not? I'm scared . . . what of? I'll stumble over words . . . everyone stumbles at some time,"* and on and on. The biggest hurdle for this interview request was the fact that I had no safety net at all—there was no pre-written script, and I could be asked anything at all! There was one thing in my favor though, and that was the fact we would be discussing ways to eliminate self-destructive patterns, something I have been researching for the past two decades! I did the interview, Caroline loved it, and she even asked me back to do another one!

Believing in Yourself
Of course, this interview had me thinking of all the techniques I have used to get me to this point. To be successful in business, you must be able to speak in public. It was a self-destructive pattern of my own that had me avoiding interviews of any kind—my own fears of making a fool of myself, not being worthy enough, not being smart enough, etc. Over the years, I have used many InnerTalk programs to change my self-talk so that instead of sabotaging my dreams and goals, my inner talk would support them. As you can see from some of the internal dialogues I had whenever presented with these kinds of situations, my self-talk did, in fact, change—and with the new supporting self-talk, I learned to face and overcome many fears and limitations.

For a few decades now, I have been using all the information contained in this book in my own life. Not long ago I suffered emotional trauma. As much as I tried, and I really gave it my all, I did not see any possible resolution. I could easily have become very depressed about it. Instead, I put in place everything I knew—the InnerTalk program titled *Coherent Emotion*, diaphragmatic breathing, exercise, a false smile on my face, etc. While this did not eliminate the problem, it eased the edges considerably. Time heals most things, but these techniques accelerated the process. This is what real self-help looks like. There is much wisdom in the saying *you cannot stop bad things happening to you, but you can choose your responses.*

Most significantly, without all the work I have done on training my mind, I would never have had the guts to agree to working on this book. What could you achieve if you followed the same path?

Reality Check

I use InnerTalk programs all the time. The fastest result I have experienced would be in an hour or two, with a shift in mood that allowed me to get my work done. The longest I have had to use a program was fifteen months, playing it every night, and then using every other mind training tool I could think of to cure myself of what would normally be an incurable condition, rheumatoid arthritis. You can read about this part of my life in my InnerTalk.com blog, titled *The Keys to Self-Healing*.[31]

Part of the controversy regarding the efficacy of subliminal self-help programs is due to some companies making the most outlandish of claims, as though the subconscious mind has incredible superpowers. As we have learned, most companies have not even done the homework necessary to figure out what a subliminal stimulus is.

For subliminal self-help programs to work, extended exposure is necessary, and what you will experience is a small shifting of beliefs in the direction of your stated desires—your reason for working with that program. As Bert Westerlundh stated in *Advances in Psychology*, "Subliminal messages are generally not read syntactically, but there seems to be a highly emotional unconscious appraisal of the words."[32]

The Subliminal Process

Subliminal information processing is a very natural everyday occurrence. Most of us have experienced being somewhere where many people were having conversations. Suddenly, in a conversation happening on the other side of the room, someone says something meaningful to you, perhaps mentioning your name, and your ears prick up. You were oblivious to their conversation, but your subconscious mind still managed to pick out your name.

Subliminal self-help programs work by easing the doubts, fears, and insecurities that frequently block your success—they assist you in achieving your best, but they do not turn you into a superbeing. For example, if you wish to improve your abilities in basketball, supporting beliefs will assist you to perform to your best ability, eliminating any self-destructive beliefs that would hold you back—but no amount of positive thinking will turn you into a Michael Jordan if the raw talent does not exist in the first place.

We are being programmed all the time; from the moment we are born. Our parents, siblings, and peer group all influence the kind of person we want to be. Television, music, entertainment, news shows, etc., all tell us how to be 'normal' and to 'fit in.' Research is constantly ongoing to figure out ways to influence your choices and we need to be alert to this. But being alert to all this information is not enough. We need to take proactive steps to remove the negativity our minds, like overly dry sponges, have sucked up and instead infuse it with positive beliefs. A correctly created subliminal program can be an important tool in this process.

NOTES

Key Points

Our subconscious mind is a repository of all our experiences. Negative experiences are stronger than positive ones. Where on a conscious level five positive experiences (e.g., expressions of love from your significant other) can counteract one negative experience (e.g., an angry exchange), this may not hold for subconscious beliefs. Plus, as a repository, our subconscious mind will hold many negative memories we have forgotten. Unfortunately, these negative experiences/beliefs continue to influence our choices today. This is a key component of self-sabotaging behaviors.

Positive affirmations are commonly used as a tool to promote positive self-beliefs. However, telling yourself something like "I am good" cannot compete with the pain of being told by a loved one that "you are worthless." Negative feedback holds more weight and as we have seen, the person who derided you would have to make at least five positive comments to cancel out the one negative comment. In many cases, this will not happen.

Over time, your stream of consciousness becomes filled with negative beliefs and your subconscious uses these as a basis to create strategies to avoid future pain. Unfortunately, these strategies may remain in place long after they are needed and can result in blocking your future success.

Research into subliminal communication has demonstrated effectiveness. Where this field became controversial in the second half of the 20th century, it was greatly due to misinformation. (See Appendix A).

Meta-analysis is the merging of the results of many studies, and using statistical methods to calculate overall results or effect. Two such meta-analyses on subliminal information processing found that the "subliminal presentation of drive-related stimuli produced significantly stronger effects on behavior than supraliminal presentation of the same stimuli"[33] and that unconscious processing not only exists but also extends to a sophisticated cognitive level.[34] So, subliminal information produces a stronger effect on behavior than supraliminal (above the threshold of conscious detection) information.

One of the issues with the subliminal self-help industry is that there is no one defined method for creating a subliminal program. By looking at some of the different techniques used, we can see why some programs have been shown to be ineffective.

Subliminal communication is a real phenomenon and is something we all experience all the time. When created correctly and used appropriately, they can be a great tool to support any self-empowerment journey.

Exercise

Think about some of the changes you would like to make in your life. Write declarative statements affirming that this change has happened and that you deserve this new reality. Then, listen carefully to the responses that come back. Do you believe these positive statements, or do you feel some resistance to them?

Subliminal self-help programs are just one of the tools in our mind training armamentarium. If you decide this is something you would like to explore, here are some questions to ask before selecting a particular brand:

- Are the affirmations written in the first person (I am vs. you are)?
- Is there any independent research supporting the efficacy of the brand?
- Are the affirmations recorded in real-time with real voices, spoken slowly and meaningfully?
- How realistic are the claims made for the said products? Do they talk about small shifts in beliefs, or do they promise incredible results?
- Are the affirmations simple and to the point, or are they complex and convoluted?
- Are you able to discern talking in the background at least some of the time or are the affirmations buried too deeply?

Selecting a subliminal self-help program requires some careful thought regarding your desired benefits. For example, rather than saying you wish to be more successful, think about what success means to you. Are you talking about success in relationships, in your studies, in your communications, relationships, parenting abilities, self-confidence, etc.? The more specific you are about your desired goal, the easier it will be for you to select the set of affirmations most likely to give you the desired results.

While it is okay to play several different programs during each day, it is best not to take on different major life changes at once. For example, you would not want to take on weight loss and stop smoking at the same time.

(To learn more about the InnerTalk technology, please visit www.inner-talk.com.)

CHAPTER TWELVE

EMPOWER YOURSELF

> Empowerment isn't a buzzword among leadership gurus. It's a proven technique where leaders give their teams the appropriate training tools, resources, and guidance to succeed.
>
> ~ John Rampton

In many ways, this chapter is the most important to me as it covers the beginning of my journey into learning how the mind works and how it can sabotage you, and the final epiphany that brought the techniques for effective mind training into a crystal-sharp focus. This epiphany led me to start working on a book that I tentatively titled *Bottling the Placebo Effect*. In time, I would overlay the ideas I had onto the manuscript that Eldon handed me and then build it out to the *Mind Training* book you are now reading.

Real, solid tools exist to assist you in maximizing your health, living a full life, and minimizing the self-sabotage that hinders your success. That is precisely what mind training is all about—science-based ideas that take you from merely accepting 'you are who you are' to taking conscious control and creating the person you choose to be. We have covered a significant number of techniques already, and now I wish to speak about hypnosis, meditation, and mindfulness. I put these into one category as I consider them variations of the same principles, especially when you add self-hypnosis. A key component of these techniques centers around slowing brainwave activity and putting the mind and body in a calm, relaxed state.

Brainwave Activity

As the cells in the brain communicate, electrical impulses are produced. All brainwaves are produced by synchronized electrical pulses from masses of neurons communicating with each other.[1] This electrical activity can be seen using an EEG (electroencephalograph) and the brainwaves are measured in cycles per second or Hertz based on their frequency or speed. Your brainwave activity will be faster when you are alert and active, and slower when you are relaxed and calm. According to the Sinha Clinic, brainwave activity is categorized as:

- *Delta brain waves* are produced when you are completely relaxed in deep sleep. Delta waves are essential for your body to heal and restore during sleep. These are the slowest brain waves and range from 1 to 4 hertz.
- *Theta brain waves* are produced when you're sleeping or daydreaming when awake. These waves are associated with relaxation and low alertness. They occur when you're lost in thought, drowsy, or sleepy. They range from 4 to 8 hertz.
- *Alpha brain waves* are produced when you're awake, but your mind is resting. They are associated with being calm and alert. They can help you during activities that require learning and coordinating. They fall right in the middle of the brain wave spectrum, ranging from 8 to 12 hertz.
- *Beta brain waves* are produced throughout your daily activities. They occur when you're awake, alert, busy, and focused. These waves range from 12 to 38 hertz and can be divided into the following subtypes:

- *Low beta waves* range from 12 to 15 hertz and occur when you're thinking.
- *Beta waves* range from 15 to 22 hertz and occur when you're active or focusing on something.
- *High beta waves* range from 22 to 38 hertz. They occur when you're excited or anxious. They also occur when you experience something new or have complex thoughts.

- *Gamma brain waves* are the fastest brain waves. They mainly occur when you're highly alert and conscious and range from 30 to 80 hertz. Gamma brain waves are associated with high levels of thought and focus.[2]

Why is slowing down brain wave activity desirable? The body has two states: growth and defense. When the mind and body are calm and relaxed, then healing and growth can occur. An analogy I like compares brain wave activity with the density of fencing.

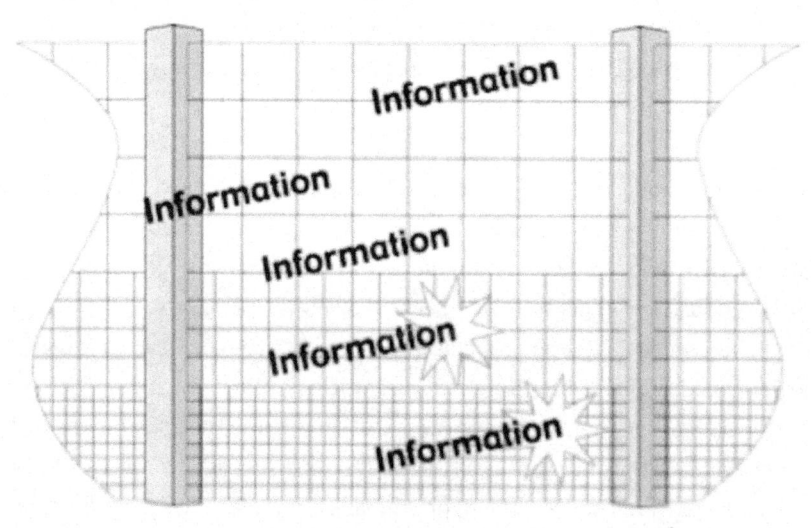

The faster the brain wave activity, the denser or tighter the fencing, therefore the less information can get through. As brain wave activity slows down, the density decreases and you find it easier to access information, such as memories, creativity, and inspiration.

Techniques

Many spiritual traditions use meditation to create a sense of peace, calm, inner harmony, and a feeling of connection to something greater. Today, though, secular meditation practices are also available, such as mindfulness, which involves attaining this calm, relaxed state and then simply observing your thoughts and accepting yourself. Self-hypnosis has some specific goal in mind, such as directing positive change in a desired area, or attempting to access information from the subconscious.

The techniques used for meditation, and self-hypnosis are very similar:

1. Controlled breathing – pacing your breath at a deeper and more relaxed rate.
2. Progressive relaxation—instructing yourself to relax systematically, perhaps from the top of the head down to the tips of your toes.
3. Visualization—picturing an outcome you may like, such as enhanced spirituality, or the ability to react calmly in a formerly tense situation.

As your body relaxes, your brainwave activity will slow. Mindfulness training will generally use step 1 and maybe step 2 before proceeding with a calm, dispassionate observation of the thoughts that emerge before gently guiding these thoughts back to a place of serenity.

A much deeper state of relaxation, however, may be achieved when an experienced hypnotherapist guides the process. While the hypnotherapist may start by using many of the same techniques as meditation and self-hypnosis, the fact that the process is being directed makes it easier to achieve deeper levels of relaxation. The hypnotherapist may also use some other tools to induce the hypnotic state, such as:

- A pendulum clock or a metronome—the slow, rhythmic ticking will entrain the brain and slow down the heart rate.
- A spinning wheel that draws the subject deeper in.
- A flashing light—again the rhythm entrains and relaxes the brain, while also drowning out distractions.
- A slower rate of speech along with a lower volume assists in slowing down thinking in the subject. The voice also becomes the guide for the journey within.

The voice of the hypnotherapist creates a safe space, making it easier for the subject to relax more deeply and to further slow brain wave activity. In some instances, the subject may enter theta or even delta levels and may even feel like they fell asleep. With careful guidance by the hypnotherapist, it may be possible for the subject to access deeper memories, heal old festering traumas, or provide ways to deal with current issues.

Benefits

The literature is rich with studies showing the benefits of these techniques, and today, doctors frequently counsel their patients to start meditating. According to the Mayo Clinic, meditation may help people manage a range of conditions, ranging from anxiety to asthma, and from heart disease to irritable bowel syndrome.[3]

Hypnosis can be used in all the same areas as well, with directed hypnosis (as opposed to self-hypnosis) being more commonly used in areas from weight loss to quitting smoking, and from anxiety reduction to uncovering suppressed memories.

As stated, a key component of all these techniques is slowing brainwave activity and putting the mind and body in a calm, relaxed state. In some ways, it is likened to rebooting a computer; everything just works better when some of the clutter is removed. As the mind rests, so does the body. Regular practices that slow down brain wave activity can have a positive rippling effect across many areas of your life, bringing health benefits, stress reduction, clearer thinking, and greater productivity.

I tend to think that the benefits of these techniques are so well established that there is little more to be gained by looking at specific scientific studies. Therefore, rather than going down the scientific route, I will share with you more of my journey into these fields and how this led to my epiphany. In this way, I believe you may gain a more practical perspective on these techniques and be provided with a clearer incentive to try them for yourselves.

Hypnosis

In the mid-'80s, I worked as a microbiologist at the Leicester Royal Infirmary's Public Health Laboratory in the UK. I was a very practical, down-to-earth kind of person, who loved the scientific method—it was only true if science could prove it to be so. One day, fliers appeared all over the hospital and labs announcing a presentation on hypnosis by a visiting anesthesiologist. I had never taken the idea of hypnosis seriously, thinking of it more as a stage trick. However, the hospital was organizing the presentation, so it had at least a quasi-endorsement from a scientific establishment.

The presentation was most interesting. I particularly remember one story the lecturer shared of a woman who had experienced pain in her arm for many years. She had seen a lot of experts, but they had been unable to figure out the source of her problem. As a last resort, she visited the anesthesiologist who was also a practicing hypnotherapist. Under hypnosis, the therapist directed her to go back in time to when the pain in her arm had started and to uncover the cause. Doing so, the woman remembered some emotional event, something she had forgotten about but that, at the time, had been extremely traumatic for her. Coming out of hypnosis, the woman dismissed the information—yes, it was interesting that she had remembered that old event, but it could not possibly be significant. The following day she phoned the therapist and reported that the pain had gone—it had disappeared the night before, but she had wanted to make sure before letting him know. I was most intrigued; how could an emotional experience cause pain in her arm? It all seemed so unrelated.

No Shills

Further verification of the whole hypnosis experience came from the fact that around seventy people working in the microbiology and virology labs attended the presentation. My colleagues all sat in different parts of the large auditorium. Coincidentally, when the lecturer chose subjects to demonstrate to us some of his different hypnotic techniques, he happened to choose three people from my lab. Under hypnosis, he made Dawn forget the number 6. Bringing her out of hypnosis he asked her to count from 1 to 10, forwards and backward, and she complied, totally omitting the number 6. Under hypnosis, he desensitized Martin to pain and stuck a pin through his arm. Martin did not flinch. I believe the lecturer had the third person do something childlike. However, as I said, this all happened close to four decades ago, and some of the details have been lost in time. For certain, three members of my lab acted as subjects and were not just shills. Martin certainly enjoyed displaying the pin that had been stuck through his arm when we were all back at work the following day.

Hypnotic Uncoverings

I found the whole thing compelling and the potential simply intriguing. I contacted a hypnotherapist and had several sessions. One of the early sessions involved age regression, where the therapist asked my subconscious mind to indicate the ages at which my 'issue' had been triggered. After hypnotizing me, the therapist counted backward from my current age to zero and asked for an ideomotor response at the important years—he asked my subconscious mind to raise my index finger to indicate when the significant events had occurred. There were quite a few of them. The following sessions then entailed going back to these events, starting at the most recent and working our way back in time. Remembering and releasing any emotional pain attached to these events was enough to reduce stress levels.

Over the next few months, I got to experience different hypnosis induction techniques and a variety of uncovering tools including hypnotic drawing and hypnotic writing. Some of these techniques spanned two sessions. So, for example, a significant event happened when I was about eight. The therapist hypnotized me, counted me back to my eighth year, and then asked my subconscious mind to *draw* the event. Once I had completed my art masterpiece, he counted me up and out of hypnosis. Looking at the piece of paper, all I saw was a jumble of squiggly lines; hypnosis had certainly not brought out some latent artistic ability.

The following week, though, the therapist repeated the process, but this time he asked my subconscious mind to let me know what the squiggles meant. At my junior school, there was an above-ground swimming pool, and throughout the summer we often went swimming while the teachers walked around the perimeter of the pool. They didn't conduct swimming lessons per se, and most of us just splashed around. One day, for some reason, I lost my footing and could not find it. I was under the water and seemingly unable to stand up—I have no real idea why; my feel just kept on slipping. Fortunately, I was at the edge of the pool, and a teacher, seeing my problem, simply reached in, and pulled me up by grabbing hold of my swimming cap.

The squiggly lines I had drawn were the pattern my feet made as they scrambled to find purchase on the floor of the pool. The significance of the event was that it had scared the daylights out of me, but I never told anyone about my level of fear. The ball of fear was locked away in my subconscious with the rest of my growing pile of insecurities and feelings of inadequacy, and just quietly seeped out into other areas of my life at inopportune times.

Negative Programming

The hypnotherapy was very effective—not 100%, but enough to bring me significant relief. The incomplete result could have been because I never really finished as I changed jobs and moved away. But the results were ample for me to see firsthand the kinds of effects negative programming had had on seemingly unrelated parts of my life.

I found the entire experience fascinating—not only was there some rhyme and reason to the workings of the mind, but it could be accessed and tweaked to enhance the quality of our lives. By the time I had just a few months of hypnotherapy, I found myself enrolled in hypnotherapy school and spent the next three years studying it for myself.

I had just started my hypnotherapy practice when I heard about a special two-day workshop being hosted by the hypnotherapy school I had attended— a workshop on subliminal information processing taught by preconscious processing expert Eldon Taylor. This one workshop led me to spend the next thirty-plus years studying the inner working of the mind with a sharp focus on very practical applications.

Meditations

As I said, meditation is akin to self-hypnosis. While meditation is often associated with spiritual practices, it is not synonymous with spirituality. If spirituality is not your thing, then please do not discard the idea of adding meditation to your repertoire of self-empowerment tools. Meditation has huge benefits, regardless of whether it is spiritual or secular—the only difference between the two meditative processes is whether you wish to add spiritual elements into the storyline as you guide your body into a more relaxed state. It comes down to personal preference.

While being far from unusual for me to come across scientific papers demonstrating the benefits of meditation, one series of papers caught my attention.

- In 2009, Dharma Singh Khalsa, M.D. president and medical director of the Alzheimer's Research & Prevention Foundation, and his colleagues showed cerebral blood flow changes during a specific chanting meditation. Significant evidence suggests that reduced cerebral blood flow is associated with higher Alzheimer's risk, as well as its rapid progression.[4]
- In 2010, a preliminary study carried out at the University of Pennsylvania Medical School by neuroscientist Andrew Newberg and colleagues showed the effects on cognitive function and cerebral blood flow in subjects with memory loss. After 8 weeks of this practice, it was shown that memory loss was reversed as compared to the control subjects.[5]
- In 2010, a study carried out by Andrew Newberg and his team showed an anti-aging effect when meditation is practiced over the long term.[6] The cerebral blood

flow of advanced meditators was compared with that of non-meditators. "The observed changes associated with long-term meditation appear in structures that underlie the attention network and also those that relate to emotion and autonomic function."[7]

- A 2012 paper by Aleezé Sattar Moss and colleagues looked at the effects of an eight-week meditation program on mood and anxiety in patients with memory loss. The study concluded that "An eight-week, twelve-minute-a-day meditation program in patients with memory loss was associated with positive changes in mood, anxiety, and other neuropsychologic parameters, and these changes correlated with changes in cerebral blood flow."[8]
- A 2013 paper by Helen Lavretsky and colleagues showed that 65% of the subjects experienced a 50% improvement in depression using the Hamilton Depression Rating scale. The improvement was "accompanied by an increase in telomerase activity, suggesting improvement in stress-induced cellular aging."[9]
- In a 2018 study, Kim Innes and colleagues found that a twelve-week meditation program was associated with improvements in cognitive function, sleep, mood, and quality of life.[10]

So according to these papers, meditation can improve many areas including memory, cognitive abilities, mood states, anxiety, depression, stress, and perhaps even aging. What drew significant attention to this series of studies was that while other studies found benefits from extensive training and long meditation periods, these studies showed that a simple twelve-minute meditation had an even stronger effect.[11] What was even more startling is that all these studies used the same twelve-minute meditation practice, and solid results were achieved after just eight weeks. But something about these studies led me to investigate further. In the process, I analyzed the mechanics behind the meditation and then personalized it according to my preferences.

Sa Ta Na Ma Meditation

I learned about the first of these papers in 2011. Eldon came into my office and told me about a study that showed how a simple meditation process resulted in memory improvements in patients suffering from dementia. He told me that the meditation involved the repeated chanting of four words plus the use of specific mudras. At that time, I had no idea what mudras were, but the four words caught my attention—Sa, Ta, Na, Ma.

Some things are just printed indelibly in your being. I was brought up a Sikh (a religion born in Punjab, India in the fifteenth century), and for a while at least, I was very devout. Just as the *Lord's Prayer* is very important to Christians, so is the *Japji Sahib* prayer to the Sikhs. The Guru Granth Sahib (the holy scriptures) begins with the Japji Sahib—the morning prayer:

IkOnkar, Sat Nam, Karta Purakh, Nirbhao, Nirvair,
Akal Moorat, Ajuni Saibangh, Gur Parsad,
Jap,
Aad Such, Jugaad Such Hai Bi Such, Nanak Hosi Bhi Such.

(God is one, True is his name, the creator, without fear, without enmity, never dies, beyond birth and death, self-illuminated, realized by the grace of the true Guru.
Repeat his name.
True in the beginning, true ever since, true now, Nanak says he will always be true.)

This part of the prayer is the Mool Mantra—the fundamental spiritual doctrine for Sikhs. This prayer is so important that in some households, children may be taught the Mool Mantra as soon as they have learned to say Dada and Mama. My upbringing was just like this, so even though I rejected formalized religion decades ago, and even when the sounds were drastically distorted, I still believed I was hearing the words that are so sacred to Sikhs: was Sa Ta Na Ma supposed to be SatNam?

Kirtan Kriya

I investigated this further. At the time, some reports were touting it as a purely secular meditation. I suppose to someone unfamiliar with the words, it would be secular—just a series of random sounds. In other accounts, the words were said to be Sanskrit for birth, life, death, and rebirth. While I had once been a devout Sikh, I was never a Sikh scholar. However, I have never heard that SatNam—true name—had any other meanings.

With a bit more digging around, I found that this meditation was created by Yogi Har Bhajan Singh, now known just as Yogi Bhajan, and is practiced by his adherents, the Sikh Dharma, also known affectionately as the *American Sikhs*. I have known about Yogi Bhajan since I was a young child and have seen him several times. While many of his practices were frowned upon by traditional Sikhs (he made a lot of stuff up and introduced ideas not based on Sikh teachings), I have always had a great admiration for his followers. The American Sikhs I met over the years all exuded a serene captivating spirituality, and I always felt I gained something from speaking with them and spending time in their company. The meditation used in all these studies was designed by Yogi Bhajan and is called *Kirtan Kriya*.

According to a White Paper put out by Dharma Singh Khalsa, one of the researchers on all the studies mentioned above, once you are in a traditional meditation mode (sitting in an upright but comfortable position, breathing naturally, and closing your eyes), there are three elements to this mediation.

First, there is the chanting of Sa Ta Na Ma – starting fully audibly for two minutes, then whispered for two minutes, then silently for four minutes, then whispered for two minutes, and then fully audibly again for two minutes. (The entire meditation takes twelve minutes.) The chanting should also be done in a sing-song voice, following the first four notes of "Mary Had a Little Lamb". So,

Ma – ry – had - a
Sa – ta – na - ma

Second, mudra, or finger movements, are performed with both hands at the same time.

Sa – touch the index finger to the thumb.
Ta – touch the middle finger to the thumb.
Na – touch the ring finger to the thumb.
Ma – touch the little finger to the thumb.

According to Khalsa, this order must always be followed and never reversed.

Thirdly, add a visualization – picture energy coming into the top of your head and then going out forwards, at the middle of your forehead – the third eye. The path of the energy following the shape of a capital L.[12]

Fact from Fiction

This meditation undoubtedly works. While Khalsa was involved in all the studies in some capacity, many other researchers were as well. The papers also appeared in highly reputable publications and journals. But it was through searching for 'why' it works that provided my epiphany.

Hypnotic Beat

Sa Ta Na Ma repeated is simply a 4/4 beat—four beats to each bar. This beat becomes a bit hypnotic, somewhat akin to the sound of a metronome. The slow even pace aids the hypnotic process. The 4/4 beat is often how I hear my feet pounding the pavement during a run—a sound that frequently puts me into a meditative state. Whether at a gentle run or in full meditation pose, this 4/4 beat works well to relax the body and keep the heart rate even and slow, while also slowing down brainwave activity. Some of my clearest thinking and best creative ideas often occur when I am on a run, listening to that 1-2-3-4, 1-2-3-4 pattern repeating over and over. (Interestingly, when I would count the 1-2-3-4s during my runs, I would use tones similar to that found in the first four notes of Mary Had a Little Lamb, emphasizing the 1, dropping the notes for 2 and 3, and then raising it again for 4.) So the hypnotic beat makes sense, but what about the words used?

Sacred Words

While you can find the 'birth, life, death, rebirth' translation in Yogi Bhajan's writings and on blogs that have not updated their information, it has now been removed from the materials put out by the American Sikhs. Today, only the original (True Name) translation is used. I can only assume that Sikh scholars objected to this alteration to the meaning and requested it be corrected. However, to believers, these words have sacred meanings, and to non-Sikhs who participated in the study, these words would gain significance simply because of their use in the experiment. Faith, whether in science or religion, can bring its own benefits, allowing for a deepening of the relaxation process.

Sacred Sounds

It was my understanding of the words and their origins that led me to conclude they are not an important element in this meditation.

OM is considered by many to be a sacred sound. In the same vein, some believe Sa Ta Na Ma to be sacred sounds too. However, Sa Ta Na Ma is a very distorted version of SatNam. Would OM remain a sacred sound if it were changed to O oo Mm eh?

According to Khalsa's White Paper, the tongue placement with the Sa Ta Na Ma mantra stimulates the eighty-four acupuncture meridian points in the roof of the mouth. This may not be the case for American Sikhs who have been taught the correct pronunciation of Sat Nam, but for those not familiar with Indian words, the sounds and tongue placement could be very different. Rather than 'Sa' as in sardonic, the correct sound is more 'Su' as in such. Rather than the 't' in 'Ta' being pronounced like the 't' in tons, with the tongue flicking the roof of the mouth, the correct sound is between 'th' as in that and 't' as in Tom and has a more plosive sound. And the sound is not Ta but more like 'teh' as in 'meh.' Na should be pronounced like 'nar' as opposed to 'nat', and Ma is more 'meh' if it is extended at all.

The power of this meditation cannot lie in sacred sounds or the activations of meridian points, for the fact remains that the meditation works for those who pronounce the words correctly with religious humility as well as those who have no idea what it means or how to pronounce them. In place of religious humility, it is possible that non-Sikh participants of the study simply believed the words must have some effect, and this belief could have contributed to the efficacy of the meditation.

Focus

One of the problems virtually everyone has when first learning how to meditate is the idea that you must clear your mind of thoughts. Most people find that, as soon as they tell themselves to stop thinking, their minds get flooded with thoughts. Repeating the sounds, though, works to focus the mind and rein in the usual non-stop inner chatter. In the same way, performing the mudras provides additional focus. A more traditional approach could be in the use of a mala, or prayer beads.

The visualization exercise could well add another layer to the focus, while also giving the mind permission to take in relaxing, purifying energy, and either releasing negativity or affirming inner strength that it projects out into the world.

If you remember earlier when I described how I practice diaphragmatic breathing, I said I would visualize the breath going up my back during the inhalation, rounding my shoulders, and then flowing down my front. When I am meditating, I send the mental energy of my breath even higher, so that rather than rounding over my shoulders, it stretches up to reach several feet above my head before flowing back down again. I actively aim to release tension and anxiety during the exhalation and reach for calmness, comfort, and positive energy during the inhalation. This is just something I do instinctively.

The mantra focuses the speech centers, the mudras focus the sense of touch, the visualization focuses the mind, the repetition calms and relaxes, and your beliefs (in the spiritual or science) empower the entire process.

Personalize

The Sa Ta Na Ma meditation, just as it is described earlier, has been extensively studied and proved effective. However, if you wish to personalize the process but still retain the essential elements, in place of Sa Ta Na Ma you could try some other four- (or eight-)beat statement you find significant. If

MIND TRAINING

you have religious leanings, you may like to use something you like from your scriptures. If I felt a need to go back to my Sikh roots, because of its habituated familiarity and childhood sense of comfort, I would work with:

Aad Waheguru, Jugaad Waheguru, Hai bhi Waheguru, Hosi Waheguru.

Wonderous God who was True in the beginning, Wonderous God who was true ever since,

Wonderous God who is still true, Wonderous God who will forever be true.

1	2	3	4	1	2	3	4
Aad	Wa-	he-	guru,	Jugaad	Wa-	whe-	guru

1	2	3	4	1	2	3	4
Hai bhi	Wa-	he-	guru,	Hosi	Wa-	he-	guru

This is sixteen beats (or four bars of 4/4 time), but the effect is the same. The additional benefit for Sikhs would be the sense of completeness as this mantra is repeated almost every time a Sikh service is held.

Catholics may like to use:

1	2	3	4
Holy	Mary	Mother of	God,

Buddhists may prefer to use:

1	2	3	4
Om	mane	padme	hum,

The jewel is in the lotus

Christians may like to use:

1	2	3	4
	Je-	sus	loves	me

Or:

1	2	3	4
Be	still	and	know

If you prefer something non-spiritual, then try something that makes you feel warm and happy. Be careful of using an affirmation, though, since, if some part of you does not believe the affirmation, this could create a little psychic tension, which is the opposite of what you are trying to achieve. Alternatively, just stick with the proven:

1	2	3	4
Sa	Ta	Na	Ma

For my Sikh version, I would not do this to the tune of Mary Had a Little Lamb. Instead, I would use the tune I heard virtually every week as a child when my family would go to the Sikh Gurudwara (temple)—a sound that still has the power to make me think of unity and awe. Interestingly, the sounds are rather like Mary Had a Little Lamb. For those who like to use the Buddhist mantra, "Om mane padme hum," it may feel even better to use "Mane padme Oo Om, Mane padem Om - " along with the tune that frequently accompanies it. Mantras often have a musical lilt to them. As such, I do not believe that the four notes that start *Mary Had a Little Lamb* have any real significance. Use them if you wish or use another of your preference.

The important part of the discussion regarding this meditation is in gaining an understanding of why the different aspects work and then finding ways to make it more comfortable for you. When you understand the mechanisms, you can remove the mystique and rituals, and instead rely on science.

Emotional Freedom Technique (EFT)

You can apply other areas to the same analytical process. One such process is the Emotional Freedom Technique (EFT), also known as tapping. Several studies have demonstrated the efficacy of Tapping as a treatment for depression,[13] PTSD,[14] anxiety,[15] and much more.[16] The research is abundant enough that it appears on WebMD[17] and amongst suggestions on Kaiser Permanente's website.[18] However, I remain skeptical, especially when I look at the quality of the studies and the kinds of publications they appear in. Most of the results are based more on anecdotal accounts, which are not scientific. My skepticism is also validated by other researchers as they believe the effects obtained are caused by other factors.

A 2013 study looking at treatments for fear was conducted by Wendy Waite (University of Lethbridge, Canada) and Mark Holder (Okanagan University College, Canada). The researchers divided 119 students into four groups: "applied treatment of EFT (Group EFT); a placebo treatment (Group P); a modeling treatment (Group M); and a control (Group C)." They found that, while the EFT group showed a "significant decrease in self-report measures at post-treatment," so did the placebo and modeling groups. The researchers concluded that "these results suggest that the reported effectiveness of EFT is attributable to characteristics it shares with more traditional therapies."[19] This conclusion makes sense. While EFT is supposed to gain part of its effect from tapping on meridians, as is the case with acupressure and acupuncture, practitioners say it does not matter where you tap, which invalidates the meridian argument. The process of tapping, though, *would* create a focus and a relaxation response (a mechanical response as we have seen with other techniques), and the question-and-answer process is then free association thinking encouraged by the tapping. Interesting responses are displayed when someone is told to say the first thing that comes to mind. Many EFT sessions also include meditations, so the slower breathing, gentle music, and soothing voice will cause the subject to feel calmer.

Labyrinth

I have also applied the same analytical approach to walking a labyrinth. Walking a labyrinth is a spiritual practice generally used for contemplation or prayer. The use of labyrinths can be found across many cultures and religions, from the Hopi Native Americans to the Celts, from Christianity to Hinduism. The oldest labyrinth is supposed to be the Cretan Labyrinth from 1200 B.C.E. Greece.

While I have never been interested in labyrinths, Eldon and I did get the opportunity to walk one a few years ago when we visited Zion National Park. The hotel we usually stayed at is very close to the entrance of the park. It was under new management, and we learned they had built a labyrinth at the back of the property. I wanted to try the labyrinth more for a laugh than anything else. The first time we went up there was just before sunset. Built right above the hotel and looking toward the park, the atmosphere itself was magical; it is obvious why Zion was considered sacred ground to the Piute Indians. At first, I simply started walking, head held high and feeling a little silly. But then I went looking for the 'something special' that many report feeling in a labyrinth. Breathing slowly and evenly, I absorbed the atmosphere of Zion through all my senses, entered the labyrinth in a state of humility, and focused on each footstep. In the process, I felt myself relax, my inner chatter diminished, and my mind emptied its clutter, allowing space for ideas and insights to flow.

Walking a labyrinth can be a very calming and healing experience, so much so they can even be found at hospitals such as the Antioch Medical Center in Northern California and Georgetown University Medical Center. According to Karen Leland, writing for WebMD, "more than 100 hospitals, hospices, and health care facilities in the U.S. have walkable labyrinths."[20] But do the benefits come from walking a certain path—how significant is the labyrinth itself?

Being outdoors, taking time to appreciate nature and the fresh air, and hopefully getting a little sun are all ways to boost the brain's serotonin production, one of the feel-good chemicals. Walking a labyrinth almost requires looking down, walking slowly, and focusing on each step, which would result in a lower heart rate and slower brainwave activity. For me, walking the labyrinth in Zion, I could also have had a boost of oxytocin—I felt connected to the spiritual part of the world, it was sunset, and I was with my husband. As I walked slowly through the labyrinth, contemplating each step, I would have entered a meditative state. As my system relaxed, inspiration had space to flow in. These all provide very scientific explanations for a spiritual experience.

What's the Deal?

So why does any of this matter? Why dissect and analyze these processes? You don't have to understand any of this for these techniques to benefit you.

Earlier I shared with you an exercise for demonstrating how mechanical the mind is. This is the exercise where you pick up your right foot and begin to move it in a clockwise circle. (This is best done in a sitting position.) Then, while your foot circles in a clockwise fashion, raise your right hand, and draw the number six in the air with your forefinger. Most people find that the foot automatically reverses course and moves in an anti-clockwise direction instead.

For me, looking behind the curtains of the Kirtan Kriya meditation was like a smack around the head in my deeper understanding of the mechanical nature of the brain. Sometimes you can have an entire picture in front of you but still not see it. For years, Eldon has been speaking of the mechanical nature of the brain and how, with a little understanding of the mechanisms, we can take ourselves (at least a part of ourselves) off automatic pilot and move into manual mode. Then, rather than going where our subconscious programming wishes to take us, we can tweak the programming so we can go where *we* choose to go.

Dissecting the Kirtan Kriya, Tapping, and Labyrinth processes gives us a greater appreciation for both the power of our minds and more importantly, the degree of control we can have if we so choose. Rather than relying on 'magical' solutions, we can use techniques backed by hard science. With both Tapping and other new age techniques, people have complained that the techniques did not work for them, only for them to be told the reason was that they did not do it 'right,' did not 'believe enough,' were 'resisting the process,' or some other comment that implied they were not worthy. They are then encouraged to just trust their teachers and continue with the process for as long as it takes to reach the appropriate stage of their development. When you take the time to understand the processes behind the techniques, you gain the ability to make the techniques work for you. You can also remove those aspects that are just smoke and mirrors—things that look impressive but that have no real function. Of equal importance, don't end up thinking you are deficient when you are told it's your fault it did not work for you.

Eldon once shared an extreme example that can highlight this concept. Say you were having open-heart surgery, and say you were on the table for six hours. To help pass the time, some surgeons have general conversations with their colleagues while they wield their scalpel in the patient's chest, and others prefer to play their favorite music. But what if your surgeon was into self-help, so the entire time you were on the operating table, unknown to you, they played a motivation program that consisted solely of creativity affirmations? We have already discussed the problems that can arise with using audible affirmations, but for you, under anesthesia, these affirmations become subliminal—no internal sentry argues against the messages. So, the surgery is over and is a complete success. Going back to work, you find that original ideas not only flow to you in abundance, but for the first time in your life, you find yourself following through and acting on these ideas. You become hugely prosperous as a result, and you tie this back directly to your surgery. Would you advocate open-heart surgery for the sole purpose of becoming rich and famous?

Understanding how the processes work gives you a greater ability to customize self-empowerment plans that work best for you and provides the tools for you to tweak the process to make it even more effective for your needs. This is empowering.

NOTES

Key Points

Like a regular physical exercise program, taking time to slow down your brainwave activity can bring benefits across the board, from health and well-being to learning and creativity.

Meditation, hypnosis (including self-hypnosis), and mindfulness all use similar techniques—controlled breathing, progressive relaxation, and visualization. The techniques vary on *what* is being visualized. In a spiritual meditation, there may be a reaching out to a religious leader or a sensing of God's presence. A secular meditation could involve focusing on the relaxation response and enjoying the sense of calm. In hypnosis, visualizations are aimed either at picturing successful outcomes or at uncovering memories or traumas. In mindfulness, there is the quiet observation and guiding of thoughts.

Kirtan Kriya—more commonly known as the Sa Ta Na Ma meditation has been shown to bring many benefits, including memory, cognitive abilities, mood states, anxiety, depression, stress, and even perhaps aging. There are also indications of its potential to slow Alzheimer's progression. There have been several studies on Kirtan Kriya, involving different researchers, that have been published in reputable journals. The full technique was provided.

Kirtan Kriya was then dissected to analyze the individual components. While non-scientists may find it unusual to question studies, this is an important part of mind training—to think about and gain an understanding of the whys and hows behind self-empowerment techniques.

In the analysis, we saw how the 4/4 beat could slow heart rate and brain wave activity, bringing a sense of calmness. We saw how giving the hands and mind something to do could reduce the inner chatter that crowds the mind as soon as we try to empty it of thoughts. We then learned how to take these elements and personalize this meditation process.

We took a quick look at how both Emotional Freedom Technique (EFT, also known as Tapping) and labyrinth walking could gain their effects. By understanding *why* these techniques can be beneficial, we are no longer bound by the mystique and rituals that often surround these kinds of teachings. Instead, you are empowered to make these processes your own, thereby opening new pathways for you to explore.

Exercise

First, try the Sa Ta Na Ma meditation for yourself. Aim to do this once a day for eight weeks. This will be easier for you to accomplish if you set a particular time for it. Before work in the morning would be ideal. Feel free to do this more than once a day if you wish—just be sure to do it *at least* once a day.

(To assist you with this meditation, we have created a few audio programs with tones at the two-minute marks. For your free copies, please visit mind-training.org.)

Journal daily and note your feelings and any changes. Pay particular attention to your anxiety/happiness levels, but also see what kind of ripple effect this exercise has on other parts of your daily life.

Next, if you so wish, try your personalized version of the meditation.

Again, journal daily and note your feelings and any changes. Pay particular attention to your anxiety/happiness levels, but also see what kind of ripple effect this has on other aspects of your daily life.

At the end of the sixteen weeks, note any differences and decide which version you will continue to use in your daily routine. (If you do try your personalized version, please write, and let me know what you used and how it worked for you.)

Check out some other meditations—many are available online. We also offer meditation and self-hypnosis programs at InnerTalk. Try out some different techniques then assess their efficacy.

CHAPTER THIRTEEN

OTHER TOOLS

The expectations of life depend upon diligence; the mechanic that would perfect his work must first sharpen his tools.

~ Confucius

I started learning how to drive in the late 1970s. Because many of my classmates were also taking driving lessons, a teacher decided to give us a special lesson and take us over the basics of engine and car maintenance. I learned about checking the oil level, making sure water was in the radiator, where the spark plugs were, including the possibility of needing to clean them periodically, where the air filter was, etc. It was only a one-off lesson, though, and I still found the car engine intimidating—something to be revered and left to the experts to fix.

Not long after I met Eldon, he took me on a trip from Las Vegas to Zion, Utah. Driving across the Mojave Desert, the car started to overheat. Eldon stopped the car a couple of times to give it a chance to cool down, and then he simply removed the thermostat. Even though he has since explained to me why this was okay to do, I still cannot fathom it. However, because he did this, the car was able to get us to the next town with an auto parts store. There, Eldon purchased a new thermostat, installed it in the car, and soon we were back on track for our weekend away. However, if Eldon had not understood how the engine worked, we would never have been able to make it to that little town—we would have broken down, and as that was before cell phones, we would have had to flag someone down for help.

Since then, I have seen Eldon do plenty of strange (to me) fixes on cars, including using zip ties and sticky tack! While many of these fixes could have me looking askance, I have also heard him speaking to several mechanic friends who agreed with his remedies—in fact, they often commended him on his ingenuity.

Today, many newer cars come with the engine covered. Rather than exposing all those intimidating elements, they have a neat black cover with cheat areas. The battery is not visible and jump-starting the car entails finding the bolt attached to the firewall, which is often colored red and with small print saying something like, 'positive battery.' You should also know to find a bolt or something to attach to the ground, but that is just a detail.

Mind/Brain

The mind, rooted in the organ brain, is intimidating to almost everyone other than perhaps neurosurgeons. For all practical reasons, I like to think of it like the covered car engine, with many easy access points that you can adjust, tweak, or tune up to enhance performance. The access points are not physical, but rather mental. Knowing how to access them can afford you many opportunities to take charge of your own life, prevent you from getting stuck, and assist you in reaching your goals/destination.

We have discussed many of the mind training techniques in detail. Here are some additional techniques that can enhance your self-empowerment journey.

Gratitude

Taking time to be grateful is currently a popular subject, but is there more to this than just the ability to feel good for a short while? According to Joshua Brown and Joel Wong (both at Indiana University Bloomington), "Many studies over the past decade have found that people who consciously count their blessings tend to be happier and less depressed."[1] But the important question here is, is it a proneness to gratitude that improves a person's life, or does actively practicing acts of gratitude cause the improvement?

In a 2016 study of gratitude at UC Berkeley carried out by Brown, Wong, and team, 293 adults who had sought university-based psychotherapy were divided into three groups. All three groups received psychotherapy, with the first group acting as the control. The second group was asked to write letters expressing their feelings about stressful experiences. The third group was asked to write letters expressing gratitude to others. When questioned four and twelve weeks after the end of the experiment, it was found that the "gratitude condition reported significantly better mental health than those in the expressive and control conditions, whereas those in the expressive and control conditions did not differ significantly."[2]

Eldon and I try every day to acknowledge gratitude for things in our lives. Eldon likes to start off each day with a "Thank you, thank you, thank you." He says starting the day this way invariably creates a better day. My own approach is more one of looking at the things I have to do and finding ways to be grateful; I actively appreciate my dishwasher when it comes to cleaning up after dinner, and when I have to run the vacuum cleaner, I frequently think of the times when people had to take their rugs outdoors, hang them on the line, and beat the dirt out of them. Before we go to sleep each night, we also invariably end up thanking each other—for being who we are, doing all that we do, being a great companion, and more. When you decide to focus on all you can be grateful for, the list will amaze you.

Laughter

In 1964, Norman Cousins, editor-in-chief of the *Saturday Review* from 1942-1972, returned from a trip to Russia with a slight fever. Within a week he found it difficult to move his neck, arms, hands, fingers, and legs and was soon hospitalized. Blood tests indicated a high level of inflammation, and it was thought he suffered from the kind of connective tissue disease found in arthritis or rheumatic conditions. His illness quickly progressed, and he soon found it difficult to move, nodules appeared over his body, and at one point his jaws were almost locked. In time he was diagnosed with ankylosing spondylitis with a 1/500 chance of recovering. Determined to increase the odds in his favor, Cousins examined everything that led up to his becoming sick—the frustrations he had experienced on his trip to Russia, the high exposure to diesel exhaust on that trip, and the amount of stress he had endured.

Cousins became unhappy with the care he received at the hospital and suspected that the treatments he was given were making him worse. Working closely with his doctor, Cousins theorized that super-high levels of vitamin C could combat the collagen breakdown he was experiencing. He also theorized that if negative emotions produced negative reactions in the body, then wouldn't positive emotions produce positive reactions? Cousins then started a regime of a vitamin C drip along with a non-stop stream of funny movies, such as the *Candid Camera* series and Marx Brothers.

Cousins states that ten minutes of genuine belly laughter had an anesthetic effect and would give him at least two hours of pain-free sleep. When the anesthetic effects wore off, he would simply turn the movies back on again. Sometimes the nurse would also read to Cousins from humorous books, such as Max Eastman's *The Enjoyment of Laughter*. Blood tests confirmed that the laughing sessions led to a decrease in Cousins' inflammation numbers. The only problem with this treatment protocol was that Cousins' laughter was disturbing the other patients. Cousins then checked himself out of the hospital and into a comfortable hotel room where he continued his treatment. His improvements continued, and though it took months, Cousins eventually returned to work. In time, he made an almost total recovery and was back playing golf and tennis.[3] In a subsequent interview, Cousins made it clear that his message could be misunderstood and oversimplified. As a clarification, he stated that "We mustn't regard any of this as a substitute for competent medical attention. But the doctor can only do half the job. The other half is the patient's response to the illness. What we really mean by a patient's responsibility is that we've got vast powers that are rarely used. It's important to avoid defeatism and a sense of panic and despair. But that's not an excuse for not seeking medical help."[4]

Norman Cousins' story is often provided as proof of the healing power of laughter, but one anecdote does not constitute proof of any kind. Several studies have since demonstrated the health benefits of laughing. Here is a small sample:

- Robin Dunbar (University of Oxford, UK) showed that laughter increased pain thresholds. Watching about fifteen minutes of comedy with a group increased pain thresholds by an average of 10%. Watching the comedies alone showed a slightly smaller increase. "The researchers believe that the long series of exhalations that accompany true laughter cause physical exhaustion of the abdominal muscles and, in turn, trigger endorphin release."[5]
- A 2011 study out of Israel found that women undergoing in-vitro fertilization were 2.67 times more likely to get pregnant if they were visited by a trained 'medical clown' for fifteen minutes immediately after the embryos were placed in the womb. The idea was to reduce the stress and thereby reap the psychological benefits.[6]
- A 2009 study found that laughter decreased arterial wall stiffness and cortisol levels while increasing the total oxidative status. Increasing stress levels had the opposite effect.[7] So laughing is good for the heart and could reduce issues related to cardiovascular disease.
- A 2001 study showed that mirthful laughter boosted the immune system by decreasing stress hormones and increasing infection-fighting antibodies, thus improving disease resistance.[8]
- A 2021 paper discusses the fact that laughter suppresses the bioactivities of epinephrine and cortisol (stress factors) while enhancing dopamine and serotonin (mood-elevating and stress-reducing factors). Laughter therapy can therefore be used to reduce anxiety and depression.[9]

But what if you don't find many things that funny? Well, it turns out that a simulated laugh can also be beneficial. A Georgia State University study looked at adding simulated laughter to a moderate-intensity group exercise program. For six weeks, the "study participants attended two forty-five-minute physical activity sessions per week that included eight to ten laughter exercises lasting thirty to sixty seconds each."[10] "Significant improvements were observed in mental health, aerobic endurance (two-minute step test), and self-efficacy for exercise."[11]

The body cannot distinguish between real, humor-based laughter, and self-initiated laughter, but making yourself laugh, especially when you engage in this exercise with others, can quickly lead to real laughter—and laughter is contagious. Regardless of whether the laughter is real or simulated, positive benefits result.

Singing

I enjoy singing, not necessarily the formal choir or solo performance kind of singing, but rather the car or shower singing. The kind of singing that happens when I am all alone. Many times I was the last to leave the office. Invariably I have been working on some project with that feeling of needing to get a lot done in a short time. Sometimes I am filled with a sense of accomplishment, and other times I am tired and need to knock off and get some rest so I will feel better to tackle more tomorrow. Regardless of how I feel, as I start to pack up and turn off the lights, I will invariably burst out into song. And not the quiet, sing-to-myself kind of thing, but rather the full-blast, fill-the-entire-building kind of song. The kind of singing that knows it matters not one iota if I miss more notes than I hit.

We instinctively seem to know that singing will release tension, open the body and lungs, and maybe even provide some feeling of connectedness. At least, that is my experience, and science backs it up.

- A 2021 study found a drop in the stress hormone cortisol in saliva after singing as compared to before. This drop was found whether the person was singing in a group or by themselves.[12] However, a similar 2015 study showed that this only held in situations that did not add their own stressors, such as in an important performance.[13] Additionally, another 2021 study showed an increase in the happy brain chemical oxytocin as a result of group singing.[14]

- The University of Helsinki carried out a study using 162 healthy older subjects, looking at cognition, mood, social engagement, quality of life, and the role of music in daily life. They found that "in healthy older adults, regular choir singing is associated with better verbal flexibility. Longstanding choir activity is linked to better social engagement and more recently commenced choir activity to better general health."[15]
- Daisy Fancourt and team (University College London, UK) studied the effects of group singing in bereavement, looking specifically at mental health, self-efficacy, self-esteem, and well-being. They found that "Participants who sang in a choir had more stable symptoms of depression and levels of well-being, as well as gradual improvements in their sense of self-efficacy and self-esteem over the twenty-four weeks. In contrast, the control group showed gradual increases in depressive symptoms, reductions in levels of wellbeing and self-esteem and no improvement in their self-efficacy."[16]
- A literature review of studies about singing and lung health showed that singing "has the potential to have a positive impact on the lives of people with lung disease, improving health status and social participation."[17] According to the *British Lung Foundation*, people with chronic obstructive pulmonary disease (COPD) have reported that regular singing led to a reduction in feelings of being short of breath and feeling more in control of symptoms.[18]
- Singing even stimulates the immune response. A 2004 study looked at the effects of singing on secretory

immunoglobulin A (S-IgA), cortisol, and emotional states. The results showed an increase in immunoglobulin A and positive mood states and a decrease in cortisol.[19]
- Another study found that, in addition to having a positive impact on relationships and emotional well-being in both dementia patients and their caregivers, singing also stimulated memory. This was not just in the patient's ability to remember the lyrics of the song, but also other life memories.[20]

Singing can often provide a way to clear out cobwebs and allow for clearer thinking. I remember as a student, I often took singing breaks. I used to play the harmonium and nothing worked better for removing the feeling of an overly full brain from exam cramming than playing a tune and belting out a song.

Awe

Although awe is defined as an emotion that is reverential respect mixed with fear or wonder, negative awe is still considered a very different emotion from positive awe. The positive awe is what I wish to discuss here.

Feelings of awe have been shown to make people feel like they have more time (they are less stressed and rushed), and as a result, they can feel more patient. Inspired by awe, people are more willing to help others and more likely to experience greater life satisfaction. The researchers in one study stated that "Awe can be elicited by reliving a memory, reading a brief story, or even watching a sixty-second commercial."[21]

In a 2018 study, researchers showed that feelings of awe proved therapeutic for military veterans, at-risk youths, and college students. In the first part of this study, veterans and at-risk youths were taken on a one- or four-day whitewater rafting trip and asked to keep a daily diary, with an emphasis on reporting emotions, cognitions, and social experiences. Improvements were found in well-being and stress-related symptoms. In the second part of this study, for fourteen days students were asked to keep a specific online diary that prompted reports on emotions, social experiences, and thoughts they experienced that day. On the days the diary accounts included aspects of being in nature, not only were there improvements in well-being and stress, but also in contentment and gratitude.[22]

It would be easy to think that experiencing awe is something that only occurs under special circumstances, like visiting the Grand Canyon, but this is not so. In a 2020 study, sixty healthy older adults were asked to take weekly fifteen-minute outdoor walks over eight weeks. The control group was simply asked to walk, while the test group was oriented to experience awe during the walk. The awe-walk group "reported greater joy and prosocial positive emotions during their walks and displayed increasing smile intensity over the study. Outside of the walk context, participants who took awe walks reported greater increases in daily prosocial positive emotions and greater decreases in daily distress over time."[23]

Experiencing awe can also have a positive effect on your health. A 2015 study found that people who experienced more awe also showed lower levels of chronic pro-inflammatory cytokines. High levels of pro-inflammatory cytokines have been associated with several chronic conditions, such as diabetes, heart disease, and depression.[24]

Another aspect of experiencing awe is that it can make you feel smaller, and in this context, this can be a good thing. Awe can make us feel like we are part of a much larger picture and feeling humbled can make us want to engage and connect more with others. In a 2018 study, those who reported experiencing awe more frequently in their daily lives were rated as humbler by their friends. Also, after experiencing awe (by watching inspiring videos), participants "acknowledged strengths and weaknesses in a more balanced way and were more likely to recognize the role of outside forces (such as luck, a greater being, or others) in their personal accomplishments (such as getting accepted into a university), compared with individuals who had not watched awe-inspiring videos."[25] As such, encouraging each other to find ways to feel awe could be a way to bring people together more harmoniously.

Taking the time to appreciate small details when you are outdoors is all you need to experience awe. While out on a walk, look for the impressive cloud formation, a beautiful and perfectly proportioned tree, a flowering weed pushing up through the tiniest crack in the asphalt, and so on. Nature offers an abundance of opportunities to experience awe. But nature does not hold the monopoly on awe, for it can be found almost anywhere and at any time. All you need do is slow down and appreciate the moment. Awe can be found in the awareness of the life that courses through you, the sounds of children playing, the joy of shared laughter, the warmth of your partner's hand, the quiet breathing of your pet while it sleeps at your feet, music that lifts your spirits or expands your awareness, art that speaks on many levels, talented performers, the perfection of a baby while it nurses or sucks on a bottle, and on and on.

Walking

Many more benefits stand to be gained from walking beyond the opportunities to experience awe. According to a *Walking for Health* Harvard article, walking for just 2.5 hours a week, that is twenty-one minutes a day, can reduce your risk of heart disease by 30%. Walking has also "been shown to reduce the risk of diabetes and cancer, lower blood pressure and cholesterol, and keep you mentally sharp."[26]

In a 2018 study, Meghan Edwards and Paul Loprinzi (both at the University of Mississippi) looked at the effects of a single bout of either meditation or walking on mood states. They found that "a ten-minute bout of brisk walking and meditation both improved mood state, when compared to an inactive control group."[27] Walking can therefore be of great benefit, particularly at stressful times when quieting the mind for meditation can prove too challenging.

A study out of Duke University found that a brisk thirty-minute walk or jog could be as effective as medications at treating depression. With all the possibilities of side effects from medications, walking, where possible, seems to be the preferable option. While the subjects who took the medications did show improvements sooner, by sixteen weeks, this difference had disappeared.[28] Some of these benefits possibly come from something known as optic flow. "Optic flow is the visual motion that results from an observer's own movement through the environment."[29] According to Andrew Huberman (Stanford University), "The actual movement of objects past us as we walk quiets some of the circuits that are responsible for stress."[30]

A Stanford University study showed that walking also enhances creativity, regardless of whether the activity happens outdoors or on a treadmill. While walking outdoors gave the biggest boost to creativity, there was still an increase when the walking occurred on a treadmill facing a blank wall. As a bonus, this increase in creative ability persisted after the conclusion of the walking activity itself. This study also showed that the effect was more directly tied to the walking process itself as this boost in creativity was not seen when the participant was pushed in a wheelchair along the same outdoor route.[31]

This last study makes perfect sense to me as I always find that walking assists me in finding solutions whenever I reach that mental block. Much of this book has been written by sessions of sitting at my desk interspersed with regular brief walking periods.

Spirituality

Spirituality and science are normally placed in different categories. Whether it includes organized religion or not, spirituality has a core value based on belief—an inner knowing and feeling of connectedness that has no problem with defying matters of science. As such, it may seem strange to include spirituality in a book on the science of mind training. However, we have already been introduced to the idea that spirituality can play a role in mind training when we discussed the power of meditation, in particular the Sa-Ta-Na-Ma meditation, and the power of experiencing awe.

The subject of religion can be confusing, especially in studies that seek to examine potential benefits. This is because, for many people, religion is a key part of their social lives and the activities they participate in. So, is it the religious beliefs that exert the positive influence, or is it due to the religious practices and community? Also, where some studies show positive benefits of religion and spirituality on mental health, others show negative effects due to "negative religious coping, misunderstanding and miscommunication, and negative beliefs."[32]

While spirituality can include sensing the presence of God, it does not have to, at least not in a religious sense. It can include feeling touched by the beauty of creation, having a sense of inner peace and harmony, feeling love for the planet, and experiencing a connection to others whether known or strangers. All of these can then lead to a feeling of a higher power or higher order in the universe we live in. A study published in the *Journal of Gerontology* found that these *everyday spiritual experiences* helped older adults better cope with negative feelings and enhanced positive feelings in daily life.[33] This study also validated an earlier study where significant benefits were found in the psychological and subjective well-being and stress in subjects who had been instructed on ways to cultivate sacred moments. These results held over the three-week study itself and six weeks later.[34] Spirituality, or intrinsic religiosity, tends to be more personal than classical religion—relying more on inner feeling than outer practice. In a 2012 study, intrinsic spirituality was related to lower levels of stress and anxiety among students approaching their exams.[35]

I am aware that when it comes to spiritual beliefs, there can be a certain snobbery in science, or at least those who state they only believe what science can prove. Those with spiritual leanings or religious beliefs often hide this side of themselves when in academic or scientific arenas. There is a strong belief that spirituality is irrational, and no one wants to be included in that category. If you find yourself feeling this way, then I would once again recommend you read Eldon's book, *Questioning Spirituality: Is it Irrational to Believe in God?* Even though Eldon has been discussing these ideas with me for decades, it was still an eye-opener. Prior to reading it, I had no idea how much inner conflict this subject produced for me. I do feel a strong connection (and responsibility) to all life, but I had also seen how irrational some can be in their beliefs and did not want to be included in that particular camp. I was surprised at how much freer I felt after reading this book. Many benefits can be gained from believing . . . in something greater than yourself.

Bringing it Together

This has been a sampling of the additional tools available to you to effect life changes. Mind training and self-responsibility go hand in hand. Now you need to keep looking out for this kind of information, with an eye to how you can make it work for you in normal daily life. Plus, keeping this kind of information in front of you will prevent you from slipping back into the old habits of thinking that *these things don't matter, they don't work well enough, so why bother?* If you take a few moments to share this information with your friends and colleagues, it can help others while reinforcing the learnings for yourself. Eldon and I like to do this—our social networking often includes the sharing of such findings, and many of our lunchtime discussions are focused on interesting tidbits of information we have come across.

As we have seen, many tools are available to start rooting out the old programming that has been holding you back. There is no longer any need to accept the status quo. Instead, you can start forging new paths for yourself—choosing the kind of person you want to be and taking actionable steps towards it. The choice is yours. None of this is easy, nothing will just get handed to you, but it will be one of the most fulfilling journeys you will ever take.

NOTES

Key Points

Studies have shown that consciously counting your blessings tends to make you happier and less depressed. A further study showed that it is the act of expressing gratitude that brings these results and not necessarily just experiencing the emotion of gratitude.

Norman Cousins credits laughter therapy for healing him from ankylosing spondylitis (a condition with a 1/500 chance of recovery). Blood tests confirmed that the laughing sessions led to a decrease in Cousins' inflammation numbers. In time, he almost totally recovered. Cousins however cautioned that this should not be used in place of professional health care but that, where possible, it should be *added* to general care.

Several studies support the value of laughter. In one study, pain thresholds increased an average of 10% after watching about fifteen minutes of comedy with a group. Laughter has also been shown to reduce stress, thereby increasing the success rate for in-vitro fertilization. Other studies showed laughter to be good for heart health, improving the immune response and reducing anxiety and depression.

Singing has been shown to cause a drop in the stress hormone, cortisol, and an increase in the happy brain chemical oxytocin. In older people, singing has been associated with better verbal flexibility. In bereavement, group singing led to more stable depression symptoms and levels of well-being, as well as gradual improvements in the sense of self-efficacy and self-esteem. According to the *British Lung Foundation*, regular singing can lead to a reduction in feelings of being short of breath and feeling more in control of symptoms. It was also found that singing can stimulate memory in both dementia patients and their caregivers.

Feelings of awe help people feel less stressed and rushed and have been shown to have health benefits. Inspired by awe, people are more willing to help others and are more likely to experience greater life satisfaction. Experiencing awe also led to improvements in well-being and stress, along with feelings of contentment and gratitude. Awe can make us feel humbler and this can lead to bringing people together in a more harmonious way.

There are many health benefits to walking including a reduction in the risk of diabetes and cancer, lowering blood pressure and cholesterol, and keeping you mentally sharp. Walking for just 2.5 hours a week can reduce your risk of heart disease by 30%. After sixteen weeks, brisk walking was shown to be as effective as medications at treating depression. (Please note this should not be taken as a recommendation to drop anti-depressants if you take them. However, with your doctor's approval, a walking routine could be beneficial.) Walking has also been shown to enhance creativity.

Spirituality can include religion and God, but it does not need to. Intrinsic spirituality relies more on inner feeling than outer practice. Intrinsic spirituality has been related to lower levels of stress and anxiety. Significant benefits have also been found in psychological and subjective well-being, and stress in subjects who had cultivated sacred moments.

Exercise

Make gratitude a daily habit. In the morning, as you write in your journal, be sure to also write down what you are grateful for. This exercise would be perfect right after your morning Sa Ta Na Ma meditation. It can also be helpful to say a silent thank you at the end of the day as you go to sleep—thank you for the day and all the good things in your life.

Ask your friends to recommend 'funnies.' These can be movies, video clips, jokes, and more. Make it a habit to end your TV watching with a short sitcom. Plan to watch a comedy movie with friends or a loved one. Create a list of comedies you would like to watch so you have them ready when needed.

Sing in the shower. Sing in the car. Sing with friends and sing alone. Play some music, sing along, and maybe dance at the same time.

Plan to go on regular walks and make it a point to observe the world around you and all its beauty. Go for walks with friends and enjoy some laughter at the same time.

While we have covered several techniques here, the beauty of these tips lies in the way many of the activities can be combined. Get creative and enjoy the process. There is an abundance of small changes you can make to your daily routines that can bring significant improvements to the quality of your life. Don't worry about trying to do them all. It can help to make a list of these techniques and pin them up in a prominent place. This will remind you of the benefits and encourage you to keep finding ways to add them to your normal routines.

CONCLUSION

THE BEST OF OURSELVES

The human body is capable of amazing physical deeds. If we could just free ourselves from our perceived limitations and tap into our internal fire, the possibilities are endless.

~ Dean Karnazes

Most people think of self-responsibility as having to do with owning up to their mistakes and striving to be productive in society. Eldon and I look at self-responsibility a little differently and a lot more deeply.

Before I elucidate on that thought, I caution that there is nothing in what we have to say here that implies blame of any kind. Bad things do happen to good people, good things do happen to bad people, bad luck is real, anyone can have health issues, etc. Blaming someone for their bad situation is never appropriate.

However, sitting back and accepting *'that's just who I am'* is frequently counterproductive to creating the best version of your life. It can be incredible how many doors of opportunities open to you when you take responsibility for everything—for who you are, your health, your personality quirks, your instincts, your experiences, etc. When something is someone or something else's fault, you can do little but react to it. If you realize that you are part of the equation, there is often something you can do. And all of this begins with appreciating quite how much power lies in your mind—a basic concept that can be found in some of the oldest teachings:

- "Jesus said, all things are possible to those who believe." ~ Mark 9:23
- "Do not conform to the pattern of this world but be transformed by the renewing of your mind." ~ Romans 12:2
- "The mind is everything. What you think you become." ~ Buddha
- "Man Jeete Jag Jeet – Master your mind and you master your life." ~ Guru Nanak Dev Ji
- You have power over your mind—not outside events. Realize this, and you will find strength. ~ Marcus Aurelius

Five Steps to Mind Mastery

We have covered a great deal of information in this book, and you may be unsure how to practice it all. As we said at the outset, the philosophy of mind training can be distilled into five main concepts. Looking at it this way makes it all more manageable:

1. *Appreciate* fully how powerful your mind is– it can hurt or heal you, sabotage you, or springboard you to success.
2. *Learn* how your mind works—how it prioritizes, takes shortcuts, and even distorts the reality you experience.
3. *Internalize* and synthesize the knowledge that your subconscious mind is a reservoir of all your experiences, along with all the information you have consumed, including media, news, entertainment, etc. Understand fully that this is the information your subconscious uses to make the decisions that run your life.

4. *Choose* to take responsibility for how your subconscious is programmed—restrict or cancel any programming that does not work for you, root out the programming that sabotages you, and reprogram with ideas and beliefs that will maximize your life experience.
5. *Implement* the little tricks and tweaks to make it all run more smoothly, efficiently, and joyfully.

As you go forward, it is worth looking back at least to the key points and exercises at the end of each of the chapters. The more you incorporate these ideas into your every day, the sooner you will habituate those habits that will put your life on a different trajectory. Don't worry about trying to incorporate everything at a time. Remember, small changes accumulate. Always remember the power of your mind and just keep on working to maximize all that you are.

How High is Up?

In 1990, Eldon wrote a book titled *Thinking Without Thinking*. I feel I have spent the last few decades thinking *about* thinking. Today I watch TV differently, ever mindful of the way Hollywood works to nudge our beliefs. I pay attention to political maneuverings, being very aware of how often they use research by social psychologists to tell us what they think we want to hear. I understand how we intake information and the extreme power enculturation has over us. Through this process, I have a better understanding of who I am supposed to be—the real me. I know too well that, while we are not in charge of the stimuli that come at us, we *are* in charge of how we respond. Daily, I work to make my mind support my goals and not hinder them. I press the correct buttons and tap the right keys to turn on the happy brain chemicals that make my life so much more fun, and my body so much healthier.

Daniel Dennett (Tufts University) has an analogy that is very fitting here. In a discussion with neuroscientist Sam Harris regarding free will, he agrees that we cannot control our genes, our environment, or other such factors that contribute to the idea that free will is an illusion. However, he compares this to sailing. As a sailor, he says he is unable to control the properties of the water, how hard the wind is blowing, or other kinds of conditions. But, as a trained sailor, he *can* control the boat. Now, someone who is not a competent sailor will not be able to do so, but he is a good sailor and therefore he can control the boat.[1]

In the same way, while we are unable to control the circumstances that life may throw at us, with a firm handle on mind training we are in a much better position to control the course of our lives. The ride may get bumpy at times, but we now have tools that can assist us in keeping our life's vehicle on the road and heading in the direction of our choosing. How well we do this will depend on how diligently we work to master the techniques.

For Eldon and me, our favorite question is *How high is up?* We would like to suggest that life is a journey with no specific destination. Instead of a destination, it has an overarching goal. The goal of the journey is to develop the best of ourselves. Experience is often our teacher, and what we don't learn the first time around will keep occurring until we catch on. Further, just as with the longest journey that begins with a single step, our learning begins with each new opportunity. What we learn today is not the end; it's only one more step.

It is a process indeed—a beautiful, empowering process that keeps stretching further and reaching higher. We encourage you to do the same.

ADDITIONAL MATERIALS

APPENDIX A

SUBLIMINAL CONTROVERSY

If the grace of God miraculously operates, it probably operates through the subliminal door.

~ William James

Today, most scientists in the field accept that information processing without awareness occurs. So, why was it considered controversial for so long? This fascinating, multi-layered story is worth looking at in some detail as it highlights some of the techniques used to sway public opinions and how misinformation gets perpetuated.

But first, I need to remind you that Eldon and I have significant skin in this game. Over 30 years ago, after carrying out extensive research, Eldon created the InnerTalk subliminal self-help technology, had it patented by the U.S. government, and invited independent researchers and private and public institutions to study it. Numerous double-blind studies—the gold standard for research as it eliminates the bias of the researchers—have demonstrated the efficacy of InnerTalk programs for priming self-talk and thereby changing the user's life experience. Eldon also participated in one of the attempts to create laws that would require informed consent for the use of subliminal messages and has testified as an expert court witness on the subject. For the past few decades, Eldon and I have been creating and using InnerTalk programs to assist people around the world in taking charge of their inner beliefs (subconscious programming), so they support their stated goals as opposed to sabotaging them.

With that disclosure out of the way (again), let's take a look at this story.

Vicary

The early research into preconscious processing was all about investigating the capabilities of the mind. However, one experiment upended the entire field as it introduced another motive to this area of research, and in so doing, brought the idea of subliminal messaging to the masses.

On September 16, 1957, *Advertising Age* wrote that James Vicary had reported using subliminal messages in a movie theatre to increase Coke sales by 18.1% and popcorn by 57.8%. The technique that Vicary used involved a tachistoscope to superimpose commercial messages as "very brief overlays of light," at a rate of 1/3,000th of a second during the movie *Picnic*. This experiment was run at a Fort Lee, New Jersey movie theatre for six weeks, during which around 45,000 people attended. The two messages used (*"Hungry? Eat Popcorn,"* and *"Drink Coca-Cola,"*) were flashed on the screen every five seconds. The *Advertising Age* article also reported that Vicary had joined with Rene Bras and Francis C. Thayer of U.S. Productions Company to form *Subliminal Projection Company* and that this company had applied for a patent on the process.[1]

Snopes

These days, when false stories are reported with reckless abandonment, it has become more important than ever to check the veracity of reports. *Snopes* has been one of my preferred fact-checking sources, and if you use it to look up *"Popcorn Subliminal Advertising,"* you will find that this story has been reported as "FALSE." It is not that the story itself was not reported, but rather that, according to the *Snopes* piece, after failing to replicate the study for the president of the Psychological Corporation, Dr. Henry Link,

Vicary eventually "confessed that he had falsified the data from his first experiments." The *Snopes* report says, "As numerous studies over the last few decades have demonstrated, subliminal advertising doesn't work; in fact, it never worked, and the whole premise was based on a lie from the very beginning."[2] However, this last statement is severely question-begging while the conclusions are most definitely not true. Plus, there is the inconvenient fact that Dr. Henry C. Link, who was an executive at Psychological Corporation from 1931 until his death, died in 1952—five years before Vicary's experiment.[3] As such, it was impossible for him to have been involved in any replication of Vicary's study—so much for the fact-checking abilities of *Snopes*!

Of greater importance for us here is that there is a lot more to this story especially when you consider any motivation Vicary may have had for lying, both with regards to the results he achieved with his ad or the fact he had even run the ad in the first place.

Outrage and Federal Hearings

A huge hue and cry resulted once the American public learned about the Vicary experiment. This fire was fueled further by Vance Packard's 1957 book *The Hidden Persuaders*, which not only covered the Vicary experiment but also highlighted the advertising industry's use of consumer motivational research and other psychological methods to persuade the public to consume their products. Norman Cousins, editor-in-chief of the *Saturday Review* from 1942-1972 and author of the book, *Anatomy of an Illness*,[4] believed subliminal technology to be so dangerous he stated that "There is only one kind of regulation or ruling that could possibly make any sense in this case; and that would be to take this invention and everything connected to it and attach it to the center of the next nuclear explosive scheduled for testing." The fear level regarding the use of this technology in the United States rose so high that it led to congressional and Federal Trade Commission hearings. Two congressional bills to penalize the use of subliminal advertising on television were introduced in 1958 and 1959. However, "Some Congressmen felt that legislation against something that could not be seen or perceived was unnecessary."[5] Both bills died in committee.[6] To date, no laws restricting subliminal transmissions have ever been passed by Congress.

State Legislation

State legislatures have also attempted to pass bills regarding the use of subliminal messages. In 1984, the California Assembly considered a bill restricting any 'person who knowingly communicates to members of the public any subliminally embedded communication without making known the existence of such communication.' This bill died in committee.[7]

In 1986, the Utah State legislature also introduced a bill that would have required informed consent to the use of subliminal communication. Eldon, himself, was involved in this legislative process, and on the day he addressed the Utah House committee, he states in his book *Mind Programming* that he found himself,

> ". . . being almost shocked by the number of professionals representing various interests, including advertising agencies, who showed up to speak against the legislation. What we thought was a local decision apparently had national and even international interest. Speakers from New York argued that the legislation wasn't needed—no one used this technology, it was too expensive, and it didn't work. The committee heard both sides and was pressed by my office and others to at least send the issue to the full House for a vote."[8]

As is too often the case, the committee never sent it to the floor for a full vote, so the bill simply died. However, there is an important detail here well worth bearing in mind as we continue to unravel this story. Why would big money invest in fighting a bill to control the use of a technology that does not work?

Limitations on Use

Even though no actual laws ban or control in any way the use of subliminal messages, the Federal Communications Commission (FCC) and the Federal Trade Commission (FTC) have both made efforts to curtail its use.

In 1957, the FCC stated that subliminal broadcasting is "inconsistent with . . . the public interest." The statutory authority to control such broadcasts is limited to enforcement against the broadcasters, and sanctions may only be imposed if the broadcaster has knowledge of the subliminal messages.[9] This would give the broadcaster so much wriggle room that the sanctions end up having no teeth to them. The FCC cannot act against the advertiser as that is the responsibility of the Federal Trade Commission (FTC), but they, too, are hobbled by restrictions. The FTC is only able to act against an advertiser if the subliminal message constitutes unfair competition or a deceptive practice as defined by the FTC and the courts.[10] Once again, so much wriggle room exists for any attorneys handling such a case that getting a case to stick would be well-nigh impossible.

Bush/Gore

You need look no further than the 2000 U.S. presidential election to realize statutory bodies lack power on the use of subliminal messages in broadcast media. During the campaigning, it was discovered that "the word *rats* appeared subliminally in a Republican political broadcast targeting Democratic health care proposals."[11] Alex Castellano, the Republican campaign manager responsible for producing the ad, denied the use of subliminal messaging, claiming that he had faded out the word bureauc*rats* to make the ad visually interesting and that it was a coincidence that the 'rats' part of the word appeared when and how it did.[12] The ad was screened 4,400 times in thirty-three different regions before a viewer spotted it so it was not in clear view.[13] According to Kathleen Hall Jamieson, author of *Dirty Politics: Deception, Distraction and Democracy*, this was the second time subliminal imagery had been used in U.S. politics as the first was another ad created by Castellano, this time for the Republican senator for North Carolina, Jessie Helms.[14]

George Bush, who would go on to become the forty-third president of the United States, downplayed the ad by saying, "The idea of one frame out of 900 hardly in my judgment makes a conspiracy."[15] The entire idea came across as even more 'silly' when Bush was unable even to pronounce the word 'subliminal,' stumbling and bumbling his way through the word as though it was just some kind of deliberate tongue-twister. Was this another deliberate tactic to avert attention from what they had attempted to do?

Politics in the U.S. is big business, and the highest stake lies in the presidential election. If there were any way the lawyers for the Democratic Party could have had Bush's campaign even formally chastised for this ad by some statutory body, they would have done so. So much for the common belief that subliminal advertising is illegal—if there are no *teeth* behind a legal ruling, then it may as well not exist.

Replication

Note that in 2008, Joel Weinberger (Adelphi University) and Drew Westen (Emory University) published a paper based on research carried out from September to November of 2000. Their research used Internet-presented subliminal primes to study the subjects' evaluation of politicians. The test subliminal prime was RATS, just as in the Republican ad. The control subliminal primes used were STAR (the exact reversal of RATS but with a different meaning), ARAB (the authors believed that at the time of this study prejudice against Arabs had not developed negative unconscious connotations in their sample), and XXXX. The subjects were asked to fix their gaze on an "X" in the middle of the computer screen, which was then replaced by a picture of a candidate. The subliminal stimulus was presented for one frame at a brightness that could be seen when unmasked but could not be detected when masked. The subliminal stimulus was then followed immediately by a photograph of a young man in a shirt and tie. The procedure was repeated three times just in case the subject happened to blink or was otherwise distracted during one of the presentations. The subjects were then asked to evaluate the 'candidate' for ten items on a seven-point scale, ranging from completely agree to completely disagree:

> "This candidate looks competent; This candidate strikes me as honest; There is something about this candidate that makes me feel positive; There is something about this candidate that makes me feel disgusted; There is something about this candidate that makes me feel angry; There is something fishy about this candidate; There is something about this candidate that makes me feel that I can trust

him; I like this candidate; I dislike this candidate; I would vote for this candidate."[16]

As predicted, the subliminal presentation of RATS led to a more negative evaluation of the hypothetical candidate than any of the other stimuli did, and this held for both men and women, and regardless of whether the participants identified as Republican or Democrat.[17] So, could the Bush campaign's RATS ad have influenced at least *some* of the voters? I would say there is little question about that.

Vicary Part II

Back to James Vicary and his *"Hungry? Eat Popcorn,"* and *"Drink Coca-Cola"* ad. Why would Vicary turnabout and say he had made it all up ... if he did so? Is it a coincidence that attempts to create laws to control the use of subliminal messages have all failed, while there is plenty of evidence that this technology is still being used in advertising, entertainment, and politics?

After announcing his success with his New Jersey theater experiment, Vicary went on to make further statements touting the efficacy of subliminal messages as an advertising tool, albeit with some caveats. The following day, an article appeared in the *Wall Street Journal* in which Vicary stated that the subliminal messages functioned as "reminder advertising" and could only work on those already familiar with a product. Vicary also stated that these messages "would not prompt a viewer to buy something he didn't consciously want."[18] So right up front, Vicary made it clear that subliminal messages, as used in his experiment, could not function as a brainwashing tool, but rather it would simply nudge the consumer in a particular direction. That said, Vicary, however, believed that with the right (stronger) psychological techniques, the entire audience would have purchased popcorn and Coca-Cola. For this reason, he and his associate Francis C. Thayer suggested that government regulation was necessary to prevent the misuse of this technique, which could be "dangerous in the wrong hands."[19] Echoing, to some degree at least, the sentiments expressed by Norman Cousins about this technology.

While Vicary's initial announcement had caused a furor that led to the congressional hearings in 1958, a lot of attention emerged from other parties interested in using this subliminal technology. Advertising inquiries flooded into Vicary and in a November 1957 interview with *Sponsor* magazine, Vicary stated that "his company [Subliminal Projection Company] was working on a subliminal projection detection device for use by a governing body."[20]

Some direct pushback arose to Vicary's claims, however, and in December 1957, an article in *Motion Picture Daily* stated that the manager of the New Jersey theatre where the *"Hungry? Eat Popcorn,"* and *"Drink Coca-Cola,"* test had been run had emphatically denied the sales increase ever happened. According to *Advertising Age*, Vicary was 'incensed' by this and visited B. S. Moss, the head of the theater chain, to show him the test data. As a result, *Motion Picture Daily* published a statement from Moss indicating that "this type of 'subconscious' advertising could help to increase sales."[21]

Replication . . . or not?

Here the story becomes even more interesting. A common theme emerges from several studies that were purportedly looking into the efficacy of subliminal communication

On January 13, 1958, 300 members of Congress, the FCC, and the Federal Trade Commission participated in a retest of the experiment. The message *"Eat Popcorn"* was used in the Civil War-themed television program, *The Gray Ghost*. However, unlike in the Jersey Theatre test, the audience was told at the start of the show that the *"Eat Popcorn"* message would be shown throughout the screening, and the message was flashed visibly on the screen before the show and the subliminal messages started. The test was judged a failure by the officials—no member of the audience expressed a desire to eat popcorn and, according to the *New York Times*, many seemed disappointed about this.[22]

Now, take a moment to think about this. In high school, we are all taught the basics of the scientific method—it is only a replication of a study if all the parameters are kept the same. Vicary never stated that the subliminal messages would force the audience to behave in a certain way. He explained to the audience before the test started that "It may remind a Democrat to go out and vote for the Democratic candidate, but it won't cause him to switch and become a Republican."[23] Also, by informing the audience of the details of the study in advance, the slight nudges in behavior could well have been replaced by a hyper-vigilance, both to the attempts made to 'see' the messages, and also by the constant internal examination along the lines of, "I wonder when I will have the urge to eat popcorn," or "I wonder what that urge will feel like."

There is also a huge difference between going out to see a movie, expecting to be entertained and relaxed by the experience, and watching a documentary while in a classroom setting. Now, I have no idea what the actual setting was for this test—was it in a theatre on the giant screen, in the cafeteria on television, or some other variation? —but the fact remains that this was a work event. Indulging while watching a movie is a common experience—many people, especially those trying to lose weight or eat more healthily, often put considerable effort into breaking the habit of reaching for snacks as soon as they settle down on the sofa in front of the TV. The experience of going to the movie is very similar—the concessions are just part of the fun experience. Watching a Civil War-themed television program with work colleagues would not put most people in a 'relax, have fun' mood.

Another detail worth considering is the increase in sales that Vicary reported. He stated that Coke sales increased by 18.1% and popcorn by 57.8%. According to a survey carried out in 2018, 34% of the audience in a movie theater are highly likely to purchase concessions, 28% were somewhat likely, 32% were somewhat or highly unlikely, and 5% had no opinion.[24] Vicary did not say that 18.1% of the audience purchased Coke; he said that there was an 18.1% *increase* in Coke sales. He did not say that 57.8% of the audience purchased popcorn; he said that there was a 57.8% *increase*. What did he base his numbers on? How did he derive his pre-test numbers to calculate the percentage increase in sales due to his test? Of those people who were likely to purchase concessions, what percentage was also likely to purchase Coke or popcorn? We do not have this information. What we do have is more evidence that subliminal information nudges beliefs and desires and will have its most visible effect on those who are on the fence about their decision or choice.

Fallout

While most of the controversy at the time centered on the work being done by James Vicary and his *Subliminal Projection Company*, another company also touted results using subliminal messages in commercial settings. *Precon Processing*, founded by Robert E. Corrigan, a former lecturer in psychology, and Hal C. Becker, claimed "ample proof" and "exhaustive experiments" had been carried out since 1950.[25] Interestingly, while both Vicary and Becker filed patent applications for their subliminal devices, only Becker's was granted.[26] In the patent, Becker's *Black Box* was described as an "apparatus for imparting useful information to an observer by subconscious stimulation and subsequently resulting in conscious purposive behavior . . ."[27]

Between the media backlash, the public outrage and hostility, and the congressional hearings to both Vicary's Lee Theater experiment and Vance Packard's book, *The Hidden Persuaders*, subliminal messages almost became taboo. As a result, both Hal Becker's *PreCon Processing* and James Vicary's *Subliminal Projection Company* suffered significant losses. Speaking to the *Wall Street Journal*, Vicary stated that the negativity surrounding subliminal advertising had affected his company financially. "'I've been taking a heck of a licking,' he said."[28]

When I considered how subliminal technology has continued to thrive since those days, I speculated, along with many others, that perhaps Vicary had been paid off by the advertising companies to keep quiet about the technology and its possible uses just so they could use it without oversight. This suspicion was fueled in part by the fact that Vicary disappeared from the scene. This, however, did not turn out to be the case.

In a December 1957 *Advertising Age* article, Vicary reported that the entire situation had caused him so much stress that he decided on a whim to visit England, his father's birthplace. However, when he came back, the entire controversy still raged. As a result, Vicary "shunned public appearances, unlisted his phone number, and feared for his life." His woes continued when the State of New York refused to grant him a psychology license. By 1962, Vicary was working for Dun & Bradstreet as a survey research director, and he made it clear that he was trying to rehabilitate his image and didn't want to be known as "Mr. Subliminal."[29]

Retraction

The Internet has brought with it great opportunities and a considerable number of challenges. While researching for this book, I have attempted as far as I could to verify sources, reading the actual papers and articles as opposed to only other people's reports. I also prefer to cite reputable sources and institutions. The problem with the Internet, though, is that an error (or lie) repeated often enough can almost become the truth. As we saw in the *Snopes* report on Vicary's experiment, a major error occurred when it was stated that Vicary was unable to replicate his results in a subsequent test for Henry Link, president of the Psychological Corporation. Dr. Link had passed away some five years prior, so this detail was false. However, if you search for this information, you will find numerous reputable sources citing the same "fact." And the same thing appears to hold for Vicary's supposed retraction.

A 2015 article in *Scientific American* states that, "Five years later he [Vicary] admitted he had faked the study."[30] 'Admitting to fakery' is a strong statement as it certainly leads the reader to dismiss everything they had learned up until this point regarding the experiment. If you care to search around, you will find that this little detail is used in several publications.

Wikipedia states that "In 1962, Vicary admitted to lying about the experiment and falsifying the results, the story itself being a marketing ploy."[31] The Wikipedia entry is worth noting as many still believe that, as stated earlier, "subliminal messages in the media are illegal, they don't work, but they are still being used." For most people, many of their opinions on subjects outside of their areas of expertise generally come from 'surface' reports, such as those cited in the general media and places like Wikipedia.

The citations used in the Wikipedia page for this detail include *The Museum of Hoaxes* by Alex Boese and *The Cargo-Cult Science of Subliminal Persuasion* by Anthony Pratkanis. We will be discussing Anthony Pratkanis' work later, so it is well worth remembering his name for he plays a significant role in the subliminal controversy. However, according to Boese:

> "During a 1962 interview with *Advertising Age*, Vicary admitted that he actually 'hadn't done any research, except

what was needed for filing a patent.' In other words, he had invented the results of the Fort Lee experiment in order to boost his business."[32]

And according to Pratkanis:

"Finally, in 1962 James Vicary lamented that he had handled the subliminal affair poorly. As he stated, "Worse than the timing, though, was the fact that we hadn't done any research, except what was needed for filing a patent. I had only a minor interest in the company and a small amount of data—too small to be meaningful. And what we had shouldn't have been used promotionally" (Danzig, 1962). This is not exactly an affirmation of a study that supposedly ran for six weeks and involved thousands of subjects."[33]

Do you read anything here that quotes Vicary as saying that he 'faked' the results, as stated in *Scientific American*, or that he had "confessed that he had falsified the data from his first experiments," as stated by *Snopes*, or that he had "invented the results" as stated by Boese, or that the study had never happened as implied by Pratkanis? To my mind, all these reports are extremely misleading if not downright false.

Vicary did call it a "gimmick that had failed,"[34] but that still does not say that the study itself failed, but rather that the publicity did not help his business in the slightest—in fact, it ruined his career. According to Kelly Crandall in their very thorough and well-researched undergraduate honors thesis for the University of Florida, "Vicary never admitted to falsifying the Fort Lee test, and in fact, reiterated that it occurred. The statement might be interpreted to mean that he had exaggerated the test data, or that a single test was insufficient to draw the bold conclusions he promulgated in 1957."[35] When you look at all of the information, I believe it is fair to say the test occurred and that the results were in the direction indicated, but that the fallout was so great that Vicary tried to downplay the story without denying any of it. I also believe that the media and the advertising industry have played a significant role in promulgating the story of the hoax and turning the entire idea into a joke—something not worth taking seriously.

Lipton Iced Tea

In 2005, Karremans, Stroebe & Claus (Radboud University and Utrecht University, The Netherlands) ran a study to see whether subliminal priming for a particular drink (Lipton Iced Tea) could influence the participants' choice and if the individual's thirst moderated this effect. This was a very thorough and tight study as it had checks in place for several factors. But let's look at a few basic details. This study did not introduce the subliminal messages in a showing of a movie or documentary, but rather they used "a visual detection task, which examined how accurate people are in detecting small deviances." The researchers also tested the subliminality of the priming technique used—making sure that none of the participants guessed the priming words, *Lipton Ice*. In the second part of the test, rather than just seeing which drink the participants chose, they were asked to indicate on the computer:

- Which of the two named brand drinks they would prefer if offered a drink right now,
- The likelihood they would choose Lipton Ice, Coke, or Spa Rood (a Dutch mineral water), and
- How thirsty they were.

The results showed that:

> "... exposing individuals subliminally to the brand name of a drink increases the probability that they will choose this drink, provided that they are thirsty. Both studies showed that subliminally exposing our participants to the brand name "Lipton Ice" increased choice for, and intention to, drink Lipton Ice only for thirsty individuals. Subliminal priming had no significant effect for participants who were not thirsty. This consistency is particularly

impressive because it emerged both with self-rated thirstiness as well as when thirst was induced by giving participants salty sweets."[36]

The researchers' conclusion also stated that:

> "Our findings suggest that consumer choices may be influenced by subliminal primes of certain means that could help people to fulfill their goals, but only if they already have the goal. Thus, when sitting on a terrace, subliminal flashes of "Lipton Ice" on a television screen next to the terrace may alter one's choice to order Lipton Ice. Or, in a computer store, subliminal primes of Macintosh may very well increase Macintosh sales. In these examples, people have the goal, respectively, to quench their thirst or to buy a computer. However, when sitting on the sofa at home, in front of the television, the goals of quenching one's thirst or buying a computer may not be highly salient (or are not present at all), and subliminal primes of a brand of drink or brand of computer are therefore unlikely to influence a person's behavior."[37]

This reiterates the view that subliminal messages won't make you do something you do not want but will simply massage your emotions and desires in a particular direction. That said, the final comments in the paper were rather amusing:

> "Although Vicary's advertising techniques appear to have existed only in Vicary's fantasies, the present findings suggest that, if certain conditions are taken into account, his fantasies may indeed become reality."[38]

It is incredible how firmly the idea that 'Vicary's experiment was just a hoax' has stuck.

Confusion

By the '80s to the early '90s, the public had become very confused about the subject of subliminal communication. In a 1985 study by Block and Vanden Bergh (Michigan State University), "330 adults were contacted to determine attitudes toward subliminal self-help products. This study revealed that consumers were skeptical of subliminal self-improvement products and were also concerned about being influenced to do something they did not wish to do.[39] They were skeptical that this technology could work and were also concerned about being influenced to do something against their wishes. What else could have caused this kind of confusion?

Subliminals in the Media

Lots of talk has pervaded the music industry about using subliminal and backmasked (reversed) messages in their compositions, most notably the Beatles, Pink Floyd, the Eagles, and ELO. In 1991 Eldon was contacted by WNCI Radio regarding satanic messages in Madonna's song *Rescue*. Analyzing her music in his studio, he found the messages/poem:

> *In the midnight smoke of yellow*
> *Hear my melodies*
> *Hail to the family*
> *It must be unknown*
> *Hail hallelujah my position . . .*

In time her people would admit they had been put there as a publicity stunt.

In 1986, Glen Pace, who at one time was probably one of the top five recording engineers in Los Angeles, spoke candidly to Eldon about having been asked by several heavy-metal rock groups to insert subliminal and backmasked messages into their music. He drew the line, though, when it came to using satanic messages.

Subliminal imagery has been used in several major movie productions, notably *The Exorcist*[40] and *Psycho*,[41] to heighten the fear response. There have also been many reports of subliminal imagery in Disney movies, and in the instance of *The Rescuers*, the discovery of a topless woman led to a recall of 3.4 million home-release videos.[42] The '80s cult movie *They Live* is all about the misuse of subliminal messages.

We must also remember all the times subliminal messages have been found in advertisements. Oftentimes they are explained away as having some other meaning, but several places exist where they are used to spoof the entire idea, from the 1959 Chevrolet advertisement with Dinah Shore and Pat Boone[43] to the parody Schweppes ad by John Cleese included in the 2002 video release for the movie *A Fish Called Wanda*.[44]

Self-Help

Another offshoot of the attention given to subliminal information processing was the use of this technology in the self-help industry. Subliminal self-help programs became mainstream with audiocassette tapes being readily available. By the late '80s, the self-help industry had burgeoned into a $50 million plus industry in self-help audio and video programs.[45] This, however, would get tipped on its head with a major news story, the Judas Priest trial. Up until now, the bulk of the research into subliminal information processing had been done on visual subliminal messages. The Judas Priest trial would bring a huge spotlight to audio subliminal messages.

Judas Priest

In 1990 much of the Judas Priest trial was televised and covered extensively in the news. The short version of the story goes this way. In 1985, two troubled young men, twenty-year-old James Vance and eighteen-year-old Ray Belknap, spent the afternoon drinking beers and playing music. One song in particular, "Better by You, Better than Me" on the *Stained Class* album by Judas Priest, caught their attention and they played it repeatedly. Chanting the phrase, "Do it," they then grabbed a 12-guage shotgun, climbed out of the window, went to the park, and attempted to commit suicide. Belknap was successful. However, Vance failed to brace the shotgun and shot off the front of his face. He would die three years later.

Vance's parent claimed that the subliminal message "Do it" that was found in "Better by You, Better than Me," had caused the boys to take their lives. The boys' parents filed a wrongful death lawsuit against CBS and the musical group Judas Priest.

The trial, which went on for seventeen days and involved more than forty witnesses, ended with Judge Whitehead ruling "that the British heavy-metal band Judas Priest was not responsible for the deaths of two youths who committed suicide after listening to the group's album, *Stained Class*."[46]

After the extensive coverage of the trial and all the expert witnesses who had been called to testify, it is fair for the public to conclude the trial proved that subliminal messages did not cause the boys to take their lives. It would be fair to believe that once again subliminal communication had been proven not to work.

Verdict

The conclusions from the trial, though, were not that clear-cut and some interesting information came to light.

First, during the pre-trial, Judge Whitehead ruled that subliminal messages were not afforded free speech protections. He said:

> "Audio subliminal communications are the antithesis of these theories. They do not convey ideas or information to be processed by the listener so that he or she can make an individual determination about its value. They do not enable an individual to further his personal autonomy. Instead, they are intended to influence and manipulate the behavior of the listener without his knowledge."[47]

This is an important point. If you remember, Eldon was involved in the attempted 1984 Utah bill that would have required informed consent.

Based on the evidence presented, Judge Whitehead ruled that "The words "Do it" were present several times on the song," and that the "Do it" commands on the record were subliminal."[48] He also said there was 'credible factual support from a lay witness' that Belknap and Vance perceived the subliminal message.[49]

Interestingly, Rob Halford, the lead vocalist for Judas Priest, said they had used backmasked messages before, but not on this album.[50] Later, Halford would say that he and his band did not even know what subliminal messages were.[51] During the trial, Halford would argue that the 'Do it' messages were just a coincidence of sound.

The attorneys for the defendants made a strong case that Vance and Belnap had social and psychological problems, "including unstable family environments, poor academic performance, drug abuse, and a history of violent and dysfunctional behavior."[52] An important line of questioning they followed was trying to ascertain *how much of a factor* the subliminal messages could have played in the actions of the boys. There cannot be a real answer to this one as such an area of research would not be acceptable to anyone.[53]

Arguments were made for and against the ability of audio subliminal messages to affect behavior. A key piece of evidence came down to a paper widely touted as proving that subliminal self-help programs did not work. This paper is not quite that straightforward, and we will look at it more deeply.

But this was a wrongful death action. Judge Whitehead said that the plaintiffs would have to show that putting the messages on the recording was a 'clear, conscious, and intentional act.'[54] With the defendants arguing that the messages were just a coincidence of sound, the only way to prove they were put there intentionally would be to listen to the master recordings. CBS put their own detective on the task of finding the master, but they were unsuccessful. However, it did come out during the trial that this detective had not been allowed to look in CBS' vault. Judge Whitehead fined CBS $40K, saying it had refused to comply with court orders to supply material needed in the case.[55]

In his conclusion, Whitehead wrote that the "plaintiffs lost this case because they failed to prove that the defendants intentionally placed subliminal messages on the album and that those messages were a cause of the suicide and attempted suicide involved in this case. However, it is unknown what future information, research, and technology will bring to this field."[56]

While Judas Priest was relieved by the verdict, Rob Halford was also disappointed because the judge did not rule that the plaintiffs' allegations were not true, but only it could not be proven . . . at this time.[57]

Influence

Now, I am not going to attempt to argue for or against the verdict in this trial; the situation was very complicated. The boys were troubled, unhappy with life, drinking too much, using drugs . . . and were listening to music that allegedly contained subliminal messages. The point of the story here is to highlight once again why the public holds such confusing beliefs regarding subliminal communication. A lot can be said for the phrase, "the truth is in the details," as without the details, the truth can truly be lost.

In this case, two trials were going on simultaneously; one was in the legal courts and the other was in the court of public opinion. In the latter case, the defendants had the decided advantage that deep pockets and influence can bring.

At the conclusion of the trial, Judge Whitehead learned that CBS had, at great expense, manipulated the media before and during the trial. On the morning of his verdict, the judge warned CBS that, "The court will be investigating this action, since some of the material given in press releases is totally improper and could constitute slander."[58]

The court of public opinion is, without doubt, easier to influence as the necessary tactics do not rely on legal arguments and effective expert witnesses. A slanted article here, some misinformation there, and a healthy dose of ridicule are really all that is needed. It may be that ridicule is the strongest technique for making sure misinformation sticks.

Ridicule

A few years ago, while Eldon was being interviewed on George Noory's *Coast to Coast AM* radio show, he told the audience that Sarah Palin, running mate for John McCain in the 2008 presidential election, had never stated that she could see Russia from her kitchen window. A few days after his interview, he received an email from one of the listeners. The email was incredibly respectful; the gentleman had enjoyed Eldon's interview very much, but he felt the need to make a correction. You see, he had heard for himself, Sarah Palin saying that she could see Russia from her kitchen window. If you do a fact-checking search, you will find several sites (including *Snopes*) that say this quote is false. It was Tina Fey on *Saturday Night Live* who said, "I can see Russia from my house." What Palin actually said was:

"They're our next-door neighbors, and you can actually see Russia from land here in Alaska, from an island in Alaska . . . I'm giving you that perspective of how small our world is and how important it is that we work with our allies to keep good relations with all of these countries, especially Russia,"[59]

Tina Fey's version, however, provided the country with the good belly laugh that firmly placed Palin in the category of 'not to be taken seriously.' Fey's version was so memorable that many are still adamant they heard Palin herself say she could see Russia from her kitchen window.

The 'belly-laugh' tactic is frequently used when the aim is to win an argument, especially when the facts may not be there. Martin Gardner, who wrote a column in *Scientific American* for twenty-five years and was one of the founders of the *Committee for the Scientific Investigation of Claims of the Paranormal* (CSICOP), said in his book, *Science: Good, Bad and Bogus*:

"In discussing extremes of unorthodoxy in science I consider it a waste of time to give rational arguments. Those who are in agreement do not need to be educated about such trivial matters, and trying to enlighten those who disagree is like trying to write on water . . . For these reasons, when writing about extreme eccentricities of science, I have adopted H.L. Mencken's sage advice: one horse-laugh is worth ten thousand syllogisms."[60]

The ridicule that results in a good belly laugh is a very effective tactic to get people to take your side, for who wants to be on the side of stupid? This tactic has long been used when it comes to subliminal information, and late-night comedians had a field day with the Judas Priest trial.

Academia

On a slightly more academic front was the article published in the *Skeptical Inquirer*. The *Skeptical Inquirer* is the official journal of *The Committee for*

Skeptical Inquiry, whose mission "is to promote scientific inquiry, critical investigation, and the use of reason in examining controversial and extraordinary claims." Their founders include Carl Sagan, Isaac Asimov, and Martin Gardner—the same Martin Gardner who prefers using humor to logical arguments. Now, the article I refer to is titled "Subliminal Tapes: How to Get the Message Across," written by Brady J. Phelps and Mary E. Exum (both at Utah State University). The authors do a stinging job in differentiating real scientists from pseudoscientists or, more specifically, scientists who work at reputable universities and such institutes versus the pseudoscientists who run studies demonstrating the efficacy of subliminal self-help programs. Here are just a few highlights from this article:

> "[pseudoscientists] do not use the same methods or have the same understanding of the importance of rigorous scientific procedures.
> . . . most important, scientists and pseudoscientists have vastly different backgrounds, different reasons and motivations for conducting and publicizing their respective findings, and very different audiences.
> . . . Such a person [real scientist] may hold a doctorate or master's degree from a university whose goal, in part, has been to teach how to conduct sound, replicable research with clearly defined independent and dependent variables and with minimal interference from confounding extraneous variables.
> . . . Countering paid advertising by pseudoscientists with paid advertisements for the validity and superiority of the scientific method is possible, but not probable, since pseudoscientists run advertisements to make money and scientists would be paying for an ad to keep people from wasting money.
> . . . Among the most widely marketed pseudoscience products today are 'subliminal' tapes."[61]

While this paper was published in 1992, after the trial, it nevertheless shows how opinions can be influenced by mocking the other side. More interestingly, though, it shows the extreme nature of the biases involved in this story. You see, the research paper used to provide evidence during the Judas Priest trial, and run by, what Phelps and Exum would describe as, 'real scientists,' has a few problems. Timothy Moore, the expert witness for the defendants who cited the research paper I'm about to share with you, also wrote another paper in 1996 that again harps on about pseudoscience: "Pseudoscience sometimes plays a role in court because of dubious 'experts' who are willing to attest to just about anything."[62]

Audio Subliminal Information

While I have spoken earlier about the vast amount of information that has demonstrated the reality of subliminal information processing, most of this was done on 'visual' subliminals, such as with Vicary's 'Coca-Cola, popcorn' experiment. With the Judas Priest trial, it became important to discredit audio subliminals and, as the market for subliminal self-help audio programs was so big, this became a primary target.

In March of 1991, a paper was published in *Psychological Sciences* titled, "Double-Blind Tests of Subliminal Self-Help Audiotapes" and was written by Anthony G. Greenwald (University of Washington), Eric R. Spangenberg (Washington State University), Anthony R. Pratkanis (University of California, Santa Cruz), and Jay Eskenazi (University of California, Santa Barbara).[63] News outlets everywhere, from *Seventeen* magazine to primetime news, picked up on this paper and ran articles saying subliminal self-help programs had been proven not to work.

Technology/Definitions

Once again, we can go back to our high school teachings where we are taught the fundamentals of a scientific experiment, with the most basic detail being the need to control the variables. In this study, the researchers decided to test subliminal self-help tapes from three different companies. The paper states that "A preliminary analysis tested for differences among the tapes provided by the three manufacturers; no differences were found, and the results below are reported for a design that did not include manufacturer as a variable."[64] However, there is no indication of what the 'preliminary analysis' entailed. I do know that subliminal self-help companies use a variety of methods to produce their programs, many of which would not be detectable just by listening to the programs. Just to remind you, because of his research, Eldon has been privy to a fair amount of inside information from subliminal self-help companies. He has learned that subliminal programs may vary in several ways, such as:

- There may be no affirmations on the program at all. In one instance, the owner of a company thought the results were all due to the placebo anyway.
- Affirmations may be recorded as much as 50 db beneath the primary carrier. This is too low a level for regular players to even pick up.
- Affirmations may be recorded in the second person (*You are good*) as opposed to the first person (*I am good*). This is an important distinction. When you hear fully audible coaching, someone else is encouraging you. When the affirmations are presented subliminally, they become part of your stream of consciousness. When this self-talk is saying 'you are good,' that only tells the individual that other people are good, and this can be deleterious on their esteem if they think everyone else is better than them.
- Formatting of affirmations is important. Short and to-the-point affirmations are more effective than long, convoluted ones. Affirmations also need to be well thought out; an affirmation such as "Ten cigarettes a day is more than enough for me," could be turned around and interpreted as "More than ten cigarettes a day is enough for me."
- Some companies believe that 'more is better' and they advertise that their programs contain millions of affirmations. There are several ways to do this:

- Have a hundred people say each affirmation simultaneously. However, it is much more difficult to understand what is being said when many people are speaking at the same time.
- Speed the affirmations up. Nothing indicates that the subconscious mind understands speech that has been sped up. Depending on the speed of the speech, it can be difficult to impossible to understand even when fully audible.
- Layer the affirmations – perhaps at 5 db, 10 db, 15 db, and so on beneath the primary track. However, there is an optimal range beneath the primary carrier where the affirmations can be detected. Any more than that is like asking a violinist to go to the other side of Los Angeles and still expecting to hear their music.

Using programs obtained from three different companies (none of which were InnerTalk) who call their products subliminal self-help programs does not take any of these technological details into account. Without the details explaining what a 'preliminary analysis' entailed, we have no assurance that these differences were even looked for. What we do know, though, is not controlling for this variable can lead to invalid results.

Subject Selection

When selecting the subject pool for this kind of study, it is important to find subjects representative of the American public. In this study, though, they used "subjects motivated to achieve the goals claimed by the tapes because such motivation is plausibly a precondition for occurrence of claimed effects and is a condition that applies generally in the marketplace."[65] While this was supposed to be a double-blind study, remembering our previous discussion regarding the Pygmalion factor, we must question what other influences were in play. This study found subjects who wanted to improve their memory, and who happened to believe in self-help programs already, and then handed them a tape that was labeled *Improve your*

Memory or something of the like. It is hard to prime the placebo effect more. Perhaps that was the study's aim. Perhaps it was designed in such a way that everything could be attributed to the placebo effect only, and this is exactly what they state in their paper: "Nevertheless, a general improvement for all subjects in both memory and self-esteem (a nonspecific placebo effect) was observed."[66] It certainly is an interesting way to discredit subliminal self-help programs.

Controls

For a study to offer meaningful results, there must be a control group. In this study, they used the recipients of the mislabeled memory program as the control for the mislabeled esteem program, and vice versa. Why did they believe this was adequate? Could this not have muted any possible effects that may have been seen using a program with subliminal messages aimed at memory or esteem?

In our line of InnerTalk programs, we also offer programs for both memory and esteem. One of the principles behind the affirmations on all the InnerTalk programs is the idea that fear of not being able to achieve your goal will hinder you from achieving it. When you believe you cannot succeed at something, you simply will not try your hardest to achieve it. Affirmations related to feeling good and calm, therefore, feature on most, if not all, the InnerTalk programs. Knowing this, you can see how a person's esteem can be improved, to some degree at least, with any of the InnerTalk programs, including *Powerful Memory*. You can also see how a subliminal program for esteem could benefit, at least to some degree, someone who is trying to improve their memory.

Adequate controls are therefore an important part of any study. In this case, if a placebo group had used a program with neutral subliminal messages, and a control group had used a program with no subliminal messages at all, then there would have been something real to compare the results with. Instead, as I have already shared, any real results were buried in the blanket statement, "a general improvement for all subjects in both memory and self-esteem (a nonspecific placebo effect) was observed."[67]

Definitions

But what does subliminal even mean? In 1988, Philip Merikle (University of Waterloo, Canada) "conducted a spectrographic analysis of several subliminal audiotapes and found no evidence for the presence of any identifiable speech sounds."[68] Is this what they were using as their definition of a subliminal program? In his paper "Subliminal Perception: Facts and Fallacies," Timothy Moore discusses the work of Merikle in which he distinguishes between subjective and objective thresholds of stimulus detection. He says conscious perception is subjective if someone reports being unaware of the subliminal stimulus, but in a forced choice scenario they select correctly at a rate better than chance—so they *were aware* of the stimulus, they just failed to report it. The stimulus is *not* detected below the objective threshold of detection.

According to Timothy Moore, "Empirical studies of subliminal perception indicate that, with rare exceptions, the phenomenon appears to be confined to a certain range of stimulus intensities (Cheesman and Merikle 1986). This range places the stimulus below a threshold of subjective or phenomenal awareness, but above an objective detection or discrimination threshold. In other words, subliminal perception is not perception in the absence of stimulus detection; it occurs when our introspective reports are at odds with or are discrepant with objective measures of detection. Subjects commonly profess to guess or to claim ignorance of a stimulus's identity when they are nevertheless making use of stimulus information."[69] None of this is discussed in the study and no attempt was made to find out where the subliminal self-help tapes from the three different companies fit in this standard. Possibly they selected programs where no audible voices could be retrieved as this seems to be how some of the researchers define 'truly subliminal.'

What Does it Mean?

So, what do we have here? A widely circulated research paper that concludes subliminal self-help programs do not work that either did not look at the actual technologies used by the different manufacturers or carefully fit a particular definition of subliminal that several researchers have shown not to work? A study that utilized subliminal tapes from three different companies so that, even if one of the programs worked, any positive result would be muted, if not drowned out, by the negative results from the other two programs? A study without any real controls, which makes all the results questionable? It also calls into question Moore, Phelps, and Exum's distinctions between real versus pseudoscientists.

For the Record

Quite honestly, I do agree there is value in Merikle's distinction between subjective and objective thresholds of stimulus detection. Eldon and I just do not call programs with no detectable affirmations subliminal. For a subliminal self-help program to work, the affirmations cannot be buried so deeply under the primary track that they cannot be detected. Therefore, Eldon refers to his InnerTalk subliminal technology as 'an audio illusion'—he uses audio techniques to distract you from consciously hearing the messages. This may also be why InnerTalk has been referred to as the unsubliminal subliminal. For us, if you cannot report hearing the affirmations, but they still work to prime your self-talk, then that is subliminal enough. Sadly, there are a lot of subliminal self-help companies making a range of claims that may be unfounded, and that use a variety of technologies that may or may not fit any sensible definition for subliminal stimuli.

Additionally, for your interest, the Greenwald, Spangenberg, et al. paper stated that "There are numerous reports of claimed therapeutic effects of subliminal audiotapes, but no such report has appeared in a competitively refereed psychology journal. Further, many of these reports have been produced by researchers associated with manufacturers of the tapes." This is an important point. We have long stated that researching your products can lead to cherry-picking results to suit your agenda. Yes, we too have conducted some research on InnerTalk, but in addition to our research, we have also made our programs available to others to study. Several double-blind studies were carried out at independent universities and institutions. One of these at least was sent to Spangenberg for his research. At the time of Greenwald's study, while these studies fulfilled thesis requirements at several universities, none were published in peer-reviewed journals. This changed in 1995 when Thomas Plante (Stanford University) and his team published their paper demonstrating the efficacy of InnerTalk programs for reducing test-taking anxiety in the *Journal of Anxiety, Stress, and Coping.*[70]

Definitions and Designs

It seems the lack of real definitions, outlandish claims, incredible fears, and big-money interests have caused confusion when it comes to subliminal messaging. Definitions are important:

- To say that subconscious perception exists is not to say that it works the same as conscious perception.
- To say we can perceive the information presented beneath the level of conscious awareness is not to say we can perceive information that is simply undetectable.
- To say that information taken in on a subconscious level can influence your feelings and choices is not to say it can force you to behave in ways contrary to your best interest.

It does not help when scientists examining this phenomenon bring in their own beliefs and biases—biases often based on decades of their own research. We saw with the work on the Pygmalion effect how the controversy raged for over thirty years because one side said the teacher's attitude could affect the students' progress and the other side was adamantly against being able to change IQ. So, the same things have occurred with subliminal research, with studies being run that belie what is being claimed.

Greenwald ran another study that tested a person's ability to identify words based on milliseconds of exposure.[71] Moore ran another study giving the subjects ten seconds of exposure and then testing if they were able to discern which of two programs were being played.[72] To me, that is like stating that coffee is believed to be a stimulant so we will place one drop of coffee on the subject's tongue and then run a test to see if factors like heart rate have increased. Even so, based on this work, Anthony Greenwald has since shifted his opinion on subliminal information processing, and now says, it "can work, but not very well."[73]

You should also note that, while the story denying *any* efficacy of subliminal messages has been widely shared, some interesting details can slip under the radar. Timothy Moore, who presented the flawed research paper as part of his expert testimony for the defendants in the Judas Priest trial is not a total disbeliever of subliminal information processing: "As Moore points out, there is considerable evidence for subliminal perception or the detection of information outside of self-reports of awareness."[74] "Can the meaning of a stimulus affect the behavior of observers in some way in the absence of their awareness of the stimulus? In a word, yes. While there is some controversy, respectable scientific evidence also exists that observers' responses can be shown to be affected by stimuli they claim not to have seen."[75]

Other researchers have also been quietly studying this phenomenon and reporting positive results. If you would like to investigate this more for yourself, Eldon's favorite book on the subject is *The Unconscious* by Joel Weinberger and Valentina Stoycheva. Earlier, we discussed the different meta-analyses that demonstrated the effectiveness of subliminal techniques when done properly. This is a powerful tool, but again, not the only one we have reviewed.

NOTES

Key Points

This has been an important chapter for a variety of reasons. At the beginning of this book, we spoke about the 'rest of the story'—how knowing additional background details can reveal an entirely different picture.

We know that humans are herd animals needing to belong. In both the Pygmalion story and the subliminal story, we have seen ridicule being used to influence opinions.

When we looked at the automatic aspects of the mind (chapter 6), we saw many ways in which our opinions could be influenced. In this chapter, we saw the use of the authority figure, framing, context, straw man fallacy, and more to influence public opinion.

By looking at the details behind studies, we have learned that just because a study purports to have made a finding in one direction does not make it necessarily valid.

Again, we have seen the power of the media to disseminate incorrect information—and the fact that a lie (or mistake) repeated often enough can gain the appearance of truth.

Hopefully, in this chapter, you have found more reason to respect your own intelligence and reasoning abilities. It took basic high school science teachings to highlight some of the issues in the study that supposedly proved subliminal communication does not work.

APPENDIX B

SCIENCE REVIEW OF INNERTALK

(Please note: Eldon's subliminal technology was originally called *Whole Brain*. This name was changed to *InnerTalk*. For ease of reading, the name, *InnerTalk,* is used in the following briefs, even though the actual papers may refer to *Whole Brain*.)

Under the direction of Maurice P. Shuman, Jr., General Director Special Programs of Instruction, a pilot study was conducted by Duval County Public School System at the Pre-trial Detention Center in Jacksonville, FL. Twenty-two incarcerated juveniles participated in a study program using InnerTalk programs designed to assist in preparation for the GED *examination*. The GED final test results show that eighteen of the twenty-two troubled students passed the full GED examination. (1997).

Kim Roche (Phoenix University) studied the effect of an InnerTalk program with children diagnosed as having *Attention Deficit Hyperactive Disorder*. Her findings indicated a significant positive effect. (1993)

Under the direction of Dr. Jose Salvador Hernandez Gonzalez and on behalf of the Institute of Mexicano Social Services (Medicas), twenty-five patients were exposed to both InnerTalk video and audio *Freedom from*

Dental Anxiety programs for thirty minutes prior to treatment and thirty minutes during treatment. The conclusion stated that the InnerTalk program was 100% effective in reducing the patient's anxiety about the treatment and the noise made by the high-speed handpiece and in reducing the pain suffered in comparison to previous experience. The report goes on to recommend the use of InnerTalk by dental surgeons. (1998)

Jane Alexander, an independent journalist and researcher in the United Kingdom, ran her own study on the efficacy of InnerTalk. Independent testers worked with *Ultra Success Power, Neat and Tidy, Attracting the Right Love Relationship,* and *Jealousy.* All the testers reported positive results. (2002)

Cosmetic Surgeon R. Youngblood and surgical staff tested the effect of the InnerTalk *Pre- and Post-Operative* program on 360 patients. They reported a 32% decrease in anesthetic requirements by volume as compared to a historical control group. (1988-1990)

Thomas Plante (Stanford University) together with Michael DiGregorio, Gerdenio Manuel and Bao-Tran T. Doan (Santa Clara University), evaluated the effect of InnerTalk on test anxiety. The statistical data significantly supported the hypothesis that the InnerTalk subliminal technology could be an effective tool in lowering *test anxiety.* (1993)

At the University of Southern California, Diana Ashley studied the effect of InnerTalk on academic achievement. Her conclusion found a significant increase in *learning* among students in the experimental group. (1993)

Patricia Galbraith and Brad Barton carried out a study at Weber State University on the effects of the InnerTalk program, *Freedom from Stress.* The psychological test results showed a significant decrease in stress. (1990)

Jane Alexander, an independent journalist and researcher in the United Kingdom, investigated several alternative methods for weight loss. Not only did she find significant weight loss using the CD for *weight loss,* but she also did a price comparison between the different alternative treatments. Her cost comparison on a per pound weight loss basis showed costs of £26/lb for acupuncture, £11.42/lb for hypnotherapy, £29.28/lb for homeopathy, and £3.28/lb for InnerTalk. (2002)

James Reid carried out a double-blind study at Colorado State University using the InnerTalk program *Freedom from Depression.* It was found that using the program for more than seventeen hours led to a significant decrease on the Beck Depression scale. This study not only shows the effectiveness of the InnerTalk program but also indicated that the effectiveness of the program was related to dosage. (1990)

Combining InnerTalk Weight Loss *audio* and *video* with *Echo-Tech* audio and a special nutritional program developed and marketed by Oxyfresh International, Harbans Sraon (University of California Irvine) conducted a ninety-day weight loss study. Sraon coached each subject to visualize their clear goal in terms of body fitness and reviewed progress weekly. Sraon reported that 90% of the subjects (ten men and fifteen women) lost significant weight. (1998)

A double-blind study conducted by Peter Kruse (Bremen University, Germany) using a specially created InnerTalk program strongly demonstrated the influence of the program on decision-making. Kruse said, "The Taylor Method" works. (1991)

In a double-blind study at the Utah State Prison performed by McCusker, Liston, and Taylor, the InnerTalk technology was deemed effective in altering *self-esteem* among inmates. As a result, the Utah State Prison installed and maintained a voluntary program library for inmates. (1985-1986)

The findings from a longitudinal study on the InnerTalk program for *Cancer* showed that 43% of the patients who used the program went into remission. For the other patients, who eventually passed away, the average life span beyond the original prognosis was significantly extended. (1988-1991)

A study carried out by Rainer Pelka (Armed Forces University, Munich, Germany) on an InnerTalk program for *weight loss*, showed average weight losses of thirteen pounds in subjects who used the program without following any other kind of diet or exercise regimen. (1991)

Experimental psychologist Julian Isaacs investigated the effects of the following InnerTalk programs: *No More Procrastination, Time Management, Confidence Power, Freedom from Stress, Positive Relationships, I Am Assertive, and High Self Esteem*. After three studies, it was concluded that the programs produced verifiable significant positive results. (1991)

Also Credited For

Numerous clinical studies with single and multiple subjects have also found effectiveness with InnerTalk in areas as diverse as anorexia to dyslexia. Additionally, InnerTalk has been credited by professional coaches for significantly contributing to winning sports events ranging from football championships to National and Olympic judo medals.

"Currently we have been playing *Spiritual Healing* twelve hours a day. You can see he (Vic Jr.) is starting to walk some, especially up the stairs. He is also starting to eat a lot more. And he has a good pulmonary function test."

~ Vic Wedel, co-inventor of ultrasound biopsy guide and founder of Civco Medical Solutions

"Your programs made the difference!"

~ Coach Mike Price, former head coach at Weber State University, Washington State University, and University of Texas at El Paso. Coach Price credited InnerTalk with taking the team at Weber State University to the Big Sky Championship for the first time and Washington State to the Rose Bowl.

"Your programs give me the boost to train and win—Thank you for training my mind for success."

~ Debbie Lawrence, World Record Holder, Olympian Racewalker for the U.S.

"No one on the National Judo Institute's team had ever won a National World or Pan Am medal until 1987, when the team began using an InnerTalk audio program as part of their training. The team's skills increased so dramatically that this year they won six Pan Am medals, one World Medal and two National medals. NJI members are now slated to fill half the spots on the 1992 Olympic Team."

~ Phil Porter, Colorado Springs, CO

"Thanks for helping our program succeed for a second straight year."

~ Gerald Carr, Football Coach, Weber State University

Testimonials

"I very often find it difficult to stay focused and motivated, but the CD really helps me concentrate. I was especially impressed at how calm I was on the day of the exams. I normally get very nervous, can't eat, and get an upset stomach but it just felt like any other day. Needless to say, I passed."

~ T. A.

"I have used the recording for 8 weeks. During this time, I have been able to lower my blood pressure to 145/78. I'm still taking my medication. Before listening to the recording, I couldn't control my blood pressure with the medication!"

~ M. M.

"It's been exactly a year since I started listening to the recordings. My thinking has drastically changed, I've stopped using drugs completely, I'm uncomfortable around anyone using them, I have changed my social activities completely. I know in my heart that I have won the Big One."

~ T. D.

"Since listening to your recordings, I have divorced my abusive husband and I have lost over 100 pounds! My self-esteem has risen dramatically!"

~ J. A.

"I am telling all my friends about your recordings. My sales have quadrupled this past year. It's the best I have ever done."

~ J. P.

Two months ago, I began my own self-improvement program with the aid of your CDs. This is what has happened so far: I have started and have been sticking to a budget. I think before I spend. I've started a savings account. I am paying off debt. It has become fun for me to manage my money. I am paying more attention to financial related news and information. My comprehension has increased tremendously and effortlessly. I have no problem learning anything. It seems that I do not have to try to learn, I just pick it up naturally. I have set many goals and each day I actually do something to get closer to achieving them. "

~ L. A.

(If you would like to read more success stories, please go to: https://www.innertalk.com/testimonials1.html)

Now, testimonials are not scientific proof, and not everyone who uses InnerTalk experiences such amazing results. But these stories do show what may be possible when the correct set of positive subliminal affirmations is used to change underlying self-destructive beliefs.

Listing of Research Papers

Ashley, D. 1993. "The Effect of Subliminally Presented Reinforcing Stimuli on Factual Material." University of Southern California.

Galbraith, P. & Barton, B. 1990. "Subliminal Relaxation: Myth or Method." Weber State University.

Gonzalez, J.S.H. 1998. Unpublished Report.

Isaacs, J. 1991 Unpublished report. Independent study carried out on behalf of *The Other 90%*.

Kruse, P. et. al. 1991. "Suggestion and Perceptual Instability: Auditory Subliminal Influences." Bremen University, Germany.

Pelka, R. 1993. "Application of Subliminal Therapy to Overweight Subjects." Armed Forces University, Munich, Germany.

Doan, B.T., Plante, T. G., DiGregorio, M., & Manuel, G. 1995. "Influence of

Aerobic Exercise Activity and Relaxation Training on Coping with Test-Taking Anxiety." *Anxiety, Stress, and Coping.* 8, 101-111.

Reid, J. 1990. "*Free of Depression* Subliminal Tape Study." Colorado State University, 1990

Roche, K. 1993. "The Effect of a Whole Brain Subliminal Program on Children Diagnosed with Attention Deficit Hyperactive Disorder." Phoenix University.

Sraon, H.S. 1997. "Weight Loss Study Produces Early Success." *Oxygram.* Vol 13, Issue II, Dec. 1997.

Taylor, E. 1990. "The Effect of Subliminal Auditory Stimuli in a Surgical Setting Involving Anesthetic Requirements." St. John's University.

Taylor, E., McCusker, C. & Liston, L. "A Study of the Effects of Subliminal Communication on Inmates at the Utah State Prison." *Subliminal Communication 2nd ed.* R.K. Books. Medical Lake, WA.

Taylor, E., & McCusker, C. 1995. "The Use of Subliminal Auditory Stimuli in Terminally Ill Oncology Patients." *International Journal of Alternative and Complimentary Medicine.* Feb. 1995.

Taylor, E. & Roche, K. 1994. "New Cognitive Therapy Successful with ADHD." *International Journal of Alternative and Complementary Medicine.* October 1994.

ENDNOTES

Introduction

1. Taylor, E. 2019. "Mind Training 101." *Eldon Taylor Blog.* July 17, 2019. https://www.eldontaylor.com/blog/2019/07/17/mind-training-101/

Chapter One: The Story of Positive Thinking

1. Taylor, E. 2015. *Gotcha! The Subordination of Free Will.* WA: Progressive Awareness Research.
2. Smillie, L. D. 2020. "Why Are There So Few Vegetarians?" *Psychology Today.* January 1, 2020. https://www.psychologytoday.com/us/blog/the-patterns-persons/202001/why-are-there-so-few-vegetarians
3. Newberg, A. & Waldman, M. 2012. "Why This Word Is So Dangerous to Say or Hear." *Psychology Today.* August 1, 2012. https://www.psychologytoday.com/us/blog/words-can-change-your-brain/201208/why-word-is-so-dangerous-say-or-hear

Chapter Two: The Power of Your Mind

1. Kanchwala, H. 2019. "Walking on Hot Coal: How Do People Firewalk?" *Science ABC.* January 22, 2022. https://www.scienceabc.com/humans/how-do-some-people-firewalk.html
2. — "Tony Robbins Firewalker." *Tony Robbins Firewalk.* https://tonyrobbinsfirewalk.com
3. — "Helpful Hints When Walking on Snow or Ice." *Iowa State University.* https://www.ehs.iastate.edu/weather/winter/walking
4. Editorial Staff. 2013. "How to Walk Across Hot Coals." *Mental Floss.* August 1, 2013. https://www.mentalfloss.com/article/52012/how-walk-across-hot-coals
5. Ross, E. 2005. "Can Firewalking Really Change Your Life?" *Associated*

Press. March 14, 2005. https://culteducation.com/group/1289-general-information/8625-can-firewalking-really-change-your-life-.html
6. Bhandari, S. 2022. "Dissociative Identity Disorder (Multiple Personality Disorder)." *WebMD.* January 22, 2022. https://www.webmd.com/mental-health/dissociative-identity-disorder-multiple-personality-disorder#1
7. Goleman, D. 1988. "Probing the Enigma of Multiple Personality." *New York Times.* June 28, 1988. https://www.nytimes.com/1988/06/28/science/probing-the-enigma-of-multiple-personality.html
and
Talbot, M. 1992. *The Holographic Universe.* NY: Harper Perennial.
8. Goleman, D. 1985. "New Focus on Multiple Personality." *New York Times.* May 21, 1985. https://www.nytimes.com/1985/05/21/science/new-focus-on-multiple-personality.html
and
Talbot, M. 1992. *The Holographic Universe.* NY: Harper Perennial.
9. Booth, C. 2005. "The Rod of Aesculapios: John Haygarth (1740-1827) and Perkins' Metallic Tractors." *J. Med. Biogr.* 13(3):155-61. https://pubmed.ncbi.nlm.nih.gov/16059528/
and
Mestel, R. 2017. "The Imagination Effect: A History of Placebo Power." *Knowable Magazine.* October 25, 2017. https://www.knowablemagazine.org/article/mind/2017/imagination-effect-history-placebo-power
10. Newman, T. 2017. "Is the Placebo Effect Real?" *Medical News Today.* September 7, 2017. https://www.medicalnewstoday.com/articles/306437
and
Tilburt, J. et al. 2008. "Prescribing 'Placebo Treatments': Results of National Survey of U.S. Internists and Rheumatologists." *British Medical Journal.* October 23, 2008. https://www.ncbi.nlm.nih.gov/pmc/articles/PMC2572204/
11. Newman, T. 2017. "Is the Placebo Effect Real?" *Medical News Today.* September 7, 2017. https://www.medicalnewstoday.com/articles/306437
12. Millard, S. 2017. "The Placebo Problem, Part 10: The Devil's in the

Details." *Premier Research*. October 20, 2017. https://premier-research.com/blog/perspectives-placebo-problem-part-10-devils-details/
13. Ibid
14. Newman, T. 2017. "Is the Placebo Effect Real?" *Medical News Today*. September 7, 2017. https://www.medicalnewstoday.com/articles/306437
15. Newman, T. 2017. "Is the Placebo Effect Real?" *Medical News Today*. September 7, 2017. https://www.medicalnewstoday.com/articles/306437
    and
    Millard, S. 2017. "The Placebo Problem, Part 10: The Devil's in the Details." *Premier Research*. October 20, 2017. https://premier-research.com/blog/perspectives-placebo-problem-part-10-devils-details/
16. Kirsch, I. & Sapirstein, G. 1998. "Listening to Prozac but Hearing Placebo: A Meta-Analysis of Antidepressant Medication." *Prevention & Treatment*. Vol. 1, Article 0002a. June 26, 1998. http://psychrights.org/research/digest/CriticalThinkRxCites/KirschandSapirstein1998.pdf
17. Ibid
18. Kirsch, I. 2014. "Antidepressants and the Placebo Effect." *Z Pscychol*. 2014; 222(3): 128–134. https://www.ncbi.nlm.nih.gov/pmc/articles/PMC4172306
19. Ibid
20. Niemi, M.B. 2009. "Placebo Effect: A Cure in the Mind." *Scientific American Mind*. Feb. 25, 2009. https://www.scientificamerican.com/article/placebo-effect-a-cure-in-the-mind/
    and
    Blakeslee, S. 1998. "Placebos Prove So Powerful Even Experts Are Surprised; New Studies Explore the Brain's Triumph Over Reality." *New York Times*. October 13, 1998. https://www.nytimes.com/1998/10/13/science/placebos-prove-so-powerful-even-experts-are-surprised-new-studies-explore-brain.html
21. Baylor College of Medicine. 2002. "Study Finds Common Knee Surgery No Better Than Placebo." *ScienceDaily*. July 12, 2002. www.sciencedaily.com/releases/2002/07/020712075415.htm
22. Harvard Medical School. 2014. "The Nocebo Response." *Harvard*

Health Publishing. March 9, 2014. https://www.health.harvard.edu/newsletter_article/The_nocebo_response

23. Ibid
24. Ibid
25. Ibid
26. Grierson, B. 2014. "What if Age is Nothing but a Mindset?" *New York Times.* October 22, 2014. https://www.nytimes.com/2014/10/26/magazine/what-if-age-is-nothing-but-a-mind-set.html

    and

    Langer, E. J. 2009. *Counterclockwise.* NY: Ballentine Books.
27. Ibid
28. Ibid
29. Staff. "Oldest Bodybuilders that Ever Lived." *Oldest.org.* https://www.oldest.org/sports/bodybuilders/
30. —. "Fauja Singh." *Wikipedia.* https://en.wikipedia.org/wiki/Fauja_Singh

    and

    Davies, C. 2011. "World's Oldest Marathon Runner Completes Toronto Race at Age 100." *The Guardian.* October 17, 2011. https://www.theguardian.com/uk/2011/oct/17/worlds-oldest-marathon-runner-100

Chapter Three: Models of the Mind

1. — "The Controversy of 'Female Hysteria.'" *Medical News Today.* https://www.medicalnewstoday.com/articles/the-controversy-of-female-hysteria
2. Devereux, C. 2014. "Hysteria, Feminism, and Gender Revisited: The Case of the Second Wave." *Association of Canadian College and University Teachers of English.* Vol. 40, Issue 1, March 2014. pp. 19-45. https://ojs.lib.uwo.ca/index.php/esc/article/view/9593/7693
3. — "The Controversy of 'Female Hysteria.'" *Medical News Today.* https://www.medicalnewstoday.com/articles/the-controversy-of-female-hysteria
4. Aleccia, J. 2008. "Without TV Ads, Restless Legs May Take a Hike." *NBC News.* May 14, 2008. https://www.nbcnews.com/health/health-news/without-tv-ads-restless-legs-may-take-hike-flna1c9463951
5. Ibid
6. Ibid

7. — "The Origins of Personality." *Open Text BC*. https://opentextbc.ca/introductiontopsychology/chapter/11-2-the-origins-of-personality/
8. Pinker, S. 1997. *How the Mind Works*. New York: W.W. Norton & Co.
9. Cherry, K. 2021. "How the Primary Process is Used in Personality." *Very Well Mind*. May 3, 2021. https://www.verywellmind.com/what-is-the-primary-process-2795474
10. Cherry, K. 2020. "The Secondary Process and Delayed Gratification." *Very Well Mind*. July 18, 2020. https://www.verywellmind.com/what-is-the-secondary-process-2795874
11. Cherry, K. 2020. "Theories and Terminology of Personality Psychology." *Very Well Mind*. December 1, 2020. https://www.verywellmind.com/personality-psychology-study-guide-2795699
12. Kelland, M. "Personality Theory." *Commons: Open Educational Resources*. July 7, 2017. https://www.oercommons.org/authoring/22859-personality-theory/15/view
13. Ismail, N.A.H. & Tekke, M. 2015. "Rediscovering Rogers's Self Theory and Personality." *Journal of Educational, Health and Community Psychology*. 2014. Vol. 4. No. 3. https://www.researchgate.net/publication/286456614_Rediscovering_Rogers's_Self_Theory_and_Personality
14. Ismail, N.A.H. & Tekke, M. 2015. "Rediscovering Rogers's Self Theory and Personality." *Journal of Educational, Health and Community Psychology*. 2014. Vol. 4. No. 3. https://www.researchgate.net/publication/286456614_Rediscovering_Rogers's_Self_Theory_and_Personality
    and
    Cherry, K. 2022. "What Is Self-Concept?" *Very Well Mind*. February 14, 2022. https://www.verywellmind.com/what-is-self-concept-2795865
15. Cherry, K. 2022. "What Is Self-Concept?" *Very Well Mind*. February 14, 2022. https://www.verywellmind.com/what-is-self-concept-2795865
16. Taylor, E. 2013. *Choices and Illusions*. Carlsbad, CA: Hay House.
17. Ibid
18. — "The Origins of Personality." *Open Text BC*. https://opentextbc.ca/introductiontopsychology/chapter/11-2-the-origins-of-personality/

19. Ibid
20. — "Freud's Model of the Human Mind." *Journal Psyche.* http://journalpsyche.org/understanding-the-human-mind/
21. Benson, H., Lehmann, J., Malhotra, M. et al. "Body Temperature Changes During the Practice of G Tum-Mo Yoga." *Nature* 295, 234–236 (1982). https://doi.org/10.1038/295234a0
22. Staff. 2002. "Meditation Dramatically Changes Body Temperatures." *The Harvard Gazette.* April 18, 2002. https://news.harvard.edu/gazette/story/2002/04/meditation-dramatically-changes-body-temperatures/
23. University of California - Los Angeles. 2011. "Is Meditation the Push-Up for the Brain? Study Shows Practice May Have Potential to Change Brain's Physical Structure." *ScienceDaily.* www.sciencedaily.com/releases/2011/07/110714091940.htm
24. Luders, E. et. al. 2011. "Enhanced Brain Connectivity in Long-Term Meditation Practitioners." *ScienceDirect.* August 15, 2011. https://www.sciencedirect.com/science/article/abs/pii/S1053811911006008
25. Andrei, M. 2015. "Man Wakes Up After 12 Years of Coma: "I Was Aware of Everything." *ZME Science.* January 15, 2015. https://www.zmescience.com/medicine/mind-and-brain/man-coma-wakes-up-14012015/ and

    Pistorius, M. 2013. *Ghost Boy: The Miraculous Escape of a Misdiagnosed Boy Trapped Inside His Own Body.* New York, NY: Thomas Nelson.
26. Mcleod, S. 2018. "Carl Jung's Theories: Archetypes, and the Collective Unconscious." *Simple Psychology.* https://academyofideas.com/2017/02/carl-jung-what-are-archetypes/
27. Steele, J. 1984. "Emerson, Hawthorne, Melville and the Unconscious." *Studies in English, New Series.* Vol. 5. Special American Literature Issue. 1984-1987. https://core.ac.uk/download/pdf/335348678.pdf
28. Frischer, L. 2022. "What is the Collective Unconscious?" *Very Well Mind.* March 18, 2022. https://www.verywellmind.com/what-is-the-collective-unconscious-2671571
29. Pearson, C. S. *The Twelve Archetypes.* https://www.uiltexas.org/files/capitalconference/Twelve_Character_Archetypes.pdf
30. — "Carl Jung: What Are the Archetypes?" *Academy of Ideas.* https://

academyofideas.com/2017/02/carl-jung-what-are-archetypes/
31. Osho. "The Great Palace of Consciousness." *Unio Mystica. https://www.osho.com/osho-online-library/osho-talks/superconsciousness-unconsciousness-collective-d70cc926-554?p=a2da8795b782c363a6078e10fcf6bcb7*
32. Bargh, J. A. 2019. "The Modern Unconscious." *World Psychiatry.* May 6, 2019. https://onlinelibrary.wiley.com/doi/10.1002/wps.20625
33. Ibid
34. McLeod, S. 2018. "Erik Erikson's Stages of Psychosocial Development." *Simple Psychology.* https://www.simplypsychology.org/Erik-Erikson.html
   and
   Cherry, K. 2022. "Erikson's Stages of Development." *Very Well Mind.* August 3, 2022. https://www.verywellmind.com/erik-eriksons-stages-of-psychosocial-development-2795740

Chapter Four: The Mechanical Brain

1. Price, M. 2009. "The Left Brain Knows What the Right Hand is Doing." *American Psychological Association.* January 2009, Vol 40, No. 1. https://www.apa.org/monitor/2009/01/brain
2. Staff. "Brain Anatomy and How the Brain Works." *Hopkins Medicine.* https://www.hopkinsmedicine.org/health/conditions-and-diseases/anatomy-of-the-brain
   and
   Price, M. 2009. "The Left Brain Knows What the Right Hand is Doing." *American Psychological Association.* January 2009, Vol 40, No. 1. https://www.apa.org/monitor/2009/01/brain
3. Rogers-Ramachandran, D., & Ramachandran, V. 2008. "Right Side Up." *Scientific American.* May 1, 2008. https://www.scientificamerican.com/article/right-side-up-2008-05/
4. Shelley, B. P. 2016. "Footprints of Phineas Gage: Historical Beginnings on the Origins of Brain and Behavior and the Birth of Cerebral Localizationism." *Archives of Medicine and Health Sciences.* 2016. 4:280-6. https://www.amhsjournal.org/text.asp?2016/4/2/280/196182
5 —2017. "Phrenology and 'Scientific Racism' in the 19th

Century." *Real Archaeology.* March 15, 2017. https://pages.vassar.edu/realarchaeology/2017/03/05/phrenology-and-scientific-racism-in-the-19th-century/

6. Shelley, B. P. 2016. "Footprints of Phineas Gage: Historical Beginnings on the Origins of Brain and Behavior and the Birth of Cerebral Localizationism." *Archives of Medicine and Health Sciences.* 2016. 4:280-6. https://www.amhsjournal.org/text.asp?2016/4/2/280/196182
7. Harlow, J. M. 1869. *Recovery From the Passage of an Iron Bar Through the Head.* Boston, MA: David Clapp & Son. https://collections.countway.harvard.edu/onview/index.php/items/show/25407
8. Twomey, S. 2010. "Phineas Gage: Neuroscience's Most Famous Patient." *Smithsonian Magazine.* January 2010. https://www.smithsonianmag.com/history/phineas-gage-neurosciences-most-famous-patient-11390067/
9. Harlow, J. M. 1869. *Recovery From the Passage of an Iron Bar Through the Head.* Boston, MA: David Clapp & Son. https://www.google.com/books/edition/Recovery_from_the_Passage_of_an_Iron_Bar/WgE2AQAAMAAJ
10. O'Driscoll, K. 1998. "'No Longer Gage': An Iron Bar Through the Head." *British Medical Journal.* December 19, 1998. 317:1673. https://www.researchgate.net/publication/13430908_'No_longer_Gage'_An_iron_bar_through_the_head_Early_observations_of_personality_change_after_injury_to_the_prefrontal_cortex
11. Harlow, J. M. 1869. *Recovery From the Passage of an Iron Bar Through the Head.* David Clapp & Son. Boston: MA. https://www.google.com/books/edition/Recovery_from_the_Passage_of_an_Iron_Bar/WgE2AQAAMAAJ
12. Ibid
13. O'Driscoll, K. 1998. "'No Longer Gage': An Iron Bar Through the Head." *British Medical Journal.* December 19, 1998. 317:1673. https://www.researchgate.net/publication/13430908_'No_longer_Gage'_An_iron_bar_through_the_head_Early_observations_of_personality_change_after_injury_to_the_prefrontal_cortex
and

ENDNOTES

      Cherry, K. 2022. "Phineas Gage: His Accident and Impact on Psychology." Very Well Mind. February 24, 2022. https://www.verywellmind.com/phineas-gage-2795244

14. Staff. 2021. "The Difference Between the Left and Right Brain." *WebMD.* https://www.webmd.com/brain/the-difference-between-the-left-and-right-brain

    and

    Staff. "The Limbic System" *The University of Queensland.* https://qbi.uq.edu.au/brain/brain-anatomy/limbic-system

    and

    Staff. "Brain Anatomy and How the Brain Works." *John Hopkins Medicine: Health.* https://www.hopkinsmedicine.org/health/conditions-and-diseases/anatomy-of-the-brain

15. Bogen, J. E. 1999. "Roger Wolcott Sperry. (20 August 1913 - 17 April 1994)." *Proceedings of the American Philosophical Society.* Vol. 143. pp. 492-500. September 3, 1999. https://www.jstor.org/stable/3181963

    and

    https://web.archive.org/web/20130509203516/http://www.its.caltech.edu/~jbogen/text/amerphil.html

16. Ibid

17. — "Corpus Callosotomy." *Cleveland Clinic.* https://my.clevelandclinic.org/health/treatments/11546-corpus-callosotomy

18. — "Michael Gazzaniga." University of California, Santa Barbara. https://people.psych.ucsb.edu/gazzaniga/michael/

19. Shen, H. H. 2014. "Discovering the Split Mind." *The Proceedings of the National Academy of Sciences (PNAS).* December 23, 2014. 111 (51). https://www.pnas.org/doi/full/10.1073/pnas.1422335112

20. Ibid

21. Ibid

22. — 2022. "Left Brain vs. Right Brain: What Does This Mean for Me?" *Healthline.* https://www.healthline.com/health/left-brain-vs-right-brain#left-brain-vs-right-brain-myth

23. — "Roger W. Sperry – Facts." *NobelPrize.org.* Nobel Prize Outreach AB 2022. Wed. 20 Jul 2022. https://www.nobelprize.org/prizes/

medicine/1981/sperry/facts/
24. Ibid
25. Carey, B. 2011. "Decoding the Brain's Cacophony." *NY Times*. October 31, 2011. https://www.nytimes.com/2011/11/01/science/telling-the-story-of-the-brains-cacophony-of-competing-voices.html
    and
    Gazzaniga, M. S. 2016. "The Brain Privileges Storytelling." *History News Network*. February 20, 2016. https://historynewsnetwork.org/article/162076
26. Harris, S. *Waking Up: A Guide to Spirituality without Religion*. New York: Simon & Schuster
    and
    Gazzaniga, M., Bogen, J.E., and Sperry, R.W. 1962. "Some Functional Effects of Sectioning the Cerebral Commissures in Man." *Proc Natl Acad Sci* USA 48 https://www.pnas.org/doi/10.1073/pnas.48.10.1765
27. Carey, B. 2011. "Decoding the Brain's Cacophony." *NY Times*. October 31, 2011. https://www.nytimes.com/2011/11/01/science/telling-the-story-of-the-brains-cacophony-of-competing-voices.html
    and
    Gazzaniga, M. S. 2016. "The Brain Privileges Storytelling." *History News Network*. February 20, 2016. https://historynewsnetwork.org/article/162076
28. Gazzaniga, M. S. 2016. "The Brain Privileges Storytelling." *History News Network*. February 20, 2016. https://historynewsnetwork.org/article/162076
29. Stroop, J. R. 1935. "Studies of Interference in Serial Verbal Reactions." *Journal of Experimental Psychology*, 18, 643-662. http://psychclassics.yorku.ca/Stroop/
30. Staff. "What the Stroop Effect Reveals About Our Minds." *Lesley University*. https://lesley.edu/article/what-the-stroop-effect-reveals-about-our-minds
31. Zhang, L. et al. 2014. "Studying Hemispheric Lateralization During a Stroop Task Through Near-Infrared Spectroscopy-Based Connectivity." *Journal of Biomedical Optics*. 19(5), 057012. https://doi.org/10.1117/1.

JBO.19.5.057012

32. Capizzi, M., Ambrosini, E., & Vallesi, A. 2017. "Individual Differences in Verbal and Spatial Stroop Tasks: Interactive Role of Handedness and Domain." *Frontiers in Human Neuroscience, 11,* Article 545. https://doi.org/10.3389/fnhum.2017.00545

33. Ben-Haim, M. S. et al. 2016. "The Emotional Stroop Test: Assessing Cognitive Performance under Exposure to Emotional Content. *J. Vis. Exp.* (112): 53720. https://www.ncbi.nlm.nih.gov/pmc/articles/PMC4993290/

34. Mitterschiffthaler, M. T. et al. 2008. "Neural Basis of the Emotional Stroop Interference Effect in Major Depression." *Psychological Medicine.* 38, 247-256. https://www.researchgate.net/publication/6015562_Neural_basis_of_the_emotional_Stroop_interference_effect_in_major_depression

35. Liu, S. et al. 2012. "Increased Intra-Individual Reaction Time Variability in Cocaine-Dependent Subjects: Role of Cocaine-Related Cues." *Addictive Behaviors.* 37(2): 193-197. https://www.ncbi.nlm.nih.gov/pmc/articles/PMC3253315/

36. Streeter, C. C. et al. 2007. "Performance of the Stroop Predicts Treatment Compliance in Cocaine-Dependent Individuals." *Neuropsychopharmacy.* 33, 827-836. https://www.nature.com/articles/1301465

37. Engelhard, I. M., Merckelbach, H. L. G. J., & van den Hout, M. A. (2003). "The Guilty Knowledge Test and the Modified Stroop Task in Detection of Deception: An Explorative Study." *Psychological Reports.* 92(2), 683-691. https://cris.maastrichtuniversity.nl/ws/files/1035258/guid-28342f18-8234-4999-9bad-4c904370908c-ASSET1.0.pdf and https://pubmed.ncbi.nlm.nih.gov/12785660/

38. Rogers, M. 2013. "Researchers Debunk Myth of 'Right-Brain' and 'Left-Brain' Personality Traits." University of Utah: Health. August 14, 2013. https://healthcare.utah.edu/publicaffairs/news/2013/08/08-14-2013_brain_personality_traits.php
and
Nielsen, J. A., Zielinski, B.A., Ferguson, M.A, Lainhart, J. E, & Anderson, J. S. 2013. "An Evaluation of the Left-Brain vs. Right-Brain

Hypothesis with Resting State Functional Connectivity Magnetic Resonance Imaging." *PLoS ONE* 8(8): e71275. https://doi.org/10.1371/journal.pone.0071275

39. Pietrangelo, A. 2022. "Left Brain vs. Right Brain: What Does This Mean for Me?" *Healthline.* https://www.healthline.com/health/left-brain-vs-right-brain

and

Nielsen, J. A., Zielinski, B.A., Ferguson, M.A, Lainhart, J. E, & Anderson, J. S. 2013. "An Evaluation of the Left-Brain vs. Right-Brain Hypothesis with Resting State Functional Connectivity Magnetic Resonance Imaging." *PLoS ONE* 8(8): e71275. https://doi.org/10.1371/journal.pone.0071275

40. Novotney, A. 2013. "Despite What You've Been Told, You Aren't 'Left-Brained' or 'Right-Brained.'" *The Guardian.* November 16, 2013. https://www.theguardian.com/commentisfree/2013/nov/16/left-right-brain-distinction-myth

41. Ibid

42. Pietrangelo, A. 2022. "Left Brain vs. Right Brain: What Does This Mean for Me?" *Healthline.* https://www.healthline.com/health/left-brain-vs-right-brain

Chapter Five: The Automatic Nature of Your Mind

1. Cialdini, R. 1984. *Influence: The Psychology of Persuasion.* New York, NY: Quill.

2. Kosslyn, S. M. & Miller, G. W. 2013. "A New Map of How We Think: Top Brain/Bottom Brain." *The Wall Street Journal.* October 20, 2013. https://www.wsj.com/articles/SB10001424052702304410204579139423079198270

and

Kosslyn, S. M. & Miller, G. W. 2013. *Top Brain Bottom Brain.* Simon & Schuster. New York: NY

and

Taylor, E. 2015. "Top Brain Bottom Brain with Stephen M. Kosslyn, Ph.D." *Provocative Enlightenment Radio.* July 29, 2015. https://www.

eldontaylor.com/provocativeenlightenment/2015-0729-top-brain-bottom-brain-with-stephen-m-kosslyn-ph-d/
3. Ibid
4. Gervais, S. J. et al. 2012. "Seeing Women as Objects: The Sexual Body Part Recognition Bias." *European Journal of Social Psychology*. 42, 743–753. June 29, 2012. https://www.researchgate.net/publication/263449107_Seeing_women_as_objects_The_sexual_body_part_recognition_bias
   and
   University of Nebraska-Lincoln. 2012. "How Our Brains See Men as People and Women as Body Parts: Both Genders Process Images of Men, Women Differently." *ScienceDaily*. July 25, 2012. https://www.sciencedaily.com/releases/2012/07/120725150215.htm
5. Ibid
6. Kahneman, D. 2011. *Thinking Fast and Slow*. Farrar, Straus, and Giroux. New York: NY.
7. Ibid
8. Gladwell, M. 2005. *Blink: The Power of Thinking Without Thinking*. Little, Brown & Co. New York: NY.
9. Ibid
10. Ibid
11. Gladwell, M. 2005. *Blink: The Power of Thinking Without Thinking*. New York, NY: Little Brown & Co.
    and
    Oskamp, S. 1965. "Overconfidence in Case Study Judgments." *Journal of Consulting Psychology*. 29(3):261-5. https://www.researchgate.net/publication/9279747_Overconfidence_in_Case_Study_Judgments
12. Kahneman, D. 2011. *Thinking Fast and Slow*. Farrar, Straus, and Giroux. New York: NY.
13. Bailey, R., & Pico, J. 2022. "Defense Mechanisms." *StatPearls Publishing*. https://www.ncbi.nlm.nih.gov/books/NBK559106/
14. Cherry, K. 2022. "What Is Repression?" *Very Well Mind*. March 1, 2022. https://www.verywellmind.com/repression-as-a-defense-mechanism-4586642
    and

Patel, J., & Patel, P. 2019. "Consequences of Repression of Emotion: Physical Health, Mental Health and General Well Being." *International Journal of Psychotherapy Practice and Research*. https://openaccesspub.org/ijpr/article/999

15. McRaney, D. *You are Not so Smart*. Gotham Books. England.
16. Latane, B., & Darley, J. 1969. "Bystander 'Apathy.'" *American Scientist*, 57, 244–268. https://www.truthaboutnursing.org/research/orig/latane_and_darley/bystander_apathy.pdf
17. Manning, R. et al. 2007. "The Kitty Genovese Murder and the Social Psychology of Helping: The Parable of the 38 Witnesses." *American Psychologist*. 62(6):555-62. https://www.researchgate.net/publication/5967912_The_Kitty_Genovese_Murder_and_the_Social_Psychology_of_Helping_The_Parable_of_the_38_Witnesses
18. Latane, B., & Darley, J. 1969. "Bystander 'Apathy.'" *American Scientist*, 57, 244–268. https://www.truthaboutnursing.org/research/orig/latane_and_darley/bystander_apathy.pdf
and
Hortensius, R. & de Gelder, B. 2018. "From Empathy to Apathy: The Bystander Effect Revisited." *The Association for Psychological Sciences*. Vol. 27, Issue 4. pp 249-256. https://journals.sagepub.com/doi/full/10.1177/0963721417749653
19. Hortensius, R. & de Gelder, B. 2018. "From Empathy to Apathy: The Bystander Effect Revisited." *The Association for Psychological Sciences*. Vol. 27, Issue 4. pp 249-256. https://journals.sagepub.com/doi/full/10.1177/0963721417749653
20. 9News. 2021. "Man Hit by Car, Left in Street While Other Cars Drive Around Him." *9News*. Feb. 11, 2021. https://www.youtube.com/watch?v=k2unMc9tEh8
21. Acevedo, N. 2021. "Riders Watched as a Woman Was Raped on a SEPTA Train but No One Called 911, Police Say." *NBC News*. October 16, 2021. https://www.nbcnews.com/news/us-news/riders-watched-woman-was-raped-septa-train-no-one-called-n1281695
22. Latane, B., & Darley, J. 1969. "Bystander 'Apathy.'" *American Scientist*, 57, 244–268. https://www.truthaboutnursing.org/research/orig/

latane_and_darley/bystander_apathy.pdf
23. Taylor, E. 2016. "The ESP Enigma with Diane Powell." *Provocative Enlightenment Radio.* May 12, 2016. https://www.eldontaylor.com/provocativeenlightenment/2016-0512-the-esp-enigma-with-diane-powell/
24. Kessler, G. 2016. "Recalling Hillary Clinton's Claim of 'Landing Under Sniper Fire' in Bosnia." *The Washington Post.* May 23, 2016. https://www.washingtonpost.com/news/fact-checker/wp/2016/05/23/recalling-hillary-clintons-claim-of-landing-under-sniper-fire-in-bosnia/
25. Martin, P. 2003. "The Twenty Lies of George W. Bush." *WSWS.* March 20, 2003. https://www.wsws.org/en/articles/2003/03/bush-m20.html
26. Kahneman, D. 2011. *Thinking Fast and Slow.* Farrar, Straus, and Giroux. New York: NY.
27. Cialdini, R. B. 1992. *Influence: Science and Practice.* New York: Harper Collins.
28. Schjoedt, U. 2010. "The Power of Charisma—Perceived Charisma Inhibits the Frontal Executive Network of Believers in Intercessory Prayer." *Social Cognitive and Affective Neuroscience.* 6(1):119-27. https://www.ncbi.nlm.nih.gov/pmc/articles/PMC3023088/
29. Ibid
30. Ibid
31. Cialdini, R. B. 1992. *Influence: Science and Practice.* New York: Harper Collins.
32. Cialdini, R. B. 1992. *Influence: Science and Practice.* New York: Harper Collins.
and
Feinberg, R. A. 1990. "The Social Nature of the Classical Conditioning Phenomena in People." *Psychological Reports*, 67, 331–334.
and
Feinberg, R. A. 1986. "Credit Cards as Spending Facilitating Stimuli: A Conditioning Interpretation." *Journal of Consumer Research.* Vol. 13, No. 3. December 1986. https://www.jstor.org/stable/2489426
33. Helzer, E. G. & Pizarro, D. A. 2011. "Dirty Liberals! Reminders of Physical Cleanliness Influence Moral and Political Attitudes."

Psychological Science. Vol. 22, No. 4 (April 2011), pp. 517-522. https://www.jstor.org/stable/25835406

and

Dingfelder, S. 2012. "The Science of Political Advertising." *Monitor.* April 2012, Vol. 43. No. 4. Page 46. https://www.apa.org/monitor/2012/04/advertising

34. Eibach, R.P., Libby, L.K. & Ehrlinger, J. 2009. "Priming Family Values: How Being a Parent Affects Moral Evaluations of Harmless but Offensive Acts." *Journal of Experimental Social Psychology.* Vol. 45. pp. 1160-1163. https://faculty.psy.ohio-state.edu/libby/lab/Publications_files/EibachLibby&Ehrlinger2009.pdf

    and

    Dingfelder, S. 2012. "The Science of Political Advertising." *American Psychological Association.* April 2012, Vol 43, No. 4, p. 46. https://www.apa.org/monitor/2012/04/advertising

35. Ibid

36. Kahneman, D. 2011. *Thinking Fast and Slow.* Farrar, Straus, and Giroux. New York: NY.

37. Musk, E. 2021. "Should Be Taught to All at a Young Age." *Twitter.* December 19, 2021. https://twitter.com/elonmusk/status/1472649556965969925

38. Seybold, M. 2016. "The Apocryphal Twain: 'Things We Know That Just Ain't So.'" *Center for Mark Twain Studies.* October 6, 2016. https://marktwainstudies.com/the-apocryphal-twain-things-we-know-that-just-aint-so/

39. O'Toole, G. 2018. "It Ain't What You Don't Know That Gets You into Trouble. It's What You Know for Sure That Just Ain't So." *Quote Investigator.* November 23, 2018. https://quoteinvestigator.com/2018/11/18/know-trouble/

    and

    Duncan, R. 2019. "What If What You Think You Know Just Ain't So?" *Forbes.* May 31, 2019. https://www.forbes.com/sites/rodgerdeanduncan/2019/05/31/what-if-what-you-think-you-know-just-aint-so/

Chapter Six: The Question of Will

1. Carey, B. 2011. "Decoding the Brain's Cacophony." *NY Times.* October 31, 2011. https://www.nytimes.com/2011/11/01/science/telling-the-story-of-the-brains-cacophony-of-competing-voices.html
   and
   Gazzaniga, M. S. 2016. "The Brain Privileges Storytelling." *History News Network.* February 20, 2016. https://historynewsnetwork.org/article/162076
2. Harris, S. 2014. *Waking Up: A Guide to Spirituality without Religion.* Simon & Schuster. New York.
3. Gazzaniga, M. S. 2016. "The Brain Privileges Storytelling." *History News Network.* February 20, 2016. https://historynewsnetwork.org/article/162076
4. Horowitz, N. H. 1997. "Roger W. Sperry." *NobelPrize.org* https://www.nobelprize.org/prizes/medicine/1981/sperry/article/
5. Harris, S. 2014. *Waking Up: A Guide to Spirituality without Religion.* New York, NY: Simon & Schuster.
6. Dingfelder, S. 2012. "The Science of Political Advertising." *American Psychological Association.* April 2012, Vol 43, No. 4. https://www.apa.org/monitor/2012/04/advertising
7. SAGE Publications. 2012. "Note to Waitresses: Wearing Red Can Be Profitable." *ScienceDaily.* August 2, 2012. https://www.sciencedaily.com/releases/2012/08/120802111454.htm
8. University of California—Berkeley Haas School of Business. 2012. "The Advantages of Being First." *ScienceDaily.* July 2, 2012. https://www.sciencedaily.com/releases/2012/07/120702210301.htm
9. Association for Psychological Science. 2013. "Warning of Potential Side Effects of a Product Can Increase Its Sales." *Science Daily.* September 24, 2013. https://www.sciencedaily.com/releases/2013/09/130924091808.htm
   and
   Steinhart, Y., Carmon, Z., & Trope, Y. 2013. "Warnings of Adverse Side Effects Can Backfire Over Time." *Psychological Science*, 2013; 24 (9): 1842. https://www.researchgate.net/

publication/255176898_Warnings_of_Adverse_Side_Effects_Can_Backfire_Over_Time

10. Yale University. 2020. "Covid-19 Vaccine Messaging, Part 1." *National Institute of Health: U.S. National Library of Medicine*. First posted July 7, 2020. https://clinicaltrials.gov/ct2/show/study/NCT04460703

11. Carey, B. 2012. "Academic 'Dream Team' Helped Obama's Effort." *The New York Times*. November 12, 2012. www.nytimes.com/2012/11/13/health/dream-team-of-behavioral-scientists-advised-obama-campaign.html

    and

    Rosenberg, M., Confessore, N. & Cadwalladr, C. 2018. "How Trump Consultants Exploited the Facebook Data of Millions." *The New York Times*. March 17, 2018. https://www.nytimes.com/2018/03/17/us/politics/cambridge-analytica-trump-campaign.html

12. Kornhuber, H.H.; Deecke, L. (1990). "Readiness for Movement – The Bereitschaftspotential-Story." *Current Contents Life Sciences* **33**: 14. https://www.researchgate.net/publication/216305523_Readiness_for_movement_-_The_Bereitschaftspotential-Story

13. Pychyl, T. A. 2011. "Free Won't: It May Be All That We Have (or Need)." *Psychology Today*. June 20, 2011. https://www.psychologytoday.com/us/blog/dont-delay/201106/free-wont-it-may-be-all-we-have-or-need

14. Smith, K. 2011. "Neuroscience vs Philosophy: Taking Aim at Free Will." *Nature* 477, 23-2. https://www.nature.com/articles/477023a

    and

    Keim, B. 2008. "Brain Scanners Can See Your Decisions Before You Make Them." *Wired*. April 13, 2008. https://www.wired.com/2008/04/mind-decision/

    and

    Soon, C.S., Brass, M., Heinze, H.J., & Haynes, J.D. "Unconscious Determinants of Free Decisions in the Human Brain."
    Nature Neuroscience. http://citeseerx.ist.psu.edu/viewdoc/download?doi=10.1.1.520.2204&rep=rep1&type=pdf

15. Smith, K. 2011. "Neuroscience vs Philosophy: Taking Aim at Free Will." *Nature* 477, 23-2. https://www.nature.com/articles/477023a

16. Ibid
17. Cave, C. 2016. "There's No Such Thing as Free Will." *The Atlantic.* June 2016. https://www.theatlantic.com/magazine/archive/2016/06/theres-no-such-thing-as-free-will/480750/
    and
    Vohs, K. D. & Schooler, J. W. 2008. "The Value of Believing in Free Will." *Psychological Science.* Vol. 19. No. 1. https://assets.csom.umn.edu/assets/91974.pdf
18. Cave, C. 2016. "There's No Such Thing as Free Will." *The Atlantic.* June 2016. https://www.theatlantic.com/magazine/archive/2016/06/theres-no-such-thing-as-free-will/480750/
    and
    Stillman, T. F. et al. 2010. "Personal Philosophy and Personnel Achievement: Belief in Free Will Predicts Better Job Performance." *Social Psychological and Personality Science* 1(1) 43-50. https://fincham.info/papers/2010spps.pdf
19. Cave, C. 2016. "There's No Such Thing as Free Will." *The Atlantic.* June 2016. https://www.theatlantic.com/magazine/archive/2016/06/theres-no-such-thing-as-free-will/480750/
    and
    Feldman, G. et al. 2016. "The Freedom to Excel: Belief in Free Will Predicts Better Academic Performance." *Personality and Individual Differences.* 90 (2016) 377-383. https://mgto.org/wp-content/uploads/2014/05/Feldman-etal-2016-free-will-academic-performance.pdf
    and
    Baumeister, R. F. et al. 2009. "Prosocial Benefits of Feeling Free: Disbelief in Free Will Increases Aggression and Reduces Helpfulness." 31 Jan 2009. *Personality and Social Psychology Bulletin* (SAGE Publications). Vol. 35, Iss: 2, pp 260-268. https://typeset.io/papers/prosocial-benefits-of-feeling-free-disbelief-in-free-will-3atvums2gq
20. Cave, C. 2016. "There's No Such Thing as Free Will." *The Atlantic.* June 2016. https://www.theatlantic.com/magazine/archive/2016/06/theres-no-such-thing-as-free-will/480750/

and

Baumeister, R. et al. 2014. "You Didn't Have to Do That: Belief in Free Will Promotes Gratitude," *Personality and Social Psychology Bulletin* 40(11). https://www.researchgate.net/publication/265557958_You_Didn't_Have_to_Do_That_Belief_in_Free_Will_Promotes_Gratitude

and

Moynihan, A. B. et al. 2018. "Lost in the Crowd: Conformity as Escape Following Disbelief in Free Will." *European Journal of Social Psychology* 49(3). https://www.researchgate.net/publication/324681457_Lost_in_the_Crowd_Conformity_as_Escape_Following_Disbelief_in_Free_Will

21. University of California-Santa Barbara. 2016. "Do We Have Free Will? A Study by UCSB Psychologists Explores How Disbelief in Free Will Corrupts Intuitive Cooperation." *ScienceDaily*. March 1, 2016. https://www.sciencedaily.com/releases/2016/03/160301103110.htm

    and

    Protzko, J. et al. 2016. "Believing There Is No Free Will Corrupts Intuitive Cooperation." *Elsevier*. February 18, 2016. https://labs.psych.ucsb.edu/schooler/jonathan/sites/labs.psych.ucsb.edu.schooler.jonathan/files/pubs/protzko_et_al._2016._fwpgg.pdf

22. Society for Personality and Social Psychology. 2017. "When It Comes to Knowing Your True Self, Believe in Free Will." *ScienceDaily*. 17 June 2016. https://www.sciencedaily.com/releases/2016/06/160617113502.htm

23. Association for Psychological Science. 2011. "Does Belief in Free Will Lead to Action?" *ScienceDaily*, 23 March 2011. https://www.sciencedaily.com/releases/2011/03/110323140233.htm

24. Ibid

25. Miles, J. 2013. "'Irresponsible and a Disservice': The Integrity of Social Psychology Turns on the Free Will Dilemma." *The British Journal of Social Psychology*. June 2013; 52(2): 205–218. https://www.ncbi.nlm.nih.gov/pmc/articles/PMC3757306/

26. Egnor, M. 2018. "Is Free Will a Dangerous Myth?" *Mind Matters*. October

4, 2018. https://mindmatters.ai/2018/10/is-free-will-a-dangerous-myth/
27. Davies, P. 2004. "Undermining Free Will." *Foreign Policy*. (144), 36-38. https://www.jstor.org/stable/4152977
28. Miles, J. 2013. "'Irresponsible and a Disservice': The Integrity of Social Psychology Turns on the Free Will Dilemma." *The British Journal of Social Psychology*. June 2013; 52(2): 205–218. https://www.ncbi.nlm.nih.gov/pmc/articles/PMC3757306/
29. Ibid
30. Raghunathan, R. 2012. *"Free Will Is an Illusion, So What?" Psychology Today*. May 8, 2012. https://www.psychologytoday.com/us/blog/sapient-nature/201205/free-will-is-illusion-so-what
31. Cave, C. 2016. "There's No Such Thing as Free Will." *The Atlantic*. June 2016. https://www.theatlantic.com/magazine/archive/2016/06/theres-no-such-thing-as-free-will/480750/
32. Harris, S. 2012. *Free Will*. New York, NY: Simon & Schuster.
33. McCusker, C. 1990. "Abstract of Findings." In Taylor, E. 1990. *Subliminal Communication" Emperor's Clothes or Panacea*. Medical Lake, WA: R. K. Books
34. Taylor, E. 2013. *Choices and Illusions*. Carlsbad, CA: Hay House.
35. Dupont C, Armant D.R., & Brenner C.A. 2009. "Epigenetics: Definition, Mechanisms and Clinical Perspective." *Seminars in Reproductive Medicine*. 27 (5): 351–7. September 2009. https://www.ncbi.nlm.nih.gov/pmc/articles/PMC2791696/
36. Manchester University. 2012.. "Personality Change Key to Improving Wellbeing." *ScienceDaily*. March 5, 2012. https://www.sciencedaily.com/releases/2012/03/120305081412.htm
37. McRay, K. 2013. "Developing Positive Emotional Habits." CEU course sponsored by *Institute for Brain Potential*. April 18, 2013.

Chapter Seven: Fine-Tuning the Brain

1. Staff. "Stress Management." *Mayo Clinic*. https://www.mayoclinic.org/healthy-lifestyle/stress-management/in-depth/stress/art-20046037
2. Ibid
3. Breuning, L.G. 2017. *The Science of Positivity*. Avon, MA: Adams Media.

4. Laurence, E. 2018. "Endorphins and Exercise: How Intense Does a Workout Have to Be for the 'High' to Kick in?" *Well and Good*. July 27, 2018. https://www.wellandgood.com/endorphins-and-exercise/
5. Cafasso, J. 2017. "Why Do We Need Endorphins?" *Healthline*. July 11, 2017. https://www.healthline.com/health/endorphins
6. Tello, C. 2019. "5 Benefits of Endorphins + How to Boost Endorphin Levels." *Selfhacked*. December 19, 2019. https://selfhacked.com/blog/endorphins/
7. Nguyen, T. 2014. "Hacking into Your Happy Chemicals: Dopamine, Serotonin, Endorphins and Oxytocin." *Huff Post*. Oct. 20, 2014. https://www.huffpost.com/entry/hacking-into-your-happy-c_b_6007660
8. Manninen, S. et al. 2017. "Social Laughter Triggers Endogenous Opioid Release in Humans." Journal of *Neuroscience*. June 21, 2017;37(25):6125-6131. https://www.jneurosci.org/content/37/25/6125

    and

    Dunbar, R.I.M. et al. 2012. "Social Laughter is Correlated with an Elevated Pain Threshold." *Proc. R. Soc. Biol Sci*. March 22, 2012. 279: 1161-1167. https://royalsocietypublishing.org/doi/epdf/10.1098/rspb.2011.1373
9. Raypole, C. 2019. "How to Hack Your Hormones for a Better Mood." *Healthline*. Sept. 30, 2019. https://www.healthline.com/health/happy-hormone
10. Dunbar, R.I.M. et al. 2012. "Performance of Music Elevates Pain Threshold and Positive Affect: Implications for the Evolutionary Function of Music." *Evol Psychol*. October 22, 2012. 10(4):688-702. https://www.researchgate.net/publication/232609675_Performance_of_Music_Elevates_Pain_Threshold_and_Positive_Affect_Implications_for_the_Evolutionary_Function_of_Music
11. Mead, M. N. 2008. "Benefits of Sunlight: A Bright Spot for Human Health." *Environ Health Perspect*. 2008 Apr; 116(4): A160–A167. https://www.ncbi.nlm.nih.gov/pmc/articles/PMC2290997/
12. Rokade, P.B. 2011. "Release of Endomorphin Hormone and Its Effects on Our Body and Moods: A Review." *International Conference on Chemical, Biological and Environment Sciences* (ICCEBS'2011) Bangkok Dec. 2011. https://moam.info/release-of-endomorphin-hormone-and-its-effects_5c3

79f11097c47d7048b45a0.html

13. Nehlig, A. 2013. "The Neuroprotective Effects of Cocoa Flavanol and Its Influence on Cognitive Performance." *Br J Clin Pharmacol*. 2013 Mar; 75(3): 716–727. https://www.ncbi.nlm.nih.gov/pmc/articles/PMC3575938/

14. Butler, N. 2020. "Some Like it Hot: 5 Reasons Spicy Food is Good for You." *Healthline*. February 4, 2020. https://www.healthline.com/health/five-reasons-to-eat-spicy-foods

15. Raypole, C. 2019. "13 Ways to Increase Endorphins." *Healthline*. Sept. 27, 2019. https://www.healthline.com/health/how-to-increase-endorphins

16. Nguyen, T. 2014. "Hacking into Your Happy Chemicals: Dopamine, Serotonin, Endorphins and Oxytocin." *Huff Post*. Oct. 20, 2014. https://www.huffpost.com/entry/hacking-into-your-happy-c_b_6007660

    and

    Buckley, C. 2012. "UConn Researcher: Dopamine Not About Pleasure (Anymore)" *UConn Today*. November 30, 2012. https://today.uconn.edu/2012/11/uconn-researcher-dopamine-not-about-pleasure-anymore

17. Sapolsky, R. 2017. *Behave: The Biology of Humans at our Best and Worst*. New York, NY: Penguin Books.

    and

    Sapolsky, R. 2011. "Dopamine Jackpot! Sapolsky on the Science of Pleasure." *YouTube*. https://www.youtube.com/watch?v=axrywDP9Ii0

18. Breuning, L.G. 2017. *The Science of Positivity*. Adams Media. Avon: MA

    and

    Breuning, L.G. 2017. *Habits of a Happy Brain*. Adams Media. Avon: MA

19. Sinek, S. 2013. "Why Leaders Eat Last." https://www.youtube.com/watch?v=ReRcHdeUG9Y

20. Reinholz, J. et. al. 2008. "Compensatory Weight Gain Due to Dopaminergic Hypofunction: New Evidence and Own Incidental Observations." Nutr Metab (Lond). 2008; 5: 35. https://nutritionandmetabolism.biomedcentral.com/articles/10.1186/1743-7075-5-35

21. Cadman, B. 2018. "Dopamine Deficiency: What You Need to Know." *Medical News Today*. January 17, 2018. https://www.medicalnewstoday.

com/articles/320637
22. Ibid
23. Scaccia, A. 2020. "Serotonin: What You Need to Know" *Healthline*. August 19, 2020. https://www.healthline.com/health/mental-health/serotonin
24. Breuning, L.G. 2017. *The Science of Positivity*. Adams Media. Avon: MA

    and

    Breuning, L.G. 2017. *Habits of a Happy Brain*. Adams Media. Avon: MA
25. Moyer, N. 2019. "Serotonin Deficiency: What We Do and Don't Know." *HealthLine*. February 27, 2019. https://www.healthline.com/health/serotonin-deficiency
26. Seo, D., Patrick, C.J. & Kennealy, P.J. 2008. "Role of Serotonin and Dopamine System Interactions in the Neurobiology of Impulsive Aggression and its Comorbidity with other Clinical Disorders." *NCBI*. https://www.ncbi.nlm.nih.gov/pmc/articles/PMC2612120/
27. Newman, T. 2018. "Boosting Memory: Serotonin Receptor May Be the Key." *Medical News Today*. May 11, 2018. https://www.medicalnewstoday.com/articles/321774
28. Perreau-Linck E, et al. 2007. "In Vivo Measurements of Brain Trapping of C-Labelled Alpha-Methyl-L-Tryptophan During Acute Changes in Mood States." *J Psychiatry Neurosci*. 2007 Nov; 32(6):430-4. https://www.researchgate.net/publication/5803649_In_vivo_measurements_of_brain_trapping_of_11C-labelled_a-methyl-L-tryptophan_during_acute_changes_in_mood_states

    and

    Young, S. 2007. "How to Increase Serotonin in the Human Brain Without Drugs." *J Psychiatry Neurosci*. 2007 Nov; 32(6): 394–399. https://www.ncbi.nlm.nih.gov/pmc/articles/PMC2077351/
29. University of California - Los Angeles. 2011. "Is Meditation the Push-Up for the Brain? Study Shows Practice May Have Potential to Change Brain's Physical Structure." *ScienceDaily*. www.sciencedaily.com/releases/2011/07/110714091940.htm
30. Sandoui, A. 2018. "What Religion Does to Your Brain." *Medical*

News Today. July 20, 2018. https://www.medicalnewstoday.com/articles/322539

31. Young, S. 2007. "How to Increase Serotonin in the Human Brain Without Drugs." *J Psychiatry Neurosci.* 2007 Nov; 32(6): 394–399. https://www.ncbi.nlm.nih.gov/pmc/articles/PMC2077351/
and
Mead, M.N. 2008. "Benefits of Sunlight: A Bright Spot for Human Health." *NCBI*. https://www.ncbi.nlm.nih.gov/pmc/articles/PMC2290997/

32. Gotter, A. 2021. "What is Tryptophan." Healthline. https://www.healthline.com/health/tryptophan

33. Lopez, V. et al. 2017. "Exploring Pharmacological Mechanisms of Lavender (*Lavandula angustifolia*) Essential Oil on Central Nervous System Targets." *Frontiers in Pharmacology.* 8:280. May 19, 2017. https://www.ncbi.nlm.nih.gov/pmc/articles/PMC5437114/
and
Brewer, S. 2017. "Lavender Oil Can Help Reduce Anxiety." Psychreg. November 23, 2017. https://www.psychreg.org/lavender-oil-reduce-anxiety/

34. – "Oxytocin." *Cleveland Clinic.* https://my.clevelandclinic.org/health/articles/22618-oxytocin

35. Magon, N. & Kalra, S. 2011. "The Orgasmic History of Oxytocin: Love, Lust, and Labor." *Indian Journal of Endocrinology and Metabolism.* Vol. 15. Issue 7. pp 156-161. https://www.ncbi.nlm.nih.gov/pmc/articles/PMC3183515/

36. Raypole, C. 2019. "How to Hack Your Hormones for a Better Mood." *Healthline.* Sept. 30, 2019. https://www.healthline.com/health/happy-hormone

37. Staff. 2018. "Can You Kiss and Hug Your Way to Better Health? Research Says Yes." *Penn Medicine.* https://www.pennmedicine.org/updates/blogs/health-and-wellness/2018/february/affection

38. Scheele, D. et al. 2012. "Oxytocin Modulates Social Distance between Males and Females." *The Journal of Neuroscience.* 14

November 2012, 32 (46) 16074-16079. https://www.jneurosci.org/content/32/46/16074
39. Burkeman, O. 2012. "Meet 'Dr. Love', The Scientist Exploring What Makes People Good or Evil." *The Guardian*. July 15, 2012. https://www.theguardian.com/science/2012/jul/15/interview-dr-love-paul-zak
40. Staff. 2018. "Can You Kiss and Hug Your Way to Better Health? Research Says Yes." Penn Medicine. January 8, 2018. https://www.pennmedicine.org/updates/blogs/health-and-wellness/2018/february/affection
41. Light, K. et al. 2005. "More Frequent Partner Hugs and Higher Oxytocin Levels are Linked to Lower Blood Pressure and Heart Rate in Premenopausal Women." *Biol Psychol*. 2005 Apr;69 (1):5-21. https://pubmed.ncbi.nlm.nih.gov/15740822/
42. Gouin, J.P. et al. 2010. "Marital Behavior, Oxytocin, Vasopressin, and Wound Healing." *Psychoneuroendocrinology*. Volume 35, Issue 7, August 2010, Pages 1082-1090. https://www.sciencedirect.com/science/article/abs/pii/S0306453010000259
43. Penn Medicine. 2018. "Can You Kiss and Hug Your Way to Better Health? Research Says Yes." *Penn Medicine*. January 8, 2018. https://www.pennmedicine.org/updates/blogs/health-and-wellness/2018/february/affection
44. Association for Psychological Science. 2011. "The Dark Side of Oxytocin." *ScienceDaily*. August 2, 2011. Retrieved September 10, 2020, from https://www.sciencedaily.com/releases/2011/08/110801160306.htm
45. Breuning, L.G. 2017. *The Science of Positivity*. Avon, MA: Adams Media.
46. Deleniv, S. 2016. "The Dark Side of Oxytocin." *Prime Mind*. June 10, 2016. https://primemind.com/the-dark-side-of-oxytocin-fb0d0124f617 and
    Dobbs, D. 2011. "The Love-Hate Hormone, Ingroup/Outgroup Wars, and the Power of Culture." *Wired*. January 11, 2011. https://www.wired.com/2011/01/the-love-hate-hormone-ingroupoutgroup-wars-and-the-power-of-culture/
47. Burkeman, O. 2012. "Meet 'Dr. Love', The Scientist Exploring What Makes People Good or Evil." *The Guardian*. July 15, 2012. https://www.theguardian.com/science/2012/jul/15/interview-dr-love-paul-zak

48. Raypole, C. 2019. "How to Hack Your Hormones for a Better Mood." *Healthline*. Sept. 30, 2019. https://www.healthline.com/health/happy-hormone
49. Mead, M. N. 2008. "Benefits of Sunlight: A Bright Spot for Human Health." *Environ Health Perspect*. 2008 Apr; 116(4): A160–A167. https://www.ncbi.nlm.nih.gov/pmc/articles/PMC2290997/
50. Beres, A. et al. 2011. "'Does Happiness Help Healing?' Immune Response of Hospitalized Children May Change During Visits of the Smiling Hospital Foundation's Artists." *National Library of Medicine*. https://pubmed.ncbi.nlm.nih.gov/21983400/
51. Staff. "Duchenne Smile: A Genuine Smile That Involves the Muscles Around the Eyes." https://www.newscientist.com/term/duchenne-smile/
52. Gunnery, S. & Hall, J.A. 2014. "The Duchenne Smile and Persuasion." *Journal of Nonverbal Behavior*. https://www.semanticscholar.org/paper/The-Duchenne-Smile-and-Persuasion-Gunnery-Hall/4fb5fc6cfdd6fca530ad97d0bd55c949a314c7da
53. Gunnery, S.D. & Ruben, M.A. 2016. "Perceptions of Duchenne and non-Duchenne smiles: A meta-analysis." *Cognition and Emotion*. 2016;30 (3):501-15. https://pubmed.ncbi.nlm.nih.gov/25787714/
54. Kraft, T.L. & Pressman, S.D. 2012. "Grin and Bear It: The Influence of Manipulated Facial Expression on the Stress Response." *Psychological Science*. 23 (11):1372-8. https://pubmed.ncbi.nlm.nih.gov/23012270/
55. Chang, J. et al. 2014. "When You Smile, You Become Happy: Evidence from Resting State Task-Based fMRI." *Biological Psychology*. 103:100-6. https://pubmed.ncbi.nlm.nih.gov/25139308/
and
Stanborough, R.J. 2019. "Smiling with Your Eyes: What Exactly is a Duchenne Smile?" *Healthline*. June 29, 2019. https://www.healthline.com/health/duchenne-smile
56. Soussignan, R. 2002. "Duchenne Smile, Emotional Experience, and Autonomic Reactivity: A Test of the Facial Feedback Hypothesis." *Emotion*. 2(1):52-74. https://pubmed.ncbi.nlm.nih.gov/12899366/
57. Lewis, M.B. 2018. "The Interactions Between Botulinum-Toxin-Based Facial Treatments and Embodied Emotions." *Scientific Reports*. October

3, 2018. https://www.ncbi.nlm.nih.gov/pmc/articles/PMC6170457/
58. Abel, E.L. & Kruger, M.L. 2009. "Smile Intensity in Photographs Predicts Longevity." *Association for Psychological Science.* 21(4) 542-544. https://journals.sagepub.com/doi/full/10.1177/0956797610363775
and
Hampton, D. 2017. "How a Simple Smile Benefits Your Brain and Body." *The Best Brain Possible.* March 12, 2017. https://thebestbrainpossible.com/how-the-simple-act-of-smiling-benefits-your-brain-and-body/
59. Harker, L. & Keltner, D. 2000. "Expressions of Positive Emotion in Women's College Yearbook Pictures and Their Relationship to Personality and Life Outcomes Across Adulthood." University of California, Berkeley. https://fliphtml5.com/vdry/fchw/basic and https://psycnet.apa.org/record/2000-14236-009
and
Hampton, D. 2017. "How a Simple Smile Benefits Your Brain and Body." *The Best Brain Possible.* March 12, 2017. https://thebestbrainpossible.com/how-the-simple-act-of-smiling-benefits-your-brain-and-body/
60. Perciavalle, V. et al. 2017. "The Role of Deep Breathing on Stress." *Neurological Science.* 2017 Mar;38 (3):451-458. https://pubmed.ncbi.nlm.nih.gov/27995346/
61. Thorpe, M. 2017. "11 Natural Ways to Lower Your Cortisol Levels." *Healthline.* April 17, 2017. https://www.healthline.com/nutrition/ways-to-lower-cortisol
62. Staff. "Learning Diaphragmatic Breathing." *Harvard Health Publishing.* https://www.health.harvard.edu/lung-health-and-disease/learning-diaphragmatic-breathing
63. Ibid

Chapter Eight: Seeing is Believing

1. Dutton, K. 2020. *Black-and-White Thinking.* New York, NY: Farrar, Straus and Giroux.
2. Loftus, E. F., & Palmer, J. C. 1974. "Reconstruction of Automobile Destruction: An Example of the Interaction Between Language and Memory." *Journal of Verbal Learning and Verbal Behavior.* Volume 13,

Issue 5, October 1974, Pages 585-589. https://www.demenzemedicinagenerale.net/images/mens-sana/AutomobileDestruction.pdf
3. Dutton, K. 2020. *Black-and-White Thinking*. New York, NY: Farrar, Straus and Giroux.
   and
   Northwestern University. "Blue, Green or 'Nol'? New Study Reveals That Even Before Infants Can Talk, Language Shapes Their Cognition." *ScienceDaily*. 18 July 2016. https://www.sciencedaily.com/releases/2016/07/160718194120.htm
4. Northwestern University. "Blue, Green or 'Nol'? New Study Reveals That Even Before Infants Can Talk, Language Shapes Their Cognition." *ScienceDaily*. 18 July 2016. https://www.sciencedaily.com/releases/2016/07/160718194120.htm
5. Ibid
6. *The Innocence Project*. https://innocenceproject.org/about/
7. Chew, S. L. 2018. "Myth: Eyewitness Testimony is the Best Kind of Evidence." *Association for Psychological Science*. https://www.psychologicalscience.org/teaching/myth-eyewitness-testimony-is-the-best-kind-of-evidence.html
8. Shapiro, A., Lu, Z., Knight, E., and Ennis, R. "The Break of the Curveball." *Best Illusion of the Year Contest*. http://illusionoftheyear.com/2009/05/the-break-of-the-curveball/
9. Schmid, R.E. 2010. "Breaking Curveball an Illusion, Scientists Say." *NBC News*. https://www.nbcnews.com/id/wbna39658106
10. Doherty, P. 1998. "How Curveballs Curve." *Exploratorium*. https://www.exploratorium.edu/video/how-curveballs-curve
11. Radford, B. 2010. "How Does a Curveball Curve." *Live Science*. July 20, 2010. https://www.livescience.com/32714-how-does-a-curveball-curve.html
12. Dockrill, P. 2020. "This Brain-Bending 3D Staircase Just Won Best Illusion of The Year For 2020." *Science Alert*. https://www.sciencealert.com/brain-bending-3d-staircase-wins-best-illusion-of-the-year-for-2020
13. Bach, M. 2012. "Motion-Induced Blindness." *Michael Bach, PhD, Scientist*.

https://michaelbach.de/ot/mot-mib/index.html
14. Simons, D. 2010. *Selective Attention Test.* https://www.youtube.com/watch?v=vJG698U2Mvo
15. Chabris, C. and Simons, D. 2009. *The Invisible Gorilla.* New York, NY: Crown Publishing.
16. Ibid
17. Simons, D. J. 2017. *Inattentional Blindness and the Illusion of Attention.* In A. G. Shapiro & D. Todorović (Eds.), *The Oxford Compendium of Visual Illusions* (p. 715–718). Oxford University Press.
    and
    Costandi, Mo. 2011. "The Illusion of Attention." *The Guardian.* August 11, 2011. https://www.theguardian.com/science/neurophilosophy/2011/aug/11/neuroscience-psychology
18. Simons, D. 2011. "Seeing the World as it Isn't" *TEDxUIUC.* https://www.youtube.com/watch?v=9Il_D3Xt9W0&feature=emb_logo
19. Costandi, Mo. 2011. "The Illusion of Attention." *The Guardian.* August 11, 2011. https://www.theguardian.com/science/neurophilosophy/2011/aug/11/neuroscience-psychology
    and
    Macdonald, J.S. and Lavie, N. 2011. "Visual Perceptual Load Induces Inattentional Deafness." *Attention Perception Psychophysics.* 2011 Aug;73(6):1780-9.
20. Costandi, Mo. 2011. "The Illusion of Attention." *The Guardian.* August 11, 2011. https://www.theguardian.com/science/neurophilosophy/2011/aug/11/neuroscience-psychology
21. Scholl, B. et al. 2003. "Talking on a Cellular Telephone Dramatically Increases 'Sustained Inattentional Blindness.'" *Journal of Vision* October 2003, Vol.3, 156. https://jov.arvojournals.org/article.aspx?articleid=2129170
22. Strayer, D. L. and Johnston, W. A. 2001. "Driven to Distraction: Dual-Task Studies of Simulated Driving and Conversing on a Cellular Telephone." *Psychological Science.* Volume: 12 Issue: 6. pp 462-466.

Chapter Nine: The Expectation Factor

1. — 1904. "Berlin's Wonderful Horse." *New York Times.* Sept. 4, 1904. https://timesmachine.nytimes.com/timesmachine/1904/09/04/101396572.pdf
2. Samhita, L. and Gross, H. 2013. "The 'Clever Hans Phenomenon' Revisited." *Communicative and Integrative Biology.* Nov 1, 2013. https://www.ncbi.nlm.nih.gov/pmc/articles/PMC3921203/
3. Ibid
4. M.K. 2011. "Clever Hounds." *The Economist.* Feb. 15, 2011. https://www.economist.com/blogs/babbage/2011/02/animal_behaviour&fsrc=nwl
   and
   Lit, L., Schweitzer, J. B. & Oberbauer, A. M. 2011. "Handler Beliefs Affect Scent Detection Dog Outcomes." *Animal Cognition.* Jan 12, 2011. 14(3): 387-394. https://www.ncbi.nlm.nih.gov/pmc/articles/PMC3078300/
5. Thomas, W. I. and Thomas, D. 1928. *The Child in America.* New York: Knopf. 571-572
6. - "The Thomas Theorem of Sociology Explained with Examples." *PsycholoGenie.* https://psychologenie.com/the-thomas-theorem-of-sociology-explained-with-examples.
7. Merton, R. K. 1948. "The Self-Fulfilling Prophecy." *The Antioch Review.* Vol. 8. No. 2. 193-210. https://www.jstor.org/stable/4609267
8. Aldean, A. 2017. "The Rat Maze: Expectations vs. Reality." *Grand Canyon University Blogs.* January 17, 2017. https://www.gcu.edu/blog/psychology-counseling/rat-maze-expectations-vs-reality
9. Rosenthal, R. and Jacobson, L. 1968. "Pygmalion in the Classroom." *The Urban Review* vol 3, pp 16-20. https://sites.tufts.edu/tuftsliteracycorps/files/2017/02/Pygmalion-in-the-Classroom.pdf
10. Rosenthal, R., Jacobson, L. 1966. "What You Expect is What You Get Teachers' Expectancies: Determinates of Pupils' IQ Gains." *Psychological Reports*, 19, 115-118. http://homepages.gac.edu/~jwotton2/PSY225/rosenthal66.pdf
    and
    Clement, C. and Portenga, A. *Famous Studies in Psychology.* https://

www.mayfieldschools.org/Downloads/Famous%20Studies%20in%20Psychology.pdf
and
Rosenthal, R. and Jacobson, L. 1968. "Pygmalion in the Classroom." *The Urban Review* vol 3, pp 16-20. https://sites.tufts.edu/tuftsliteracycorps/files/2017/02/Pygmalion-in-the-Classroom.pdf

11. Rosenthal, R. and Jacobson, L. 1968. "Pygmalion in the Classroom." *The Urban Review* vol 3, pp 16-20. https://sites.tufts.edu/tuftsliteracycorps/files/2017/02/Pygmalion-in-the-Classroom.pdf
12. Ibid
13. Spitz, H. H. 1999. "Beleaguered Pygmalion: A History of the Controversy Over Claims That Teacher Expectancy Raises Intelligence." *Intelligence, 27*(3), 199–234. https://docplayer.net/174290158-Beleaguered-pygmalion-a-history-of-the-controversy-over-claims-that-teacher-expectancy-raises-intelligence.html
14. Elashoff, J. D. and Snow, R. E. 1971. *Pygmalion Reconsidered*. CA: Wadsworth Publishing Company. https://www.gwern.net/docs/statistics/bias/1971-elashoff-pygmalionreconsidered.pdf
15. Ibid
16. Ellison, K. 2015. "Being Honest About the Pygmalion Effect." *Discover Magazine.* October 28, 2015. https://www.discovermagazine.com/mind/being-honest-about-the-pygmalion-effect
17. Spitz, H. H. 1999. "Beleaguered Pygmalion: A History of the Controversy Over Claims That Teacher Expectancy Raises Intelligence." *Intelligence, 27*(3), 199–234. https://docplayer.net/174290158-Beleaguered-pygmalion
18. 1997. "Richard E. Snow." *Human Intelligence.* https://www.intelltheory.com/snow.shtml
19. Spitz, H. H. 1999. "Beleaguered Pygmalion: A History of the Controversy Over Claims That Teacher Expectancy Raises Intelligence." *Intelligence, 27*(3), 199–234. https://docplayer.net/174290158-Beleaguered-pygmalion-a-history-of-the-controversy-over-claims-that-teacher-expectancy-raises-intelligence.html
20. Rosenthal, R. 2009. "Vita." http://rosenthal.socialpsychology.org/cv/

Rosenthal.pdf
21. Staff. 2002. "Eminent Psychologists of the 20th Century." *American Psychological Association.* https://www.apa.org/monitor/julaug02/eminent
22. Elashoff, J. D. and Snow, R. E. 1971. *Pygmalion Reconsidered.* CA: Wadsworth Publishing Company. https://www.gwern.net/docs/statistics/bias/1971-elashoff-pygmalionreconsidered.pdf
23. Spitz, H. H. 1999. "Beleaguered Pygmalion: A History of the Controversy Over Claims That Teacher Expectancy Raises Intelligence." *Intelligence,* 27(3), 199–234. https://docplayer.net/174290158-Beleaguered-pygmalion-a-history-of-the-controversy-over-claims-that-teacher-expectancy-raises-intelligence.html
24. De Meyer, K. 2016. "The Mind of the Educator." King's College, London. *ResearchGate.* https://www.researchgate.net/publication/284702497_The_Mind_of_the_Educator
25. Jussim, L. and Harber, K. 2005. "Teacher Expectations and Self-Fulfilling Prophecies: Knowns and Unknowns, Resolved and Unresolved Controversies." *Personality and Social Psychology Review.* Vol 9, No. 2, 131-155. https://www.researchgate.net/publication/7869791_Teacher_Expectations_and_Self-Fulfilling_Prophecies_Knowns_and_Unknowns_Resolved_and_Unresolved_Controversies
26. De Meyer, K. 2016. "The Mind of the Educator." King's College, London. *ResearchGate.* https://www.researchgate.net/publication/284702497_The_Mind_of_the_Educator
27. De Meyer, K. 2016. "The Mind of the Educator." In book: *The Palgrave International Handbook of Alternative Education* (pp. 17-30) https://www.researchgate.net/publication/284702497_The_Mind_of_the_Educator
28. Spitz, H. H. 1999. "Beleaguered Pygmalion: A History of the Controversy Over Claims That Teacher Expectancy Raises Intelligence." *Intelligence,* 27(3), 199–234. https://docplayer.net/174290158-Beleaguered-pygmalion-a-history-of-the-controversy-over-claims-that-teacher-expectancy-raises-intelligence.html
29. Ibid
30. Eden, D. 1992. "Leadership and Expectations: Pygmalion Effects." *The*

Leadership Quarterly. Volume 3. Issue 4. pp 271-305. https://www.yumpu.com/en/document/read/48237473/eden-1992-leadership-and-expectations-pygmalion-effects-and-other-self-fulfilling-prophecies-in-organizations

and

Livingston, J. S. 2003. "Pygmalion in Management." *Harvard Business Review.* https://hbr.org/2003/01/pygmalion-in-management

and

Bezuijen, X. M. et al. 2009. "Pygmalion and Employee Learning: The Role of Leader Behaviors." *Journal of Management.* Vo. 35. Issue 5. pp 1248-1267.

31. Herrell, J. M. 1971. "Galatea in the Classroom: Student Expectations Affect Teacher Behavior." *Proceedings of the 79th Annual Convention of the American Psychological Association.* https://files.eric.ed.gov/fulltext/ED056331.pdf

32. Livingston, J. S. 2003. "Pygmalion in Management." *Harvard Business Review.* https://hbr.org/2003/01/pygmalion-in-management

33. Eden, D., & Shani, A.B. 1982. "Pygmalion Goes to Boot Camp: Expectancy, Leadership, and Trainee Performance." *Journal of Applied Psychology.* 67, 194-199.

and

Eden, D. 1992. "Leadership and Expectations: Pygmalion Effects." *The Leadership Quarterly.* Volume 3. Issue 4. pp 271-305. https://www.yumpu.com/en/document/read/48237473/eden-1992-leadership-and-expectations-pygmalion-effects-and-other-self-fulfilling-prophecies-in-organizations

34. Eden, D. 1992. "Leadership and Expectations: Pygmalion Effects." *The Leadership Quarterly.* Volume 3. Issue 4. pp 271-305. https://www.yumpu.com/en/document/read/48237473/eden-1992-leadership-and-expectations-pygmalion-effects-and-other-self-fulfilling-prophecies-in-organizations

35. Shendow, W. 2014. "The Pygmalion Effect and Public Administration." *The Torch.* Volume 87, Issue 3. http://www.ncsociology.org/torchmagazine/v873/shendow.html

36. Livingston, J. S. 2003. "Pygmalion in Management." *Harvard Business Review*. https://hbr.org/2003/01/pygmalion-in-management
37. Ibid
38. Whitehead, S. 2019. "Pygmalion Effect and Burnout: When Employees are Pushed too Hard." *Panmore Institute*. http://panmore.com/pygmalion-effect-and-burnout-when-employees-are-pushed-too-hard
39. Livingston, J. S. 2003. "Pygmalion in Management." *Harvard Business Review*. https://hbr.org/2003/01/pygmalion-in-management
40. Babad, E. Y., Inbar, J. & Rosenthal, R. 1982. "Pygmalion, Galatea, and the Golem: Investigations of Biased and Unbiased Teachers." *Journal of Educational Psychology*, 74(4), 459–474. https://psycnet.apa.org/record/1983-01891-001
41. Michaelson, J. "Golem." *My Jewish Learning*. https://www.myjewishlearning.com/article/golem/
42. Livingston, J. S. 2003. "Pygmalion in Management." *Harvard Business Review*. https://hbr.org/2003/01/pygmalion-in-management
43. Ibid
44. Spitz, H. H. 1999. "Beleaguered Pygmalion: A History of the Controversy Over Claims That Teacher Expectancy Raises Intelligence." *Intelligence*, 27(3), 199–234. https://docplayer.net/174290158-Beleaguered-pygmalion-a-history-of-the-controversy-over-claims-that-teacher-expectancy-raises-intelligence.html
45. Ellison, K. 2015. "Being Honest about the Pygmalion Effect." *Discover Magazine*. October 28, 2015. https://www.discovermagazine.com/mind/being-honest-about-the-pygmalion-effect
46. Ibid
47. Rosenthal, R. and Jacobson, L. 1968. "Pygmalion in the Classroom." *The Urban Review* vol 3, pp 16-20. https://sites.tufts.edu/tuftsliteracycorps/files/2017/02/Pygmalion-in-the-Classroom.pdf
48. Livingston, J. S. 2003. "Pygmalion in Management." *Harvard Business Review*. https://hbr.org/2003/01/pygmalion-in-management
49. Eden, D. 1992. "Leadership and Expectations: Pygmalion Effects." *The Leadership Quarterly*. Volume 3. Issue 4. PP 271-305. https://www.

yumpu.com/en/document/read/48237473/eden-1992-leadership-and-expectations-pygmalion-effects-and-other-self-fulfilling-prophecies-in-organizations

50. Dvir, T., Eden, D. and Banjo, M.L. 1995. "Self-fulfilling Prophecy and Gender: Can Women be Pygmalion and Galatea?" *Journal of Applied Psychology.* 80(2), 253-270.
51. Livingston, J. S. 2003. "Pygmalion in Management." *Harvard Business Review.* https://hbr.org/2003/01/pygmalion-in-management
52. Eden, D. 1992. "Leadership and Expectations: Pygmalion Effects." *The Leadership Quarterly.* Volume 3. Issue 4. pp 271-305. https://www.yumpu.com/en/document/read/48237473/eden-1992-leadership-and-expectations-pygmalion-effects-and-other-self-fulfilling-prophecies-in-organizations
    and
    Eden, D. and Ravid, D. 1982. "Pygmalion Versus Self-Expectancy: Effects of Instructor- And Self-Expectancy on Trainee Performance." *Organizational and Behavior and Human Performance.* Vol. 30, Issue 3. December 1982. Pages 351-364. https://www.sciencedirect.com/science/article/abs/pii/0030507382902252?via%3Dihub
53. Baumeister, R.F. et all 2001. "Bad is Stronger Than Good." *Review of General Psychology.* Vol. 5. No. 4. 323-370. https://assets.csom.umn.edu/assets/71516.pdf

Chapter Ten: The Positivity Quotient

1. Assari, S. & Lankarani, M. 2016. "Depressive Symptoms are Associated with More Hopelessness among White than Black Older Adults." *Front Public Health.* Vol. 4. No. 82. https://www.ncbi.nlm.nih.gov/pmc/articles/PMC4854870/
2. Richter, C. 1957. "On the Phenomenon of Sudden Death in Animals and Man." *Psychosomatic Medicine.* Vol. XIX, No. 3. https://www.aipro.info/wp/wp-content/uploads/2017/08/phenomena_sudden_death.pdf
3. Ibid
4. Richter, C. 1957. "On the Phenomenon of Sudden Death in Animals and Man." *Psychosomatic Medicine.* Vol. XIX, No. 3. https://www.aipro.info/

wp/wp-content/uploads/2017/08/phenomena_sudden_death.pdf
and

Hallinan, J. T. 2014. "The Remarkable Power of Hope." *Psychology Today*. May 7, 2014. https://www.psychologytoday.com/us/blog/kidding-ourselves/201405/the-remarkable-power-hope

5. PETA 2020. "Eli Lilly's CEO Refuses to Ban Near-Drowning of Small Animals." PETA. https://support.peta.org/page/7704/action/1
6. Kirsch, I. 2014. Antidepressants and the Placebo Effect. https://www.ncbi.nlm.nih.gov/pmc/articles/PMC4172306
7. Hallinan, J. T. 2014. "The Remarkable Power of Hope." *Psychology Today*. May 7, 2014. https://www.psychologytoday.com/us/blog/kidding-ourselves/201405/the-remarkable-power-hope
and

Li, J. et al. 2002. "Myocardial Infarction in Parents Who Lost a Child: A Nationwide Prospective Cohort Study in Denmark." *Circulation*. Sept. 24, 2002. 106 (13):1634-9. https://pubmed.ncbi.nlm.nih.gov/12270855/
and

Li, J. et al. 2003. "Mortality in Parents After Death of a Child in Denmark: A Nationwide Follow-Up Study." *The Lancet*. 361 (9355):363-7. Feb. 1. 2003. https://pubmed.ncbi.nlm.nih.gov/12573371/

8. Fang, F., et al. 2012. "Suicide and Cardiovascular Death after a Cancer Diagnosis." *N Engl J Med.*, 366(14): 1310-7. https://pubmed.ncbi.nlm.nih.gov/22475594/
and

Hallinan, J. T. 2014. "The Remarkable Power of Hope." *Psychology Today*. May 7, 2014. https://www.psychologytoday.com/us/blog/kidding-ourselves/201405/the-remarkable-power-hope

9. Fang, F., et al. 2012. "Suicide and Cardiovascular Death after a Cancer Diagnosis." *N Engl J Med.*, 366(14): 1310-7. https://pubmed.ncbi.nlm.nih.gov/22475594/
and

Hallinan, J. T. 2014. "The Remarkable Power of Hope." *Psychology Today*. May 7, 2014. https://www.psychologytoday.com/us/blog/kidding-ourselves/201405/the-remarkable-power-hope

10. Leach, J. 2018. "'Give-up-itis' Revisited: Neuropathology of Extremis." *Med. Hypotheses.* Nov; 120:14-21. https://www.newswise.com/pdf_docs/153745548338429_Leach%20Give%20Up%20Itis%20paper.pdf
11. Maier, S. F. & Seligman, M. E. P. 2016. "Learned Helplessness at Fifty: Insights from Neuroscience." *Psychological Review, 123*(4), 349–367. https://www.ncbi.nlm.nih.gov/pmc/articles/PMC4920136/
12. Ibid
13. Ibid
14. Hiroto, D.S. & Seligman, M. E. 1975. "Generality of Learned Helplessness in Man." *Journal of Personality and Social Psychology.* 31 (2): 311–27. https://www.appstate.edu/~steelekm/classes/psy5150/Documents/Hiroto&Seligman1975-learned-helplessness.pdf
15. Breuning, L.G. 2017. *The Science of Positivity.* Avon, MA: Adams Media.
    and
    Breuning, L.G. 2017. *Habits of a Happy Brain.* Avon, MA: Adams Media.
16. Marks, H. "Stress Symptoms." *WebMD.* https://www.webmd.com/balance/stress-management/stress-symptoms-effects_of-stress-on-the-body
17. Lyubomirsky, S., King, L., & Diener, E. 2005. "The Benefits of Frequent Positive Affect: Does Happiness Lead to Success?" *Psychological Bulletin.* 2005, Vol. 131, No. 6, 803– 855. https://www.apa.org/pubs/journals/releases/bul-1316803.pdf
18. Danner, D. et al. 2001. "Positive Emotions in Early Life and Longevity: Findings from the Nun Study." *Journal of Personality and Social Psychology.* 2001, Vol. 80, No. 5, 804-813. https://www.apa.org/pubs/journals/releases/psp805804.pdf
19. — "The Power of Positive Thinking." *Johns Hopkins Medicine.* https://www.hopkinsmedicine.org/health/wellness-and-prevention/the-power-of-positive-thinking
20. Dwyer, M. 2016. "Optimism May Reduce Risk of Dying Prematurely Among Women." *Harvard T.H. Chan School of Public Health Press Release.* December 7, 2016. https://www.hsph.harvard.edu/news/press-releases/optimism-premature-death-women/
21. Peterson, C., Seligman, M.E., & Vaillant, G.E. 1988. "Pessimistic

Explanatory Style is a Risk Factor for Physical Illness: A Thirty-Five-Year Longitudinal Study." *Journal of Personality and Social Psychology*, 55(1), 23–27. https://psycnet.apa.org/record/1988-29571-001

22. Taylor, E. 2012. *Self-Hypnosis and Subliminal Technology*. Carlsbad, CA: Hay House.

    and

    Visintaines, M. 1982. "Immune System Suppressed?—Cancer Linked to Helplessness." *Brain Mind Bulletin*. Vol. 7. No. 11B. Originally reported in *Science* (216: 437–440).

23. Taylor, E. 2012. *Self-Hypnosis and Subliminal Technology*. Carlsbad, CA: Hay House.

    and

    Williams, R. 1989. "Trusting Hearts Last Longer: Hostility May Be a Type of Toxin." *Brain Mind Bulletin*. Vol. 14. No. 6G.

24. Taylor, E. 2012. *Self-Hypnosis and Subliminal Technology*. Carlsbad, CA: Hay House.

    and

    Eysenck, H. J. 1989. "Personality Predicts Early Death." *Brain Mind Bulletin*. Vol. 14. No. 6B. Also published as "Personality, Stress and Cancer: Prediction and Prophylaxis." *British Journal of Medical Psychology*. 61:57–75. https://www.healmindbody.com/wp-content/uploads/2019/02/Personality-Stress-Cancer-Eysenck-1988.pdf

25. Taylor, E. 2012. *Self-Hypnosis and Subliminal Technology*. Carlsbad, CA: Hay House.

    and

    Goodkin, K., Antoni, M. H., Sevin, B., & Fox, B. H. 1993. "A Partially Testable, Predictive Model of Psychosocial Factors in the Etiology of Cervical Cancer I. Biological, Psychological and Social Aspects." *Psycho-Oncology*. Vol 2. Issue 2. pp 79–98.

26. Fredrickson, B. L., & Joiner, T. 2002. "Positive Emotions Trigger Upward Spirals Toward Emotional Well-Being." *Psychological Science*, 13(2), 172–175. https://psychology.ecu.edu/wp-content/pv-uploads/sites/216/2019/03/Fredrickson-Joiner-2002.pdf

27. Lee, L. O. 2022. "Optimism, Daily Stressors, and Emotional Well-Being

Over Two Decades in a Cohort of Aging Men." *The Journals of Gerontology: Series B.* https://academic.oup.com/psychsocgerontology/advance-article/doi/10.1093/geronb/gbac025/6542099

and

Boston University School of Medicine. 2022. "Optimism May Promote Emotional Well-Being by Limiting How Often One Experiences Stressful Situations." *Science Daily.* March 7, 2022. https://www.sciencedaily.com/releases/2022/03/220307082334.htm

28. Taylor, E. 2012. *Self-Hypnosis and Subliminal Technology.* Carlsbad, CA: Hay House.

    and

    Goodkin, K.; Antoni, M. H.; Sevin, B.; and Fox, B. H. 1993. "A Partially Testable, Predictive Model of Psychosocial Factors in the Etiology of Cervical Cancer I. Biological, Psychological and Social Aspects." *Psycho-Oncology.* Vol 2. Issue 2. pp 79–98.

29. University of Bath. 2020. "Time to Get Real on the Power of Positive Thinking." *Science News.* July 7, 2020. https://www.sciencedaily.com/releases/2020/07/200707113230.htm

    and

    David de Meza, D., & Dawson, C. 2020. "Neither an Optimist Nor a Pessimist Be: Mistaken Expectations Lower Well-Being." *Personality and Social Psychology Bulletin.* 47(4). https://www.researchgate.net/publication/341658045_Neither_an_Optimist_Nor_a_Pessimist_Be_Mistaken_Expectations_Lower_Well-Being

30. Bargh, J. A., Chen, M., & Burrows, L. 1996. "Automaticity of Social Behavior: Direct Effects of Trait Construct and Stereotype Activation on Action." *Journal of Personality and Social Psychology.* 71(2), 230–244. https://doi.apa.org/doiLanding?doi=10.1037%2F0022-3514.71.2.230

    and

    Chivers, T. 2019. "What's Next for Psychology's Embattled Field of Social Priming." *Nature.* December 11, 2019. https://www.nature.com/articles/d41586-019-03755-2#

31. Chivers, T. 2019. "What's Next for Psychology's Embattled Field of Social Priming." *Nature.* December 11, 2019. https://www.nature.com/articles/

d41586-019-03755-2#

32. Taylor, E. 2018. "Before You Know It: The Unconscious Reasons We Do What We Do with Professor John Bargh." *Provocative Enlightenment Radio*. October 11, 2018. https://www.eldontaylor.com/provocativeenlightenment/2018-10-11-before-you-know-it-the-unconscious-reasons-we-do-what-we-do-with-professor-john-bargh/

33. Ramscar, M. et al. 2015. "Why Many Priming Results Don't (and Won't) Replicate: A Quantitative Analysis." Unpublished paper. https://www.sfs.uni-tuebingen.de/~mramscar/papers/Ramscar-Shaoul-Baayen_replication.pdf

34. Ramscar, M. et al. 2015. "Why Many Priming Results Don't (and Won't) Replicate: A Quantitative Analysis." Unpublished paper. https://www.sfs.uni-tuebingen.de/~mramscar/papers/Ramscar-Shaoul-Baayen_replication.pdf
and
Doyen, S. et al. 2012. "Behavioral Priming: It's All in the Mind, but Whose Mind?" Plos One. January 18, 2012. https://journals.plos.org/plosone/article?id=10.1371/journal.pone.0029081

35. Ramscar, M. et al. 2015. "Why Many Priming Results Don't (and Won't) Replicate: A Quantitative Analysis." Unpublished paper. https://www.sfs.uni-tuebingen.de/~mramscar/papers/Ramscar-Shaoul-Baayen_replication.pdf

36. Weingarten, E. et al. 2016. "From Primed Concepts to Action: A Meta-Analysis of the Behavioral Effects of Incidentally Presented Words." Psychological Bulletin. Vol. 142, No. 5, 472–497. https://www.ncbi.nlm.nih.gov/pmc/articles/PMC5783538/

37. Dai, W. et al. 2022. "Priming Behaviors vs. Ideas: A Meta-Analysis of the Effects of Behavioral and Nonbehavioral Primes on Overt Behavioral Outcomes." Psychological Bulletin – In press. https://www.researchgate.net/publication/363485171_Priming_Behavior_A_Meta-Analysis_of_the_Effects_of_Behavioral_and_Nonbehavioral_Primes_on_Overt_Behavioral_Outcomes

38. Weingarten, E. et al. 2016. "From Primed Concepts to Action: A Meta-Analysis of the Behavioral Effects of Incidentally Presented Words."

Psychological Bulletin. Vol. 142, No. 5, 472–497. https://www.ncbi.nlm.nih.gov/pmc/articles/PMC5783538/

39. Richter, M. et al. 2010. "Do Words Hurt? Brain Activation During the Processing of Pain-Related Words." *Pain*. Vol. 148. Issue 2. https://www.sciencedirect.com/science/article/abs/pii/S0304395909004564

40. Lodge, J., Harte, D. K., & Tripp, G. 1998. "Children's Self-Talk Under Conditions of Mild Anxiety." *J. Anxiety Disord*. March-April 1998;12 (2):153-76. https://pubmed.ncbi.nlm.nih.gov/9560177/

41. Coudin, G. & Alexopoulos, T. 2010. "'Help Me! I'm Old!' How Negative Aging Stereotypes Create Dependency Among Older Adults." *Aging and Mental Health*. Vol. 14. Issue 5. https://www.researchgate.net/publication/44609289_'Help_me_I'm_old'_How_negative_aging_stereotypes_create_dependency_among_older_adults
    and
    Cherry, K. 2021. "Priming and the Psychology of Memory." *Very Well Mind*. June 18, 2021. https://www.verywellmind.com/priming-and-the-psychology-of-memory-4173092

42. Hagood, E. W. & Gruenewald, T. L. 2018. "Positive Versus Negative Priming of Older Adults' Generative Value: Do Negative Messages Impair Memory?" *Aging and Mental Health*. Vol. 22. Issue 2. https://pubmed.ncbi.nlm.nih.gov/27783535/
    and
    Cherry, K. 2021. "Priming and the Psychology of Memory." *Very Well Mind*. June 18, 2021. https://www.verywellmind.com/priming-and-the-psychology-of-memory-4173092

43. Newberg, A. & Waldman, M. 2012. "Why This Word Is So Dangerous to Say or Hear." *Psychology Today*. August 1, 2012. https://www.psychologytoday.com/us/blog/words-can-change-your-brain/201208/why-word-is-so-dangerous-say-or-hear

44. Ibid

45. Newberg, A. & Waldman, M. 2012. *Words Can Change Your Brain*. Avery: New York, NY.

46. Losada, M. & Heaphy, E. 2004. "The Role of Positivity and Connectivity in the Performance of Business Teams: A Nonlinear Dynamics Model."

American Behavioral Scientist. Vol. 47. Issue 6. February 1, 2004. https://journals.sagepub.com/doi/10.1177/0002764203260208 and http://www.factorhappiness.at/downloads/quellen/s8_losada.pdf
and
Newberg, A. & Waldman, M. 2012. "Why This Word is So Dangerous to Say or Hear." *Psychology Today.* August 1, 2012. https://www.psychologytoday.com/us/blog/words-can-change-your-brain/201208/why-word-is-so-dangerous-say-or-hear

47. Eagleson, C. et al. 2016. "The Power of Positive Thinking: Pathological Worry is Reduced by Thought Replacement in Generalized Anxiety Disorder." *Behaviour Research and Therapy.* Volume 78, March 2016, Pages 13-18 https://www.sciencedirect.com/science/article/pii/S0005796715300814

48. Dwyer, M. 2016. "Optimism May Reduce Risk of Dying Prematurely Among Women." *Harvard T.H. Chan School of Public Health Press Release.* December 7, 2016. https://www.hsph.harvard.edu/news/press-releases/optimism-premature-death-women/
and
Kim, E. S. & Hagan, K. A. et al. 2016. "Optimism and Cause-Specific Mortality: A Prospective Cohort Study," *American Journal of Epidemiology.* December 7, 2016. https://academic.oup.com/aje/article/185/1/21/2631298

49. Selk, J. 2013. "Habit Formation: The 21-Day Myth." *Forbes.* April 15, 2013. https://www.forbes.com/sites/jasonselk/2013/04/15/habit-formation-the-21-day-myth/

50. Lally, P. 2009. "How Are Habits Formed: Modelling Habit Formation in the Real World." *European Journal of Social Psychology.* Vol. 40. Issue 6. Pages 998 – 1009. https://centrespringmd.com/docs/How%20Habits%20are%20Formed.pdf

51. Tierney, J. & Baumeister, R. F. *The Power of Bad: How the Negativity Effect Rules Us and How We Can Rule It.* Penguin Press: New York, NY.

Chapter Eleven: Subconscious Controls

1. Losada, M. & Heaphy, E. 2004. "The Role of Positivity and Connectivity

in the Performance of Business Teams: A Nonlinear Dynamics Model." *American Behavioral Scientist.* Vol. 47. Issue 6. February 1, 2004. https://journals.sagepub.com/doi/10.1177/0002764203260208 and http://www.factorhappiness.at/downloads/quellen/s8_losada.pdf
2. Benson, K. 2017. "The Magic Relationship Ratio, According to Science." *The Gottman Institute.* October 4, 2017. https://www.gottman.com/blog/the-magic-relationship-ratio-according-science/
3. Black, John. 2013. "Asklepion and the Use of Dreams for Curing Diseases with the Help of the Gods." November 21, 2013. *Ancient Origins.* https://www.ancient-origins.net/ancient-places-europe/asklepion-and-use-dreams-curing-diseases-help-gods-001049
4. Christopoulou-Aletra, H., Togia, A. & Varlami, C. 2010. "The 'Smart' Asclepieion: A Total Healing Environment." *Archives of Hellenic Medicine.* 27. 259-263. https://www.researchgate.net/publication/297832922_The_smart_asclepieion_A_total_healing_environment
5. Ibid
6. Warren, C. 2009. "Subliminal Stimuli, Perception, and Influence." *American Journal of Media Psychology.* Vol. 2, Nos. ¾ (Summer/Fall 2009) https://www.researchgate.net/publication/313236697_Subliminal_Stimuli_Perception_and_Influence
7. Ibid
8. Ibid
9. Pam, N. 2013. "Poetzle Phenomenon." *Psychology Dictionary.* https://psychologydictionary.org/potzl-phenomenon-poetzl-phenomenon/
10. Shevrin, H., & Luborsky, L. 1958. "The Measurement of Preconscious Perception in Dreams and Images: An Investigation of the Poetzl Phenomenon." *The Journal of Abnormal and Social Psychology, 56*(3), 285–294. https://psycnet.apa.org/record/1959-09534-001
11. Fisher, C. 1988. "Further Observations on the Poetzl Phenomenon: The Effects of Subliminal Visual Stimulation on Dreams, Images, and Hallucinations." *Psychoanalysis & Contemporary Thought, 11*(1), 3–56.

12. — 1984. "Hearing Before the Subcommittee on Transportation. Aviation and Materials of the Committee on Science and Technology. U.S. House of Representatives. Ninety-Eighth Congress. Second Session." No. 1051. https://books.google.com/books?id=7Xd-wwEACAAJ&printsec=frontcover#v=onepage&q&f=false
13. Ibid
14. Ibid
15. Ibid
16. Ibid
17. Ibid
18. Ibid
19. Ibid
20. — 1984. "Hearing Before the Subcommittee on Transportation. Aviation and Materials of the Committee on Science and Technology. U.S. House of Representatives. Ninety-Eighth Congress. Second Session." No. 1051. https://books.google.com/books?id=7Xd-wwEACAAJ&printsec=frontcover#v=onepage&q&f=false
21. Taylor, E. 2020. "The Unconscious Part 2 With Professor Joel Weinberger." *Provocative Enlightenment Radio.* https://www.eldontaylor.com/provocativeenlightenment/2020-06-22-the-unconscious-part-2-with-professor-joel-weinberger/
22. Taylor, E., Bey, R. & Sadana, R. 1990. *Peripheral Perception Via Subliminal Stimuli Desk Reference.* Progressive Awareness Research. https://progressiveawareness.org/research_desk_reference/Peripheral_Desk_Reference.html
23. Kahneman, D. 2011. *Thinking Fast and Slow.* Farrar, Straus, and Giroux. New York: NY.
    and
    Whalen, P. J. et al. 2005. "Human Amygdala Responsivity to Masked Fearful Eye Whites." Science. 306(5704):2061. https://www.researchgate.net/publication/8126364_Human_Amygdala_Responsivity_to_Masked_Fearful_Eye_Whites
24. Bornstein, R. F. 1990. "Critical Importance of Stimulus Unawareness for the Production of Subliminal Psychodynamic Activation Effects: A

Meta-Analytic Review." *Journal of Clinical Psychology.* Mar:46(2):201-10. https://pubmed.ncbi.nlm.nih.gov/2139041/

25. Van den Bussche, E. 2009. *The Mechanisms of Subliminal Stimuli: A Meta-Analysis and New Experiments.* Katholieke Universiteit Leuven. https://www.researchgate.net/publication/28360860_The_mechanisms_of_subliminal_stimuli_A_meta-analysis_and_new_experiments

26. Doan, B.T., Plante, T. G., DiGregorio, M., & Manuel, G. 1995. "Influence of Aerobic Exercise Activity and Relaxation Training on Coping with Test-Taking Anxiety." *Anxiety, Stress, and Coping.* 8, 101-111. https://www.researchgate.net/publication/240236134_Influence_of_aerobic_exercise_activity_and_relaxation_training_on_coping_with_test-taking_anxiety

27. Pelka, R. 1993. "Application of Subliminal Therapy to Overweight Subjects." Armed Forces University, Munich, Germany.

28. Ashley, D. 1993. "The Effect of Subliminally Presented Reinforcing Stimuli on Factual Material." University of Southern California.

29. Galbraith, P. & Barton, B. 1990. "Subliminal Relaxation: Myth or Method." Weber State University.

30. Reid, J. 1990. "*Free of Depression* Subliminal Tape Study." Colorado State University.

31. Taylor, R. 2016. "The Keys to Self-Healing." *InnerTalk Blog.* March 30, 2016. https://www.innertalk.com/blog/2016/03/30/the-keys-to-self-healing/

32. Westerlundh, B. 2004. "Defense Mechanisms." *Advances in Psychology.* https://www.sciencedirect.com/topics/neuroscience/subliminal-stimuli

33. Bornstein, R. F. 1990. "Critical Importance of Stimulus Unawareness for the Production of Subliminal Psychodynamic Activation Effects: A Meta-Analytic Review." *Journal of Clinical Psychology.* Mar:46(2):201-10. https://pubmed.ncbi.nlm.nih.gov/2139041/

34. Van den Bussche, E. 2009. *The Mechanisms of Subliminal Stimuli: A Meta-Analysis and New Experiments.* Katholieke Universiteit Leuven. https://www.researchgate.net/publication/28360860_The_mechanisms_of_subliminal_stimuli_A_meta-analysis_and_new_experiments

Chapter Twelve: Empower Yourself

1. — "What are Brainwaves?" *Sinha Clinic*. https://www.sinhaclinic.com/what-are-brainwaves
2. — "What to Know About Gamma Brain Waves." *WebMD*. https://www.webmd.com/brain/what-to-know-about-gamma-brain-waves
3. — "Meditation: A Simple, Fast Way to Reduce Stress." *Mayo Clinic*. https://www.mayoclinic.org/tests-procedures/meditation/in-depth/meditation/art-20045858
4. Khalsa, D. S. 2015. "Yoga and Medical Meditation as Alzheimer's Prevention Medicine: A White Paper." *Alzheimer's Research and Prevention Foundation*. https://www.alzheimersprevention.org/downloadables/White_Paper.pdf
   and
   Khalsa, D. S. et al 2009. "Cerebral Blood Flow Changes During Chanting Meditation." *Nuclear Medicine Communications*. 30 (12):956-61. https://kundaliniresearchinstitute.org/wp-content/uploads/2022/09/Khalsa-2009-Nucl-Med-Commun.pdf
5. Khalsa, D. S. 2015. "Yoga and Medical Meditation as Alzheimer's Prevention Medicine: A White Paper." *Alzheimer's Research and Prevention Foundation*. https://www.alzheimersprevention.org/downloadables/White_Paper.pdf
   and
   Newberg, A. B. et al. 2010. "Meditation Effects on Cognitive Function and Cerebral Blood Flow in Subjects with Memory Loss: A Preliminary Study." *Journal of Alzheimer's Disease*. 20(2):517-26. https://www.researchgate.net/publication/41466103_Meditation_Effects_on_Cognitive_Function_and_Cerebral_Blood_Flow_In_Subjects_with_Memory_Loss_A_Preliminary_Study
6. Khalsa, D. S. 2015. "Yoga and Medical Meditation as Alzheimer's Prevention Medicine: A White Paper." *Alzheimer's Research and Prevention Foundation*. https://www.alzheimersprevention.org/downloadables/White_Paper.pdf
7. Newberg, A. B. et al. 2010. "Cerebral Blood Flow Differences Between Long-Term Meditators and Non-Meditators." *Conscious

Cognition. 19(4):899-905. https://static1.squarespace.com/static/52402ca4e4b0b7dd2fafe453/t/52613943e4b090ca0008e43b/1382103363060/cerebral-blood-flow-differences-between-long-term-meditators-and-non-meditators.pdf

8. Moss, A. S. et al. 2012. "Effects of an 8-Week Meditation Program on Mood and Anxiety in Patients with Memory Loss." *Journal of Alternative Complementary Medicine.* 18(1):48-53. https://www.researchgate.net/publication/221769816_Effects_of_an_8-Week_Meditation_Program_on_Mood_and_Anxiety_in_Patients_with_Memory_Loss

9. Lavretsky, H. et al. 2013. "A Pilot Study of Yogic Meditation for Family Dementia Caregivers with Depressive Symptoms: Effects on Mental Health, Cognition, and Telomerase Activity." *Int. Journal of Geriatric Psychiatry.* 28(1):57-65. https://www.ncbi.nlm.nih.gov/pmc/articles/PMC3423469/

10. Innes, K. E. et al. 2018. "Effects of Meditation and Music-Listening on Blood Biomarkers of Cellular Aging and Alzheimer's Disease in Adults with Subjective Cognitive Decline: An Exploratory Randomized Clinical Trial." *Journal of Alzheimer's Disease.* 66(3):947-970. https://www.ncbi.nlm.nih.gov/pmc/articles/PMC6388631/

11. Khalsa, D. S. 2015. "Yoga and Medical Meditation as Alzheimer's Prevention Medicine: A White Paper." *Alzheimer's Research and Prevention Foundation.* https://www.alzheimersprevention.org/downloadables/White_Paper.pdf

12. Ibid

13. Church, D. 2012. "Brief Group Intervention Using Emotional Freedom Techniques for Depression in College Students: A Randomized Controlled Trial." *Depression Research and Treatment*, vol. 2012, Article ID 257172, 7 pages. https://www.hindawi.com/journals/drt/2012/257172/
and
Nelms, J. A. & Castel, L. 2016. "A Systematic Review and Meta-Analysis of Randomized and Nonrandomized Trials of Clinical Emotional Freedom Techniques (EFT) for the Treatment of Depression." *Explore (NY).* 2016 Nov-Dec, 12(6):416-426. https://pubmed.ncbi.nlm.nih.

gov/27843054/

14. Church, D. et al. 2013. "Psychological Trauma Symptom Improvement in Veterans Using Emotional Freedom Techniques: A Randomized Controlled Trial." *Journal of Nervous and Mental Disease.* February 2013. Volume 201. Issue 2. pp 153-160. https://journals.lww.com/jonmd/Abstract/2013/02000/Psychological_Trauma_Symptom_Improvement_in.14.aspx

15. Clond, M. 2016. "Emotional Freedom Techniques for Anxiety: A Systematic Review with Meta-analysis." *Journal of Nervous and Mental Disease.* May; 204 (5):388-95. https://pubmed.ncbi.nlm.nih.gov/26894319/

16. — "EFT Tapping Research." *EFT Universe.* https://eftuniverse.com/research-studies/eft-research/

17. — Brennan, D. 2021. "What Is EFT Tapping?" *WebMD.* https://www.webmd.com/balance/what-is-eft-tapping

18. — "Emotional Freedom Technique (EFT)" *Kaiser Permanente.* https://healthy.kaiserpermanente.org/health-wellness/health-encyclopedia/he.emotional-freedom-technique-eft.acl9225

19. Waite, W., & Holder, M. 2003. "Assessment of the Emotional Freedom Technique: An Alternative Treatment for Fear." *The Scientific Review of Mental Health Practice.* Summer 2003, Vol. 2, No. 1. http://www.srmhp.org/0201/emotional-freedom-technique.html

20. Leland, K. – "Labyrinths: Ancient Aid for Modern Stresses." *WebMD.* https://www.webmd.com/balance/features/labyrinths-for-modern-stresses

Chapter Thirteen: Other Tools

1. Brown, J. & Wong, J. 2017. "How Gratitude Changes You and Your Brain." *Greater Good Berkeley.* June 6, 2017. https://greatergood.berkeley.edu/article/item/how_gratitude_changes_you_and_your_brain

2. Wong, Y. J. et al. 2016. "Does Gratitude Writing Improve the Mental Health of Psychotherapy Clients? Evidence From a Randomized Controlled Trial." *Psychotherapy Research.* 28(2), 1-11. https://www.researchgate.net/publication/301826526_Does_gratitude_writing_

improve_the_mental_health_of_psychotherapy_clients_Evidence_from_a_randomized_controlled_trial
3. Cousins, N. 1979. *Anatomy of an Illness*. New York, NY: Norton. https://www.cc-seas.columbia.edu/sites/dsa/files/cousins.pdf
4. Colburn, D. 1986. "Norman Cousins, Still Laughing." *Washington Post*. October 21, 1986. https://www.washingtonpost.com/archive/lifestyle/wellness/1986/10/21/norman-cousins-still-laughing/e17f23cb-3e8c-4f58-b907-2dcd00326e22/
5. Welsh, J. 2011. "Why Laughter May Be the Best Pain Medicine." *Scientific American*. September 14, 2011. https://www.scientificamerican.com/article/why-laughter-may-be-the-best-pain-medicine/
and
Dunbar, R.I.M et al. 2011. "Social Laughter is Correlated with an Elevated Pain Threshold." *The Royal Society Publishing*. September 14, 2011. https://royalsocietypublishing.org/doi/epdf/10.1098/rspb.2011.1373
6. Szalavitz, M. 2011. "You're Kidding! Medical Clown Increases Pregnancy Rates with IVF." *Time*. Jan 31, 2011. https://healthland.time.com/2011/01/31/youre-kidding-medical-clown-increases-pregnancy-rates-with-ivf/
and
Friedler, S. et al. 2011. "The Effect of Medical Clowning on Pregnancy Rates After In Vitro Fertilization and Embryo Transfer." *Fertility and Sterility*. 95(6):2127-30. https://www.sciencedirect.com/science/article/abs/pii/S0015028210029584
and
Kreit, B. 2013. "Clowns, Placebos and the Future of the Care Effect." *Open Mind BBVA*. February 7, 2013. https://www.bbvaopenmind.com/en/science/bioscience/clowns-placebos-and-the-future-of-the-care-effect
7. Vlachopoulos, C. et al. 2009. "Divergent Effects of Laughter and Mental Stress on Arterial Stiffness and Central Hemodynamics." *Psychosomatic Medicine*. 71(4):446-453. https://pubmed.ncbi.nlm.nih.gov/19251872/
8. Berk, L.S. 2001. "Modulation of Neuroimmune Parameters During the Eustress of Humor-Associated Mirthful Laughter." *Alternative Therapies*

in Health and Medicine. March; 7(2) 62-72, 74-76. https://pubmed.ncbi.
nlm.nih.gov/11253418/
and
— "Laughter is the Best Medicine." *Help Guide.* https://www.helpguide.
org/articles/mental-health/laughter-is-the-best-medicine.htm
9. Akimbekov, N. A., & Razzaque, M. 2021. "Laughter Therapy: A Humor-Induced Hormonal Intervention to Reduce Stress and Anxiety." *Current Research in Physiology.* Vol. 4. Pages 135-138. https://www.researchgate.net/publication/351237891_Laughter_therapy_A_humor-induced_hormonal_intervention_to_reduce_stress_and_anxiety
10. Georgia State University. 2016. "Laughter-Based Exercise Program for Older Adults Has Health Benefits, Georgia State Researchers Find." *Georgia State University.* September 15, 2016. https://news.gsu.edu/2016/09/15/laughter-based-exercise-program-health-benefits-georgia-state-researchers-find/
11. Greene, C. M. et. al. 2017. "Evaluation of a Laughter-based Exercise Program on Health and Self-efficacy for Exercise." *The Gerontologist.* Volume 57, Issue 6, December 2017, Pages 1051–1061.
12. Good, A. & Russo, F. 2021. "Changes in Mood, Oxytocin, And Cortisol Following Group and Individual Singing: A Pilot Study." *Psychology of Music.* October 2021. https://www.researchgate.net/publication/355608127_Changes_in_mood_oxytocin_and_cortisol_following_group_and_individual_singing_A_pilot_study
13. Fancourt, D., Aufegger, L., & Williamon, A. 2015. "Low-Stress and High-Stress Singing Have Contrasting Effects on Glucocorticoid Response." *Frontiers in Psychology.* September 4, 2015. https://www.frontiersin.org/articles/10.3389/fpsyg.2015.01242/full
14. Good, A. & Russo, F. 2021. "Changes In Mood, Oxytocin, And Cortisol Following Group and Individual Singing: A Pilot Study." *Psychology of Music.* October 2021. https://www.researchgate.net/publication/355608127_Changes_in_mood_oxytocin_and_cortisol_following_group_and_individual_singing_A_pilot_study
15. Pentikainen, E. et al. 2021. "Beneficial Effects of Choir Singing on Cognition and Well-Being of Older Adults: Evidence from a

Cross-Sectional Study." *Plos One.* February 3, 2021. https://journals.plos.org/plosone/article?id=10.1371/journal.pone.0245666

16. Fancourt, D. et al. 2019. "Group Singing in Bereavement: Effects on Mental Health, Self-Efficacy, Self-Esteem and Well-Being." *BMJ Supportive & Palliative Care.* June 26, 2019. https://spcare.bmj.com/content/early/2019/06/26/bmjspcare-2018-001642

17. Lewis, A. et al. 2016. "Singing For Lung Health—A Systematic Review of the Literature and Consensus Statement." *NPJ Primary Care Respiratory Medicine.* 26, 16080. https://www.nature.com/articles/npjpcrm201680#citeas

18. British Lung Foundation. 2020. "How Can Singing Improve My Wellbeing?" https://www.blf.org.uk/support-for-you/singing-for-lung-health/improve-your-wellbeing

19. Kreutz, G. et al. 2004. "Effects of Choir Singing or Listening on Secretory Immunoglobulin A, Cortisol, and Emotional State." *Journal of Behavioral Medicine.* December 2004. 27(6):623-35. https://pubmed.ncbi.nlm.nih.gov/15669447/

20. Osman, S. E. et al. 2016. "'Singing for the Brain': A Qualitative Study Exploring the Health and Well-Being Benefits of Singing for People with Dementia and Their Carers." *Dementia (London).* November 2016. 15(6): 1326–1339.
    and
    Healthline. 2020. "10 Ways That Singing Benefits Your Health." *Healthline.* https://www.healthline.com/health/benefits-of-singing

21. Rudd, M., Vohs, K.D., & Aaker, J. 2012. "Awe Expands People's Perception of Time, Alters Decision Making, and Enhances Well-Being." *Psychological Science.* 23(10) 1130-1136. August 10, 2012. https://journals.sagepub.com/doi/abs/10.1177/0956797612438731
    and
    https://www.bauer.uh.edu/mrrudd/download/AweExpandsTimeAvailability.pdf

22. Anderson, C. L., Monroy, M., & Keltner, D. (2018, June 21). "Awe in Nature Heals: Evidence from Military Veterans, At-Risk Youth, and

College Students." *Emotion.* June 21, 2018. https://www.sierraclub. org/sites/www.sierraclub.org/files/program/documents/Anderson,%20 Monroy,%20Keltner2018_Awe%20in%20nature%20heals-%20 Evidence%20from%20military%20veterans,%20at-risk%20youth,%20 and%20college%20students..pdf

23. Sturm, V.E. et al. 2020. "Big Smile, Small Self: Awe Walks Promote Prosocial Positive Emotions in Older Adults." *Emotion.* https://doi.apa. org/doiLanding?doi=10.1037%2Femo0000876

24. DiGiuliom S. 2019. "Why Scientists Say Experiencing Awe Can Help You Live Your Best Life." *NBC News.* February 19, 2019. https://www. nbcnews.com/better/lifestyle/why-scientists-say-experiencing-awe- can-help-you-live-your-ncna961826

    and

    Stellar, J.E. et al. 2015. "Positive Affect and Markers of Inflammation: Discrete Positive Emotions Predict Lower Levels of Inflammatory Cytokines." *Emotion.* 15(2):129-33. https://pubmed.ncbi.nlm.nih. gov/25603133/

25. DiGiuliom S. 2019. "Why Scientists Say Experiencing Awe Can Help You Live Your Best Life." *NBC News.* February 19, 2019. https://www. nbcnews.com/better/lifestyle/why-scientists-say-experiencing-awe-can-help-you-live-your-ncna961826

    and

    Stellar, J.E. et al. 2018. "Awe and Humility." *Journal of Personal and Social Psychology.* February 2018. 114(2):258-269. https://pubmed.ncbi. nlm.nih.gov/28857578/

26. Harvard. – "Walking for Health." *Harvard Health Publishing.* https:// www.health.harvard.edu/exercise-and-fitness/walking-for-health

27. Edwards, M.K. & Loprinzi, P.D. 2018. "Experimental Effects of Brief, Single Bouts of Walking and Meditation on Mood Profile in Young Adults." *Health Promotions Perspectives.* 8(3): 171–178. https://www.ncbi. nlm.nih.gov/pmc/articles/PMC6064756/

28. Duke University, 1999. "Exercise May Be Just as Effective as Medication for Treating Major Depression." *Science Daily.* October 27, 1999. https://

www.sciencedaily.com/releases/1999/10/991027071931.htm
29. Wurtz, R. H. 1998. "Optic Flow: A Brain Region Devoted to Optic Flow Analysis?" *Current Biology*. Vol. 8. Issue 16. https://www.cell.com/current-biology/fulltext/S0960-9822(07)00359-4
30. Erickson, M. 2020. "Setting Your Biological Clock, Reducing Stress While Sheltering in Place." *Stanford Medicine*. https://scopeblog.stanford.edu/2020/06/03/setting-your-biological-clock-reducing-stress-while-sheltering-in-place/
31. Oppezzo, M, & Schwartz, D. 2014. "Give Your Ideas Some Legs: The Positive Effect of Walking on Creative Thinking." *Journal of Experimental Psychology*. Vol. 40, No. 4, 1142-1152. https://www.apa.org/pubs/journals/releases/xlm-a0036577.pdf
32. Weber, S.R. & Pargament, K. 2014. "The Role of Religion and Spirituality in Mental Health." *Psychiatry*. Vol. 27. Issue 5. pp 358-363. https://journals.lww.com/co-psychiatry/Abstract/2014/09000/The_role_of_religion_and_spirituality_in_mental.9.aspx
33. Whitehead, B.R. & Bergeman, C.S. 2011. "Coping with Daily Stress: Differential Role of Spiritual Experience on Daily Positive and Negative Affect." *The Journals of Gerontology*. Series B, Volume 67, Issue 4, July 2012, pp 456–459. https://academic.oup.com/psychsocgerontology/article/67/4/456/567333
34. Goldstein, E.D. 2007. "Sacred Moments: Implications on Well-Being and Stress." *Clinical Psychology*. Vol. 63. Issue 10. pp 1001-1019. https://onlinelibrary.wiley.com/doi/abs/10.1002/jclp.20402
and
Whitehead, B.R. & Bergeman, C.S. 2011. "Coping with Daily Stress: Differential Role of Spiritual Experience on Daily Positive and Negative Affect." *The Journals of Gerontology*. Series B, Volume 67, Issue 4, July 2012, Pages 456–459. https://academic.oup.com/psychsocgerontology/article/67/4/456/567333
35. McMahon, B.T & Biggs, H.C. 2012. "Examining Spirituality and Intrinsic Religious Orientation as a Means of Coping with Exam Anxiety." *Society, Health & Vulnerability*. Vol 3. Issue 1. https://www.tandfonline.com/doi/full/10.3402/vgi.v3i0.14918

Conclusion

1. Harris, S. 2023. "Making Sense of Free Will." *Making Sense with Sam Harris.* Episode 5. https://www.samharris.org/podcasts/essentials/making-sense-of-free-will

Appendix A: Subliminal Controversy

1. Santora, T. 2020. "Does Subliminal Messaging Really Work?" *Live Science.* March 14, 2020. https://www.livescience.com/does-subliminal-messaging-work.html
and
Mikkelson, D. "Popcorn Subliminal Advertising." *Snopes.* https://www.snopes.com/fact-check/subliminal-advertising/
and
— 1957. "'Persuaders' Get Deeply 'Hidden' Tool: Subliminal Projection." *Advertising Age.* Sept. 16, 1957. https://muse.jhu.edu/article/193862/figure/fig03
and
Barr, W. M. 2005. "'Subliminal' Advertising." *Advertising and Society Review.* Vol. 6, Issue 4. https://muse.jhu.edu/article/193862
2. Mikkelson, D. 1999. "Popcorn Subliminal Advertising." *Snopes.* July 1, 1999. https://www.snopes.com/fact-check/subliminal-advertising/
3. —Crandall, K. 2006. "Invisible Commercials and Hidden Persuaders: James M. Vicary and the Subliminal Advertising Controversy of 1957." *Undergraduate Honors Thesis. University of Florida.* http://plaza.ufl.edu/cyllek/docs/KCrandall_Thesis2006.pdf
and
-- "Henry Charles Link." *Prabook.* https://prabook.com/web/henry.link/3764028
4. Eric Pace (December 1, 1990). "Norman Cousins, 75, Dies; Edited The Saturday Review". *The New York Times.* https://www.nytimes.com/1990/12/01/obituaries/norman-cousins-75-dies-edited-the-saturday-review.html
5. Barr, W. M. 2005. "'Subliminal' Advertising." *Advertising and Society Review.* Vol. 6, Issue 4. https://muse.jhu.edu/article/193862

6. Silverglate, S. 1990. "Subliminal Perception and the First Amendment: Yelling Fire in a Crowded Mind?" *University of Miami Law Review*. Vol. 44. No. 5. https://repository.law.miami.edu/cgi/viewcontent.cgi?referer=&httpsredir=1&article=1987&context=umlr
7. Silverglate, S. 1990. "Subliminal Perception and the First Amendment: Yelling Fire in a Crowded Mind?" *University of Miami Law Review*. Vol. 44. No. 5. https://repository.law.miami.edu/cgi/viewcontent.cgi?referer=&httpsredir=1&article=1987&context=umlr
8. Taylor, E. 2009. *Mind Programming: From Persuasion and Brainwashing to Self-Help and Practical Metaphysics*. Carlsbad, CA: Hay House.
   and
   Taylor, E. 1990. *Subliminal Communication: Emperor's Clothes or Panacea?* WA: R.K. Books.
9. Silverglate, S. 1990. "Subliminal Perception and the First Amendment: Yelling Fire in a Crowded Mind?" *University of Miami Law Review*. Vol. 44. No. 5. https://repository.law.miami.edu/cgi/viewcontent.cgi?referer=&httpsredir=1&article=1987&context=umlr
10. Ibid
11. Borger, J. 2000. "Dirty Rats Leave Gore a Subliminal Message." *The Guardian*. September 12, 2000. https://www.theguardian.com/world/2000/sep/13/uselections2000.usa
12. — 2006. "Gore Campaign Calls 'Rats' Ad 'Bizarre.'" *ABC News*. January 7, 2006. https://abcnews.go.com/US/story?id=95789&page=1
13. Borger, J. 2000. "Dirty Rats Leave Gore a Subliminal Message." *The Guardian*. September 12, 2000. https://www.theguardian.com/world/2000/sep/13/uselections2000.usa
14. Ibid
15. Ibid
16. Weinberger, J. & Westen, D. 2008. "RATS, We Should Have Used Clinton: Subliminal Priming in Political Campaigns." *Political Psychology*. Vol 29, Issue 5. https://onlinelibrary.wiley.com/doi/10.1111/j.1467-9221.2008.00658.x
17. Gale Group. 2003. "Campaign Ad May Have Swayed Voters Subliminally. (Dirty RATS)." *The Free Library*. https://www.thefreelibrary.com/

Campaign+ad+may+have+swayed+voters+subliminally.+(Dirty+RATS)-a098977985

18. Crandall, K. 2006. "Invisible Commercials and Hidden Persuaders: James M. Vicary and the Subliminal Advertising Controversy of 1957." *Undergraduate Honors Thesis. University of Florida.* http://plaza.ufl.edu/cyllek/docs/KCrandall_Thesis2006.pdf

    and

    Carter Henderson, "A Blessing or a Bane? TV Ads You'd See Without Knowing It." *Wall Street Journal.* 13 September 1957.

19. Crandall, K. 2006. "Invisible Commercials and Hidden Persuaders: James M. Vicary and the Subliminal Advertising Controversy of 1957." *Undergraduate Honors Thesis. University of Florida.* http://plaza.ufl.edu/cyllek/docs/KCrandall_Thesis2006.pdf

20. Ibid

21. Crandall, K. 2006. "Invisible Commercials and Hidden Persuaders: James M. Vicary and the Subliminal Advertising Controversy of 1957." *Undergraduate Honors Thesis. University of Florida.* http://plaza.ufl.edu/cyllek/docs/KCrandall_Thesis2006.pdf

    and

    George Schutz, "Just Whom Did Invisible Advertising Sell?" *Motion Picture Daily.* 16 December 1957.

22. Crandall, K. 2006. "Invisible Commercials and Hidden Persuaders: James M. Vicary and the Subliminal Advertising Controversy of 1957." *Undergraduate Honors Thesis. University of Florida.* http://plaza.ufl.edu/cyllek/docs/KCrandall_Thesis2006.pdf

    and

    "Subliminal Ad is Transmitted in Test but Scores No Popcorn Sales." *Advertising Age.* 20 January 1958.

23. Crandall, K. 2006. "Invisible Commercials and Hidden Persuaders: James M. Vicary and the Subliminal Advertising Controversy of 1957." *Undergraduate Honors Thesis. University of Florida.* http://plaza.ufl.edu/cyllek/docs/KCrandall_Thesis2006.pdf

24. — 2018. "How Likely Are You to Buy Concessions, Such as Soda, Candy or Popcorn, When You Go to a Movie

Theater?" *Statista*. https://www.statista.com/statistics/815506/likelihood-buy-concessions-movie-theater-us/

25. Crandall, K. 2006. "Invisible Commercials and Hidden Persuaders: James M. Vicary and the Subliminal Advertising Controversy of 1957." *Undergraduate Honors Thesis. University of Florida.* http://plaza.ufl.edu/cyllek/docs/KCrandall_Thesis2006.pdf

26. Ibid

27. Crandall, K. 2006. "Invisible Commercials and Hidden Persuaders: James M. Vicary and the Subliminal Advertising Controversy of 1957." *Undergraduate Honors Thesis. University of Florida.* http://plaza.ufl.edu/cyllek/docs/KCrandall_Thesis2006.pdf

    and

    Corrigan, R. E. et. al. 1962. "Apparatus for Producing Visual Stimulation." U.S. Patent No. 3,060,795. October 30, 1962

28. Crandall, K. 2006. "Invisible Commercials and Hidden Persuaders: James M. Vicary and the Subliminal Advertising Controversy of 1957." *Undergraduate Honors Thesis. University of Florida.* http://plaza.ufl.edu/cyllek/docs/KCrandall_Thesis2006.pdf

    and

    Peter S. Bart, "'Hidden' Commercials, Launched by Fanfare, Now Flounder Quietly: Public Opposition Stalls TV, Movie Ads That Aim at Viewer's Subconscious Mind," *Wall Street Journal.* 14 January 1959.

29. O'Barr, W. M. 2005. "'Subliminal' Advertising." *Advertising and Society Review.* Vol. 6. Issue 4, 2005. https://muse.jhu.edu/article/193862

30. Stern, V. 2015. "A Short History of the Rise, Fall and Rise of Subliminal Messaging." *Scientific American* Sept. 1, 2015. https://www.scientificamerican.com/article/a-short-history-of-the-rise-fall-and-rise-of-subliminal-messaging/

31. — "Fort Lee, New Jersey" *Wikipedia.* https://en.wikipedia.org/wiki/Fort_Lee,_New_Jersey

32. Boese, A. — "#19: Subliminal Advertising" *The Top 40 Hoaxes of All Time.* http://hoaxes.org/Top/P10

33. Pratkanis, A. R. 1992. "The Cargo-Cult Science of Subliminal Persuasion." *Skeptical Inquirer.* Vol. 16.3. Spring 1992. https://cdn.centerforinquiry.

org/wp-content/uploads/sites/29/1992/04/22165159/p50.pdf
34. Crandall, K. 2006. "Invisible Commercials and Hidden Persuaders: James M. Vicary and the Subliminal Advertising Controversy of 1957." *Undergraduate Honors Thesis. University of Florida.* http://plaza.ufl.edu/cyllek/docs/KCrandall_Thesis2006.pdf
35. Ibid
36. Karremans, J. C., Stroebe, W. & Claus, J. 2005. "Beyond Vicary's Fantasies: The Impact of Subliminal Priming and Brand Choice." *Journal of Experimental Social Psychology.* 42 (2006) 792–798. https://citeseerx.ist.psu.edu/viewdoc/download?doi=10.1.1.464.4958&rep=rep1&type=pdf
37. Ibid
38. Ibid
39. Block, M. P., and Vanden Bergh, B. G. 1985. "Can You Sell Subliminal Messages to Consumers?" *Journal of Advertising.* 14 (3), 59-62. Michigan State Univ. https://www.scholars.northwestern.edu/en/publications/can-you-sell-subliminal-messages-to-consumers
and
Taylor, E. 1988. *Subliminal Learning: An Eclectic Approach.* WA: RK Book.
40. Rossen J. 2016. "The Terrifying Subliminal Image Hidden in *The Exorcist*" *Mental Floss.* October 10, 2016. https://www.mentalfloss.com/article/87245/terrifying-subliminal-image-hidden-exorcist
41. Shaw-Williams, H. 2015. "Shocking Subliminal Messages Hidden in Popular Movies." *Screen Rant.* Sept. 12, 2015. https://screenrant.com/secret-movie-hidden-subliminal-messages/
42. Ibid
43. Commercial for 1959 Chevy's with Dinah Shore & Pat Boone 1. https://www.youtube.com/watch?v=DzipGOKPP4w
44. "Schweppes Subliminal Advertising - John Cleese" https://www.youtube.com/watch?v=bMCsm1IFkds
45. Pratkanis, A. 1992. "The Cargo-Cult Science of Subliminal Persuasion." *Skeptikal Inquirer.* Vol. 16. No. 3. https://skepticalinquirer.org/1992/04/the-cargo-cult-science-of-subliminal-persuasion/

46. Reuters. 1990. "Band is Held Not Liable in Suicides of Two Fans" *New York Times*. August 25, 1990. https://www.nytimes.com/1990/08/25/arts/band-is-held-not-liable-in-suicides-of-two-fans.html
47. Daus, M.W. 1992. "Subliminal Messages in Music: Free Speech or Invasion of Privacy?" *University of Miami Entertainment and Sports Law Review*. October 1, 1992. https://repository.law.miami.edu/cgi/viewcontent.cgi?article=1096&context=umeslr
48. Ibid
49. Ryan, C.Y. 1990. "Judge Rejects Subliminal Message Suit Against Judas Priest." *UPI*. August 24, 1990. https://www.upi.com/Archives/1990/08/24/Judge-rejects-subliminal-message-suit-against-Judas-Priest/2397651470400/
50. Ibid
51. — 2020. "How a Suicide Pact Was Almost the End of Judas Priest." *Metal Hammer*. April 22, 2020. https://www.loudersound.com/features/how-a-suicide-pact-was-almost-the-end-of-judas-priest
52. — 1990. "Rock Group Cleared in Suicide Case." *Washington Post*. August 25, 1990. https://www.washingtonpost.com/archive/lifestyle/1990/08/25/rock-group-cleared-in-suicide-case/956fb48e-525e-4a07-808b-21629f22bddb/
53. Trial transcripts of "Vance, J., Vance, E.J.R., Vance, P., Robertson, A. -vs- Judas Priest, CBS et al. Case No. 86-5844 and 86- 3939.
54. Ryan, C.Y. 1990. "Judge Rejects Subliminal Message Suit Against Judas Priest." *UPI*. August 24, 1990. https://www.upi.com/Archives/1990/08/24/Judge-rejects-subliminal-message-suit-against-Judas-Priest/2397651470400/
55. — 1990. "Band is Held Not Liable in Suicides of Two Fans." *New York Times*. August 25, 2990. https://www.nytimes.com/1990/08/25/arts/band-is-held-not-liable-in-suicides-of-two-fans.html
56. — 1990. "Rock Group Cleared in Suicide Case." *Washington Post*. August 25, 1990. https://www.washingtonpost.com/archive/lifestyle/1990/08/25/rock-group-cleared-in-suicide-case/956fb48e-525e-4a07-808b-21629f22bddb/

ENDNOTES

57. Grow, K. 2015. "Judas Priest's Subliminal Message Trial: Rob Halford Looks Back." *Rolling Stone*. August 24, 2015. https://www.rollingstone.com/music/music-features/judas-priests-subliminal-message-trial-rob-halford-looks-back-57552/
58. Taylor, E. 1995. *Thinking Without Thinking*. RK Books.
59. Sivak, D. 2018. "Fact Check: Did Sarah Palin Say, 'I Can See Russia from My House'?" *Check Your Facts*. https://checkyourfact.com/2018/03/14/fact-check-did-sarah-palin-say-i-can-see-russia-from-my-house/
60. Gardner, M. 1986. *Science, Good, Bad, and Bogus*. Amherst, NY: Prometheus Books.
61. Phelps, B. J. and Exum, M. E. 1992. "Subliminal Tapes: How to Get the Message Across." *Skeptical Inquirer*. Vol. 16. Spring, 1992. https://skepticalinquirer.org/1992/04/subliminal-tapes-how-to-get-the-message-across/
62. Moore, T. E. 1996. "Scientific Consensus and Expert Testimony: Lessons from the Judas Priest Trial." *Skeptical Inquirer*. November/December 1996. https://cdn.centerforinquiry.org/wp-content/uploads/sites/29/1996/11/22165027/p32.pdf
63. Greenwald, A.G. et al. 1991. "Double-Blind Tests of Subliminal Self-Help Audiotapes." *Psychological Science*. Vol. 2, No. 2, March 1991. https://faculty.washington.edu/agg/pdf/Gwald_Spang_Pratk_Esk_PsychSci_1991.OCR.pdf
64. Ibid
65. Ibid
66. Ibid
67. Ibid
68. Phelps, B. J. and Exum, M. E. 1992. "Subliminal Tapes: How to Get the Message Across." *Skeptical Inquirer*. Vol. 16. Spring, 1992. https://skepticalinquirer.org/1992/04/subliminal-tapes-how-to-get-the-message-across/
69. Moore, T. E. 1996. "Scientific Consensus and Expert Testimony: Lessons from the Judas Priest Trial." *Skeptical Inquirer*. November/December 1996. https://cdn.centerforinquiry.org/wp-content/uploads/sites/29/1996/11/22165027/p32.pdf

70. Doan, B.T., Plante, T. G., DiGregorio, M., & Manuel, G. 1995. "Influence of Aerobic Exercise Activity and Relaxation Training on Coping with Test-Taking Anxiety." *Anxiety, Stress, and Coping.* 8, 101-111. https://www.researchgate.net/publication/240236134_Influence_of_aerobic_exercise_activity_and_relaxation_training_on_coping_with_test-taking_anxiety
71. Abrams, R., Klinger, M, & Greenwald, A. 2002. "Subliminal Words Activate Semantic Categories (Not Automated Motor Responses)" *Psychonomic Bulletin and Review.* 2002, 9 (1), 100-106. https://faculty.washington.edu/agg/pdf/Abrams_Klinger_Greenwald_PBR2002.pdf
72. Moore, T. 1995. "Subliminal Self-help Auditory Tapes: An Empirical Test of Perceptual Consequences." *Canadian Journal of Behavioural Science.* 1995, 27:1, 9-20. https://www.researchgate.net/publication/232427601_Subliminal_self-help_auditory_tapes_An_empirical_test_of_perceptual_consequences
73. Mullen, W. 1996. "Study Challenges Freud's Theory of Subconscious." *Chicago Tribune.* Sept. 19, 1996. https://www.chicagotribune.com/news/ct-xpm-1996-09-20-9609200240-story.html
74. Pratkanis, A. 1992. "The Cargo-Cult Science of Subliminal Persuasion." *Skeptikal Inquirer.* Vol. 16. No. 3. https://skepticalinquirer.org/1992/04/the-cargo-cult-science-of-subliminal-persuasion/
75. Moore, T. E. 1992. "Subliminal Perception: Facts and Fallacies." *Skeptical Enquirer.* Volume 16. Spring 1992. https://cdn.centerforinquiry.org/wp-content/uploads/sites/29/1992/04/22165159/p58.pdf?_ga=2.40058146.1819408869.1665102514-422267812.1665102514

ACKNOWLEDGMENTS

Two people in our lives made everything we do possible. Our work, including this book, would never have been possible without the encouragement and support of Roy and Lois Bey. Roy and Eldon started Progressive Awareness Research, Inc. in 1984, prompted by a desire to create a business that truly helped people. It was Roy's sister Lois who suggested the InnerTalk technology be patented. When Roy passed away in 1991, Lois did everything she could to continue the support of Roy's dream, providing advice and recommendations, serving on the board of Progressive Awareness, and being the best cheerleader possible. Lois passed away in 2017. However, both Roy and Lois will remain forever in our hearts. Thank you, Roy and Lois.

ABOUT THE AUTHORS

Ravinder and Eldon Taylor have each worked in the field of personal empowerment for over 30 years. While Eldon has been the front face, releasing numerous best-sellers, developing and patenting his InnerTalk technology, and communicating with audiences around the globe, Ravinder has worked primarily in the background, researching, editing, and ghost-writing parts of Eldon's books. This approach has changed with their latest book, *Mind Training: The Science of Self-Empowerment*, where Ravinder has taken the lead role, overlaying her perspective on their decades-long work of discovering and refining techniques for creating a self-empowerment program based on solid scientific principles.

Eldon Taylor

Eldon is the New York Times best-selling author of *Choices and Illusions*. The subjects of his books range from exposing the darker sides of mind programming and brainwashing to the spiritual search for life's meaning. Some of his other works include *I Believe, What If? What Does That Mean? Mind Programming, Gotcha!* and *Self-Hypnosis and Subliminal Technology*. Eldon is also the author of over 300 personal motivation audio and video programs. His books and audio/video programs have been translated into many languages and are sold worldwide.

Eldon is an expert in preconscious information processing and has served as an expert trial witness with regards to both subliminal communication and hypnosis. As a practicing criminalist for over ten years, he supervised and conducted investigations and testing to detect deception. His earliest work with changing inner beliefs was conducted from this setting, including a double-blind study conducted at the Utah State Prison from 1986 to 1987.

Eldon has earned doctorates in clinical and pastoral psychology. He is an ordained interdenominational minister, a Fellow in the American Psychotherapy Association, and a Certified Master Chaplain by the American Board for Certification in Homeland Security.

Ravinder Taylor

For the past 30 years, Ravinder has been researching and analyzing self-help modalities. She has utilized her learning in thousands of interactions with individuals seeking guidance for breaking through blocks to success in their lives. Many have praised her insights and reported great success when following her recommendations.

In addition to working alongside Eldon on each of his books, Ravinder is the co-author of over 200 personal motivation audio programs and two books, *Motivational Nudges to Empower Your Life* and *Peripheral Perception via Subliminal Stimuli*.

Ravinder has a Bachelor of Science degree in microbiology (University College of Wales, Aberystwyth) and is an ordained interdenominational minister. She was also trained in hypnotherapy at the National College of Hypnosis and Psychotherapy in the U.K.

••••

MORE INFORMATION

If you enjoyed this book and would like to learn more about the tools suggested to help you become the person you were meant to be, visit www.mind-training.org or scan:

Printed in Dunstable, United Kingdom